White Logic, White Methods

To MICHAEL

with respect & admiration,

Your BIICAN* brother,

[illegible signature]

*BLACK- PUERTO RICAN

White Logic, White Methods

Racism and Methodology

Edited by Tukufu Zuberi
and Eduardo Bonilla-Silva

ROWMAN & LITTLEFIELD PUBLISHERS, INC.
Lanham • Boulder • New York • Toronto • Plymouth, UK

ROWMAN & LITTLEFIELD PUBLISHERS, INC.

Published in the United States of America
by Rowman & Littlefield Publishers, Inc.
A wholly owned subsidiary of The Rowman & Littlefield Publishing Group, Inc.
4501 Forbes Boulevard, Suite 200, Lanham, Maryland 20706
www.rowmanlittlefield.com

Estover Road
Plymouth PL6 7PY
United Kingdom

British Library Cataloguing in Publication Information Available

Library of Congress Cataloging-in-Publication Data

White logic, white methods : racism and methodology / edited by Tukufu Zuberi and Eduardo Bonilla-Silva.
p. cm.
ISBN-13: 978-0-7425-4280-8 (cloth : alk. paper)
ISBN-10: 0-7425-4280-7 (cloth : alk. paper)
ISBN-13: 978-0-7425-4281-5 (pbk. : alk. paper)
ISBN-10: 0-7425-4281-5 (pbk. : alk. paper)
1. Race relations—Research—Methodology. 2. Racism. 3. Prejudices. 4. United States—Race relations—Research—Statistical methods. 5. African Americans—Research—Statistical methods. I. Zuberi, Tukufu. II. Bonilla-Silva, Eduardo, 1962–
HT1521.W445 2008
305.8—dc22 2007046456

Printed in the United States of America

∞™ The paper used in this publication meets the minimum requirements of American National Standard for Information Sciences—Permanence of Paper for Printed Library Materials, ANSI/NISO Z39.48-1992.

Contents

I

INTRODUCTION

1

Toward a Definition of White Logic and White Methods

Eduardo Bonilla-Silva and Tukufu Zuberi

> The best available methods of sociological research are at present so liable to inaccuracies that the careful student discloses the results of individual research with diffidence; he knows that they are liable to error from the seemingly ineradicable faults of the statistical method, to even greater error from the methods of general observation, and, above all, he must ever tremble lest some personal bias, some moral conviction or some unconscious trend of thought due to previous training, has to a degree distorted the picture in his view. Convictions on all great matters of human interest one must have to a greater or less degree, and they will enter to some extent into the most cold-blooded scientific research as a disturbing factor.
>
> —W. E. B. Du Bois, *The Philadelphia Negro: A Social Study* (1899)

In most respects, social science today is unrecognizably different from what it was in the years when W. E. B. Du Bois wrote his classic book *The Philadelphia Negro*. The social sciences have developed a whole series of methods of observation and analysis, and on the basis of these developments, have proceeded to describe the social world with a degree of confidence and consensus that only a few optimists could have expected in Du Bois's time. Many more social scientists are engaged in research, and the resources available for social research have also greatly increased from the thousands to the billions. The political conformity and development of convincing methods have led to the marriage of social research with social policy to an extent that was not possible in Du Bois's time, especially for a social scientist who was also an African American. The passage of years and positive turn of events have not, however, reduced the relevance of W. E. B. Du Bois's concerns with sociological methods.

Nevertheless, some readers will ask us, "Why did you folks write a book on White logic and methods?" They will likely be incensed and demand to know why we have titled our book *White Logic, White Methods*. The methodologically inclined will say, "Methods are objective research tools beyond race, gender, and class." They will argue that "social science methodology, like genetics, can be applied impartially regardless of the racial background of the individual conducting the investigation." Before we address these burning questions and points of view, we need to explain our motivations for editing a book such as this one. Thus, we begin this book in a very personal way with two vignettes from our own experiences in academia. We do so because we believe that our experiences showcase how "White logic" and "White methods" work in practice and how they blind (or severely limit) many social scientists from truly appreciating the significance of "race" (or, properly speaking, racial stratification). This book, accordingly, is not just the product of our sociological practice; it also grows out of our concerns with how the White racial logic influences the life chances of all "racial subjects" (Goldberg 1997, 104–9) and the "sociological imagination."[1] This book is also "personal" in so far as we, like other sociologists of color, have felt the impact of racial stratification in our own flesh throughout our entire lives—inside and outside of academia. Thus, we regard this as our first collaborative effort to attack White supremacy in contemporary research on race as well as in the methods most sociologists employ to examine, according to the logic that parades as "objectivity," the so-called race effect. In this book, we will challenge the artificial distinction between analysis and analysts, individuals doing research and the world of scholarly knowledge, methods, and theory, a fiction of modern social analysis (Agger 2002).

In what follows, we do three things. First, we provide vignettes from our experiences in our respective sociological domains that show how White logic and White methods have affected us. Second, we conceptualize White logic and White methods and explain the problems they pose for sociology and its practitioners. Lastly, we conclude this introductory chapter with a brief description of each of the chapters in the book and explain what each brings to the methodological table.

TUKUFU ZUBERI ON WHITE LOGIC AND WHITE METHODS

In the first set of vignettes, Tukufu Zuberi discusses the reactions to his book Thicker Than Blood: How Racial Statistics Lie.

Since the publication of *Thicker Than Blood* in 2001, I have been invited by the major sociology and population departments in the country to discuss what I meant by writing such a book. In these discussions, there is always a question asked by some through scientific curiosity and by others through the difficulty of coming to terms with the history of racism among social scientists. Most scholars in attendance, nevertheless, think around these questions. They raise their hands in a half-hesitant sort of way, looking at me with a strange curiosity, and then instead of saying directly "Are you calling us racist?" they ask, "Are you suggesting social scientists practice racism when they use statistics?" or "Are you suggesting that the logic of statistical methods is racist?" I answer restating the basic argument presented in the book.

Are you calling us racist?

I typically answer this first question by stating that in *Thicker Than Blood* I do not call anyone a racist. Rather than label individuals, or impute motive I provide an analysis of the history and logic of statistical analysis. I believe that social science is at its best when it is self-critical and relentlessly self-correcting. In order to be self-correcting we must be open to a critical evaluation of the methods we use and the conclusions that we have come to. In *Thicker Than Blood* I outline how statistical analysis was developed alongside a logic of racial reasoning. That the founder of statistical analysis also developed a theory of White supremacy is not an accident. The founders developed statistical analysis to explain the racial inferiority of colonial and second-class citizens in the new imperial era. I critically evaluate the history and practice of racial statistics to suggest ways in which social statisticians correct their practice.

Are you suggesting social scientists practice racism when they use statistics?

I usually begin answering this question by stating that I use statistics in my research. In fact, I feel that I have earned the right to critique the use of statistics by my long history of using statistics and demographic methods.[2] In others words, I say, "I have sinned, thus I can speak." I then explain that in my view the historical trajectory of the application of statistical methods to the study of society developed in relation to European contact, colonization, trade, and domination of peoples thought to be beyond modern civilization. In *Thicker Than Blood,* I demonstrate how the current uses of statistical methods in the social sciences were developed as part of the eugenics movement. No one can deny this fact. A careful reading of the history of social statistics reveals that it was born when mathematical statistics and evolutionary theory met in the racially bent eugenic mind of Francis Galton.[3] Galton was obsessed with explaining the racial hierarchy in social status and achievement.

In these discussions I always point out that the idea that racial differences are the cause of individual social status and achievement grew out of colonialism and the enslavement of Africans and Native Americans. The rise of democracy occurred at the same time as enslavement and colonialism. The establishment of European colonies in Africa, Asia, and America distinguished the beginning of the twentieth century. When Africans were emancipated from slavery in the West, colonization and segregation ruled the day in Africa and Asia. These apparent contradictions needed justification, and the birth of racial statistics gave scientific credibility to justifications of racial inequality.

Usually it is at this point that someone in the audience points out that statistics have not been used exclusively by supporters of racist policies. They argue that, particularly in more recent times, social scientists have regularly used statistics to refute racist arguments. I agree with them on this important point; however, I mention that by employing racial statistics incorrectly they legitimate the use of methodologies that perpetuate the problem. In part, this is a result of a faulty understanding of the meaning of race, and a misuse of statistical methodology.

I remind the audience that the top journals in sociology routinely publish articles in which the authors discuss the "effect of race." This use of causal language has important implications for how racial data are interpreted.[4] In almost all of the articles in these journals race is viewed as an unalterable characteristic of an individual. This social construction of race as an unalterable characteristic places a conceptual limitation on the researcher's ability to understand racial dynamics. I argue that the very definition of race has changed over time; thus, to understand the impact of race one would need to understand the impact and nature of these changes in the definition of race. As a variable, race is not consistently defined as a variable across time and space, and thus comparing race over time is in reality a comparison of the changing social meaning of race.

I point out that social scientists are typically not prepared to answer the basic questions of "how do you interpret the meaning of the 'effect of race?'" It is at this point that I typically ask a rhetorical question: "What does it mean when a researcher writes something like, 'The effect of being Black on mortality is equivalent to over five years of increased age?'" In this hypothetical case does the author mean that the "effect of being Black" refers to the color of the person's skin, in which case the blacker the person the more intense the impact, or do they mean to imply that Black persons have a higher propensity to engage in some particular behavior? In both of these cases race, not racial relations, is seen as the causal factor, and in both cases the researcher's answer is not based on the data.

I suggest that when we discuss the "effect of race," we are less mindful of the larger social world in which the path to success or failure is influenced. Usually someone in attendance argues that "race causes a person to be in a certain condition." This is like arguing that race is a proxy for an individual's biological makeup, or like smoking causes cancer. Alternatively, I suggest that we place statistical analysis of race within a historical and social context. It is not a question of how a person's race causes disadvantage and discrimination. The real issue is the way the society responds to an individual's racial identification. The question has more to do with society itself, not the innate makeup of individuals. Racial identity is about shared social status, not shared individual characteristics. Race is not about an individual's skin color. Race is about an individual's relationship to other people within the society. While racial identification may be internalized and appear to be the result of self-designation, it is, in fact, a result of the merging of self-imposed choice within an externally imposed context. When we forget or make slight of this point, social science becomes the justification for racial stratification.

To this end, I argue that race is a social construct. Within this construct, the person of color does not exist outside of his or her otherness. It is the international belief in race as real that makes race real in its social consequences. Nevertheless, a belief is not a fact, and we should question how and why we believe something to be real. We must demystify aspects of currently accepted notions of racial statistics by showing the extent to which this research has been shaped by extrinsic factors such as the interests and social position of particular scholars/researchers and debated issues long since forgotten. The views and social position of researchers have a lot to do with how they interpret racial statistics. As our example with the "effect of race" discussed above, researchers reach beyond the data when they interpret their statistical results. Data do not tell us a story. We use data to craft a story that comports with our understanding of the world. If we begin with a racially biased view of the world, then we will end with a racially biased view of what the data have to say. Data may indeed speak to some users of statistics; however, it only speaks to the rest of us in the voice of the research.

Are you suggesting that the logic of statistical methods is racist?

First, we must keep in mind that the numbers of mathematics and the numbers of statistics (including those of economics, sociology, and demography) are quite different. Mathematics is a system of statements that are accepted as true.[5] Mathematical statements follow one another in a definite order according to certain principles and are accompanied by proofs. The numbers from mathematics are the result of logical calculations. In mathematics, the numbers are either exact or have a known or estimable error. Statistics is a system of estimation based on uncertainty. Statistics is a form of applied mathematics. Often statistics are no more than the axioms applied, and they do not suggest the conditions of the correct applicability of the methods in the real world. Particular statistical methods' applicability to social problems is determined by the users of social statistics.

The language of statistics is full of terms and symbols that have no meaning to social scientist across disciplines and usually are not important to anyone who is not an expert in the specific discipline's practice of statistics. But the foundations of statistical applications to the study of society are the same and can be understood and debated on the basis of basic mathematics and logical statements. Yet there is no set logic in the methods themselves that lead to them being used by sociologist, economist, or political scientist. These various disciplines use statistics in particular ways because of a consensus among the practitioners. Thus, the accepted practices of statistical analysis unfortunately are not the result of the logic of the methods, but a result of the consensus-making process within the discipline.

I elaborate on this point by pointing out that current statistical methodologies were developed as part of the eugenics movement and continue to reflect the racist ideologies that gave rise to them. Early in its development, social statistics were inextricably linked to the numerical analysis of human difference. Eugenic ideas were at the heart of the development of statistical logic. This statistical logic, as well as the regression-type models that they employed, is the foundation on which modern statistical analysis is based.

In these cases, I ask the audience to think of the example of the statistical relationship between an individual's race and intelligence. I ask them to imagine that a researcher poses the question: *"Is a person's level of intelligence the result of their race?"*[6] I suggest that the researcher establishes what we can study by how they have asked the question. This hypothetical question requires that we accept that both intelligence and individual racial identity can be measured using some type of instrument. In the social sciences, the instrument of measurement is a survey, or written examination. Thus, this hypothetical case requires us to believe that we can measure an individual's racial identity and intelligence by the use of a survey questionnaire or examination. By its very design, this hypothetical question has forced us to accept the logic of understanding the nature and relationship between race and intelligence. Both race and intelligence are presented as individual attributes. We are forced to consider the statistical relationship as something that can be learned from the data. But, in fact, the statistical relationship between the two variables is a result of how they have been designed and our acceptance of them as appropriate for statistical analysis. That is, we are not learning from the data, we are in fact presenting data that we have generated by our own biases. We believe that race can be measure by an individual, and that this measurement is objective and consistent across individuals. We also must accept that intelligence can be measure by a test. Both systems of collecting data and using statistics to analyze them were born in the intellectual movement of eugenics.

By this time the audience usually becomes a little upset with my insistence that what appears to be real is in fact a socially constructed fact based on our own views. And, typically in defense of remaining practical, someone from the audience argues that statistical analysis is the best way for social scientists to make public policy statements. He or she argues that statistical models allow us to elaborate on how and what produces particular effects. I answer that this may be true, but human knowledge is uncertain and imperfect, and it is not clear how statistical models contribute to understanding how and what produces a particular social outcome.[7] I point out that interpreting the results of a statistical analysis is connected to an underlying theory. Statistical results, themselves, do not prove anything beyond the numerical relationship between two or more lists of numbers or variables. The connection of these variables in the real world requires a causal theory. The language used by social scientists is usually reflective of an unarticulated causal theory. It is irrelevant whether the social scientist is aware of the theory.

I ask the audience to recognize the obvious fact that theories of society not statistical methods guide how we interpret social data. It is important to remember that what social scientists see as the strengths of statistical analysis in other sciences have more to do with the strength of their theory than with their statistical methods. Empirical results may be a way to understand what is happening; however, these same data tell us very little about why it happens.

After the above points are made, the questioner usually nods his or her head in agreement, but, unfortunately, silence follows. This important debate has for the most part been silenced in social science. And, unfortunately, this silence has led to a kind of paralysis of effort by some—as they continue to use statistics as if the old positivist paradigm had never been questioned—and a burst of passionate and intemperate support by others. In fact, among social statisticians the debate about causation has raged as if the emperor had clothes.

My second experience resulted from my response to the rising use of notions of race in population research.[8] The year before the publication of *Thicker Than Blood*, Edwin J. C. J. van den Oord and David C. Rowe (2000) published an article in the journal *Demography* entitled "Racial Differences in Birth Health Risk: A Quantitative Genetic Approach." The editors sent me a copy of a comment on the article that they were going to publish in response to the appearance of the article in *Demography*. I was given the task of advising the editors on whether they should publish the response to the article in the journal. Finally, the editors asked if I would also like to write a response to the article. They were aware of my forthcoming publication, *Thicker Than Blood*, and thought that I might have something to say on this issue. I wrote the editors that if given the opportunity I would write a comment on the misuse of racial statistics in the article, and I would start by considering that despite its misuse of statistics this article was successful in the review process and published in the flagship journal of American demography. I told the editors that I would argue that this is not the first or last time this will happen, given the scientific criteria used for the review of research and the lack of a clear distinction between causal effects and causal theory among quantitative social scientists using racial statistics. To their credit, the editors of *Demography* were eager to publish my response.

In my response, I argued that the Edwin J. C. G. van den Oord and David C. Rowe article was a combination eugenic thinking about race and a misuse of statistical analysis. However, I praised the authors' effort to integrate biological and social factors into their analysis. It did not take much to recognize that biological data were increasingly available for demographic research; furthermore, I suggested that these data allowed researchers the opportunity to examine the relationship between biology and population processes. After praising the article for doing these things, I pointed out the weakness of the authors' research. Like many social scientists, van den Oord and Rowe presented an anachronistic theory of racial differences and even misused the statistical methods. Their misuse of statistical methods in the analysis of race is routinely allowed in social science journals.

The authors defined races as "genetic entities because generations of 'reproductive isolation' have led to differences in gene frequency across racial groups" (van den Oord and Rowe 2000, 286). They based their measure of race on the mother's self-reported racial identification. Consequently, their measure of race is indirect, and based on their socially constructed decision. Indirect self-reporting of race is the standard practice in the social sciences, because there is no scientific way to measure this socially constructed idea. Like all other social scientists, van den Oord and Rowe could not directly measure their so-called idea of the genetic aspect of race. In fact, the basis on which the mothers reported their racial identification is a social system that uses skin color as the criterion for classification. Theoretically we can group human populations on the basis of skin color. Such a grouping, however, is based on our arbitrary distinctions. The difference in skin color between people of African and European origin is believed to be the result of a melancortin 1 receptor (MC1R) (Harding et al. 2000). Yet, the relationship of skin color to health outcomes obviously remains unknown. Health is not simply a social construction. That is, our health is as much a result of our biological, environmental, and psychological realities as it is about how we are socially organized. However, race is a social construction.

When we say that race is socially constructed, it has implications for how we use statistical methods. Human biological variation is real, yet race is a distorted way of organizing this variation. This point is important because it contradicts race-based perspectives about the physical reality of race. Racial stratification is real, but biology is not its root cause. Race is often referred to as either a biological (anthropological) or a demographic characteristic; in reality it is neither. Van den Oord and Rowe misunderstood the meaning of race. They viewed race as a biological and demographic part of each individual. Part of the absurdity in this kind of definition, which is quite popular among both social and biological scientist, is that while biology points to an individual, demography refers to a population and does not point to an individual attribute like the proposed definition of race used in racial statistics.

Second, the authors employed the statistical methods incorrectly to the data. The quantitative genetic approach used by van den Oord and Rowe is based on a false notion of heredity and, in fact, is governed by knowledge (or processes) at a different level. Their analysis is not based on a genetic understanding of race. From a genetic point of view race is not an appropriate basis for discussing biological differences.[9] The results of van den Oord and Rowe's study refer to a statistical model and its system of equations, not to the "racial genetics" that they suggest are the empirical basis of their findings. The authors incorrectly use racial statistics as a scientific justification of their wrongheaded ideas.

Nothing in van den Oord and Rowe's article depends on the statistical analysis because their causal inferences are not open to empirical testing. In other words, they have failed to understand the conditions of the correct applicability of the statistical methods in the real world. Their conceptualization of race is fundamental to their subsequent uses of racial statistics, and they were not cautious when using race as a variable. The authors, like many others, do not demonstrate an understanding of the fact that the numbers in social statistics are unique. Social statistics is a system of estimation based on uncertainty. Statistics is a form of applied mathematics; however, the power of the results should not be considered as a mathematical proof. In their response to my critique of their article, the authors argued that race was socially, biologically, and demographically real. Van den Oord and Rowe's results are no more than the axioms applied, and pay little attention to the conditions of the correct applicability of the methods in the real world. In part, this is because their theory of race is other-worldly; however, this other-worldliness is not enough to prevent an article that articulates old-fashioned (prerecognition of Africans as humans) racial ideas from being published.

This debate in the pages of *Demography* had very little impact on research practice. During the next few years, two articles were published on racial differences in birth weight. They were entitled "Low Birth Weight, Social Factors, and Developmental Outcomes among Children in the United States" (Boardman et al. 2002) and "An Investigation of Racial and Ethnic Disparities in Birth Weight in Chicago Neighborhoods" (Sastry and Hussey 2003).

Neither of these articles cited van den Oord and Rowe's original article or the exchange that it stimulated on the measurement of race in such research. This lack of citation can be read as a form of silence, and an acceptance of the practice of the misuse of race as a variable. More importantly, these articles demonstrate how powerful racial statistics are in the current academic environment.

This silence about race and methods should not be misconstrued as being of merely academic significance. Statistical conceptions of race play a critical role in guiding and justifying both private belief and public policy. Almost all of the racial statistics conducted in the social sciences and sponsored by billions of dollars, from the federal government and private foundations, deal with causal inferences. Because such statistics look and sound scientific and are usually promulgated by reputable scholars, great weight is accorded them, even if their import is in fact distorted by subjective predispositions. If the statistics are misleading, inappropriate, or false, or if the methodology incorporates false assumptions, few scholars or public officials are in a position to detect it.

Today we are witnessing a revival of the biological idea of race in medicine and science, even though some social scientists have argued for years that race is a socially complex matter and that subjective predispositions and biases, more than biology or demography, govern our definitions and categories of racial difference. The van den Oord and Rowe article shows how some scholars developed their ideas under the sway of eugenic theories of race. Eugenics developed by using complex statistical models to justify racial reasoning. This is in fact, how the practice of statistics found its way into the social science. The publication of the van den Oord and Rowe article, and the subsequent publication of articles with similar points of view, demonstrates the continued acceptance of these theories in social science. However, it is the silence about the misuse of racial statistics as a cover for wrongheaded ideas about race across academic disciplines that remains at the heart of the problem.[10] This silence also reflects how our disciplinary journals have done researchers a great disservice.

The misuse of methods in the study of race demands our attention. This issue needs deliberate and conscious study; we must analyze and provide answers. By recognizing that the researcher is as important as what they study we enhance our ability to contribute to an understanding of society. We are not Martians from another time or place, thus we cannot study society as outsiders. We are part of the world and study society from the inside. As we study, as we investigate, we must offer solutions that solve, and the world justifiably must demand not a lack of values and convictions, but rather the dedication to justice and an ability to present the truth as we understand it regardless of the challenges it may present.

EDUARDO BONILLA-SILVA ON WHITE LOGIC AND WHITE METHODS

In the second set of vignettes, Bonilla-Silva addresses how colleagues at Michigan reacted to his analysis of the material and ideas that later appeared crystallized in his book Racism without Racists *(2006)*[11] *as well as to how they reacted to a talk he gave on the diversity challenge to sociology.*

When whiteness becomes normative, it works like God, in mysterious ways. For example, while analyzing data for my *Racism without Racists,* I made a presentation on my preliminary findings at the "house of methodological correctness": the Sociology Department at the University of Michigan. Most of the questions my colleagues asked me were "White questions"[12] hidden behind the cover of (White) methodology. Following are a few of the questions I got on that occasion, and I hope to show the whiteness that seeped through the (racial) cracks in all the questions.

Eduardo, who coded these data? Did you have White or Black coders? And what was the intercoder reliability index?[13]

My answer to this question was that I indeed had independent raters, that some were White and some were Black, and that my intercoder reliability index was close to 80, which is deemed acceptable (Tinsley and Weiss 2000). But I also asked the person if he asked such questions across the board or only to researchers saying that race *matters*! I also asked him how many times he had asked White sociologists about the reliability of their data on racial matters. How often, for example, did he push them to reveal the racial identity of their coders and to examine if their racial identity affected in any way their interpretation of the data, thus potentially affecting the reliability and validity of the data they presented? My colleague, as you can imagine, was not too happy with this answer, but one always has to be ready to "speak truth to power"[14] no matter what.

Since you do not have longitudinal data and are dismissive of survey results on racial attitudes, why should anyone believe your interpretation of these interviews?

My reply to this second question was that I combined survey and interview data to make my case and used a "face off" approach—cross checking the survey and interview findings or what is called in methodology circles as "triangulation"—to uncover consistencies and inconsistencies in the views respondents claimed to endorse.[15] This strategy allowed me to document that many of the White respondents who looked "good" (i.e., tolerant) based on their answers to multiple-choice-type survey questions on race, looked quite different in their answers to in-depth questions on the same subject (see Bonilla-Silva and Forman 2000). I also stated that the expectation of having longitudinal data on race had one huge and very problematic assumption: In order for the comparison of survey results from the 1960s and 1970s with those of today to be meaningful, we had to believe that "racism" and the racial problematic in the United States were constant items. If, in contrast, we believe, as I do, that "racism" (or, to be technically accurate, the dominant racial ideology of the social system) and the racial problematic in the United States have changed in fundamental ways, the comparison of survey results from the 1960s and 1970s with results from today would be all but meaningless and bound to produce a felicitous view of racial matters in America. My colleague dismissed my answer as further evidence of my lack of "scientific rigor." Ah, whiteness grants the gift of *eternal objectivity* to its grantees!

Why do you question the obvious angst and ambivalence of your respondents on these highly sensitive matters? For instance, you seem to question Whites' sincerity when they state concerns about the children of interracial marriages, and aren't they right? Don't these children suffer a lot in this world? If this is the case, why do you make these Whites look "racist"?

My answer to the final set of questions was that I addressed the ambivalence and angst of my respondents but differently from the way mainstream analysts have done it. A common way of interpreting Whites' racial attitudes, embodied in the work of Howard Schuman et al.[16] (1997), suggests Whites are ambivalent about racial matters, which can be seen in the fact that they agree with the principles of integration (e.g., school integration) but disagree with most of the policies developed to accomplish these goals (e.g., busing). This interpretation seems to me to be profoundly naive, but, as some have argued, Whites' naiveté and "ignorance" of racial matters is structured[17] (Mills 2003). Whites express theoretical (or, in Schuman's terminology, *normative*) support for the principles of integration in contemporary America yet maintain systemic privilege by failing to do *anything* about racial inequality. This amounts to telling people of color, "I believe you should have the same life chances as I, but disagree with all the policies that can make this reality possible" and is akin to one telling one's kids, "You can go to the beach but please do not get wet!"

On the seemingly "sensitive" matter about Whites stating that the children of interracial couples experience discrimination, I said that I believe this is in fact the case. However, I also pointed out that this contradicts Whites' belief that we have become a color-blind society. Why would the color-blind children of color-blind parents be mocked by other color-blind children raised by color-blind parents in a color-blind world? This could only be a serious problem if ours is *not* a truly color-blind world. And, if this is the case, as I believe it is, Whites' protestations seem like a cover to express their objections to this type of relations (for a detailed analysis, see the discussion of the "White habitus" in chapter 5 of Bonilla-Silva 2006).

The second experience happened in a brown-bag panel in the sociology colloquium dealing with the diversity challenge to sociology. My colleagues Professor Mayer Zald, who talked about universalism as the solution to the diversity challenge; Professor Yu Xie, who lectured on good methodology as the solution to the diversity challenge; and I were the invited panelists. My talk was about Whiteness in sociology, and I discussed the history of exclusion of people of color in sociology, the slow and recent process of integration of minority scholars in the discipline, and how the White imagination still blocked sociologists from doing things such as including W. E. B. Du Bois or Oliver C. Cox as "classics" or precluded them from fully seeing how race worked in contemporary America. And guess what happened? I got creamed! My colleagues accused me of calling them "racist," of making race "real," of fanning the racial flames, and of talking about something for which I did not have systematic data.[18] I told them they all sounded like first-year college students in a sociology class. I made a structural claim about the effects of race in sociology, and they all heard me calling them "racist."[19] The discussion produced more heat than light, and, although I believe I stood my ground, that event marked the beginning of the end for me as a professor at Michigan.[20]

TOWARD A DEFINITION OF "WHITE LOGIC" AND "WHITE METHODS"

> For concepts and notions are never innocent, and by employing the notions of the adversary to reply to him [*sic*], one legitimizes them and permits their persistence.
>
> —Nicos Poulantzas (1972, 241)

We provide these vignettes from our experiences to facilitate our more formal discussion and definition of the concepts of "White logic" and "White methods." We offer four fundamental problems that White logic and White methods pose for sociology and its practitioners. *First,* Whites in the United States are the dominant group in the racial hierarchy and maintain an interest in keeping the racial order in place. Racial stratification means the differentiation of a given population into hierarchically superposed racial groups. Its basis and very essence consist in an unequal distribution of rights and privileges among the members of a society (Bonilla-Silva 1997). This numerical situation has conceptual implications. Not only are Whites a dominant population, the dominant perspective in sociology has been defined by a view of reality that privileges Whites in the United States and Europe (Zuberi 2001a and 2006). The espousal of the study of race was motivated by the need to support the racially stratified industry and the colonial efforts; but to the watching world it sounded like the carefully thought-out result of experience and reason. And because of this, it was singularly disastrous for social science, and for government and social policy.

Second, the physical and social sciences have actively aided in the development of racial stratification as a scientifically legitimate and socially acceptable concept. In the beginning the social sciences were an all-White affair (Aguirre 2000; Moody 2004; Stanley 2006; Antonio 2002; Nussbaum 1997; Benson et al. 2007), and this numerical reality did not change until very recently. Social scientists and the discipline itself reflected the dominant racial views of the time, and these views impacted their analysis (see McKee 1993; Collins 1998, chapter 3; Smith 1999, chapter 3; Zuberi 2001a, chapters 4, 5, and 6). The new social sciences developed as part of the efforts to justify racial stratification. This is why we question the objectivity in the analysis of race. The social sciences developed alongside the practice of racial stratification, in fact, they were developed as part of the system of racial stratification.

Third, even after the "integration" of a few scholars of color the social sciences remained numerically, logically, and methodologically a discipline led and structured by White males (Morris 2002). Integration of the academy did not invite a transformation of the ways of thinking about social life. In fact, many social scientists thought that the integration would produce White scholars with Black faces. Most preintegration scholarship that passed as objective study, under the guise of ethnographic excerpts or statistical analysis, was in fact ideologically White supremacist. This led a group of first-generation Black integrators to challenge the scientific claims of sociological practice in the 1973 classic volume edited by Joyce A. Ladner entitled *The Death of White Sociology*. This volume sparked a tradition that was followed by John H. Stanfield II and Rutledge M. Dennis (1993); Patricia Hill Collins (1998); Linda Tuhiwai Smith (1999); France Winddance Twine and Jonathan W. Warren (2000); and Tukufu Zuberi (2001a). W. E. B. Du Bois's (1899) critique of sociological methods and the works of Max Weber (1949) preceded this challenge by the integrators; however, this work did not force social scientists to confront their racial biases in their research. Parallel to this critique by the integrators is the work by several mainstream White scholars who appear to have once again not cited the work of the integrators. For example, see Stanley Lieberson (1985), Vaughn R. McKim and Stephen P. Turner (1997), and Loïc Wacquant (2002). While we might forgive the philosophers McKim and Turner for not being aware of this earlier work, it is difficult to understand how Lieberson and Wacquant did not make the direct connection of their critique to the work of these integrators.

Lastly, sociology has been—and still is—a White-led and White-dominated field and, therefore, it should not surprise anyone that the logic of analysis and methods used to investigate racial matters reflect this social fact. It is in this context that we venture to define what we mean by White logic and White methods. We do so fully cognizant that some readers will, to use a sociological cliché phrase from surveys, "strongly disagree" with the very idea that there are such things as *White* logic and *White* methods. However, as we suggest above, this reaction is expected. Most White sociologists, reflecting their dominant position in the discipline, have complained that sociologists of color are "biased" and thus do not take seriously their work or their criticisms. Conversely, many sociologists of color, reflecting their subordinate position in sociology, have doubted the research findings by white sociologists to explain the standing of people of color in America.[21] The list of books and articles by minority scholars and by few white sociologists (few in proportion to the size of the population of white sociologists) criticizing the whiteness of sociology is quite long. To avoid over-referencing, we mention here a partial list of the names of sociologists who have done some of this critical work: W. E. B. Du Bois, Hylan Lewis, Joyce Ladner, Patricia Hill Collins, Aldon Morris, James Blackwell, Bruce Hare, Thomas Pettigrew, Charles V. Willie, Margaret Anderson, Morris Janowitz, John Stanfield, Howard Winant and Michael Omi, France Winndance Twine, Joe R. Feagin, James B. McKee, Robert Blauner, Stephen Steinberg, and Stanford Lyman. On this point, the words of Albert Murray, legendary essayist, novelist, and social critic, in his contribution to *The Death of White Sociology* ring as true today as when they were first stated four decades ago.

> There is little reason why Negroes should not regard contemporary social science theory and technique with anything except the most unrelenting suspicion. There is, come to think of it, no truly compelling reason at all why Negroes should not regard the use of the social science statistical survey as the most elaborate fraud of modern times. In any event, they should never forget that the group in power is always likely to use every means at its disposal to create the impression that it deserves to be where it is. And it is not above suggesting that those who have been excluded have only themselves to blame. (Murray 1973, 112)

By speaking of *logic* we refer to both the foundation of the techniques used in analyzing empirical reality, and the reasoning used by researchers in their efforts to understand society. *White logic,* then, refers to a context in which White supremacy has defined the techniques and processes of reasoning about social facts. White logic assumes a historical posture that grants eternal objectivity to the views of elite Whites and condemns the views of non-Whites to perpetual subjectivity;[22] it is the anchor of the Western imagination, which grants centrality to the knowledge, history, science, and culture of elite White men and classifies "others" as people without knowledge, history, or science, as people with folklore but not culture. Therefore, White logic operates to foster a "debilitating alienation" (Oliver

2004) among the racially oppressed, as they are thrown "into a world of preexisting meanings as [people] incapable of meaning making" (15).[23] Conversely, White logic fosters the obverse feeling on Whites (elite or not): a sense of superiority,[24] a sense they know things, as well as the "White man's burden"—the urge so many Whites feel to educate and "civilize" non-Whites, which has served historically as the moral and intellectual foundation for colonialism[25] and "internal colonialism" (Blauner 1969).

Some readers will be shocked by this claim because it deeply challenges the idea that social science studies the real world. How could there be White logic in one world, one objective reality independent from observers?[26] Some readers will argue that the logic of social science, like mathematics and physics, is without racial biases, and can be applied regardless of racial and other individual considerations. However, as we have argued, all scientific endeavors transpire in a world where race, gender, and class are important not only as subjects for investigation, but as structural factors that partly shape researchers and their scientific gaze.[27] Furthermore, as critics of science and the social sciences (what Foucault called the "sciences of man") have argued, the normative order of the sciences was and is White, male, bourgeois, and heterosexual (see chapter 5 in Young 1990; Smith 1999, chapter 3; Collins 1998, chapter 3; Zuberi 2001a).

And to be clear, we are not suggesting that racial subalterns, simply because of their position in the racial order, are better able to understand the social world. In fact, most racial subalterns (as many chapters in this book will suggest), along with their White colleagues, have for the most part employed the White logic and White methods in their analysis of "racial" matters and thus helped reproduce the racial status quo. White logic and White methods can be—and have been—used by members of all racialized groups and the critique (and defense) of them comes from all quarters.[28] Nevertheless, for the reasons we articulated above, the critique of White logic and White methods has historically been done mostly by racial subalterns and, similarly, the defense of normative sociological practice has historically been done mostly by White sociologists. Hence, whereas the knowledge/experience basis of Whites, as a group, leads them to produce racial knowledge that tends to reproduce the racial order, the knowledge/experience of non-Whites, as groups, leads them to produce racial knowledge that uncovers social relations of domination, practices of exclusion, and the like (Mills 1998; Moya 1997; c.f., Scott 1999).

White methods are the practical tools used to manufacture empirical data and analysis to support the racial stratification in society. *White methods* are the various practices that have been used to produce "racial knowledge" (Goldberg 1997) since the emergence of White supremacy in the fifteenth and sixteenth centuries and of the disciplines a few centuries later. These practices remain connected to White logic and, as such, cannot be easily divorced, no matter what their practitioners murmur or shout vociferously, from racial domination. In fact, the more researchers deny the connection of White logic to methods of research the more entangled they become in the morass of justifying the legacy of White supremacy. Only by recognizing this connection can we begin to develop the best practices that avoid the legacy of White supremacy.

For years, these practices were mostly argumentative and based on overt racist readings of the people Europeans dominated and their cultures.[29] Thus, Europeans made (and still make) statements about the reputed inferiority of "primitive," "underdeveloped," or "minority" people in the world. In the United States, for example, the author of one of the first sociology books reviled those who favored the emancipation of Blacks because, "slavery here relieves him (referring to Blacks) from a far more cruel slavery in Africa, or from idolatry and cannibalism, and every brutal vice and crime that can disgrace humanity" (Fitzhugh 1854, 84). As sociology matured as a discipline, views like these were "scientifically" defended through data produced by phrenologists, ethnologists, eugenicists, IQ testers, and criminologists (for a review of race and criminology, see Covington [2002]; for a review of the eugenicists and IQ see Zuberi [2001a]). Foundational sociologists such as William G. Sumner, Lester Ward, Small, Giddings, Edward A. Ross, many members of the Chicago School (most notably, Robert Park), Charles H. Cooley, Charles Ellwood, and many others reproduced in research and arguments the racial common sense about racial minorities of their time (that racial minorities were inferior to Whites) (Hayes 1973; Morris 2007; Bonilla-Silva, Baiocchi, and Horton forthcoming) and helped in the "art of savage discovery" (Ryan 1972).[30] Some sociologists reproduced this view by following the biological view of race, while others followed a cultural perspective that has been labeled by Fredrickson (1971) as "accomodationist racism." Very few sociologists between the 1880s and 1930s were not affected by the "social force" of racism, but let's not forget sociologists reformers such as Jane Addams and, most notably, the forgotten Frances Kellor, who, despite contradictions, sang and played a different tune than their contemporaries (Osofsky 1964).

In contemporary sociology, as we will expose in this tome, the arsenal of practices to generate racial knowledge has been expanded and refined to include tools such as surveys, ethnography, various demographic indices, genetics, scholastic aptitude tests, and comparative history, among others. Notwithstanding that White logic and White methods have been dominant in society, in academia, and in sociology, they have never been monolithically dominant. Hence, the old maxim, "wherever there is domination there is resistance," applies to society and to sociology as well. In sociology the work of Du Bois represented early fundamental challenges to the eugenic views that ruled these disciplines, and the criticisms and internal rebellions that have plagued sociology historically suggest that resistance remains strong (Zuberi 2001a; Morris 2002; 2007; Winant 2007. See also list of authors critical of the "sociology of race relations" in footnote 21).

Resistance, as we will articulate in the concluding chapter, is the way to topple the reign of White logic and White methodology in sociology and in the social sciences. In sociology, for instance, without the fighting spirit and personal sacrifices of the first Black sociologist, Ida B. Wells, and the first formally trained Black sociologist, W. E. B. Du Bois, as well as the fire that has been kept alive by those who followed them in sociology, there would not be scholars of color in academia. And, more importantly, without the social protests of people of color in the United States and in sociology (e.g., Black Caucus, Latino Caucus, etc.), the climate would not have been created for White academics to accept the need for diversity within the discipline.

THE CHAPTERS IN THE VOLUME

The chapters in this tome criticize many aspects and iterations of White logic and White methods. Part 2 ("Race as a Variable") begins with chapter 2 by Angela James. In her chapter James addresses how social research, specifically research based on census data, follows the racial common sense on racial groups; that is, researchers treat race as fixed, thus reifying the category and, by extension, ignoring the existence of a racial stratification order. James argues that most social scientists studying race matters downplay the making and remaking of the category (the racialization process) hence naturalizing race and racial inequality. In chapter 3 Carole Marks presents an update of her 1993 piece on race and methodology (Stanfield 1993). Marks shows that since 1993, social scientists (she focused on sociologists, but her claims fit the various fields in the social sciences) have continued neglecting race and worked quite hard to eliminate racism as a topic worthy of research. In chapter 4, Akil K. Khalfani and his collaborators shift our attention to the development of the national system of data collection and racial classification in the Republic of South Africa. The authors examine both the apartheid and postapartheid periods.

The first chapter in part 3 ("Logic of the Method") is chapter 5, by Paul Holland. He argues that given the fact that determining the "race" of subjects is such a complex matter riddled with social and political implications, it makes no sense to use "race" as a *causal* variable. Accordingly, when researchers conceptualize race as something with the ability to cause, this idea raises a question of methodological soundness, and, therefore, Holland suggests that extreme caution should be used when "race" is inserted in statistical models as the independent variable. Chapters 6, by Quincy Stewart, and 7, by Tukufu Zuberi, highlight additional problems with using quantitative methods to explain racial inequality. For Stewart, the central problem is quantitative researchers' neglect of the interactive (i.e., structured) processes that create and maintain racial inequalities. Using a "swim meet" (where one team always swims upstream and another downstream) as an allegory for how analysts examine race matters, Stewart elaborates a critique of the narrow, straightforward modeling that analysts often do. He highlights what is missing in these studies and offers a new way of thinking about how to model structured interactions *within* social institutions and the covariation of racially structured interactions *across* institutions. Similarly, Zuberi questions in his chapter quantitative researchers' interpretations of the "race effect." Zuberi first exposes the centrality of racist thinking in the development of the field of (racial) statistics and, second, shows how that thinking led to causal modeling in statistics. Zuberi, following his pivotal 2001 book, renews his plead for the complete deracialization of statistics, and of "race" itself.

Part 4 ("Interpreting the Problem") is led by chapter 8, authored by Eduardo Bonilla-Silva and Gianpaolo Baiocchi. In their chapter they do a blitzkrieg on contemporary sociological studies on race (both quantitative and qualitative) and show how the methods used to examine race matters end up producing "the declining significance of race," a view they contend both reflects and reproduces Whites' racial common sense. In chapter 9 Carla Goar examines how experimental social psychologists have reified prevailing notions on race and racism over the years. Goar argues that as a result of the current ideology of color-blind racism, experimental researchers inadequately consider or fail to even examine race in their studies, even when the subject matter clearly necessitates it. In chapter 10, Charles Gallagher lists epistemological and methodological concerns that researchers who study Whites' perspectives on race should keep in mind. He ends his chapter with nine valuable and specific take-home points for researchers studying White racial attitudes. Finally, in chapter 11 Alford Young Jr. exposes the methodological problems associated with White-led and -oriented (as we mentioned above, White analysis need not be done by Whites) ethnographic research on race. Young also exposes how this type of White ethnography of minority communities helps maintain the dominant pathological views of people of color and their communities.

Part 5 ("Dimensions of Segregation and Inequality Typically Missed") is led by a chapter by Brent Berry. In chapter 12 Berry articulates a critique of the traditional methodology associated with research on residential segregation, particularly the multiple problems with our main demographic index to assess segregation: the index of residential dissimilarity. Berry argues for retooling the existing quantitative measures of segregation because they do not take adequately into account the "meso-" and "micro-" level interactions (or lack there of) of segregation. He advocates using multiple indices and strategies to assess the total effect of segregation in communities. In chapter 13 Walter Allen and his coauthors argue for more rigorous research that emphasizes theory and methodology in the area of education, particularly in studies dealing with scholastic achievement. Allen et al. argue that the traditional methods employed by educational researchers rationalize and maintain the racial status quo. Therefore, they conclude with a number of specific suggestions based on Project CHOICES, an in-depth study of race/ethnic inequities in school achievement across a select set of California high schools conducted by the authors. In chapter 14, by Hayward Horton and Lori Sykes, the authors critically examine traditional demographic methods of measuring racial discrimination. They suggest a new approach based on the critical demography paradigm developed by Horton as a more suitable strategy to capture the full impact of racism. Lastly, in chapter 15 by Jennifer Bratter and Tukufu Zuberi, the authors center their attention on the subject of interracial marriage. They criticize the assumptions that the social distance between Whites and other minorities can be narrowed with increased racial diversity, as this diversity will depend on how groups are classified in the racial order. In their analysis, they document how increased "racial diversity" has not been translated directly into a higher level of interracial contact and how the old Black-White divide is still fundamental to explain why some groups, rather than others, exhibit higher (or lower) levels of interracial marriage.

Chapter 16 by John Stanfield is the first in part 6 of this tome, "The Practice of Racial Research." John Stanfield provides a deep critique of how cultural hegemonic attributions about race predict the research outcomes and analysis produced by what he labels as the "feel-good sociology of race relations." Stanfield criticizes the "scientific" claims about race made by sociology in the last 100 years or so and argues, quite cogently, that sociology has not even dealt with the profound changes in the world that have transpired in the last few decades. Hence, he claims, sociology may become a useless discipline. In chapter 17, William Tucker offers a critical analysis of the funding endeavors of the Pioneer Fund, an organization known for its racist stance on all race-related matters. He traces his case study back from the publication of *Race, Evolution, and Behavior*, by J. Philippe Rushton, and uncovers the long trajectory of racist funding, publications, and agendas of this group. His analysis forces us to look more carefully at the working of the racist right-wing foundations and institutes (e.g., Heritage Foundation, Manhattan Institute, etc.) that are in place with the goal of funding research and researchers working to undo the reforms brought forth by the Civil Rights movement.

In chapter 18 Oscar Gandy Jr. provides insight on the various uses of statistical data and analysis to frame public issues. Gandy, a communications scholar, argues that increasingly journalists and other public intellectuals, as a result of greater competition or concern with the bottom line, are faced with presenting alternative and misleading statistics as a method designed to stimulate controversy and generate a readership. Hence, as the song from

Public Enemy suggested, "Don't believe (the media) hype!" Finally, in chapter 19 Regina Austin argues that although racialized crime statistics may help us challenge persisting racial stereotypes regarding Blacks and Latinos, in most instances they are used to reinforce racist perceptions of minorities. She documents how these statistics are used in courts across the nations, as well as by many criminologists, without controlling for class, wealth, education, and other relevant variables to represent trends (e.g., minority overrepresentation in certain kinds of criminal activities) as "racial."

CONCLUSION

As we have outlined in this introductory chapter and in the summary of the chapters, our goals with this volume are scientific (we firmly believe that new methods and optics are needed to capture the effects of racial stratification in society) but, more importantly, political. We see this edited volume as part of the long march of resistance to White domination in society and in academe. The chapters in this volume cover many of the ways in which White logic and White methods shape the production of racial knowledge and, thus, can serve as stop signs (or at least as a cautionary tale) for a new generation of sociologists. Furthermore, we hope the volume serves the all-important task of raising the sociological self-esteem of those pursuing new ways of thinking, of analyzing, of framing race-related matters. For as Charles W. Mills has argued (1997; see also Collins 1999; Alexander and Talpade Mohanty 1997), in order for anyone to attain epistemic liberation from the White logic,

> [o]ne has to learn to trust one's own cognitive powers, to develop one's own concepts, insights, modes of explanation, overarching theories, and to oppose the epistemic hegemony of conceptual frameworks designed in part to thwart and suppress the exploration of such matters; one has to think *against the grain*. (119)

This is our small contribution toward the lofty goal of liberation from White logic and White methods in sociology and the social sciences. We expect—and are prepared for—criticisms from the usual suspects, but hope the readers who find the book useful use it as ammunition in the war of position against the manifestations of White supremacy in the social sciences.

NOTES

1. C. Wright Mills's notion of the "sociological imagination" has become the standard to define the sociological enterprise. However, sociologists have not

extended the logic of his arguments to the project of sociology. Had they done that, sociology as a discipline, and sociologists as its practitioners, would not look as heroes, and the "promise" Mills wrote about would be viewed as a nightmare.

2. As of 2007, for examples of my statistical and demographic publications under the name Antonio McDaniel see my numerous articles, and the book *Swing Low, Sweet Chariot: The Mortality Cost of Colonizing Liberia in the Nineteenth Century* published by the University of Chicago Press; under the name Tukufu Zuberi, see my numerous articles, and the edited volumes Tukufu Zuberi (Guest editor), *Racial Statistics and Public Policy*, Special issue of *Race and Society*, Tukufu Zuberi, Amson Sibanda, and Eric Udjo (editors), *The Demography of South Africa*, Volume 1 of the *General Demography of Africa* series, and my 2001 book entitled *Thicker Than Blood: An Essay on How Racial Statistics Lie*.

3. Francis Galton wrote in the preface to his classic work *Hereditary Genius: An Inquiry into Its Laws and Consequences* (1892): "The idea of investigating the subject of hereditary genius occurred to me during the course of a purely ethnological inquiry, into the mental peculiarities of different races; when the fact, that characteristics cling to families, was so frequently forced on my notice as to induce me to pay especial attention to that branch of the subject" (23).

4. For more on this see Tukufu Zuberi, *Thicker Than Blood* (2001a), chapters 5, 6, and 7.

5. See chapter 1 of Alfred Tarski's (1941) *Introduction to Logic*.

6. This was a core question among the eugenic researchers in 1892 when Francis Galton published *Hereditary Genius: An Inquiry into Its Laws and Consequences*, and more recently in Herrnstein and Murray's popular *The Bell Curve* (1994) over a hundred years after Galton's work.

7. Clifford Clogg and Adamantios Haritou argue that "without assumptions or knowledge that cannot be determined from or validated with the data in hand, we cannot tell whether a given model gives a biased estimator of the causal effect of X or Y due to omitted variables or due to included variables, or whether any partial regression coefficient is unbiased, or indeed whether any of the possible models permit unbiased estimation to any of the causal effects" (1997, 104).

8. See Zuberi (2001c).

9. While the Human Genome Project has not ended biological readings of "race," many scientists avoid this concept and favor the term "population groups." On how this project has not done away with "race" and "racism," see McCann-Mortimer, Augustinos, and Lecouteur, "'Race' and the Human Genome Project: Constructions of Scientific Legitimacy" (2004). On how this continued use of race is contrary to current science see Jonathan Marks (1995); Jonathan Marks (2002; especially chapter 3; Joseph Graves (2004).

10. An interesting exception can be found among mathematically oriented statisticians who have begun to question the use of racelike variables in statistical analysis (for examples, see Holland 1986; Sobel 1995; Cox 1992; Rosenbaum 1984).

11. For examples of the kind of questions I receive from my mostly White readers and how I answer them, see chapter 10 in the second edition of *Racism without Racists* (2006).

12. What is a "White question"? To answer this I first have to assert that Whites form a group or social collectivity (for details on this point, please see Bonilla-Silva

2001). Thus, as a majority group in America, Whites develop collective views and interests and, thus, not surprisingly, one can talk about a "White question," or a question that reflects the majority viewpoint on racial matters. For example, whenever I lecture on my book *Racism without Racists*, invariably a White person asks me, "How come you did not present any data on Blacks?" I tell the person that I have a chapter dealing with Blacks' views and describe my findings (that Blacks are partially directly but mostly indirectly affected by color-blind racism). But this answer does not usually satisfy the person because this is not what the person wishes to hear. Thus, I proceed to answer the question behind their question as follows: "I know that what you, and maybe other members of this audience, want to address is the idea that Blacks are as racist, if not more, than Whites. To this I say that Blacks can be prejudiced—albeit survey research suggests that compared to Whites, they are less prejudiced toward Whites than Whites are toward them—but they do not have, and are very unlikely to develop, a social system based around their prejudices that will give them down the road systemic social, economic, political, and psychological advantages." For more on this, see chapter 10 in the second edition of *Racism without Racists* (2006).

13. Intercoder reliability is the widely used term for the extent to which independent coders evaluate a characteristic of a message or artifact and reach the same conclusion (Tinsley and Weiss 2000).

14. This was one of the charges given to the Friends (Quakers) in the eighteenth century and popularized by similar statements made by Frederick Douglass in the nineteenth century.

15. Lawrence Bobo, one of the most distinguished survey researchers on racial matters, has used this approach recently in his book *Prejudice in Politics* (Bobo and Tuan 2006). However, he used open-ended questions, rather than formal interviews, to cross-validate his survey findings on the Wisconsin Treaty-Rights controversy of the late 1980s.

16. To avoid any misunderstanding here, I believe this consensus was fundamentally based on the ideas of my former colleague Howard Schuman, who had made similar arguments since the late 1960s. Some of the coauthors of the famous *Racial Attitudes in America*, Maria Krysan and, most notably, Lawrence Bobo, developed their own, unique arguments and their ideas differed substantially from those of Schuman.

17. Many astute social scientists become ridiculously simple-minded when analyzing racial matters. I have personally seen how, for example, they buy into nonracial interpretations of "White flight" (Whites leaving neighborhoods experiencing a racial transition) such as that developed by David Harris (2001); how they love the culturalist interpretations of Black life such as those of Wilson (1978, 1987), Anderson (1999), and many others; or how they almost salivate when a minority scholar says that race is no longer as significant in America as it was in the past.

18. Professor Donald Deskins, one of the few Black professors in the department at the time, jumped in when I was questioned about the "data" and told the professor who asked me the question the following: "How many Blacks you need to see hanging in trees before you think we have a racial problem?" Professor Deskins has retired since and is now an emeritus professor.

19. One of the best, most direct, and clear discussions on this matter can be found in Alan Johnson's book *The Forest and the Trees* (1997).

20. I had plenty of invitations to "do lunch" after this talk. This would have been great and a direct challenge to some of the things I addressed in my talk had it not been for the fact that all the colleagues who invited me used the opportunity to chastise me one-on-one in private. I distinctly remember telling one of them, "How come you did not say what you are telling me now during the talk?" My colleague replied: "Ah, had I done that, some of the graduate students there would have thought I was a racist." My reply: "Then maybe your views are *really* racist." Common decency prevents me from printing my colleague's reply.

21. The list of books and articles by minority scholars and by a few White sociologists (few in proportion to the size of the population of White sociologists) criticizing the Whiteness of sociology is quite long. To avoid overreferencing, we mention here a partial list of the names of sociologists who have done some of this critical work: W. E. B. Du Bois, Hylan Lewis, Joyce Lardner, Patricia Hill Collins, Aldon Morris, James Blackwell, Bruce Hare, Thomas Pettigrew, Charles V. Willie, Margaret Anderson, Morris Janowitz, John Stanfield, Howard Winant and Michael Omi, France Winndance Twine, Joe R. Feagin, James B. McKee, Robert Blauner, Stephen Steinberg, and Stanford Lyman.

22. We would be remiss if we did not mention that objectivity has also been gendered as a masculine attribute. For en early statement on this point as well as for a wonderful critique of sexism in research, see Eichler, *Nonsexist Research Methods* (1991).

23. For an early statement of how Whites' research on race affected Black researchers, see Rhett S. Jones, "Proving Blacks Inferior: The Sociology of Knowledge" (1972).

24. Fanon explained best this dialectic between colonizer and colonized: "The feeling of inferiority of the colonized is the correlative to the European's feeling of superiority. Let us have the courage to say it outright: *It is the racist who creates his inferior* (1967, 93).

25. For a discussion of how Rudyard Kipling's 1899 poem and his *oeuvre* was used to justify imperialism and why it is gaining popularity today, see Foster, "Kipling, 'The White Man's Burden,' and US Imperialism" (2003).

26. Today, few philosophers of science would agree in *toto* with this objectivist and realist stand. Most would agree with Fay (1996, 204) when he writes: "Facts don't speak for themselves; nature is never encountered in an unvarnished way; experience, sensations, and other perceptions require *a priori* conceptual resources in order to occur; and the language in which we think and articulate our thoughts is inherently permeated by our conceptual commitments." Yet, one needs not end in the relativist, perspectivist, and postmodernist trap of arguing that, because of the above, all knowledge is the mere expression of power relations and as such, is just "representation" (e.g., Lyotard, Baudrillard, etc.) We contend that science and scientists (social or otherwise) can be responsible, responsive to community needs, and, hopefully, multicultural (Fay 1996). We believe in the possibility of developing a new sociology "concerned with careful explication of what *is* in order to ultimately liberate us from the destiny of what *has been*" (Brown 1994, 320).

27. For an examination of the deep connection between the emergence of biology and "race," see McWhorter, "Scientific Discipline and the Origins of Race: A Foucaltian Reading of the History of Biology" (1995).

28. On this point, we agree fully with pedagogical philosopher and educator, Gloria J. Ladson-Billings, when she writes, "[T]he issue is not merely to 'color' the scholarship. It is to challenge the hegemonic structures (and symbols) that keep injustice and inequity in place. The work is not about dismissing the work of European-American scholars. Rather, it is about defining the limits of such scholarship" (2000, 271).

29. The case of Puerto Rico is illustrative. When the island was "discovered," the Spaniards described the "natives" as either peaceful Indians (the Tainos) or warring cannibals (the Caribs). In the second imperial invasion of the island, the Americans described the natives as criminal, indolent, half-breeds, and childlike in need of supervision. On the former, see Badillo (1978), and, on the latter, see Santiago-Valles (1994).

30. We are well aware that many of these foundational sociologists have been canonized and, therefore, that some readers will interpret this statement as sociological sacrilege. However, a systematic review of the works of all these writers done by Eduardo Bonilla-Silva for his forthcoming book *Anything but Racism* reveals that none of them escaped the racial mores of their times. And the question for us, as sociologists, is why would we expect otherwise?

II

RACE AS A VARIABLE

2

Making Sense of Race and Racial Classification

Angela James

On March 7, 2001, the *Washington Post* published preliminary figures from Census 2000 and announced that the Hispanic population of the United States had "drawn even" with the African American population in size. Whereas the Hispanic population constituted 12.5 percent of the total U.S. population, the Black population was "only" 12.3 percent. Of course, that finding was true only if Blacks who responded as identifying with more than one race were not counted as Black, and if Blacks who also identified themselves as Hispanic origin were counted solely as Hispanic. The tone of this headline however presages the outlines of emergent racial processes. Who "counts" in public policy is represented as being determined by which "minority" group could post the largest population counts. In this manner, marginalized groups are pitted as competitors over scarce social resources. Few ask why the ethnic designation "Hispanic" is usually compared with a racial designation. Would it be equally relevant to compare the number of people with "British" ethnic ancestry in New England with the number of Blacks in that area? Or does the comparison between Blacks and Hispanics merely reflect an emergent popular understanding of Hispanic/Latino as constituting a racially distinct group? The journalistic "fact" of Hispanics "overtaking" Blacks is as much a fabrication of racial designation as it is of the demographic growth of the emerging group (Goldberg 1997).

As social scientists, race scholars, and demographers, how do we begin to make sense of recent changes in the system of racial classification, as well as of the popular response to those changes? This chapter explores the lacuna between popular and contemporary theoretical understandings of race. I begin by reviewing the idea of race as a social construct, as well as presenting a brief history of racial classification in the United States. Next, the role of social research in perpetuating flawed, essentialist understandings of race is critically examined. This chapter ends with an assessment of the question of how race can be most reasonably and effectively used in social research. I argue that there are two major ways of understanding race and that these contrasting understandings are the underlying basis of the different ways in which social scientists approach the examination of race in the social world. Specifically, race can be understood as a social construction, or as a fixed characteristic. Although contemporary theoretical views of race flow from its being understood as a social construction, this insight is lost in statistical analyses of race, which most often use the construct as if it were a fixed characteristic. There are significant political and social costs associated with the continued use of race as a fixed construct in statistical analyses. This chapter highlights those costs, along with suggestions for how race should be employed in statistical analysis.

RACE AS SOCIAL CONSTRUCTION

Race is an exceedingly slippery concept. Although it appears in social life as ubiquitous, omnipresent, and real, it is hard to pin down the construct in any objective sense. This is because the idea of race is riddled with apparent contradictions. For example, while race is a *dynamic* phenomenon rooted in political struggle, it is commonly observed as a *fixed* characteristic of human populations; while it does not exist in terms of human biology, people routinely look to the human body for evidence about racial identity; while it is a biological *fiction*, it is nonetheless a social *fact*.

The Origin of Race

The emergence of contemporary understandings of race coincided with European colonization and domination of native peoples around the world. When English voyagers first laid eyes upon African natives after 1550, for example, the stage was set for the race relations that have unfolded in the United States ever since. As the historian Winthrop Jordan (1974) has noted:

> Englishmen actually described Negroes as *Black*—an exaggerated term which in itself suggests that the Negro's complexion had powerful impact upon their perceptions (emphasis original).

In other words, the early English read the African body as "text" (Hall 1988), as a signifier of important meanings about the nature of the souls (or lack thereof) contained within. The labeling of African bodies as "Black," of course, became all the more meaningful because the label represented the perfect contrast to the ideal with which the English imagined themselves. Adds Jordan:

> It was important, if incalculably so, that English discovery of Black Africans came at a time when the accepted English standard of beauty was a fair complexion of rose and White. Negroes seemed the very picture of perverse negation. (1974, 7)

The role of this "perverse negation" in the subsequent history of race in America cannot be overstated. It is a history rooted in the nature of "binary oppositions" (Hall 1988), specifically between the opposites "Black" and "White." Because the meaning of an object is always established in relation to another object, that is, through the differences between the objects, meaning is most efficiently and effectively expressed through comparisons between binary opposites (e.g., day and night, male and female, Black and White). Eventually, the basic White (English)/Black (African) distinction would give birth to a pair of extended chains of related equivalences: English = civilized = Christian = superior = free; African = uncivilized = heathen = inferior = unfree. The African thus became the foil against which the English defined who they wished to be. Indeed, the rationalized morality of the slavery system ("unfree" labor) depended upon these distinctions, which also worked to pacify poor Whites ("free" labor) with the relatively higher levels of status it bestowed upon them. In a very real sense, America's emerging racial order was predicated on this binary and continues to be organized by it today, despite the rise of other-raced groups.

The Nature of Race

In our earliest conceptualizations of race, scientists and common folk alike understood race to be a matter of "bloodlines." In other words, racial characteristics were considered to be "in the blood" and tied to an individual's ancestry as well as appearance. Following the early European voyagers, observers generally accepted race as a fact of nature, as a biological, fixed essence that could be used to objectively distinguish one human group from another.

Even though commonsense notions of race continue to echo this early view of racial differences, being rooted in biological distinctions between groups, most scholars today understand race as a "social construction," the ongoing, dynamic product of political contest (Omi and Winant 1994). In practical terms, to say that race is "socially constructed" means that it is *neither* "mere illusion," and thus irrelevant, *nor* something that should be viewed as "objective" and "fixed." As a social phenomenon, race is rather unique in its marriage of fictitious and factual attributes. Even though there are physical characteristics that one can point to in distinguishing among various groups, most social scientists would agree that the physical differences are much less significant than the social meanings attached to them (e.g., recall the chains of equivalences associated with the Black/White binary). In fact, researchers have shown that there is often more phenotypic variation *within* so-called racial groups, than there is *between* the groups (Marks 1994). This is why race as a social phenomenon is distinct, although not entirely disconnected, from observable physical differences.

At the same time, the social construction of race refers to the process by which people, both individually and collectively, negotiate their identities and related interests in an environment of scarce resources. That is, race entails subjective attachments of the individual to a racially defined group—a dominant racial group that uses its power to subordinate other racial groups defined as inferior (i.e., "racism"), or subordinate racial groups whose members join forces to challenge the racial status quo (i.e., "antiracism"). In this sense, race acts as a proxy for a common set of historical experiences and contemporary interests shared by individuals (Guinier 1995). What it "means" to belong to a race at any given moment is created intertextually as part of an ongoing, ideological struggle over societal boundaries, inclusion, and equity (Hunt 1997; Hall 1988). These constructions are both the product of the racial subject as well as racial others. Each is intricately connected to the racial structuring of society, as well as to ongoing interactions with each other.

In short, social events, both past and present, are key to the formation of any racialized context. Economic, political, and cultural factors continually shape the definitions of race and of racial groups in the United States (Omi and Winant 1994). It is impossible to understand contemporary social debates about race and racism without considering how they are deeply imbedded in the specifics of the moment. At the same time, the social meaning of race today, although somewhat different from past understandings, cannot be entirely disconnected from this history; it can be most fruitfully considered as part of a long-standing, dynamic process of racial formation (Omi and Winant 1994). While the human body informs the roles people play in this process, it does not determine the outcome.

Current research on human origins emphasizes common ancestors that branch off into separate subpopulations. This view contrasts sharply with the commonly employed concept of four "racial groups" (Black, White, American Indian, and Asian), which have been used in the United States.

This view of four races (putting aside for the moment the current project of racialization among Latinos) relies on a view of separate, unmixed racial populations. Each group can only be viewed as constituting distinct "populations" by ignoring the substantial and ongoing intermingling between groups. For example, in order to discuss the demise and/or disappearance of the Native American population from Mississippi, one has to accept that Blacks and Whites in Mississippi with known Native American ancestry are *not* Native Americans. Membership in a given category, especially if that category was "Black,", has in the past been to the exclusion of membership in any other racial category.

Table 2.1, based on data from the 2000 census, illustrates a more fluid understanding of race. In this census, for the first time, respondents were allowed to identify with more than one racial category.

Here each racial group can be represented in terms of those who identify with only one racial group, as well as those who identify with any other group(s). While this representation results in population counts exceeding the number of "warm bodies" in the United States, it has the advantage of allowing a view of the relative permeability across groups. At the same time, this representation of all racial groups in nonexclusive terms underscores the socially constructed nature of racial definitions.

THE HISTORY OF THE UNITED STATES CENSUS AND ITS USE OF THE CONCEPT OF RACE: CLASSIFICATION

The process of classification is necessary because of the political and social centrality of race in American society. As the previous section on the history

Table 2.1. Representing Race: 2000 Census

For United States:	*White*	*Black*	*Native American*	*Asian*	*Other*
White	**98**	2.2	26.3	7.3	12
Black	.4	**95**	4.4	.9	2.3
Native American	.5	.5	**60**	.4	.5
Asian	.4	.3	1.3	**61**	1.3
Other	.7	2	8	30.4	**83**
Total %	100%	100%	100%	100%	100%
Total Number	216,930,975	212,564,542	359,983,124	13,896,728	18,521,486

Source: Census 2000 Summary File 1 (SF 1) 100-Percent Data.

of race demonstrates, oppression predated the naming of differences among races. It is incredibly naive to believe that simply by eliminating classification racialized hierarchies would fall. However, although classification may be necessary, it is also necessarily problematic. Because race is a socially constructed concept with no fixed reality, all classification efforts are fraught with imprecision. Classification schemas are always a set of imperfect choices made in response to a given set of political agendas and imperatives. The institutionalization of these choices over the long run always has the effect of "naturalizing" particular understandings of race. That is why there generally has been a great deal of struggle associated with changes in census classification, and why it is necessary to interrogate change and continuities in categorization.

Beginning with the first census in 1790, the federal government has always measured race in some form. Although the categories have changed over time along with the rationales given for the collection of this information, Whites, Blacks, and Indians have been in various ways designated as "separate races" from the inception of the republic (Rodriguez 2000). The census itself has been entangled in the nation's racial dilemmas from the beginning, when the U.S. Constitution instructed that slaves be "counted" as three-fifths of a person, to current debates over the identity and representation (Anderson and Fienberg 1999; Skerry 2000). Indians "not taxed" were not to be enumerated, while those who "renounced tribal rule" were to have their "color" described as Indian (Anderson and Fienberg 1999). In 1870, the census initiated a new category for "Chinese," which was followed politically by the Chinese Exclusion Act of 1882. Japanese, Filipino, Hindu, and Korean categories were all added in response to successive immigration waves. In fact, some have argued that the history of the Census Bureau's attempts to classify the populace can be read as an ongoing debate over inclusion and exclusion of various parts of the population from full participation in the nation-state (Anderson and Fienberg 1999).

Until 1960, the racial classification of individuals in the census relied upon the reports and observations of the census enumerator (Anderson and Fienberg 1999). Race during most of this period was viewed as both self-evident and fixed. Significantly, where there was ambiguity enumerators were instructed to look for other social signifiers (Rodriguez 2000). For example, in the 1870 census, enumerators were instructed to use the socially dependent criteria of residential community to classify "half-breed" Indians. So, if such persons lived with Whites, and had the "habits of life" of Whites, they should be classified as Whites. If however, they lived among Indians they were to be classified as Indian (Rodriguez 2000).[1]

For the last several decades, an individual's racial classification has reflected self-identification into one of a fixed set of categories. This change reflected a conceptualization of race as socially constructed, although it still implied that race was fixed for individuals. Further, this technique of racial classification did not include any recognition of the possibility of mixed racial heritage. This, of course, reflected a social understanding that mixed-race individuals were not White, and that other racial distinctions were less important. According to this schema, when a mixed-race person identified as White, they were "passing."

In the most recent census taken in 2000, for the first time individuals were instructed to identify themselves using as many racial categories as they chose. This recent change came about as a result of intense political pressure by multiracial advocates, as well as in continued recognition of the fluid and subjective nature of race for a given individual, as well as across individuals. This change was met with opposition from advocates of several "single" race groups. In Los Angeles, for example, several local Black politicians and community leaders urged its constituents to simply "check the Black box," particularly if their direct parentage was Black. This campaign was undertaken in recognition that there is strength in numbers. Debates and political struggles over classification schemes are not a mere matter of academic debate. The ideological and political significance given to numeric representations insures that any changes to the system of classification will have substantial ramifications. Indeed, recently a local reporter called to ask me about the social and cultural consequences of Black population decline in the city of Los Angeles. The reporter described a 75,000-person decline in the number of Blacks in the city of Los Angeles between the decade of 1990 and 2000. After probing for the source of the numbers with which he was working, I discovered that the numbers were deflated by only including those Blacks who had reported a single race. If all persons listing Black as a part of their racial identity were instead included in the "Black" category, the decline in the number of Blacks from the city of Los Angeles drops to a level easily explained by movement within the same metropolitan area. Although this particular article on the impact of Black decline in Los Angeles was never written, its genesis is a reflection of a widely held view of declining Black influence in Los Angeles. The results of this view range from support of Blacks in the city for a White mayoral candidate over a Latino candidate, to the recent loss of the Black police chief.

Race vs. Ethnicity in the Census

The treatment of race by the Census Bureau stands in direct contrast to how ethnicity has been handled. The manner in which race and ethnicity is treated by the census, as well as by the popular media, tells us a great deal about the tortured history of race in American thought. Whereas sections on ethnicity and ethnic ancestry have long incorporated questions about the respondent's own country of birth along with the country of birth of each of their parents, race has been assumed fixed across generations. Similarly, in 1980 and 1990 the Census Bureau asked respondents to identify which ancestry *or* ancestries with which they most closely identified. Notably, this question never asked the respondent for an exclusive ethnic identity. In this manner, the question of ethnic identity has never been conceived as a matter of fixed identity. Further, whereas the ancestry sections of the questionnaire are clearly labeled as such, respondents are nowhere in the questionnaire alerted to the fact that they will be asked to identify their race. The respondent is asked to simply complete the sentence, "This person is . . ." followed by four racial categories, White, Black, Native American, and Asian/Pacific Islander, and one residual category "other." Hence even the manner in which the race question is displayed demonstrates the institutional discomfort with the project of race classification. In fact, there is a determined rebuke of the understanding of race as a physical/biological fact, as opposed to understanding race as a social fact. The description of race and the race question as presented by the Office of Management and Budget is as follows:

> The concept of race as used by the Census Bureau reflects self-identification; it does not denote any clear-cut scientific definition of biological stock. The data for race represent self-classification by people according to the race with which they most closely identify. Furthermore, it is recognized that the categories of the race item include both racial and national origin or sociocultural groups. (U.S. Census Bureau 2000)

This statement underscores the subjective and social-political nature of the data being collected. Census officials have explicitly distanced themselves from any understanding of race rooted in biology.

FROM ETHNICITY TO RACE? CONTEMPORARY RACIAL FORMATION AND HISPANICS

As the previous discussion highlights, the census continues to be inextricably bound to issues of race and representation. As such, the manner in which groups are continually redefined and "racialized" reflects broader conceptualizations of racial formation. For example, Hispanic Americans have been defined as an ethnic group whose population could be any race. However, in the last several decades 50–60 percent of Hispanic Americans responded that they are racially "White"; much smaller percentages respond that they are Black (3.6 percent), American Indian (1 percent), or Asian (1 percent), and over 40 percent of Hispanic Americans mark "other" in response to the racial question (Rodriguez 2000).

The racially ambiguous status of Hispanics is becoming an increasingly important part of the racial self-portrait that is the census. Alongside the social and political contestations of people from "mixed" racial heritage the difficulty of classifying Hispanics is transforming the boundaries of race in U.S. society. However, in the United States, the political discourse about race has been most fundamentally shaped by the definitions of who is "Black" and who is "White" in American society (Davis 1991). The Black category has long been defined as someone with "any known Black ancestry," otherwise known as the "one-drop rule" (Myrdal 1944; Williamson 1984; Davis 1991). Anthropologists use the term "hypo-descent rule" to describe the one-drop rule and to elaborate on the meaning to encompass a system whereby people with mixed ancestry are assigned the social status of the subordinate group (Harris 1964). Although there have been at various times attempts to describe intermediate racial statuses with terms like "mulatto, quadroon, or octoroon," these terms have been merely descriptive of differing degrees of Black ancestry and have never carried any legal or social significance. Other racial groups in the U.S. context have not been subjected to the one-drop rule. These groups represent "intermediate" categories in the U.S. racial stratification schema (Hacker 1992). The degree to which "racially-mixed" persons *without* Black ancestry have been accorded the lower racialized status has been linked to both appearance and class. In general, these other groups of racially mixed people have been treated as assimilated after the first generation of "miscegenation" (Davis 1991). Whether Hispanic Americans will become a "race" or whether they, like other "ethnic" groups in the United States, will experience gradual incorporation and assimilation is an open historical question.

Racial classification is a dominant feature of all social interactions, both personal and institutional in the United States. Along with gender, knowledge of a person's racial origins influences both the terms and the manner in which individuals are likely to interact. Racial classification systems are the systemic and official accounting of salient social distinctions. As such, recent changes in racial classification schemas deserve attention insomuch as they reflect broad understandings of what race means in the contemporary American context.

In the United States, racial categories reflect our own particular political and economic struggles. There are several other racialized contexts, with very different historical trajectories with regard to race, most notably in Latin America, Brazil, and South Africa (Rodriguez 2000; Degler 1986; Marx 1988). In many of these contexts, race is defined in terms of appearance and class, rather than ancestry. While racial stratification with Whites at the top and Blacks at the bottom of the status hierarchy characterizes each of these other contexts, the boundaries separating races are not as rigidly drawn. For example, it is not uncommon in many parts of Latin America to find within the same family, members who are "Moreno" (dark-skinned) and others who are "Jabao" (high-yellow) (Rodriguez 2000; Degler 1986). The categories are not meaningless; they are attached to differential treatment and life circumstances (Rodriguez 2000). Categories also reflect the dominance and value of White "racial" characteristics over those of Blacks and Indians. However, it is appearance rather than ancestry that determines an individual's experience of race and racism (Rodriguez 2000; Degler 1986).

Most research in this area has found that Hispanic Americans understand "race" to mean some combination of nationality, national origin, ethnicity, culture, and skin color (Rodriguez and Codero-Guzman 1992). Further, Hispanics tend to see race along a continuum, rather than in dichotomous terms of "White" or "Black."

Increasingly, Latin American conceptualizations of race are having an impact on the ongoing race formation process in the U.S. context. Only in one federal census (1930) have Hispanic Americans been classified as a racial group.[2] This classification was resisted and has never been repeated. However, since 1970 Hispanic-origin persons have had two opportunities to identify themselves, once in the ancestry question included in the long form, and also on the Hispanic origin question included in the short form. In this manner, although Hispanic origin is officially represented as an ethnicity, the political treatment suggests some ambiguity as to whether and how Hispanic ethnicity is connected to overarching racial understandings. As such, census treatment of Hispanic groups in the United States exemplifies the social constructedness of race (Rodriguez 2000). The vast majority of respondents marking "other" in response to the question of racial identity are of Hispanic origin, demonstrating their sense that the racial taxonomies of the United States do not match their own identities.

In addition to the mismatch between the U.S. and Hispanic American conceptualizations of race, the exclusionary nature of the concept of "Whiteness" should be acknowledged. Despite several historical changes in racial categorization in the United States, there has been an overriding concern with marking the truly White. Beginning with concern over how to classify mixed-race individuals at the turn of the twentieth century, keeping separate the "non-Whites" has been a concern. Contemporary race representations suggest that this is still a concern. On March 30, 2001, CNN broadcast a news report saying, "non-Hispanic Whites now a minority in California." Many racial projections predict the "browning" of America. This concern suggests that Hispanic Whites are not seen as really White. The implied difference of non-Hispanic from Hispanic Whites suggests that Hispanics may be an emerging racial group, and that this process of racial formation is related to both internal and external group pressures.

MIXED RACE AND RACIAL STRATIFICATION

Another important social challenge in the ongoing struggle over the social meaning of race has been issued from "mixed-race" or "multiracial" individuals. Like Hispanics, this group has grown increasingly large and has been able to successfully argue that they do not fit into the traditionally rigid set of racial categories employed in the U.S. Census. In recent years, parents of mixed-race children and multiracial individuals continuing in the spirit of self-identification, have argued that selecting one race forced individuals to deny the racial heritage of one parent. As a consequence, the major change introduced in the 2000 census was with regard to racial identification. For the first time, individuals were instructed to classify themselves with all the racial categories with which they identified. As suggested by this description, persons responding with multiple racial categories should not be seen as revealing either their parentage, or their full ancestry. Rather, respondents' choices merely indicate the groups with which they feel social identity.

The historical progenitors of contemporary treatment by the census of "mixed-race" individuals can be found in decisions and rules governing the enumeration of "mulattos, quadroons, and octoroons" among people with some African American ancestry, as well as the somewhat reverse, "blood quantum" enumerations of American Indians in the early part of the last century. Mulattoes were counted for the first time in 1850 (Williamson 1984). Concern with the fluidity of the first category was expressed in the instructions for enumerators in 1870 advising them to be "particularly careful in reporting the class mulatto." The word is generic and includes quadroons, octoroons, and all persons having any discernable trace of African blood. By contrast, in 1860 "half-breeds" were listed separately from Whites and Indians. In 1870 this issue was debated as census officials questioned: "shall they be classified with respect to the superior or to the inferior blood?"(Rodriguez 2000). It was decided that the criteria applied to the "former slave population" should not be applied to Indians. Ultimately, in what was perhaps the first recognition of the socially situated nature of racial meaning, the census chose to classify "half-breeds" as White if they lived among Whites, and Indian if they lived among Indians.

THE STRANGE HISTORY OF RACE IN SOCIAL SCIENCE RESEARCH

Given convoluted and contradictory understandings of race, the treatment of race in the social sciences is perhaps not so strange. Race and racial identity are both treated by social scientists variously as a primordial characteristic, or as a fluid and situational characteristic. The study of race in the social sciences can be divided into two major groupings: those who study race and racial dynamics, and those who routinely use the concept of race in their studies. This division largely mirrors the division in the conceptualization of race.

Those who study race and ethnicity as social phenomena understand race as dynamic and situational (Waters 1990; Omi and Winant 1994; Hunt 1997; Espiritu 1992). In this vein of research, race is seen as a profoundly social characteristic. The dynamisms and fluidity of race are often used to better understand related social processes. For example, in Hunt's (1997) study of the 1992 Los Angeles uprisings, he focused on the process by which race is reconstructed in media as well as how media perceptions are shaped by race. Similarly, in Espiritu's (1992) study of Asian Americans, she focuses on the process by which pan-ethnicity, or broader ethnic bonds are forged in response both to political threats and opportunities. In each of these examples of contemporary race scholarship, race is seen as an ongoing social process. Racial differences, according to this conceptualization, are delineated as the effect of historical patterns of racial hierarchy imbedded in ongoing interactions, both spectacular (as in the case of a civil uprising) and mundane.

On the other hand, those who *use* race or ethnicity in their research, as opposed to those who *study* race, tend to treat it as a primordial or fixed characteristic (for an extended critical discussion of this tendency in statistical research see Zuberi 2000). Despite the widespread academic understanding of race as a social construction, most studies using race in quantitative analysis treat race as a function of fixed differences between "populations." In this way, race, as it is used in most quantitative studies, is most often conceptualized as a *cause* of myriad social processes and distinctions (Zuberi 2000). From SAT scores, to out-of-wedlock births, race is presented as part of a causal explanation of various social distinctions. Essentialized understandings of race are frequently made rather explicitly, as in the 1994 book by Herrnstein and Murray, which argued that racial differences in IQ reflected genetic differences in endowment between groups, or in a recent article in *Demography* which found strong environmental influences shaped racial differences in birth weight and then argued for the role of an unmeasured "genetic component" in determining racial differences in birth weight (van den Oord and Rowe 2000). Most commonly, however, the understanding of race as a fixed characteristic is expressed implicitly, as in an article in a recent issue of the *American Sociological Review*, which presents an analysis in which a dummy variable distinguishing "Black couples from non-Black couples" is included as an "independent" or causal variable explaining marital dissolution (South 2001). In another example from the same journal, researchers use "race" as a "control" variable to explain variation in children's well-being. In all of these examples, the causal mechanism by which race has an effect on social outcomes is not examined directly. In the first two examples, genetic differences are identified as racially distributed and these genetic differences are considered the causal mechanism by which racial differences impact the various outcomes under consideration. In other words, race is conceptualized as a fixed characteristic, rooted in biological or genetic differences between easily distinguishable "groups."

Explicit arguments about the presumed biological or genetic basis of race are not normally articulated. In that sense, the second set of examples is far more ubiquitous in the social sciences. In each of this second set of examples, race is used as an independent variable, which aids in the explanation of some other social phenomena. Often race is presented as a "demographic" or "control" variable, implying a theoretical neutrality not supported by the substance of the arguments or techniques used in the research. In this way, race has become, to use a bad pun, the "black hole" of social scientific research. To illustrate this point with recent issues of major research journals, in the fall 2001 issues of the *American Sociological Review*, *Demography*, *Social Forces*, and *American Journal of Sociology*, 67 percent of the articles that mention race make use of race as a disembodied variable in a regression model. The use of race as a control variable flattens out the meanings of racial differences and replaces it with a generic notion of difference. This technique represents a seemingly atheoretical and presumed neutral *usage* of race. However, using race as an independent variable without any contextualization or explanation implies that the causal mechanism for social differences lies in the categories themselves. This is most definitely not a "neutral" assumption. When race is presumed to *cause* differences in family behavior, test-taking, and psychological well-being—that is, without comment or argument about how or why the experience of race in U.S. society may result in different outcomes for individuals who face different racialized experiences—conceptual understanding of race as a fixed characteristic is being promoted.

CONCLUSION

Virtually everyone in America is of mixed racial origins. The long and continuing history of race "mixing" does not imply that such mixing will solve the race problem. In fact, an extensive mulatto population was enumerated as early as the census of 1850. High proportions of Black Americans are thought to have some White ancestry, and a nontrivial proportion of White Americans likely have some Black ancestry. However, such long-standing genealogical legacies have not dismantled the Black-White divide in social,

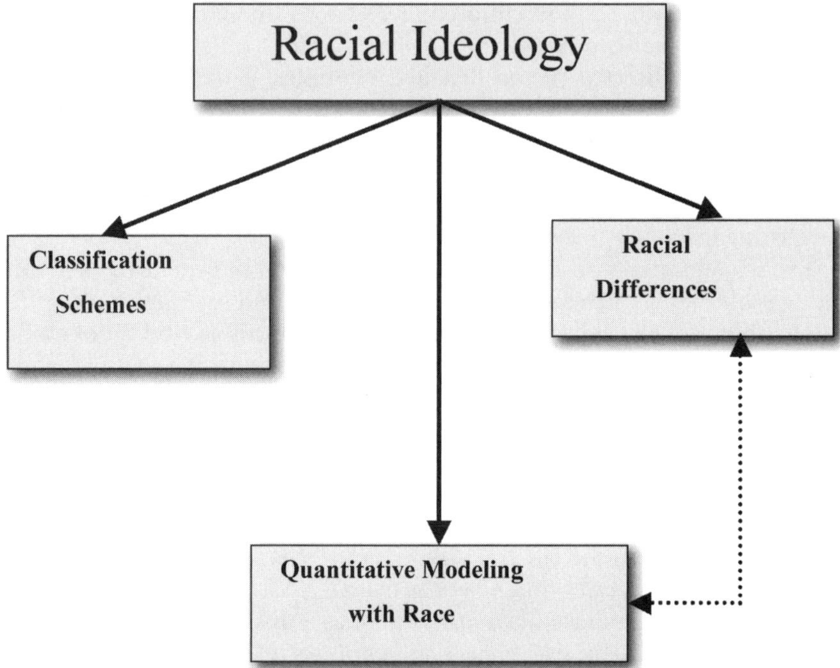

Figure 2.1. Conceptualizing the Linkages: Race, Categorization, and Statistics

political, and economic life. Similarly, history suggests that changes to the system of racial classification will not itself reform the way people understand race. Census racial classifications have changed with almost every decade without sparking a social movement, or even a perceptible shift in common understanding. However, classifications and the struggle over racial classification are not meaningless. There are important interrelationships between racial ideology, racial classification, and social scientific research using race.

While I view racial ideology as logically prior to classification schemas and research, each has ongoing impact on the other in what Omi and Winant (1994) describe as the ongoing political contestation over racial meanings.

This chapter has focused on the use of race in studies and statistical models of individual characteristics and behavior. I argue that social scientists and in particular, those using statistical models that include race as an independent variable, have contributed to the conceptualization of race as a fixed characteristic.

There are several ways to incorporate a more socially and historically situated view of race into models of social behavior. First and foremost, the use of race as a "demographic, control" variable must be contested. The atheoretical use of race as a demographic "background" variable is misleading and promotes an essentialized understanding of race by hiding the social underpinnings of presumed racial differences. When racial differences are found in a model of social behaviors, or attitudes, I argue that it is incumbent upon the researcher to interrogate possible sources for this difference. Instead of merely "controlling" for the difference of the aberrant "others," racial differences should be assessed and grounded in the set of historical and social circumstances that give meaning to the race concept. To do otherwise is to suggest that differences are rooted in the characteristics or "nature" of the groups themselves.

The use of separate models and interaction terms may help establish where broader patterns of social processes are similar or different based on racial group identity/membership. However, the most important step toward incorporating a more grounded conceptualization of race in social research is to adequately theorize race as a social and a historical fact in our thinking about racial effects.

NOTES

1. Notably, by 1950 enumerators were given the following instructions: "A person of mixed Indian and Negro blood should be returned as a Negro, unless the Indian blood very definitely predominates and he is accepted in the community as an Indian" (Ruggles et al. 2004 Enumerator instructions in Vol. 3, Counting the Past—IPUMS). This illustrates the peculiar marginalization of African Americans.

2. In the 1930 census the Census Bureau listed "Mexican" as a possible answer to the "color or race" question (Anderson and Fienberg 1999).

3

Methodologically Eliminating Race and Racism

Carole Marks

Over time, there has been a methodical elimination of the topic of race (defined as "a concept that signifies and symbolizes sociopolitical conflicts and interests in reference to different types of human bodies") and the topic of racism (defined as "a system of advantage based on race") in mainstream sociological work (Winant 2000, 172). This removal, rather than being viewed with regret or embarrassment, has instead been embraced and at times celebrated by many sociologists. Reflecting the standpoint of much of White America, sociological research confirms the majority view that civil rights laws have ended racial inequality, that discrimination is in the descendancy and redress readily available for those wronged. This is, I think, the heart of the elimination process.

Titling an article "Methodologically Eliminating Race and Racism" suggests that the topics of race and racism in the field of sociology were at some point or are now methodically included in published work. Such is not the case, and I am not arguing it. A better characterization might be that much of the time the sociological study of race has been haphazard and quixotic. I am not arguing that either, and it is important to state that at the outset.

I am arguing that in a White majority ideological construct, the concept of race, to use Howard Winant's terms, "is finally obviated" and replaced by color blindness and racial pluralism (2000, 171). An array of scholars, including many sociologists, accept this position. Labeled "racial realists" by Alan Wolfe, they claim that "America has made great progress in rectifying racial injustice in the past thirty-five years" (Brown et al. 2003, 7). Race still matters, they contend, because ill-conceived and unnecessary race conscious politics have exaggerated animosities. The failure to "live by the content of our character" is due to alienation and identity politics, encouraged by disaffected Blacks and the "condescension of well-meaning Whites." Thus, for these scholars, the reality is that racial exclusion and inequality are diminishing and racism is a thing of the past.

Underlying this thinking has been an assumption by many, as Stanford Lyman once observed, that "the good society will be brought about by increments, each one alleviating some suffering, establishing some benefit, until the last and final vestige of oppression, injustice, and wretchedness has been eliminated" (1993, 377). This is the thinking at the heart of the traditional sociological imagination. It is also a key ingredient in what I call the elimination process, a practice that predicts and then finds the declining significance of racism, declares victory over the evil past, and moves on to new debates. The legitimacy of political authority and the power of economic structures, that is, the basic structures of society, are not in question. Those individuals who claim the continuing presence of racial signification and the persistence of racial stratification are wrong, these scholars conclude.

Evidence of the "realist's" notion of racial progress is strong. "In almost every realm of American life, from sports and entertainment to universities, corporate boardrooms and the military," historian Eric Foner told the court in *Gratz, et al. v. Bollinger, et al.* in 2002, "an unprecedented racial diversity has been achieved and nonwhites play roles inconceivable only a few decades ago." That sociologists should then seek to document this apparent declining significance of race is not surprising. But there is also evidence that racial progress is still mixed with failure. Brown et al. in *White-Washing Race,* for example, wrote, "Studies provide consistent evidence not only that race still matters in the justice system but also that discrimination in the justice system has a rippling effect on blacks' life chances across every other institution in American life" (2003, 135). As Foner (2002) also reported in *Gratz,* the median wealth of Black families remains far below White counterparts, Black unemployment continues at twice the rate of White, Black persistent poverty is widespread, and life expectancy and health gaps between the races are staggering.

Producing meaningful explanations for simultaneous progress and stagnation are difficult. At the heart of the problem is the question of how much access to education, employment, and housing, for example, is still based on a system of racial advantage. Over time, public opinion polls have suggested that racist attitudes have declined. Is the attitudinal decline related to progress and stagnation, to something else other than race? Or is it simply the case, as sociologist Albert Memmi once observed, that despite progress, "racism persists, real and tenacious" (2000, 3).

EARLY CONSTRUCTIONS OF RACE AND RACISM

Sociology, like any science, operates within dominant paradigms that center on accepted practices: variable analysis, objectification, a political and a historical standpoint, and quantitative indices. These accepted practices are developed to create what Tilly called "useful tools of sociological analysis" and become the stuff of cutting-edge research published in mainstream journals and in many books and manuscripts. To be effective, tools of analysis need a theoretical base. Without them, results fall in between lies, damn lies, and statistics.

While "race has always been a significant sociological theme," Howard Winant pointed out in a 2000 article in the *Annual Review of Sociology*; it is a theme that never developed a convincing theoretical foundation. The concept of race was present in the literature from the beginning, he observed "though often in an inchoate, undertheorized, and taken-for-granted form" (159). Over time, I argue, these problems have magnified rather than lessened, and much about race remains unexplained. Without a convincing theoretical foundation, elimination is not surprising.

It was the "Chicago School" in the early twentieth century that gave significance and meaning to the study of *race relations* for the discipline. At the most basic level, this race-relations perspective, Joe Feagin has suggested, explored "relations between distinctly constituted groups, especially blacks and whites . . ." (2001, 100). Robert Park, chair of the department at Chicago, conceived of these race relations as "fixed and enforced by custom, convention and the routine of an expected social order." Park did not mean by this that the social order was static but rather that it operated by a system of evolving rules. By and by, according to him, through distinct stages the "others" would be assimilated into the mainstream and the last vestige of difference would disappear (1950, 81).

The scholars at the University of Chicago were not the first to think about race. W. E. B. Du Bois had been writing and thinking about race since the 1890s. Lester Ward thought and wrote about races in the South as castes and William Graham Summer viewed racism as a product of mores, long before Park and his colleagues.

But it was the Chicago School, as member E. Franklin Frazier indicated, that first systematically combined meaning and method to the concept of race, "developing precise quantitative methods in order to measure degrees of separation" (1968, 70). They studied groups in cities with reference to organization, competition, and distribution, ecological factors that described if not explained the notion of difference. Frazier was ultimately disappointed in the work because its major emphasis was upon social psychological aspects of race relations with little attention to the study of social structure. He argued that racial differences were ultimately rooted in economic relations and the political institutions that emerged from them and that these topics were missing from the Chicago research.

Even earlier Du Bois had expressed a more basic despair at the nature of the sociological inquiry. Said Du Bois: "Between me and the other world there is ever an unasked question: unasked by some through feelings of delicacy; by others through the difficulty of rightly framing it. How does it feel to be a problem? To the real question, How does it feel to be a social problem? I answer seldom a word" (1903, 15).

Frazier and Du Bois were lonely voices in the 1940s and 1950s, trying to move their fellow sociologists beyond a social-psychological, social-problems perspective on race. They were on the margins of the discipline, often shouting into the wilderness. More typical of the mainstream was Lester Ward, who, according to Lyman (1993, 375), was not sure whether the "lower races" could ever achieve the same moral, material, and intellectual levels as the "higher, occidental ones." The calls for historical context, a dynamic rather than a fixed system of classification, and perhaps most of all a debunking of what others assumed were minor irritants in a basically healthy social system went unnoticed.

RACE MEANING AT MID-TWENTIETH CENTURY

Over time, events and processes would force more and more sociologists to join the view of Du Bois and Frazier that race relations and race itself were significant and that their presence in the United States represented a systemic malady not a minor hiccup. Race mattered in large-scale political projects—wars, international immigration, social movements—and in minute everyday practice. "In the aftermath of WWII," Winant would later explain, "with the destruction of European colonialism, the rise of the Civil Rights movement and the surge of migration on a world scale, the sociology of race became a central topic" (2000, 170).

Still, making the leap from realizing its importance to attaching it to a theoretical foundation was a formidable task. "Theories too are products of their times and places," Winant has been quick to point out, "but their total absence impedes the ability to explain" (2000, 179). In the short term what was done was to figure out a way to study the social fact of race, a thing that most agreed was fixed and writ in black and white. The methods used to examine the facts of race relations were frequently introduced and almost as frequently, challenged. In *Dusk of Dawn*, Du Bois summarized the concerns. "The best available methods of social research are at present so liable to inaccuracies that the careful student discloses the results of individual research with diffidence," he said. Du Bois was convinced that there were differences between Blacks and Whites "but just what these differences are, is known to none with an approach to accuracy" (1940, 59).

Taking on the challenge, though probably unaware of Du Bois's concerns, empirical researchers in the 1960s and 1970s nonetheless redoubled their efforts to apply rational thought and greater scientific accuracy to the study of race relations. "There was growing respect for science," Joel Best noted, "and statistics offered a way to bring the authority of science to debates about social policy." Best suggests that researchers had two goals: one, to provide "a true description of society and the other, more hidden, to support particular views about social problems" (2001, 13).

This task was also fraught with problems. "Quantitative research," Evelyn Glenn wrote, "treated race as a preexisting 'fact' of social life, an independent variable to be correlated with or regressed against other variables" (2002, 9–10). Race was pragmatically studied by dividing individuals into distinct groups, defined by phenotypic markers such as skin color, and counting the differences between them.

The findings were unimaginative. They suggested, for example, that on average dark skins had lower education, less wealth, and lower incomes. "Race" studies, in fact, became crude measures of social class, a thing also "difficult to define and measure" (Best 2001). Since class was not fixed in mobile America, these findings "proved" what everyone already knew, that middle-class people have more income than the working poor, live in nicer neighborhoods, and give more money to their children. Adding Blacks to the equation with sophisticated measurement techniques perhaps increased "scientific accuracy" but produced little understanding. Race did give findings a little spice, and held out hope for some that something about race, some residual, could cause it to become salient without having to resort to biological determinism.

Biological determinism had been abandoned because many if not most natural scientists argued that race had little biological meaning and explanations based on things like phenotypic markers and genetic predispositions were not supportable. Racial classification systems, it was suggested, "were arbitrary, conventional and imply no hierarchy at all" (Gordon 1999, 99). The sociological acceptance of the biological determinism of race in the past had contributed to its fixity. Once removed, questions were raised about its genealogy. What was race, it was asked? A social construction was the response, unsteady, shifting, and capable of being transformed and dissolved. The problem, then, was to figure out how to study a fiction, what Ruben Rumbaut called a "pigment of the imagination," that had social meaning (Gordon 1999, 99). It was not an easy task. As Winant observed, "the most notable and intriguing feature of race is its ubiquity, its presence in both the smallest and the largest features of social relationships, institutions and identities" (2000, 171).

MAKING RACE COUNT

Overwhelmed or perhaps unpersuaded, many sociologists decided to ignore the fiction that they thought was, in any case, almost impossible to study. The question "What is race?" was left to the more speculative terrain of qualitative gazers and journalists. In empirical research, the favored approach was to study systematically the question "What is difference?" As Albert Memmi has observed, the problem with doing difference is that "difference is made to be a quality in and of itself" whereas differences are not in themselves good or bad. "They may be wholly conceptual, or simply invented and imposed on designated groups like a veneer," he wrote. In this case, they are used "as weapons against its victims, to the advantage of the victimizer." Difference has been noticed, he stated, for the purpose of denigration and not for some importance prior to that purpose (2000, 3).

Narrowing the focus in this way was a practice easily achieved because as Maxine Baca Zinn et al. have commented, "Most of the scholarly research and writing that takes place in the United States are conducted at a relatively small number of institutions" (1986, 290). The production of knowledge about race (and gender and class) is controlled by a small, mostly male, mostly White elite who perpetuate their power by designating, among other things, good and bad scholarship. Good scholarship on race, using large data sets and sophisticated "scientific" techniques, gets published.

The "official, flagship" journals, in doing difference only in the study of race, became increasingly technical and for many, unreadable. Race studies were particularly obtuse, the purview and the method of the few. As Leslie McCall pointed out in a 2001 *American Sociological Review* (*ASR*) article, research on racial inequality became "increasingly specialized, often focusing on a single explanation and subgroup of the population." And much earlier, Wilburt Moore observed that in focusing on more limited studies, almost any thesis can be made to conform to a curve.

The narrow focus led to accusations of abandonment, neglect, and exclusion from those who chose other methods of research. Inquiries into journal practices revealed that much of the absence was both accepted and explained. An *ASR* editor pointed out, without apology, "Many important developments in contemporary society receive little or no attention in sociology journals." Joe Feagin, in his presidential address in 2001, referred to a study of over 2,500 articles in *ASR* from 1936 to 1984. The study examined major social and political events for five time periods and found that overall only 1 in 20 articles dealt with the "major events examined for these periods." (Feagin 2001, 9).

The charge of narrowness also introduced the issue of exclusion. It was noted that African American sociologists, in particular, indeed many of the most well known, had never published in the "cutting-edge journals." Flags were raised. Why did these scholars rely instead on university presses and academic trade publishers? The question was, were those not published in the flagship journals denied acceptance, or were they intentionally by-passing this major edge of the discipline, or some combination of the two?

One reason was that reliance on a narrow range of methods and themes made many inquiries impossible. Typical of the problem was a comment by Erik Wright in his award-winning book *Class Counts*, a massive research project administered by telephone and face-to-face interviews in six countries, involving national random samples "of the labor force who are currently employed." Wright explained, "Aside from relatively brief sections in Chapter 2 and Chapter 14, there is almost no discussion of race and class in the book. . . . Given how salient the problem of race is for class analysis in the United States," Wright observed, "this is a significant and unfortunate absence." Wright's justification for the absence is to the point. "The relatively small sample size meant that there were too few African Americans in the sample to do the sophisticated analyses of the interaction of race and class" (1997, xxxi). The message was clear. Race had to be sacrificed in order to do sophisticated analysis.

Hampton and Gelles (2000) found, in a similar vein, that battered women's literature often ignored the experiences of nonmajority women by failing to mention the race of the women studied, by acknowledging that only majority women are included, or by including some women of color but not in the proportions comparable to their numbers in the population. The authors attributed three explanations to this neglect. First, the size in the sample was too small, à la Wright. Second, fear that the research would lead to negative assumptions about the minority group, especially African Americans, a liberal guilt explanation. Third, was a lack of interest in the topic of nonmajority battered women (196). Unfortunately these represent disparate reasons with but one effect, the elimination of race.

In a 2000 article, "Color-Blind: The Treatment of Race and Ethnicity in Social Psychology," published in the *Social Psychology Quarterly*, Hunt et al. did a content analysis of the extent to which "race and ethnicity" have been incorporated in social psychological scholarship. They examined over 900 articles published in three journals over a twenty-five-year period and coded them as to whether race/ethnicity was mentioned in the data and methods, whether it was used in the analysis, and whether it was seriously considered. They found that while the mention of race, the least substantive focus, increased dramatically between 1970 and 1999, a shift from 8 percent to 41 percent, the number of articles that seriously considered race during the same time period only increased from 6 percent to 10 percent. That is, there was an increase in the number of articles where race was a variable but few in which race was the subject.

The American Sociological Association (ASA) underwent a bitter controversy about the editorship of its major journal in 1999 that centered on an unwritten standard that an editor should have published in the journal. Attempting to investigate the concern, the association examined the issues of who publishes and what is published. A task force of ASA Council members, journal editors, and other scholars was formed to study the mainstream journals and their practice. Of particular interest was the question of how often articles about race appeared in the journal. Their findings, while not celebratory, suggested that the track record was much better than many feared, though still inadequate on a number of levels. Articles about race in particular appeared with some frequency, they found, although they were unable to make the distinctions of content outlined in the *Social Psychology Quarterly* article.

The ASA felt compelled, as a result, to issue an official statement on race. It said in part, "Sociologists have long examined how race—a social concept that changes over time—has been used to place people in categories. Some scientists and policymakers now contend that research using the concept of race perpetuates the negative consequences of thinking in racial terms. Others argue that measuring differential experiences, treatment, and outcomes across racial categories is necessary to track disparities and to inform policymaking to achieve greater social justice. The American Sociological Association finds greater merit in the latter point of view" (American Sociological Association 2002, 6). Laudable goals, but ultimately the result is more elimination.

One of the concerns of the task force was to discover if submission and acceptance processes were discriminatory. Former associate *ASR* editor Andrew Walder outlined the criteria that the committee heard fairly frequently from other editors. "The review process," he wrote, "tends to favor certain kinds of work: work that it firmly grounded in evidence, carefully framed in a significant sociological literature, and well-argued and well-written" (Camic et al. 2001, vii).

CURRENT CONSTRUCTS: BATTLING FOR THE HIGH GROUND

In the 2000–2001 period, published journal articles on race roughly fell into three categories. The first involved testing, with large data sets, some previously accepted theory. This was the most popular method of "doing difference" by using race as an epiphenomenon. The second involved exploring historical archival data with the intent of illuminating some specific event of the past with implications for the present. The third involved theoretical debates about the construction of race and their intersection with micro- and macrostructures. The latter two areas were clearly underrepresented in many mainstream journals, although their presence in "new or cross-disciplinary" journals was more pronounced.

The historical research area is the most recent contribution to race studies. As one *ASR* editor expressed it, "Many of the most intriguing questions these days occur at the disciplinary intersections, whether among various social sciences, social and natural sciences, or social sciences and humanities and art" (Camic et al. 2001, vi). But intriguing questions seem more likely to be raised, when published, by senior scholars, a luxury perhaps of longevity or power. More typical was the year 1999, the year the controversy began, when two articles appeared both reflecting the "doing difference" category. The first article was about property values and race. The second was about White attitudes toward racial inequality. Both used large data sets and sophisticated measurement tools.

The article on property values and race attempted to determine if "people might be adverse to black neighbors because of pure discrimination or racial proxy." The issue, as the author defined it was, "if whites avoid blacks because they are black, then stable integration is unlikely; no matter what policy is pursued, whites will still object to living near blacks," that was called pure discrimination. Alternately, if Whites avoid Blacks because of characteristics associated with being Black, then stable integration can be achieved through policies that promote racial integration while minimizing undesirable nonracial characteristics. That was called racial proxy. The author used national data on housing prices and for neighborhoods, census tracts (Harris 1999a).

He found that "evidence of a preference for high SES neighbors, combined with the lack of a significant net effect of percent black, provides strong support for the racial proxy hypothesis. Clearly, housing is more valuable in less integrated neighborhoods largely because people prefer well-educated, affluent neighbors, and each of these traits is more prevalent among whites than among blacks." The author's separation of pure discrimination from racial proxy is based on competing traditions within the field. Pure discrimination has been championed by Bobo et al., and racial proxy first by Taeuber and recently by others from Chicago. One basis for viewing these as opposites, according to the author, is that pure discrimination suggests little can be done while racial proxy (nonracial factors) suggests that "when black residents and their neighbors have similar socioeconomic statuses, increasing levels of integration should have little effect on property values, and white flight should not ensue" (Harris 1999a, 476). This is a process of elimination by structure of the debate. The choice is (1) you don't wish to live near Blacks because they are Black or (2) you don't wish to live near Blacks because they are poor. In the first case change is not possible because of bigotry. In the second case, change is possible if White people are convinced that not all Blacks are poor. The author concluded that the evidence does not support the notion of out-and-out racism, "lack of a significant net effect of percent black," so it may be eliminated from the discussion. The issue is not White racism, because Whites do not *significantly* flee neighborhoods that contain Blacks of similar socioeconomic status (Harris 1999a, 476).

In the year 2000, six articles appeared in which "race" was the subject, as well as one research exchange about the nature and presence of race categories in introductory texts. Two of the articles attempted a kind of fusion of empirical testing with historical archival evidence. Three relied on more traditional methods. An article entitled "Lost in the Storm" used integrated public-use microdata series (IPUMS) data to show the neglect of the Black working class in sociological literature. The article was critical of past race studies but its own limitations were also apparent. The authors used an occupational/income variable to identify three classes within the Black community in the South in the 1870s and 1880s and showed that the working class was the largest group and yet the least studied. To test the validity of their categories, the authors ran tests of where "laborers" fit and found that in over 95 percent of the cases they were located in the working class. They also found that in the 1870s and 1880s a higher percentage of Blacks than Whites were in the "working class" and a higher percentage of Whites than Blacks were in the "bottom class." This "surprising" finding was stated but left unexamined. The fact that the region had not yet industrialized at that time was not mentioned. The authors also failed to discuss what the Black and White "laborers" were actually doing and how many of the Whites in the "bottom" were farm owners, contradictory locations that often plague Southern labor studies (Horton et al. 2000).

The other three articles were less innovative. One suggested that "when African Americans and Whites have similar low levels of concentrated disadvantage, the effects of disadvantage and homeownership are relatively comparable" (Krivo and Peterson 2000, 547), and a second, "that a decline in the spatial proximity to employment is associated with an increase in the unemployment rate for blacks" (Mouw 2000, 730). The third, an article on the racial gap in health, concluded that "socioeconomic conditions, not health risk behaviors," explained the racial gap in chronic health conditions, a rather modest conclusion (Hayward et al. 2000, 927). The authors also examined the claim of previous research "that blacks and whites differ in their ability to transform socioeconomic resources into good health," and dismissed it. "The fundamental meaning and importance of socioeconomic circumstances in influencing chronic health problems, is the same for blacks and white," they found (Hayward et al. 2000, 927). Realizing perhaps that in making this claim they were rejecting strong evidence of racist medical practice toward the Black middle class, they explained that "institutional racism operates indirectly through the trajectories of socioeconomic achievement." Eduardo Bonilla-Silva has called such a methodological procedure "making race vanish in statistical air." (2006). In an article entitled "Leveraging the State: Private Money and the Development of Public Education for Blacks," the authors identified a strategy of combining private funds and public funds that Black communities used, in the face of disenfranchisement and hypersegregation, to secure public education. The authors, revisiting the Booker T. Washington–Du Bois debate, argued that the strategy was successful in obtaining social rights but not political or civil ones. This is not a sociology that takes risks.

The sixth article, "Ethnicity and Sentencing outcomes in U.S. Federal Courts: Who Is Punished More Harshly?" explored one of the most plentiful sources of research in the field, research on race and crime. The article introduced the use of data to reify an ethnic queue and concluded that there is a continuing significance of both race and ethnicity in sentencing in American society. That is the brave part. But they also found, "consistent with theoretical hypotheses, that ethnicity has a small to moderate effect on sentencing outcomes that favors white defendants and penalizes Hispanic defendants, black defendants are in an intermediate position." This represents a two-step elimination strategy. Step one, discrimination is there but not dramatically so. Step two; some folks have it worse than Blacks, a new bottom.

Despite the limitations, all of these articles satisfied the ASA's stated goal to "provide scientific evidence over the social consequences of the existing categorizations and perceptions of race; allow scholars to document how race shapes social ranking, access to resources, and life experiences; and advance understanding of this important dimension of social life, which in turn advances social justice." (American Sociological Association 2002, 5). Unfortunately, in the best of circumstances, the research also seemed to reify three forms of elimination. First, if samples of the "others" are too small, ignore them. Second, if the evidence does not support the presence of widespread racism, racism must be disappearing. And lastly, if some "others" have it worse, don't complain.

But more tellingly, Tukufu Zuberi, in his analysis of racial statistics, argued that "models that present race as a cause are really statements of association," because since an individual's race does not vary, race cannot be treated as a cause (Zuberi 2001a). James McKee, in his examination of race studies over time, addressed this problem in even broader terms when he observed that it was not simply a failure of empirical research but that "the fault lay with the assumptions and themes, the values and biases, in short, the worldview that gave direction and plan to research" (1993, 338).

THE OTHER SIDE

Empirical studies in mainstream journals were not the only examinations made of race and racism. Research and writing in other venues abounded in the 1980s and 1990s. The elimination of race and racism from the social scientific radar was found in one of the most respected and prolific race scholars. In the *Declining Significance of Race* (1978), William J. Wilson argued that racial barriers of the past are less important than present-day class attributes in determining the life chances of African Americans, a point he explored at length in *The Truly Disadvantaged* (1987). Wilson was not arguing that racism was disappearing, though many used his work to support that claim, but he was suggesting that economic opportunity varied significantly within the Black community. This spawned a new model minority, the Black middle class, well trained and educationally competitive, who faced less structural discrimination. Highly touted in the media, their hard work and success were used to discipline the growing pool of untrained and unskilled inner-city poor Blacks. According to Wilson, the racial disadvantage of both groups, while not absent, was on the decline. Critiques of these claims also arose. Oliver and Shapiro in *Black Wealth, White Wealth* argued that examination of wealth rather than income erased much of the advantage of the Black middle class. "The highest earning black households," they found, "possess twenty-three cents of median net financial assets for every dollar held by high-income white households" (1995, 101).

From the nonempirical side, a consensus emerged that new language and understandings were needed to correct the contradictions. One direction was acceptance that an increasing significance of class did not mean a decline in racism. Racism was ubiquitous and taken for granted. Another direction was the challenge to the binary constructions of race. Both sociologists and historians argued that racial categories created by sociohistorical processes have changed over time. James Davis (1991) pointed out the simple question "Who is Black?" did not have simple answers. Another was in the episodic composition of race. In 1994, Omi and Winant, in their path-breaking book on racial formation, insisted that race was a "fixed axis of social organization not an epiphenomenon of some other category" and that racial categories, could be "created, inhabited, transformed and destroyed" (55).

Historians revealed that international immigration at the turn of the twentieth century forced the expansion of the concept of "whiteness," as European ethnics joined Anglo-Saxon Protestants in the "American discourse of positively valued Whiteness and negatively charged Blackness" (West 1993). In *The Great Arizona Orphan Abduction*, Linda Gordon wrote tellingly of the Irish orphaned children leaving New York in 1904: "They did not grasp that this trip was to offer them not only parents but upward mobility. Even less did they know that mobility took the form of a racial transformation unique to the American Southwest, that the same train ride had transformed them from Irish to White" (19). As Cornel West pointed out, European immigrants had to learn that they were White principally by adopting this American discourse (1994, 29).

Again, after 1965, international migration affected the problematic of categorization. Where do we put dark-skinned Asians, it was asked? Are they like Blacks, subject to the same mistreatment, inheritors of the same social locations? And should they advance more rapidly in terms of levels of income, education, and employment, as many Japanese Americans have; must we return to some biological imperative after all? "From its inception," Loïc Wacquant argued, "the collective fiction labeled 'race' . . . has always mixed science with common sense and traded on the complicity between them" (2002, 1507). Whether duplicitous or not, this miscegenation created "findings" about race that were unremarkable and confessions about race that seemed unique and ungeneralizable.

Describing race, unsteady and contested, as a "fixed axis" of social organization introduced more questions. What were the origins and structure of racial categories? What about issues of identity, language, and representation? The introduction of terms like "intersectionality" and "multiple oppression" has allowed some researchers to explore the dynamic, independent, yet intersecting hierarchies of identity that characterize what Cornell West called, "a new cultural politics of difference of our present moment" (West 1994, 29). But they have done so at a price. They do little to explain how race conflict emerges and expresses itself over time or what general practices influence its development.

Exploration of ruling ideas, particularly the taken-for-granted, imperious ideas used to drug "the others," as Gramsci's use of the term "hegemony" implied, served as an important corrective to the notion that subordinate groups were both thoughtless and powerless victims. Michel Foucault once noted that "power invests (those who do not have it), is transmitted by them and through them; exerts pressure on them, just as they resist . . . the grip it has on them" (Foucault 1980, 99).

The implication that racial categories could be contested or even destroyed led to questions about the reactions of the *others*, including their ability to say no, to struggle, oppose, and sometimes change things. A spectrum of responses was observed. At one end, what Aldon Morris (1993) called "oppositional consciousness," a set of insurgent ideas and beliefs developed by the oppressed to challenge their domination. For some African Americans, it meant developing a discourse to counter White supremacy. At the other end, there was "internalized oppression," African Americans and *others* believing the negative and distorted messages about themselves. Sometimes there arose mixtures of the two, to quote Du Bois, "warring ideals in one dark body."

The instability of the category of race led to the substitution of terms like "racialized group," which stood for structures, ideologies, and attitudes historically instilled with "racial meaning" and also contingent and contested. This usage attempted to circumvent the contradiction of a socially constructed group that existed objectively, even before the process of categorization. *Racialized group* eliminated race, the biological fiction, but retained racism, the lived experience. The advantage of such a category was that it was not fixed, had a historical context, did not ignore social structures, and yet was "real," a fact that Bonilla-Silva has convincingly argued on several occasions (1999, 899).

But arguing for a real and subjective social construction is not the same as producing a convincing theory. As Winant suggested, over time Jim Crow was defeated, apartheid abolished, colonialism discredited, and yet racial classification and subordination persist (2000, 81). What do we know about the reality of race? The historian Barbara Fields (1990) went so far as to suggest that "race is a category without content, unrooted in material reality, a lens through which people view and make sense of their experiences" (118). Fields was not suggesting an absence of all material reality, but rather the presence of multiple ones. Stuart Hall (1986) went even further. "It may be true that the self is always, in a sense, a fiction," he said, "just as the kind of closures which are required to create communities of identification—nation, ethnic group, families, sexualities—are arbitrary closures and the forms of political action whether movements, or parties, these too are temporary, partial, arbitrary" (69). Paul Gilroy, who acknowledges both the privileges attached to the beneficiaries of racial hierarchy and the complex tradition of "politics, ethics, identity, and culture" built by oppressed groups in response to that hierarchy, nonetheless calls for the demise of "race." He suggests that "something worthwhile will be gained from a deliberate renunciation of race as a basis for belonging" (2000a, 12).

In the end, this new construction is highly individualized, idiosyncratic and shifting. Poet Audre Lorde described it as a mythical norm. "Somewhere, on the edge of consciousness," she said, "there is a mythical norm which each one of us within our hearts knows 'that is not me.' In America, this norm is usually defined as White, thin, male, young, heterosexual, christian, and financially secure." It is an *other* so large it could encompass most of the society, if not the world. Lorde talks about the need to "see whole people in their actual complexities," an agenda that seems more like an act of religious faith than scientific inquiry. There is power and strength in an identification of the actual complexities of racial reality, but it gets us to a place that does not easily lend itself to systematic analysis.

How "groupness" is experienced in this context also remains unknown. Mara Loveman, in a response to Bonilla-Silva, pointed out that "no leverage is provided for exploring the variable relationship between categories, identities, and the 'groupness' experienced because the analytical distinction between categories and groups is not maintained." Loveman's solution was at once attractive and appalling: "To avoid these pitfalls and to understand more fully how 'race' shapes social relations and becomes embedded in institutions, 'race' should be *abandoned as a category of analysis*" (1999, author's emphasis).

In her schema, borrowing from Barth and Bourdieu, race is studied as a category of practice, which seems to mean the "exploration of methods of 'groupmaking' in general, which keep open the possibility that social relations constituted by the concept of 'race' may entail distinct patterns, logic, or consequences" (Bourdieu 1990; Barth 1969). Keeping it open, of course, suggests that the concept of race may not have distinct patterns, logic, or consequences and that "the analytical leverage" led us again to the notion that race is not real. And so, the elimination is complete.

CONCLUSION

Standing at the crossroads, both empirical and nonempirical race studies have become fractured and disembodied. The question remains of what is to be done. John Stanfield, in an article in the *American Journal of Evaluation*, concluded that it is impossible to discuss adequately the more technical issues of technique and measurement, until we grasp the epistemological and biographical problematic of social sciences and their uses (1999).

Grasping a biological let alone epistemological problematic seems daunting. Yet it reminds me that I entered the major of sociology many years ago to study about my family and "to look at myself" and never did. I became a sociologist some years later, intending to write about my family and never did. I read voraciously to hear about my family and rarely do. Baca Zinn et al. expressed a similar lament in their 1986 *Signs* article. "As women who came to maturity during the social upheavals of the late sixties and early seventies," they wrote, "we entered academia to continue—in a different arena—the struggles that our foreparents had begun centuries earlier. We sought to reveal untold tales and unearth hidden images, and we believed (or at least hoped) that, once illuminated, the truths of the lives of our people—Black, brown, and working class White—would combat the myths and stereotypes that haunted us" (290).

In a symposium that appeared in *Contemporary Sociology* at the end of 2000, Walter Allen and Angie Chung ("Your Blues Ain't Like My Blues") issued a challenge to researchers studying about race, ethnicity, and social inequality in America that provides an important blueprint for new reflection. They begin by affirming "the unique significance, status, and power of race/ethnic identity as 'anchor' or 'master' factors in the U.S. system of 'racialized' social equality." Recognizing the anchor is, I think, the first step in conducting research on race and racism. As Bonilla-Silva stated, race is real. At the same time, "racialized groups" have socially constructed identities that, in Allen and Chung's words "vary across time, space, situation, and perception." The problem, they rightly suggest, is that this quality introduces "ambiguities into the debate" (2000, 796).

As Allen and Chung conclude, "Given the shifting meaning and structure of race, contemporary scholars must focus less on which forms of stratification do or do not exist, [which I read as measuring difference] and more on how these forms may predominate in certain contexts while continuing to be intertwined with other systems of stratification in others" (2000, 796). It is not simply that race is socially constructed but that it is embedded in a system of knowledge and reality that are as well.

The call for the abandonment of traditional thinking and measures is not easy. Yet new interpretations are necessary for our survival. As early as 1997, Bonilla-Silva argued that social relations can be understood best through intensive, participatory observation of social interaction and experiences that shape individual and collective status, self-perceptions, social relations, workplace and institutional experiences (1997, 470). These are not tasks we take on gladly.

I am again reminded of Du Bois. When he published *Souls of Black Folk* in 1903 he talked of "double consciousness," "the sense of always looking at one's self through the eyes of others, of measuring one's soul by the tape of a world that looks on in amused contempt and pity. One ever feels his two-ness." He wrote, "an American, a Negro; two souls, two thoughts, two unreconciled strivings; two warring ideals in one dark body, whose dogged strength alone keeps it from being torn asunder" (1903, 17).

Du Bois began a dialogue we must continue. We must move toward creation of a "convincing racial theory that addresses the persistence of racial classification and stratification." It must begin with an intelligible construction of the concept of race. Zen masters talk of the idealism of "inseparable opposites," like life and death, good and evil, whose reality is not the anchors themselves, which do not in fact exist, but the "between." Perhaps this is the place to begin. The real race, in black and white, is the ambiguous "between" of identity, representation, and structure that places people in categories that change over time and influence how systems of advantage are manifested and sustained.

4

Race and Population Statistics in South Africa

Akil Kokayi Khalfani, Tukufu Zuberi, Sulaiman Bah, and Pali J. Lehohla

Population statistics measure the changing dynamics of a given population. Births, deaths, migration, the relative population size, composition, and distribution all play key roles in the formation of population statistics. Statistical measurements can provide a snapshot of a population at a particular time and place, or a view of a relative population over time. However, these same statistics may say more about the politics, policies, or culture of those who produce and disseminate them than about the population being analyzed. One only has to look at the history of the field of statistics to gain an understanding of the potential dangers of using statistics and various statistical methods to describe and analyze a people (Zuberi 2001a).

In this chapter we examine the systems that provide a foundation for population statistics in South Africa. Population statistics are produced from limited, but essential data sources—censuses, civil and vital registration systems (including population registries), and various surveys. We make use of two aspects of South African population statistics—the modern censuses and the civil and vital registration systems (including the population register).[1] The South African government and certain NGOs have conducted numerous surveys, such as the October Household Surveys, and various DHS and WFS-type surveys, to assess the status of the population.[2] Although these types of surveys are important contributors to population statistics, they will not be discussed in this chapter.[3] We divide our examination into two sections. In the first section we use a historical and sociological approach to look at the system of racial classification in South

Africa's censuses from 1911 to 1996. In the second section we analyze the systems of civil and vital registration used in South Africa.

RACIAL CLASSIFICATION AND THE MODERN CENSUS

Population enumerations in southern Africa began with the settlement of Dutch colonists at the Cape of Good Hope in 1652 (Zuberi and Khalfani 1999). These enumerations expanded in type and depth over the centuries as the colonists continued to migrate northward, consuming the territory of and impinging upon the rights of indigenous people. The modern census in South Africa began in 1911, after the formation of the Union of South Africa in 1910, and has continued to the present. One fact remains consistent throughout almost 350 years of enumeration in the region: *Administrators have racialized every population enumeration in South Africa by subclassifying the population into races.* Thus, population statistics produced from their enumerations reflect the racialized agendas of the various administrations. In this section, we place South Africa's policies of legitimating racial classification in the context of official state policy. We examine the modern systems of racial classification in South African censuses from 1911 to 1996 as part of the state's population statistics program.[4]

The Meaning of Race

Census administrators and scholars have defined the boundaries of race as biological realities. In an important article, South African physical anthropologist Phillip V. Tobias concluded that the "concept of race is valid as long as we are dealing with groups of people; racial features are the average of a large number of individuals' features" (Tobias 1953, 122).[5] From a policy perspective, Census Director C. W. Cousins argued, "One of the most vital questions to be faced in South Africa is whether the White population numerically and otherwise is to hold its own. Distinguished authorities have given a negative reply to the question, and it is clear that the answer, if certainty is possible, can only be secured from the recurring censuses" (Cousins 1923, vi). South African demographers, administrators, and physical anthropologists tended to accept the notion of race. However, unlike the demographers and administrators, anthropologists may not have been directly involved in providing scientific support for the government's racial classification in census enumeration (Tobias 1985; Dubow 1995). As Saul Dubow (1995, 106) notes, "Because the changed meaning of the term was registered indirectly rather than in an explicit theoretical sense, typological models of racial difference were not consistently dispensed with." We suggest that racial classification in population enumeration is a tradition of convenience and that this tradition has been used to justify racial stratification.

Racial classification systems assume that race refers to groups of human beings characterized by common anthropometric measurements of skin color, hair type, eye color, or cranium size. When these criteria are not sufficient, common heredity is used as the determinative trait, despite wide ranges of physical traits within the groups. Such topological thinking is static and based on arbitrary categories that depend on the history of social relationships, as opposed to biological relationships (Jackson 2000). This type of thinking characterizes the history of racial classification in racially stratified societies such as South Africa, and census taking is one of the instruments that the South African state used to foster this stratification.

The process of racial classification in South Africa involved at least four facets of government—the legislature, the judiciary, the secretary of internal affairs, and the Classification Board. The legislature wrote and revised the statutes that dictated the classification process and standards. Many of these statutes were conflicting, unclear, and/or unspecific. In fact, van Wyk (1984) argues:

> Race (color, ethnicity) has had an almost incalculable effect on the law. Adding to the problem is the fact that "racial" provisions are more often than not to be found in obscure, even unlikely, pieces of subordinate legislations. (387)

Later, he continues,

> The conclusion seems to be well founded that a classification in terms of the Population Registration Act may cause a reflection on, but does not itself create or affect, personal status. A person's classification only becomes meaningful in relation to a particular statute. To put it in simple and more concrete terms: *a White person in terms of the Population Registration Act need not be a White person for the purposes of the Immorality Act, the Prohibition of Mixed Marriages Act, or the Group Areas Act.* (400, emphasis added)

Whereas they may have only presented some confusion or frustration for Whites, the classifications affected the life chances and quality of life for others (Davenport 1991; Pogrund 1990; van Wyk 1984). Where there was great confusion the legislature sometimes drafted new laws or amendments to existing ones. Possibly understanding the complexity, importance, and confusion surrounding the racial classification process, the legislature gave the secretary of Internal Affairs the authority and responsibility to classify all individuals on the Union's population register.

The judiciary interpreted the various laws related to cases on racial classification brought before them for adjudication. The system of racial classification presented the judiciary with many challenges. However, the legislature established yet another intervening body—the Classification Board (Union of South Africa 1950b, 283–87)—to review disputes about racial classification. This three-person panel, which included a judge or ex-judge of the South African Supreme Court, or a magistrate, was mandated to hear all requests for reclassification. This formal process allowed that "any person who considers himself aggrieved by his classification by the Director in terms of section *five* and any person who has any objection to the classification of any other person in terms of the said section, may at any time object in writing to the Director against that classification" (Union of South Africa 1950b, 283 [section 11, subsection 1]).[6] The importance here was that, "The decision as to a person's classification is, under the laws of this country, of cardinal importance to him since it affects his status in practically all fields of life, social, economic and political. An incorrect classification can in all of those fields have devastating effects upon the life of the person concerned" (Van Winsen 1974, as cited in van Wyk 1984, 404).

Racial classifications have developed along the dimensions of physical difference. The racial classification scheme employed in the Republic of South Africa used skin color and ancestry as the criteria. This was problematic in the case of European-origin populations because, "it would appear that in defining a 'White,' the legislature was faced with the dilemma that descent would obviously not be a proper primary test in view of the fact that many Whites in South Africa are indeed from mixed stock; *appearance and acceptance would remain as the only viable alternatives*" (van Wyk 1984, 406 emphasis added) for determining that someone was "truly" White. "However, to keep the 'lineage' as pure as possible, persons who by their own admission identified themselves as of mixed or Colored descent, were ruled out, while others who could show that both their parents have been classified as White, were ruled in, regardless of the definition" (van Wyk 1984, 406). So theoretically, if a person's grandparent was mixed, but both of his or her parents had been classified as White, then that person (the grandchild) would be classified as White regardless of the other classification requirements. That is, even if the grandchild did not "look" White or was not normally considered to be White, as called for in the statute, she or he would be classified as White. Obviously, the biological ability to reproduce interracially is at odds with the social desire to maintain the boundaries of racial classification. Thus, the system of racial classification has been based on socially accepted or imposed criteria of difference, and biology has been necessarily irrelevant.

Race is an ascribed characteristic and, in theory, racial groups cannot change their racial identity. However, in reality, one racial group may assimilate into another; such has been the case with segments of the Hispanic and Asian populations in the United States (see Barringer, Gardner, and Levin 1993; Ignatiev 1995; McDaniel 1995a; Zuberi 2001b). In South

Africa, two years after Afrikaners, by way of the National Party, came to power in 1948, the government instituted the formal process for reclassification stated above. A. J. Christopher (1994, 104) notes that in the 1980s many people made use of this reclassification process. The outcome for that decade was that 3,455 Cape coloreds changed their racial classification to White and 1,827 Africans changed their racial classification to colored. Watson poignantly illustrates the nature and problem of the social construction of race and racial classification in South Africa. He argues, "Races and the divisions which exist among them in South Africa reveal the hidden hands of nothing more elemental than the bureaucracy of Pretoria. If this is kept firmly in mind, there is no cause for bewilderment in the facts that brothers and sisters can belong to different *races*, that *White* adults can start life as *Colored* children, that men can live as *Coloreds* but work as *Whites*" (Watson 1970, xiii).

In the discussion about race another important factor is often neglected, completely forgotten, or thought not to be an issue. Ethnicity should not be confused with race because race is a distinctly different concept from ethnicity. The two types of group distinctions are used differently in society, especially in racially stratified ones (Hanchard 1994; Wade 1993; Zuberi 2001a). Generally, ethnic identity is a way of distinguishing culturally distinct members within a particular population. Thus, English, Dutch, Germans, French (Huguenots), and Afrikaners are ethnically or nationally different, yet all have been considered White, European, inhabitants, or Christians, within official South African governmental statistics (Zuberi and Khalfani 1999). We can refer to them as European-origin populations (Zuberi 2001a, 106–10).

How race is defined depends on the nature of the state. Racial classification is a social process used to direct social stratification. Thus, racially classifying the population is an effort for or against the processes of racial stratification and domination. *If the state advances a policy of racial stratification, the use of race facilitates the administration of racially marginalized populations. Contrarily, if the state advances a policy against racial stratification, then the use of race facilitates the state's fight against racial stratification by providing the empirical data necessary to vindicate past misdeeds. And, if the state advances a policy against racial distinctions, the use of racialized data becomes part of a process to end the everyday practices of racism, which necessitates race.*

White Supremacy

As the European-origin population increased in South Africa, so did their political domination. And, as Europe achieved hegemony throughout the world, South African settlers of European origin became the link between the southern African region and the modern world economy (see Patterson

1975; Ross 1989). The indigenous population was stifled in every way in their attempts at interstate and international commerce and communication (Gerhart 1978). Some scholars describe the situation as a dual economy for the benefit of Europeans (Cell 1982).

The first decade of the twentieth century marked the period that European settlers established dominion over the indigenous inhabitants of South Africa (Thompson 1995, 163–64). Before 1910, southern Africa was composed of various colonies, territories, and protectorates, including the Basutoland, Bechuanaland, Cape of Good Hope, Natal, Orange River Colony or Orange Free State, South West Africa, Swaziland, and Transvaal. Eight years after their successful campaign in the Second Anglo-Boer War, the British government consolidated the Cape of Good Hope, Natal, Orange Free State, and Transvaal colonies under a single authority.[7]

The new state was named the Union of South Africa. The new administration immediately galvanized the former colonial governments' ideologies and policies. Under the auspices of White supremacy, the Union government applied a comprehensive program of racial segregation and discrimination, gained control over the land, and transformed the indigenous inhabitants into wage laborers and land tenants.

The political discourse about race helped forge a common racial identity for the two dominant European ethnic groups—Afrikaner and British. In this discourse, race and ethnicity were seen as distinct realities. Indeed, they served two distinct purposes. Ethnic identity was important during the Afrikaner struggle for national autonomy and hegemony. The Trek Boers were attempting to expand their dominance throughout the southern portion of the African continent. Likewise, the British Empire wanted to continue its efforts at global hegemony, with Cecil John Rhodes striving for a unified Pan Africa under the auspices of the British flag, while simultaneously repressing Afrikaner ambitions to do the same. Hence, wars ensued between the British and the Afrikaner settlers. After the Afrikaners lost the two Anglo-Boer wars, the two groups did not have great affinity or trust for one another. However, they did agree that their survival "depended on the maintenance of white supremacy. On that question no compromise was possible. White must be on top" (Cell 1982, 47). And in that vein, "Generals Botha and Smuts saw Afrikaners and English-speaking Whites as flowing together in 'one stream'" (Giliomee 1995, 191).

Between 1910 and 1960, English and Afrikaner political parties maintained a policy of cooperation. However, the English settlers wanted to maintain a formal relationship with the British Empire, while the Afrikaners desired republican independence. In 1961 the Afrikaners realized their republican ambitions when South Africa broke away from the British Commonwealth, forming the Republic of South Africa. The tacit fact here is that in a racially stratified society the ethnic diversity of the dominant group is unimportant when the issue of racial dominance is afoot. That is, if state policies support racial stratification and domination, ethnic allegiances are necessarily second in the face of racial solidarity.

Racial Classification and the Census, 1911–1996

The modern South African system of racial classification has its roots in the establishment of European political, social, and economic hegemony. Policies of the European-origin population served as the basis for racial identity and the system of apartheid in South Africa in the twentieth century.[8] For example, pass laws were first utilized in the Cape Colony in 1809, and a reserve, or quasi-reserve, system, was initially used in the late eighteenth and early nineteenth centuries to minimize conflicts between Boers on the frontier and various groups of Africans.[9] The first oppressive laws of the Union were designed to benefit European laborers, while segregating and controlling Africans. Examples of these laws are the Mines and Workers Act of 1911, Natives Labour Regulation Act of 1911, Natives Land Act of 1913, and Native Affairs Administration Bill of 1917. The philosophical and policy foundations of European domination crystallized with the passing of apartheid legislation in the 1940s and 1950s.

The first census of the Union of South Africa was conducted in 1911, the year following the establishment of the Union. The two-tier parliamentary government—the House of Assembly and the Senate—passed the Census Act and the 1914 Statistics Act. The Census Act provided for the taking of a quinquennial enumeration of the European population for electoral purposes and a decennial enumeration of the entire population (Office of Census and Statistics 1925a). As Director of the Census J. B. Moffat noted, "All that is required for redistribution purposes is the number of European male adults in each Province" (Moffat 1911). Again the enumeration process facilitated racial stratification and in this case gender stratification as well. The census legislators provided a context in which the discourse about racial stratification took place.

Changes in the composition of the population result from a combination of differential fertility, differential mortality, net immigration, and, if race exists, racial classification. In South Africa, racial classification has had a direct impact on the social position of different members of the population. Table 4.1 presents the racial classifications used in the Union/Republic of South Africa censuses from 1911 to 1996. Table 4.2 presents the sizes of these racial groups estimated by the Central Statistical Service (CSS, currently known as Statistics South Africa).

The Office of Census and Statistics was responsible for collecting and compiling census enumerations and other statistical data. *The Statistical Council discussed the census structure and developed the various racial classifica-*

Table 4.1. Racial Classifications in the Union/Republic of South Africa, 1911–1996[a]

Year	*African*	*Indian/Asian*	*Colored*	*European/White*
1911	Bantu[d]		Mixed and Other Colored[e]	European/White
1918[b]				European/White
1921	Native (Bantu)	Asiatic	Mixed and Other Colored	European
1926[b]				Europeans
1931[b]				European
1936	Natives	Asiatics	Colored	Europeans
1941[b]				European
1946	Natives (Bantu)	Asiatics	Mixed and Other Colored	European (White)
1951	Natives	Asiatics	Coloreds	Whites
1960	Bantu	Asiatics	Coloreds	Whites
1970	Bantu	Asiatics	Coloreds	Whites
1980	Blacks	Asians	Coloreds	Whites
1985[c]	Blacks	Asians	Coloreds	Whites
1991	Blacks	Asians	Coloreds	Whites
1996[f]	African/Black	Indian/Asian	Colored	White

Source: Official census reports and questionnaires.

Notes:
[a]South Africa became a Republic in 1961.
[b]Census of the European population only.
[c]Household census only.
[d]The Bantu classification consisted of the following subclassifications: Baca, Bachuana, Basuto, Bavenda, Bomvana, Daffir (unspecified), Damara, Fingo, Hlangweni, Ndebele, Northern Rhodesian Tribes, Nyasaland Protectorate Tribes, Other Tribes, Pondo, Pondomise, Portuguese East African Tribes, Southern Rhodesian Tribes, Swazi, Tembu, Tonga (alias for Bagwamba including Tshangana), Xesibe, Xosa, and Zulu.
[e]The Mixed and Colored other than Bantu classification consisted of the following subclassifications: Afghan, American colored, Arabian, Bushman, Chinese, Creole, Egyptian, Griqua, Hottentot, Indian, Koranna-"Hottentot Races," Krooman, Malagasy, Malay (Cape), Mauritian, Mixed, Mozambique, Namaqa-"Hottentot Races," Other, St. Helena, Syrian, West Indian, Zanzibari.
[f]Statistics South Africa collected data for the Griquas separately in 1996, but combined them with the Coloreds in the published tables.

tions used in the censuses. The population statistics from the first census of the Union contained data on three major racial classifications: "European or White," "Bantu," and "Mixed and Colored other than Bantu." The census was composed of an extensive set of racial subcategories.

The "Bantu" and the "Mixed and Colored other than Bantu" categories were each composed of twenty-three "racial" subclassifications. The extensiveness of these racial classifications illustrates the degree to which the notions of race, nationality, and ethnicity were confounded in the collection of census data. For example, European settlers saw the San and Khoikhoi as being from a different "race" than the Bantu-speaking people they encountered in the 1770s. In fact, this distinction continued to be a major issue

Table 4.2. South African Population: 1911–1996

	Racial Classifications				
Year	*Africans*	*Indians/ Asians*	*Coloreds*	*Europeans*	*Total*
1911[a]	4,019,066		678,146	1,276,242	5,973,454
1921	4,697,813	165,731	545,548	1,519,488	6,928,580
1936	6,596,689	219,691	769,661	2,003,857	9,589,898
1946	7,831,915	285,260	928,484	2,372,690	11,418,349
1951	8,560,083	366,664	1,103,016	2,641,689	12,671,452
1960	10,921,922	477,932	1,510,143	3,078,050	15,988,047
1970	15,339,975	630,372	2,050,699	3,773,282	21,794,328
1980	21,078,600[b]	818,380	2,686,720	5,589,660	30,173,360
1985	24,449,800[b]	821,361	2,832,705	4,568,739	32,672,605
1991	28,397,171[b]	986,620	3,285,718	5,068,110	37,737,619
1996	31,127,631	1,045,596	3,600,446	4,434,697	40,583,573[c]

Sources: Official South African census reports for various years; census microdata for 1991; and Sadie1988 for 1980.

Notes:
[a]In 1911, the Indian/Asian population was included in the Colored population.
[b]These estimates include numbers from the TBVC areas (6,401,390 for 1980; 6,084,400 for 1985; and 6,750,700 for 1991).
[c]Total includes 375,204 unspecified/others. These are excluded from the calculations in the remaining tables.

among physical anthropologists well into the twentieth century (Dubow 1995, 33–65; Tobias 1985).

Several national censuses in the Republic of South Africa included only the European population, or else dropped the race question and predetermined race. The 1918, 1926, 1931, and 1941 censuses were only for the European settler population. For the 1921 census, the enumerators used separate schedules for each racial group. That year, the state determined racial identity for both individuals and households prior to the enumeration.

Part of the confusion surrounding race and racial classification in South Africa is directly related to the established definition of the various racial groups. In 1950, the legislative basis of apartheid was established. Particularly important for census enumerations were the Population Registration Act and the Group Areas Act. The 1950 Population Registration Act defined a "'colored person' [as] a person who [was] not a White or a native" (Union of South Africa 1950b, 277). This effort to clarify the racial classification of "Colored" persons led to the conclusion that "some discrepancies are reflected in the . . . Colored and Bantu population figures for certain districts of the Cape Province. *This must be ascribed to apparent erroneous classification*" (Republic of South Africa 1968, vii; *emphasis added*).

Before 1950, Europeans were defined as White persons who were pure descendants of Europe. From 1950 to 1991, the European population was defined as "Persons who in appearance or who are generally accepted as White persons, but excluding persons who, although in appearance obviously White, are generally accepted as Colored persons" (Union of South Africa 1950b, 277). The colonial administrations assumed that physical appearance was not enough to make a person White. The social context of being "generally accepted" as White was seen as being more important than physical appearance. Moreover, the effort here was to keep White identity separate from that of other races. Additionally, the definition for White identity was designed to keep coloreds from "passing" as White or being mistakenly counted as White. This definition for the European classification has always been arbitrary, and illustrates how racial classifications are socially constructed for the benefit of the dominant group.

By the 1960 census, coloreds were defined as "All persons not included in any of the three [other] groups," including Cape Malays (Republic of South Africa 1961, v). As previously mentioned, the "Colored" population was particularly difficult to enumerate because it was composed of many mixed-race persons. Africans were defined as aboriginal races or tribes of Africa, and Asians as natives of Asia and their descendants. Historically, the European-dominated colonial administration sought to distinguish between itself, the European-origin population, and others, the African- and Asian-origin populations, along with the mixed, or colored races.

The next major development in the censuses of the Republic occurred at the start of the 1991 census. Just prior to the administration of the 1991 census the government decided to abandon the collection of race-based data and to repeal the Population Registration Act of 1950 with the enactment of the Population Registration Act Repeal Act of 1991.[10] This change in policy had an impact on the census, vital registration, and other statistics collected and produced by the government. The passing of the act was an effort to appease Africans, trade unions, and others who were the victims of racial discrimination and who wanted to eliminate racial bias. However, the director of the Central Statistical Service (CSS), with the support of some of the leading scholars in the country, decided to collect data on race even though doing so was no longer government policy. The CSS defended its decision to collect racial data on television, in newspapers, and in press releases. They said that the information was needed for demographics and statistical purposes and not political ones. "From a statistical point of view ignoring population group information can do more harm than good. . . . It is not as if population differences will suddenly cease to exist and that the demographic characteristics of all population groups [races] will henceforth be the same" (Bureau for Information 1991). The Bophuthatswana statistics branch made the same argument for its 1991 census (Republic of Bophuthatswana 1991).

The 1996 South African Census Committee decided that the racial classifications for the 1996 census should remain the same as the 1991 census classifications. However, it was decided that the category for Africans would be relabeled "African/Black" instead of just "Black." This was done to distinguish between the Afrikaners and the indigenous Africans, both of whom refer to themselves as Africans.[11] The other categories were "Indian/Asian," "Colored," and "White." The decision to maintain these classifications was justified by the claim that most people in the country recognized and understood the categories. Notwithstanding this, Statistics South Africa enumerated the Griquas as a separate racial group because the group argued that they did not fit into any of the other racial categories; in the published statistics, however, they were included with the coloreds.

From 1921 to 1996 the South African government used four broad racial categories in multiracial censuses. The use of these four classifications was determined at a Statistical Council (SC) meeting in November 1921 (Statistical Council 1921). One of the council members suggested the use of a fifth classification—Eurafricans. This term had been used earlier in the 1910 Johannesburg municipal census. However, the other council members suggested that a Eurafrican population would be difficult to identify, thus the suggestion was abandoned.

A Closer Look at the Last Apartheid Census

The CSS took the last census of the apartheid era in 1991. They enumerated the 1991 Republic of South Africa (RSA) population on a de facto basis. The 1991 census was the first de facto census. All previous censuses were collected on a de jure basis, meaning RSA citizens as well as foreigners present within the boundaries for more than three months were enumerated. The CSS distributed census questionnaires to the population beforehand and collected completed returns after March 8, 1991. If the respondent was unable to complete the questionnaire or requested assistance in completing the questionnaire a census enumerator aided in the completion of the form.

Apartheid, as a system, produced extreme levels of residential segregation (Christopher 1992). It was part of a system that disorganized African communities, led to European acquisition and occupation of the land, and to White control of African labor (Christopher 1983; Magubane 1979, 142–43). Consequently, by 1991 a comprehensive door-to-door survey was not possible for areas populated by Africans. In fact, the CSS found that "88 areas country-wide" were inaccessible "during the preparations for the enumeration of the census" (Republic of South Africa 1992b, ix).

The CSS asked the Human Sciences Research Council (HSRC) to estimate the population in these "inaccessible" areas by using a combination of sampling and aerial photographs. The HSRC took a "sample" based on a set of assumptions regarding the number of residents interviewed by a team of eight census enumerators, and inflated the population estimates in accordance with the aerial adjustment factors.[12] The CSS then employed the services of J. L. Sadie and the Bureau of Market Research to produce the estimates for underenumeration. Table 4.3 gives an indication of the extent to which these adjustments affected the published population estimates. The estimates in the table were computed using the 1991 South African census microdata and the various weights used by the CSS.

Table 4.3 shows that the CSS enumerated only 64 percent of the total population. Such a large underenumeration reflected the political discontent and opposition of various groups and political organizations to the enumeration, especially the African National Congress (ANC). As late as March 8, 1991, the *Star* newspaper reported, "a stand-off between the

Table 4.3. Percentage of Population Estimated by Method, 1991

Race	*Census*	*Survey*	*Aerial*	*Demographic*[a]	*All Methods*	*Final Estimate*	*HSRC*[b]
Male							
African	52.58	0.69	27.59	19.13	100.00	10,864,932	28.29
Colored	86.82	0.07	1.38	11.73	100.00	1,605,811	1.45
European	88.13	0.00	0.01	11.86	100.00	2,519,833	0.01
Indian/ Asian	84.07	0.25	2.72	12.96	100.00	488,952	2.97
All	62.91	0.50	19.60	16.99	100.00	15,479,528	20.10
Female							
African	55.05	0.75	29.71	14.49	100.00	10,781,538	30.46
Colored	88.38	0.08	1.55	10.00	100.00	1,679,907	1.63
European	90.28	0.00	0.01	9.71	100.00	2,548,278	0.01
Indian/ Asian	85.16	0.24	2.67	11.94	100.00	497,669	2.91
All	65.41	0.54	20.91	13.14	100.00	15,507,392	21.45
All							
African	53.81	0.72	28.65	16.82	100.00	21,646,470	29.37
Colored	87.62	0.08	1.46	10.85	100.00	3,285,718	1.54
European	89.21	0.00	0.01	10.78	100.00	5,068,111	0.01
Indian/ Asian	84.62	0.24	2.69	12.44	100.00	986,621	2.94
All	64.16	0.52	20.25	15.06	100.00	30,986,920	20.78

Source: 1991 South African census microdata. Estimates do not include TBVC areas.

Notes:

[a]The Demographic method represents the estimation for underenumeration.

[b]Human Sciences Research Council (HSRC) estimated both the survey and aerial methods. By combining the effects of these two methods, the HRSC column illustrates the impact the council's inflations had on the final population estimates for the 1991 census.

African National Congress and the Government over the census continued yesterday, with the ANC sticking to its demand that the R60 million surveys be postponed." In addition to the ANC opposition, the *Star* also reported that there were "reports questioning the fact that members of the public would be asked to state their race—in spite of the announcement that the Population Registration Act was to be scrapped."[13]

The apartheid censuses of 1980, 1985, and 1991 all excluded the former homelands—Transkei, Bophuthatswana, Venda, and Ciskei (TBVC). But the CSS made at least one effort to estimate the size of the Republic of South Africa and the TBVC states (Republic of South Africa 1992a). This effort produced estimates of the size of the population that served as the basis for estimating the level of underenumeration, and also as the basis for the weights used in the microdata tapes produced by CSS for the 1991 census (see table 4.2). The Self-Governing Territories (SGT) were not clearly demarcated into Enumeration Areas (Republic of South Africa 1997). Teams of enumerators were used to "sweep" through these areas without controls of demarcated boundaries or lists.

The method of enumeration had a profound impact on the estimated population. Table 4.4 presents the estimated sex ratio by the method of estimation. Women appear to be overrepresented in the census enumeration. The aerial and survey methods decreased the sex ratio for Africans and coloreds and increased it for other population groups. That these methods estimated a larger African female population suggested that African males were absent from the areas where the aerial and survey methods were used. This interpretation is consistent with apartheid-imposed patterns of labor and internal migration. The demographic inflation, which estimated the undercount, increased the sex ratio for all population groups, suggesting that males, in general, were underenumerated and that, in particular, African males were considerably underenumerated.

The final estimates of the population sex composition reflect the impact of these inflations. The impact of these changes is most pronounced on the African male population. The sex ratio of the demographic inflation is 132.03, and indicates a significant inflation of the male population by this

Table 4.4. Sex Ratio by Estimation Method, 1991

Race	*Census*	*Survey*	*Aerial*	*Demographic*	*Estimate*
African	95.52	92.09	92.88	132.03	100.77
Colored	98.24	93.08	88.79	117.36	95.59
European	97.62	113.39	100.19	122.14	98.88
Indian/Asian	98.73	103.58	102.07	108.54	98.25
All	96.18	93.05	93.73	129.30	99.82

Source: Table 4.3 in this chapter.

method. So significant is the inflation that it produces a deficit of women. While this may reflect the "true" sex ratio of the African population, it also reflects the fact that the African sex ratio is a factor of the inflation methods and not the actual enumeration. The sex ratio for the 1996 census was 92.68 for the entire population. If we compare the sex ratios for the total population for both the 1991 and the 1996 censuses, assuming that the latter is much more representative, as we discuss below, it is clear that the CSS's estimates for the 1991 census do not accurately characterize the size or distribution of the population. In fact, to go from a sex ratio of 99.82 in 1991 to 92.68 in 1996 suggests that men, African men in particular, were not enumerable in 1991 and that the only way to estimate the potential size of their population was through demographic estimation techniques in addition to the enumeration process. These demographic estimations are in no way perfect and potentially overinflated the African male population to justify certain social and political objectives, as has been argued about the use of racial statistics and racial stratification (Zuberi 2000, 2001a).

Transkei, Bophuthatswana, Venda, and Ciskei Censuses of 1980, 1985, and 1991

The Afrikaner constitutions of the Orange Free State, in 1854, and the Transvaal, in 1860, established in law the principle of inequality between Africans and Europeans in church and state (Thompson 1995, 100–103). When Dr. D. F. Malan led the National Party government to power in 1948, the banner of apartheid was raised high and the future of the principle of European superiority was legally established. By 1950, the state policy of partition unfolded (Christopher 1994, 66–73). Under the policy of state partition, all Natives in South Africa would become members of an "independent" nation. The objective was to eliminate racial diversity—in particular to eliminate the African political presence in the most economically well-off areas. These TBVC states served primarily as symbols of domination, as less than 40 percent of the African population lived in the new states by 1951. In 1959, the Promotion of Bantu Self-Government Act created a hierarchy of local governments for the rural reserves. Traditional authorities (such as chiefs and headsmen) assumed power in these "homelands." The South African Native Trust Lands designated certain areas as Native Reserves. With the exception of Ciskei and Transkei, the Native Reserves of Trust Land were grouped together on a linguistic basis and brought under the supervision of the Chief Commissioner. Christopher reports "Census enumerators in the Black states tended to find the characteristics of the dominant group rather than the minority while compiling the census data, thereby statistically reducing the extent of the minority problem" (Christopher 1994, 69). The Republic of South Africa continued these apartheid policies and introduced several consolidation plans that amounted to no more than efforts to resettle African populations without compensation.

The 1970 Bantu Homelands Citizenship Act assigned all Africans to one of the ten homelands that included the four independent states—Transkei, Bophuthatswana, Venda, and Ciskei (TBVC). The Republic of South Africa included six "Self-Governing Territories" (SGT): Gazankulu, KaNgwane, KwaNdebele, KwaZulu, Lebowa, Qwaqwa, and the Common Area (CA), which included the rest of the country. The Republic established the TBVC states as racial- and ethnic-specific geopolitical units. The populations within the TBVC states and the SGT areas were predominantly African, and they continued to serve as the dominant labor force within the Republic of South Africa. Many of the laborers had temporary residences in South Africa or they commuted to work. The Republic of South Africa granted the TBVC states "independence" in the following years—Transkei in 1976, Bophuthatswana in 1977, Venda in 1979, and Ciskei in 1981.

Transkei, Boputhatswana, and Venda conducted their first population censuses in conjunction with the Republic's 1980 population census. Ciskei's first census was in 1985. The independent statistical offices of the TBVC states conducted the enumerations, but the Republic's statistical department processed the raw data and produced the tabulations. CSS had the physical, personnel, and financial resources to manage this task, but the government also had a vested interest to ensure that the results were favorable to the administration. The tabulated results went back to the individual states, which in turn published them, but not without debate. The census results were used to determine how much money the Republic of South Africa paid these governments from customs revenues. The amount given was determined by the size of the population, so both the Republic and the TBVC states tended to challenge the final results.

In 1985, all four TBVC states conducted population enumerations. The Transkei's census was a de jure estimate of the population and was derived from a sample. The Transkei sample was based on 1,400 aerial photographs. Bophuthatswana and Venda's censuses were modeled after the Republic of South Africa's and, as before, the CSS processed the data and produced the tabulations.

In 1991, the Republic—via the HSRC—monitored the TBVC enumerations. Officials considered the Venda census to be a very accurate enumeration. Ciskei had a 50 percent response rate and used a sample, based on aerial photos of houses in the area, to inflate the population. Data on the racial classifications of the population were collected and tabulated in the censuses for the Republic of South Africa, Bophuthatswana, and Venda.

Table 4.5. Estimated Undercount by Race, Percent, and Year

Race	*1980**	*1985**	*1991**	*1996*
African	22.00	20.40	46.20	10.50
Colored	3.20	3.50	12.40	10.50
European	8.50	5.50	10.80	9.00
Indian/Asian	4.40	6.50	15.40	6.10

Source: Repuplic of South Africa 1992a, 1998a; table 4.3 in this volume.

Note: *The estimate of undercount for these years does not include TBVC areas. All numbers are rounded.

The Postapartheid Census

In April 1994, South Africa held its first fully democratic elections. Afterward, the Republic of South Africa reincorporated the six SGT and the four TBVC states. In October 1996, the CSS conducted the first census in the Republic of South Africa where the majority of the South African population was not under the oppressive control of a minority population. Table 4.5 presents estimates of underenumeration by race between 1980 and 1996. The 1996 census may be the most complete enumeration ever taken in South Africa.

Compared to the previous censuses, the 1996 population census was a huge success. Statistics South Africa (Stats SA) enumerated 93 percent of the population. (In September 1998, the Central Statistical Service changed its name to Statistics South Africa.) Such a large improvement in the enumeration reflected the political success of the reformed South African government and the capable efforts of a reformed statistical department as part of the new administration. Increased support for the enumeration process by South Africans also contributed to the success of the 1996 census. Stats SA counted more than 88 percent of African men and about 90 percent of African women. The coloreds were counted at about the same rate as Africans with Indians/Asians being the most completely enumerated racial group (94 percent of men and 95 percent of women); 91 percent of Whites were enumerated.

THE CIVIL, VITAL, AND POPULATION REGISTRATION SYSTEMS

The civil registration and vital statistics systems are essential elements in South African population statistics.[14] Here we intend to explore the intricacies of that system from a historical approach and in doing so we will call upon our examination of the population registration system in the first part of this chapter. In the South African context, one cannot comprehensively discuss one system without discussing the other.

The Civil Registration and Vital Statistics System Prior to the Population Register

The existence of a civil registration and vital statistics system in South Africa, in a decentralized form, predated the formation of the Union of South Africa in 1910. In fact, colonial registries, journals, and diaries, as well as the Opgaafrols and Monsterrollen van Vrije Lieden (Muster Rolls of Vryliede) served as systems of enumeration and registration of colonial populations from the mid-1600s until the early 1900s (Zuberi and Khalfani 1999). The main purposes of those early systems were to identify taxable and voting populations and population control. Subsequent to the formation of the Union, Act 38 of 1914 established a national statistical office for South Africa. This resulted in the centralization of the collection of vital statistics. However, uniformity in vital registration throughout the Union was only achieved after the Births, Deaths and Marriages Registration Act (Act 17 of 1923) came into effect in 1924. Under Act 17 of 1923, registration of vital events was made compulsory for Africans living in urban areas but was voluntary for Africans/Blacks living in rural areas. This was in line with the Urban Areas Act of 1923. Mamdani argues:

> Section 10 [of the Act] defined the few blacks with legal permission to live in cities and large towns not as having the right to do so, but as exempt from the provisions of the act. For a black person residing in rural areas who wished to move to a city the law prescribed a definite path. (1996, 228)

Initially vital statistics were published only for Whites. In 1937, official vital statistics for coloreds became available and a year later they were published for Indians/Asians. During this period, no official vital statistics were produced for Africans.

An African Population Register?

In the 1950s, influx control, a set of laws that monitored and controlled the movements of Africans, became a compulsory policy throughout South Africa (Evans 1997). The Population Registration Act of 1950 was an integral part of this control. It assigned every person an identity number that sealed his or her fate as a South African—either improving or diminishing that individual's life chances. Under the Act, there were only three racial classifications: "White," "Colored," and "Native." The latter two were classified additionally according to ethnic group. Oddly missing here is the classification for Asians or Indians. Even though they were not directly pointed out in the act, this group has always been separately classified in the censuses, except for the 1911 census, which obviously predates this act.

The aim of the 1950 act was to make provision for the compilation of a register of the population of the Union, primarily for issuing identity cards. Under the act, anyone whose name was included in the register was assigned an identity number and population group. The register was divided into three parts. One part was for South African citizens, the second part was for permanent residents, and the third part was for temporary residents. The South African Population Register dealt with births, deaths, identity, marriages, divorces, and movements of all South African citizens and permanent residents. Part of the identity number

> was a racial classification: thus 00 meant a White South African, 01 a colored, 02 a Malay, 04 a Chinese, 05 an Asian, down to a 09 for a Nama of South West Africa. Two sections, 06 for "Other Asian" and 07 for "Other colored," provided for those who could not be fitted in elsewhere, a sort of miscellaneous of the human race. Those vital two digits were intended to, and did, affect life from birth to death, with every detail specified and fixed by law: in which hospital you could be born; in which suburb you could live. (Pogrund 1990, 79)

Several complicated laws hindered the compilation of vital statistics among Africans. For example, the Native Laws Amendment Act of 1952 mandated that Africans carry reference books (detailed identification books). These reference books consolidated fingerprints, information about the bearer's residency rights in the urban areas, tribal affiliation, employment history, tax payments, and any infractions of urban labor control laws and regulations. These documents were seen as a new type of pass (Mamdani 1996). The reference book was used as a tool of oppression that curtailed African rights. The reference book was also extended to women in the late 1950s. But here it met with much resistance. African women were "unshakably" suspicious of the reference book and quickly learned that the acceptance of it rendered them virtually powerless (Evans 1997). These passes had to be shown when requested by authorities, and failure to do so or a refusal to carry a pass meant imprisonment, a fine, or both. Non-Africans were not subjected to these intense forms of tracking.

In a detailed study of bureaucracy and race during the 1950s, Evans (1997) made several interesting observations regarding this system. The details of the African population were severely underrepresented in the manual South Africa population register (m-SAPR). The systems continued to function in this fashion, more or less, for two decades. The SAPR was computerized in 1972. At that time, only the details of Whites, Coloreds, and Indians/Asians were kept on the new system. This electronic population register (e-SAPR) operated alongside the m-SAPR and did not serve as a replacement for it.

In response to considerable domestic and international protest and sanctions, influx controls were abolished in 1986. The sustained political pressure and resulting economic strain on the country led to additional restrictive laws being abolished (Davenport 1991). Eventually, African data were entered into the e-SAPR in 1986, and Africans were issued uniform identity documents. After 1986, several acts, such as the Population Registration Act of 1991 (Act 114 of 1991) and the Births and Deaths Registration Act, 1992 (Act 51 of 1992), were amended to improve the coverage and content of the population register.

The Roles of the Population Register in the Civil Registration and Vital Statistics Systems

The civil registration system is the source for both the population register and the vital statistics system. Since the Department of Home Affairs is responsible for both the population register and the civil registration system, it keeps several databases that relate to different aspects of civil registration records but which are not, strictly speaking, the population register. When the clerks at the various offices of the Department of Home Affairs (DHA) capture the information about a birth, for example, they do so directly onto the database at the Nucleus Bureau (the data processing center for the DHA). These transactions are used to update the population register database as well as the birth register. The population register is cumulative, while the vital statistics system is periodic. Details on non–South African citizens or permanent residents could be obtained from the civil registration system but not from the population register. One would say that the vital statistics system was related to the m-SAPR and the different vital registration databases kept by DHA. The e-SAPR hardly fed into vital statistics in the past. Recently however, the vital statistics system began to include details extracted from the e-SAPR. This complementary system holds the key for the rapid production of vital statistics, but is yet to be fully exploited and analyzed.

The Development of the South African Vital Statistics System

The standing aim in publishing official vital statistics is to report on all vital events that have taken place during the period under consideration. When the completeness of registration of vital events is very low in certain geographic areas of the country or among certain population subgroups within the country, there are different ways of handling the situation. First, these subgroups could be omitted from the vital statistics until the coverage has reached sufficiently high levels. This was the route used in the Union of South Africa during the early stages for developing the vital registration areas. Alternatively, the low reported vital events would be included but commented upon. In the case of South Africa, Stats SA took a combination of both options. The statistical agency published vital statistics exclusively on Whites from 1910 to 1935. As mentioned earlier, from 1937, particulars on coloreds were included, while those of Indians/Asians were included in 1938.

The CRB was established in the 1950s to serve as a pseudo Bureau of Census and Statistics for Africans. However, there is no evidence that the official national statistical office ever tapped into the resources of the CRB in order to obtain vital statistics data on Africans. Officials used the civil registration forms filed in the Office of the Registrar-General of Births, Marriages and Deaths for Africans prior to 1960. These returns were very meager. From January 1960, the safekeeping of vital registration forms was transferred to the Bantu Reference Bureau falling under the Department of Bantu Administration and Development.

In 1963, the Births and Deaths Registration Act (Act 81) was passed. Under this act, registration of births and deaths for Africans at the district level was to be handled by the Bantu Affairs commissioner while for all other population groups it was to be handled by the district registrar. In districts where there were no registrars, the magistrates served as district officers. It was the information that went through the district registrar that formed the mainstream civil registration and vital statistics system. Details of births were kept in the "births register" and those of deaths were kept in the "deaths register." The act made no link between these registers and the population register as outlined in the 1950 act.

Starting in 1968, a separate mortality report was issued for Africans in selected urban magisterial districts. This series continued up to 1977. From 1978, a new series of reports was issued covering deaths of Africans throughout the country. At this stage, the function of civil registration among Africans fell under the jurisdiction of the Department of Co-operation and Development. These series continued up to 1990. For the years 1979 and 1980, information regarding African births was collected and processed. However, due to the underregistration of these births and the high percentage of late registration that occurred, the figures were not published for those years. Subsequently, the collection of information on African births was discontinued in 1981. In July 1989, the collection and processing of information on African births was reinstated. Again, because of continuing problems of incompleteness and lateness, the figures for African births were not published for 1990.

As mentioned earlier, with the enactment of the Population Registration Act Repeal Act of 1991, the population group identifier was dropped from the civil registration system. This affected both the population register and vital statistics. The crucial legal framework for collecting vital statistics for all people living in South Africa is the Births and Deaths Registration Act of

1992 (Act 51 of 1992). This was a logical successor following developments that started in 1985 with the abolition of influx control.

After 1991, vital statistics could no longer be broken up into population groups. The long series of uninterrupted vital statistics for Whites, coloreds, and Indians/Asians came to an end. With the redrawing of provincial boundaries in 1993 (Act 200 of 1993), geographic breakdown became the primary axis for disaggregating vital statistics.

Operation of the Current System

In South Africa today, the DHA manages vital registration. Informants are required to produce some form of identification at the time of registration of the event. The registration of deaths has changed considerably over time. The old system used two individual forms, a single-page death register (form BI-7) and a single-page medical certificate for deaths and stillbirths (form BI-12). Form BI-7 contained the demographic information about the deceased. Form BI-12 was completed by a medical professional and contained more detailed cause-of-death information. The causes-of-death information on the BI-7 sometimes differed from that reported by the physician on the BI-12 form. In the new system, forms BI-7 and BI-12 have been combined into form BI-1663.

In the past, different departments used different forms. The DHA mainly used the information on form BI-7. The statistical service relied, primarily, on the causes-of-death information stated by the physician on form BI-12. In this form, the physician was not obliged to state the cause of death if the death was due to unnatural causes. This was done for so-called practical reasons, as the DHA faced administrative difficulties in following up cases under investigation. This procedure was maintained with regard to the new forms. However, the physician is now required to state if the cause of death is under investigation.

Along with the introduction of the new form, there has been an attempt to increase the accuracy, timing, and completion rate of both birth and death forms. To this end, nurses have been employed to assist in the completion of birth registration forms. Likewise, for the registration of deaths, nurses, undertakers, and pathologists have been sought to aid in the completion of the forms. These individuals are not required to take responsibility for the forms' content.

Efforts to Improve the System during the Second Half of the 1990s

After the 1994 election, the Reconstruction and Development Programme (RDP) became known as the blueprint for the redistribution of resources and services to redress the inequalities of the previous administrations. The time frame for the implementation of the RDP was from 1995 to 2000. The various departments of the new government drafted their own RDP White papers to further the goals of the ANC. The Department of Health, for instance, saw improvement of vital statistics in South Africa as a serious priority in aiding the RDP. "While the Department of Health previously appeared to have reneged on its public health responsibility and has not engaged in the process, it has now clearly committed itself to improving the situation" (Bradshaw et al. 1998).

The Department of Health established the National Health Information System for South Africa (NHIS/SA) Committee in 1994. The broad objective of the committee was to develop a National Health Information System for South Africa that begins at the local level and feeds into district, provincial, and national levels and includes the private and public sectors. The committee's discussion paper, "Towards a National Policy and Strategy for a National Information System for South Africa," identified birth and death legislation as impeding the successful implementation of the revised health information system. The births and deaths legislation governing vital records needed to be changed if the newly proposed system was to be successful.

The essence of the NHIS/SA principles regarding vital statistics was that their efforts should begin at the local level and feed into the provincial and national levels. The NHIS/SA should incorporate all the former TBVC states as well as the former self-governing territories. The principles stressed the importance of substantial coordination between the relevant role players, namely DHA and Stats SA. Part of the aim of the information system is to enable the Department of Health to identify and monitor the disparities in health status generated largely by apartheid. NHIS/SA would take into account issues of confidentiality and would endeavor to distribute information quickly to allow decisions to be made and to monitor and evaluate national health policy. Numerous strategies were outlined for carrying out these principles. For vital statistics, four strategies were most relevant. First, information should be developed through a national process involving representatives of provincial and district authorities, community representatives, nongovernmental organizations, scientific communities, and academic institutions. These groups would work together to develop health objectives, health indicators, new data collection forms, health information systems, and the supporting computer and telecommunication methodology and technology. Second, the indicators to be developed should be disaggregated in such a way as to allow for monitoring of apartheid-generated disparities in access to health services. For example, specific levels of breakdown would include race, sex, age, geographic location, and socioeconomic status. Third, information should be disseminated widely to all stakeholders ranging from local authorities to provincial governments. Lastly, NHIS/SA saw its resulting database as an asset to be shared with researchers, whose requests would be cleared through an ethical committee.

Another prominent stakeholder that has emerged during this era could broadly be described as "advocacy groups." In practice, these groups get their message across through one or more of several consultative processes available through cooperative governance. One such mechanism is that instituted by the South African Law Commission (SALC).[15] SALC's main mandate is law reform, to change laws to keep in step with society's changing needs. Any person or body is free to submit proposals to the SALC for the reform of any aspect of South African law. If the proposal warrants law reform, the commission's research staff will prepare a discussion document on the subject. These documents are distributed free of charge and the public is invited to comment on the proposals they contain. After extensive consultation and debate a final report is submitted to the Minister of Justice for consideration. As a result, new laws may be enacted or old ones amended. Of interest to the subject of this chapter is the commission's investigation on HIV/AIDS and death registration.

The commission held a workshop on February 7, 1997, entitled "Medical certificates in respect to HIV/AIDS-related deaths." The workshop brought together the Department of Health, Stats SA, a "broad group of researchers," epidemiologists, HIV/AIDS advocacy groups, medical practitioners, lawyers, and human rights activists to debate the issue of a patient's right to privacy with regard to filling out and processing of the medical certificate with respect to the cause of death. While different views were expressed, in the end the advocacy groups achieved their aims. The second page of the new death notification form (the "Health page") had the following instruction written on the top: "After completion *seal* to ensure *confidentiality*." Subsequent to the adoption of the new death notification form, other researchers expressed reservations about the usefulness of this approach (Wood and Jewkes 1998). SALC's relationship with vital statistics gives it an open mandate to investigate any aspect of vital statistics for the purpose of legislative reform.

The Stats SA provincial offices agreed to partake in the vital registration process, and consequently, a bimonthly newsletter was started called the *Villages and Townships Vital Statistics Network* (VTVSN). This newsletter is a collaborative venture between the Stats SA subdirectorate of vital statistics and the Stats SA provincial offices. Its stated aim is the improvement of vital registration in villages and townships. The main strategy for accomplishing this was "networking." The Stats SA provincial offices joined the existing vital statistics steering committees in their provinces (comprised of the Department of Health, DHA, and other relevant stakeholders) and took part in their efforts. The officers report their activities in the newsletter, thereby informing members of the wider network the issues addressed and the progress being made.

Of all the challenges facing the South African vital statistics system, the two most pressing are to improve the coverage of vital events in nonurban areas and to produce timely death statistics for the purpose of monitoring the impact of mortality resulting from HIV/AIDS and other important causes of death. The first concern falls under what Linder (1981) refers to as "relatively intractable problems." These are problems that take a long time to solve and do not have "quick-fix" solutions.

The second problem is solvable, and Stats SA has taken positive steps to do so. One strategy Stats SA is adopting is to use the e-SAPR to produce advance release of death statistics and to use the microfilm of the death notification forms and medical certificates as the primary source for capturing details on causes of death. The captured information will then be processed through a system automatically coding the causes of death. The microfilms are readily available, as is the software. Steps are being taken to interface the automatic coding software with Stats SA's data-capturing system. When the system is fully functional, advance release data could be published within two months after any reference year or month and cause-of-death data could be produced one year after the reference year. Figure 4.1 shows the framework designed by Stats SA for the rapid processing of cause-of-death statistics.

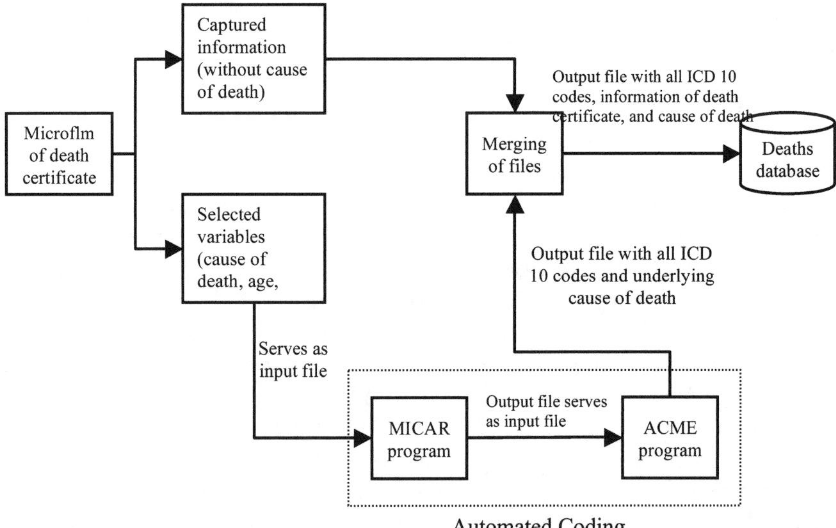

Figure 4.1. Statistics South Africa's Strategy for Implementing Automatic Coding of Causes of Death

Source: Bah 2002.

CONCLUSION

Race becomes a fact of identity in racially stratified societies. Even the members of the marginalized racial group feel compelled to maintain the racial classifications. The logic of the racial classification becomes obvious even to these marginalized groups. As mentioned above, the statistics director for Bophuthatswana stated in the 1991 census report that in spite of the negative history of classifying the "four ethnic groups, Whites, Coloreds, Asians and Blacks . . . it does make *demographic sense to retain the classifications* . . . to the extent that one finds more homogeneity within the groupings than differences, and this is crucial to the study of demography amongst other disciplines" (Republic of Bophuthatswana 1991, iv).

The history of the development of the South African state and Afrikaner identity played an important role in the development and the composition of the country that is today known as the Republic of South Africa. As one Afrikaner leader noted, "The Afrikaans Language Movement is nothing less than an awakening of our nation to self-awareness and to the vocation of adopting a more worthy position in world civilization."[16] In fact, the Afrikaans Language Movement was to become a major opponent in the struggle against apartheid by the Black Consciousness Movement. Unlike the English-speaking White identity, with its internationalistic identification with European imperialism, Afrikaans and Afrikaner racial identity was based on a specific notion of bringing and developing civilization in South Africa. European origin was equated with civilization, and the new Afrikaner culture was seen as the most recent manifestation of this cultural transformation (Giliomee 1995; Zuberi and Khalfani 1999). Thus, if Afrikaans became the language of the nation, it would also result in a modernization of the population's "self-awareness." This ethnocentric concern with language served as a model for partisan demographic research as well (for an example see Sadie [1949]).

Official classifications influence personal identities as well as social science research. Given the influence of the government on society, these classifications leave an important imprint on society. The impact of a government classification process is not unique to South Africa. There is abundant evidence around the globe that a government's employment of a racial classification system has an impact on various social and political aspects of that society (Cox 1948; Nascimento and Nascimento 2001; Wade 1993; Zuberi 2001b). But also, official classifications change as a result of changes in the social and political structure. Therefore, there is a symbiotic relationship between the state's efforts to develop and use racial classifications, and the society's use of, adherence to, and development of these classifications.

Racial classification of the South African population has been used for political purposes. In particular, apartheid used racial classification to signify

African "otherness" and African marginalization. On a broad level, apartheid laws sought to ensure that Whites maintained social, economic, and political control over the country and over Africans. This was deemed necessary since the African population greatly outnumbered the White citizenry.

Race expresses and symbolizes two different kinds of social things. Race is the outward and visible form of socially salient physical differences; it is also the flag of the population—the sign by which each racial population distinguishes itself from others, the visible mark of its distinctiveness, and a mark that is borne by everything that emanates from the race. Race is the symbol of both stratification and population identity, because both are aspects of society. Thus racial identity becomes part of a group's collective identity and its sense of history and culture, but *the group transfigured and imagined in the physical form of skin color is what appears as race.* The modern South African census illustrates how important race can be in a political context.

On a surface level the South African data sets represent the distribution of the population at different times by age, sex, race, and geographic location. On another level, they reflect a history of governmental policies of racial discrimination in South Africa. We must remember that the purpose of population statistics and their analysis "is the reduction of data. Census or survey micro-data are of such a quantity that analysis is impossible without some process of summarizing the data" (Zuberi 2001a, 101). However, these analyses and reduction processes are not devoid of the cultural, political, or social influences of the collectors and processors of such data (de Graft-Johnson 1988; Zuberi 2001a; Zuberi and Khalfani 1999). Hence, we need to be thoughtful when using or producing such statistics. As in the United States, South Africa "provides an excellent example of how historical origins and race are interrelated in racially stratified societies. Racial data have been used in many ways . . ." however, "[r]acial data are necessary for viewing the effects of racial prejudice . . ." in a society plagued by institutionalized racial stratification and racial discrimination (Zuberi 2001b, 163).

NOTES

1. See Zuberi and Khalfani (1999) for a discussion of censuses and other enumerations in southern Africa prior to 1911.

2. See Udjo (2005) for a discussion of the October Household Surveys. South Africa also conducted fertility surveys modeled on international Demographic and Health Surveys (DHS) and World Fertility Surveys (WFS).

3. Johan van Zyl (1994) of the Human Sciences Research Council in South Africa presented an unpublished paper at the annual Population Association of America meeting in 1994 that outlined many of the surveys conducted and analyzed by this government organization from 1966 to 1994. See also the South African Data Archive, which is available online at www.nrf.ac.za/sada/.

4. As this volume goes to press, the South African government is preparing to release the results of the 2001 census; hence, the 2001 census results are not incorporated into our analysis.

5. This is the same Philip V. Tobias (1970) who published the landmark study undermining the scientific basis of "claims that races of man have been shown to differ in quantity of brain-substance and especially, of grey matter in the cerebral cortex." However, even at this late date Tobias maintained a racialized view of human difference.

6. The title of this office was amended from director to secretary by Act 30 of 1960 in the government Gazette No. 6402 on April 1, 1960. Section five of the Population Registrations statute stated that all persons included in the population register will be classified by the secretary of interior, or one of his officers, as either a white person, a colored person, or a native. The latter two groups were to be further subclassified according to ethnic or other group according to the secretary. The statute further stated that the governor-general could by proclamation add or amend the colored or native classification as he saw necessary. Lastly, the secretary was empowered with the ability to racially reclassify individuals (after notifying them) that he thought were erroneously classified.

7. In addition to the four colonies that composed the Union of South Africa in 1910, Botswana (Bechuanaland Protectorate), Lesotho (Basutoland), Malawi (Nyasaland), Swaziland, Zambia (Northern Rhodesia), and Zimbabwe (Southern Rhodesia) were considered for incorporation into the Union during its formation, as they were either British colonies or protectorates, or territorial possessions of the Cape Colony.

8. As Hermann Giliomee notes, "South Africa's institutionalized racism . . . can best be understood as a product of the Afrikaners' conception of their distinct place in the social structure" (1995, 190).

9. The reserve system consisted of areas on the border of the colonies where Africans resided. These groups of Africans, like the Fingoes, often served as buffers and intermediaries between the European colonists and other groups of Africans (see Zuberi and Khalfani 1999). The reserve system was the precursor to the homeland system later developed by the Nationalist Party.

10. Although the census was administered on March 7, 1991, the Population Registration Act Repeal Act of 1991 did not officially go into effect until June 28, 1991. Therefore, technically and legally the CSS was still obligated to collect racial data. However, the popular understanding that the Population Registration Act Repeal Act of 1991 was soon to be signed into law created an atmosphere of conflict between the CSS and the various groups who were opposed to the use and collection of racial data by the government.

11. Interview of Wole Adegboyega with Akil Kokayi Khalfani. Adegboyega is the United Nations Population Fund's (UNFPA) Census Advisor to the South African Central Statistical Service. December 8, 1995.

12. "The HSRC's field workers and organizers, each with a team of census enumerators, visited the indicated premises and shacks on the ground and ensured that each resident was enumerated. The particulars obtained in this manner were then projected in accordance with the number of dwelling structures to obtain an estimate of inter alia the population number in the specific area. For instance, if

the particulars show that for 10 dwelling/structures the average occupancy rate is six persons per dwelling, then a hundred dwellings will have an estimated six hundred occupants" (Republic of South Africa 1992a, ix).

13. There were many news articles on the politics of the 1991 census. For a few additional examples, see the *Transvaler*, February 8, 1991, and the *Star*, March 6 and 7, 1991.

14. The civil registration system and the system put in place for generating vital statistics are known as the vital statistics system.

15. "The South African Law Commission was established by the South African Law Commission Act 19 of 1973. . . The Commission is an advisory body whose aim is the renewal and improvement of the law of South Africa on a continuous basis" (www.server.law.wits.ac.za/salc/objects.html).

16. D. F. Malan, cited in Giliomee (1995, 192). Malan, along with General Hertzog, was one of the original Afrikaner nationalists prominent at the beginning of the century.

III

LOGIC OF THE METHOD

5

Causation and Race

Paul W. Holland

For over 2000 years, ideas about causation have been discussed, classified, and criticized. To mention only a few of the most influential authors: in philosophy there are Aristotle, Hume, and Mill; in medicine there are Koch and Henle (Yerushalmy and Palmer 1959) and Sir A. Bradford Hill (1965); and in social science research and program evaluation there are Campbell and Stanley (1963). With all this work explaining, refining, and clarifying what causation means and how to distinguish it from "mere association," it is still worth repeating the maxim: before one leaps to a causal conclusion, one needs to consider first the other noncausal explanations and eliminate them.

Two of the most commonly occurring alternatives to causal explanations are reverse causation and common causes (or hidden confounding). Following are two examples that are easy to identify, yet continue to cause problems in educational policy discussions.

Example 1 (Reverse Causation): It is easy to find data, for example from the National Assessment of Educational Progress (NAEP), in which widely accepted educational materials and practices (such as dividing classes into reading groups, using work sheets, and repetitive drill and practice) are associated with lower student performance on NAEP. The causal explanation is that these practices inhibit student learning and need to be replaced in school reform efforts. The noncausal explanation is that those who need more help may get it in a caring and student-oriented system of instruction and their low test performance is only indicative of their need, and not of the result of the practices. The noncausal explanation is "reverse causation" in the sense that the apparent effect, that is, low test scores, is actually a measure of the cause, that the students are being taught in particular ways, rather than being the real effect of these practices.

Example 2 (Common Causes): It is equally easy to find NAEP data that shows that socially desirable educational practices (such as smaller classes, computers, and low teacher turnover) are associated with higher student test performance. The causal explanation is that these desirable things are desired because they are good for students and help them to succeed academically. The noncausal alternative explanation is that what we are really seeing is social segregation and socioeconomic status (SES) differences, which, like it or not, are associated with (might even cause!) both higher scores and more socially desirable schooling conditions. The common cause is SES differences. In this example it is possible that the educational practices are making a positive difference in the education of the students, but until the effect of SES is sorted out, the amount of this difference is difficult to know.

These examples of the problems with causal explanations are only two from a long list, but they are easy to identify and understand. Both are special cases of Simpson's paradox, which has perplexed users of statistics for over 100 years (Simpson 1951; Pearl 2000). Simpson's paradox says that a correlation or association between two variables can change in quite dramatic ways when the effect of a third variable is taken into consideration. A famous U.S. example is the claim by the UC Berkeley student newspaper that graduate student admissions at Berkeley were biased against women. The data showed exactly that. The Berkeley-wide rate of acceptance of women graduate students was lower than that of men. However, when the departments to which the students were applying were examined it was discovered that men and women applied to different departments and, interestingly, the different graduate programs admitted students at different rates. Women tended to apply to the departments where the acceptance rates were lower. In fact at the department level, there was a slight tendency to admit women at a higher rate than men (Bickel, Hammel, and O'Connell 1975). The third variable here was "department applied to," and a third variable, associated with the two of interest (gender and admission), can do amazing things with the original association.

I think one way to understand Mark Twain's attribution to Queen Victoria's prime minister, Benjamin Disraeli, of that famous put-down, "Sir! There are three kinds of lies—lies, damn lies and Statistics!" is as the blustering reaction of a great politician to someone's (mis)use of statistics to trash one of his pet policies. Simpson's paradox no doubt abounded in the trade and currency data that Disraeli and others needed for policy analysis in the middle of the nineteenth century. Who knows what the "third variable" was or the data presented or Disraeli's pet policy (Twain never tells us), but rest assured, no matter how gifted an orator he was, Disraeli was doomed to naught but uttering pure bluster if it was Simpson's paradox he was up against. British statisticians Pearson and Yule were the first to understand the workings of Simpson's paradox but only did so years after Disraeli had left office.

However, the topic of this chapter is not about the type of misplaced causal thinking that reverse causation, common causes, and Simpson's Paradox exemplify. My interest here is one that has concerned me for some time (Holland 1988b) and that is of an order different from the simple misidentification of association for causation. The problem I wish to address is: What is the causal role of variables such as "race" in social science research?

Every day, an economist, a sociologist, or a political scientist "runs" a regression analysis in which some variable denoting the race of the person who is the unit of analysis appears as a predictor (along with other predictors) of some outcome variable. Every day, the analyst interprets the coefficient of this race variable as the "effect of race" on the outcome variable. Is there a "causal interpretation" to this race effect?

My answer to this question is that race is not a causal variable and for this reason "race effects" per se do not have any direct "causal" interpretation. It is also clear, however, that race does play an important role in some causal studies and that more clarity as to what this role is will help us understand concepts like "discrimination" and "bias" in ways that make fruitful use of causal ideas. In the rest of this chapter I will give the details of my argument and point of view, and illustrate it with an example of biased tests in a later section.

One warning. Those who wish a serious discussion of the meaning of race will have to look elsewhere. I take racial categories, however determined, as given. This is also the plight of the analyst who runs his or her regressions. For the most part, someone else determines the definition of the race variable and the analyst has to use the available data. I do not apologize for this superficiality on my part, because it is the common superficiality of those who employ race as a variable in their analysis. While not satisfactory for every situation, this approach to race is good enough for many purposes, or at least, the alternatives are even less satisfactory.

For the record, I regard race as a socially determined construction with complex biological associations. I also believe that it is very naive to disregard the durability and power of social constructions. Be that as it may, race is not a neutral concept and its many consequences for social interaction and other activities are the subject of a vast literature to which this chapter will not contribute.

CAUSATION

In this section I will give a relatively brief discussion of a few essential points about causation that are germane to my point of view. Related discussions are in Holland (1986, 1988a, 1988b, 2001). To begin, it is useful to distinguish between two classes of scientific studies in the social sciences: descriptive and causal studies.

Descriptive Studies

Descriptive studies have the goal of describing some phenomenon or state of affairs. Typical examples are ethnographic studies of a social system, detailed classroom observations, or sample surveys of characteristics of a population. The most ubiquitous type of purely descriptive study in American life is the opinion poll. Polls have the sole purpose of describing current opinion/sentiment of some population on some set of relevant issues. In education research the most important current descriptive studies are the National and State surveys collectively called the National Assessment of Educational Progress (NAEP). An early important education survey was the "Coleman Report" (Coleman 1966) and there are also important longitudinal surveys as well, such as High School and Beyond and the various versions of The National Educational Longitudinal Study (NELS).

It sometimes helps to classify questions in terms of the interrogatives of English. Those most relevant to descriptive studies are "Who? What? Where? and When?" The output of a descriptive study is a description, be it a "thick description" of some event or phenomenon or merely a mean, a distribution, or a correlation. An important contribution of statistics to descriptive studies is the twentieth-century invention of the sample survey employing random selection. "Careful observation and description" does, however, have ancient scientific credentials.

The Slippery Slope toward Causation

Description often results in comparisons, and a comparison often invites one to ask the other kinds of interrogatives, in particular, Why? or How? While these causal questions are, in some sense, more fundamental than those related to description, I remind myself regularly that, at least in the social sciences, casual comparisons inevitably initiate careless causal conclusions.

It is not unusual for our desire to know "Why?" to outstrip our ability to provide an adequate answer. For example, we may know that there are a variety of replicable differences in test performance between various groups of examinees (e.g., males and females or ethnic/racial groups), but why these differences consistently arise often eludes serious explanation. In a related setting, NAEP's descriptive data are used time and again to address causal questions, and absurd conclusions can result from the failure to recognize the survey/descriptive nature of NAEP. The two examples, of reverse causation and common causes, given earlier are typical of this overenthusiasm for causal explanations.

Different types of research studies can make it more or less difficult to clearly distinguish between description and causation. We have somewhat pejorative language for this failure: "Correlation does not necessarily imply causation" and "mere correlational research." In my opinion, however, good descriptive studies, which lay out important dimensions of some social science phenomena, are highly underrated. On the other hand, there is a sense in which all studies are just descriptive studies and all that is ever observed in any study is "mere correlation." In this view some of these correlations have causal relevance while others do not. As my colleague Howard Wainer once quipped, "Where there is correlational smoking there may be causational cancer."

Causal Studies

I do not think that it is very useful to try to make an exhaustive catalog of all possible causal studies. Rather I think it is more helpful to try to recognize when a study has a "causal" focus, rather than being solely concerned with pure description of phenomena. Even studies that start out as purely descriptive can be given an apparent causal focus as we slide down the slippery slope initiated by casual comparisons. In such situations it is best to be wary of the slippage from description to causation.

Again, the interrogatives of English can begin to help us (though they have limitations). Questions of Why? or How? invite causal explanations. I believe, however, that there are really three distinct types of causal questions, with Why? and How? associated with only two of them. Confusing the three types of causal questions (or their answers) can make causal discussions confusing and contentious.

I call the answers to the three types of causal questions (a) Identifying Causes, (b) Assessing Effects, and (c) Describing Mechanisms. Let me amplify each of these in turn.

Identifying Causes. This is the usual answer to Why? A singular event occurs, and we seek its cause. "Why did the car (or stock market) crash?" "What caused his death?" "Why are test scores down?" There can be an element of blame in answers to Why-questions. For example, "Test scores are down because our curricula are a mile wide and an inch deep!" Legal responsibility can also be involved, as in assessing financial responsibility for an accident. Causal identification is often a form of speculative postmortem.

Assessing Effects. This is the answer to the missing type of causal question alluded to above. I think that "What if?" better describes the questions whose answers require the assessment of the effects of certain causes. Likewise, "What is?" is the proper form of the "What" questions that descriptive studies can address. When we ask a What-if question we seek to know the effect of some cause or intervention that we might contemplate making. "Will test scores go up if we reduce class size?" "What will happen to dropout rates if we end social promotion as we know it?" I think that the questions that are most relevant to the intersection of social science and public policy are these What-if questions whose answers involve assessing effects of causes or interventions.

Perhaps the simplest image that underlies our understanding of causal attribution is the comparison of two identical units of study, one exposed to one experience and the other exposed to another experience, which are then subsequently compared on an identical outcome criterion. Because these units of study are identical/similar to begin with and are evaluated in an identical/similar manner at the end, whatever difference is observed between them in the outcome is attributable to the differences they had in their intervening experiences and to nothing else.

An important contribution of statistics to the study of causation is the other twentieth-century invention of the randomized comparative experiment. Such study designs remove the need for finding "identical" units of study. They started in agriculture and quickly spread to many areas of science where uncontrollable variation in experimental material—the weather, the fertility of the earth, population, and so on—is a fact of scientific research life. In my opinion, such studies are very good at addressing What-if questions, but, on occasion, when coupled with predictions, they may indirectly address the speculations of Why? and How? as well.

There are deep formal connections between sample surveys that employ random selection of units for inclusion in the sample and comparative experiments that employ random assignment of units to experimental conditions. These two types of studies, however, address very different types of questions (the former descriptive, while the later causal) and ought not to be confused with each other.

Describing Mechanisms. This is the answer to How? We see that some effect follows from some cause and we want to know "How does it work?" "How does the effect arise from the action of the cause?" "How do smoke-rings form?" "How will class size reduction improve test scores?" "How does aspirin reduce heart attacks?" Understanding and identifying causal mechanisms is, perhaps, the primary driving force of science. Causal mechanisms are the closest things to "theory" that I will discuss here. Furthermore, causal mechanisms are almost always involved in that hallmark of science, prediction. "Describing causal mechanisms," like "identifying causes," almost always involves some element of speculation—sometimes a very healthy dose of it.

The description of a causal mechanism can be completely wrong while at the same time the effect of the cause is clear and replicable. A well-known medical example concerns taking aspirin to reduce one's risk of heart attacks. The data on the reduction are clear and well established by a large randomized clinical trial. But at first the mechanism by which the reduction was achieved was in question. Was it aspirin's blood-thinning effect or its inflammation-reduction effect? Early explanations emphasized blood thinning, but later experimental work confirmed inflammation reduction. However tentative, causal mechanisms are often useful ways to encode our thinking about causal relationships (e.g., the germ theory of disease).

I think that it is important to be clear as to what type of questions a study is trying to or can answer: descriptive or causal; and, if causal, which type? One of the problems of communication between social scientists and policy makers is related to the distinction I make between assessing effects and describing mechanisms. Understanding some aspect of a causal mechanism often advances science (i.e., theory), whereas the needs of public policy often require an answer that assesses the effects of an intervention, rather than reasons or speculations as to how these effects come about. If class size reduction results in better student learning, a policy maker might argue that it does not matter if this effect is due to more time for individualized instruction, fewer classroom disruptions, or something else. On the other hand, the mechanism might matter to the policy maker if other reform policies besides class size reduction are of interest. Knowledge of the causal mechanism could indicate that other policies would be supportive or possibly contraindicated when classes are small. My view is that both positions need to be clearly delineated and not confused with each other.

Causal Variables

It should be clear, but it often is not, that the language of causation is more precise when we are concerned with assessing effects than when we are concerned with either identifying causes or with proposing causal mechanisms. In the latter two cases, "anything" can be a cause, because we are just talking rather than doing. When we design an experiment, however, the only things that can qualify as causes are "treatments" or "interventions." I think that putting limits on "what a cause can be" by using What-if questions to do this is useful and a very important step because it focuses on "doing" rather than on the (sometimes casual) causal talk of identifying causes and proposing causal mechanisms.

Long ago, Donald Rubin and I made up the slogan: No causation without manipulation (Holland 1986). Its purpose was to emphasize the ambiguity that arises in causal discussions when things that were not treatments or interventions of some sort are elevated to the status of "causes." Not everyone agrees with this point of view (Marini and Singer 1988), but I still think it is a sound position and reiterate it here.

Our slogan closely corresponds to the following basic image, already mentioned, for understanding causation. Two identical/similar units of study, one exposed to one experience and the other exposed to another experience, which are then subsequently compared on an identical/similar outcome criterion. In this basic setting, the attribution of cause is to the different experiences (to which either unit could have been exposed), and not to some other characteristic of the units of study, because the units are "identical/similar." We can manipulate these experiences and thus attribute to them causation of any subsequent observed differences without necessarily suggesting a mechanism to explain the resulting difference. Thus, we return to my insistence that causes are experiences that units undergo and not attributes that they possess: No causation without manipulation!

Causal variables are those that reflect such manipulations or varying experiences between units of study. For a causal variable it is meaningful to ask about both (a) the result that obtained under the experience the unit was actually exposed to; and (b) the result that would have obtained had the unit been exposed to another experience. This is the essence of the definition of a causal effect. It inherently involves the use of counterfactual conditional statements (the result that would have obtained had the unit been exposed to another experience) (Lewis 1973). Properties or attributes of units are not the types of variables that lend themselves to plausible states of counterfactuality. For example, because I am a White person, it would be close to ridiculous to ask what would have happened to me had I been Black. Yet, that is what is often meant when race is interpreted as a causal variable.

There is no cut-and-dried rule for deciding which variables in a study are causal and which are not. In experiments, in which we actually have the control to manipulate conditions, there is usually no problem in identifying the causal variables (but even there, however, "what was actually manipulated" may not be so clear—perhaps the most famous examples being those involved with placebo effects).

Causal studies may also involve many types of nonexperimental settings in which we do not have control over which units are exposed to which experiences. In these cases it can become a challenge to determine what qualifies as a causal variable in the sense that I am using the term. The only rule I have is that if the variable could be a treatment in an experiment (even one that might be impossible to actually pull off due to ethical or practical issues) then the variable is probably a cause, and correctly called a causal variable. From this point of view, attributes of individuals such as test scores, age, gender, and race are not causes and their measurement does not constitute a causal variable.

Causation as a status symbol: We might ask why is it important to make a distinction between causal and noncausal variables? A biostatistician, whose name I have unfortunately misplaced, once made the telling point to me that in medical research it is highly valued to be able to assert that an association between one thing and another is "causal." However, he argued, as far as action is concerned it often does not matter whether the association is causal or noncausal. In medicine, "risk factor" refers to either case. Is high blood pressure causal in its association with heart disease, or are they both just due to a common cause? No matter, try to lower your blood pressure by diet, exercise, or drugs and you will probably be healthier. Being able to assert that the association is based on a causal connection is, in many circumstances, merely a status symbol, one that confers importance to the finding without any consequence for improved public health. Causes are sometimes easily related to action and noncauses are often not. For example, the physician can help you stop smoking, but not get younger!

From this point of view, which I believe is a healthy antidote to the search for a causal "Good Housekeeping Seal of Approval" on associations, it is the use of an association for important purposes that is its enduring value, and not its status as a causal variable.

IS RACE A CAUSE?

From the arguments of the last section, it should be clear that variables like race are not easily thought of as describing manipulations, and so, in my opinion, they do not qualify as causal variables. In this sense race is not a cause. It is important, however, to state the limitation of this assertion. Race is not a cause because race variables do not have causal effects as defined above. "What would your life have been had your race been different?" is so far from comprehensible that it is easily viewed as a ridiculous question. Few experimenters have manipulated race and, when they try to, it is a poor imitation of the real thing.

It is possible to find various apparent counterexamples to this last assertion. John Howard Griffin's book, *Black Like Me*, and Grace Halsell's *Soul Sister* are examples of individuals' reporting what happened to them when they changed their outward appearances to experience, for a while, some aspects of life as a member of a different race. There are other studies where nearly identical résumés are sent to businesses. The only difference between the résumés is an indication of the race of the person applying for the job. Both of these are instances where some aspect of race was manipulated for a real or hypothetical individual. These are experimental treatments, there is no doubt about that. Their relevance to the use of race in social science research is, however, almost nil. Self-reported racial categories used to define a variable in a regression analysis are very different from these purported counterexamples.

On the contrary, these examples show how complex the manipulation of race really is. Grace Halsell may have changed the color of her skin, but by her own admission she could not change the fact that she was raised a southern White woman, with all of the experiences and beliefs that such an upbringing implies. In the résumé studies, it is only the race on the résumé that is changed, the altering of provided information, not the life experiences that accompany a résumé in real life. Although not entirely irrelevant, this is a far cry from changing the race of a "real" individual.

In my opinion, race does play an important descriptive role in identifying important societal differences such as those in wealth, education, and health care. The attribution of cause to race as the producer of these differences is, to me, the most casual of causal talk and does not lead to useful action.

So, relieved of the burden of raising the research status of race to that of a causal variable, I can now address the more important issue of what role race should play in causal analyses. I will discuss two related issues. The first concerns how to think about causation in racial (and other types of) discrimination. The second is how race and a true causal variable can connect in a causal study. I will illustrate this second point in more detail below in the section on biased tests.

Causation and Discrimination

If race is not a causal variable, how do we analyze issues of racial discrimination in causal terms, if at all? We certainly do think of racial discrimination in causal terms because many of us think racial discrimination is something that could be changed, reduced, or in some way altered. There are those who dream of a day when racial discrimination is a thing of the past and long forgotten. What is it that has to change? Certainly not the color of people's skin or some other physical characteristic. Clearly discrimination is a social phenomenon, one that is learned; it is taught and fostered by a social system in which it plays a complex part. When we envision a world without racial discrimination we thus envision it as a whole social system that must be different in a variety of ways from what we now see before us. One almost has to envision a parallel world, so to speak, in which things are so different that what we recognize in our own world as racial discrimination does not exist in this other parallel world. How might we detect this state of affairs in the parallel world?

I ask the reader's indulgence in my pursuing a little fantasy involving more perfect worlds that are "parallel" to our own. Something like the following might suffice to show that racial discrimination does not exist in that parallel world. Suppose we take several persons who, in the real world, have experienced what they regard as racial discrimination, and transport them into this other parallel world. There they meet their "parallel selves" and the two "selves" can exchange views about various things, including their experiences about discrimination based on race. They might have very different stories to tell each other, the parallel selves finding the stories of the original selves horrible to hear and difficult to understand from their experiences. Would that be enough to establish that racial discrimination did not exist in the parallel world? Maybe, but I think the case would be strengthened if we suppose that we also found other persons in the real world who had not had the experience of racial discrimination. Perhaps they are White, privileged, and oblivious to the plight of others? Then we transport them to the parallel world, introduce them to their parallel selves, and listen in on the resulting conversations. To put this fantasy into the simplest terms, we might then discover that the parallel selves of these privileged persons also did not report any experiences with racial discrimination.

The point of my fantasy is that racial discrimination should be viewed as how society treats different people differently in a rather complicated way. It is not just that different groups of people have different experiences, which is what statisticians would call the "main effect of race." It is the statistical interaction of race with an appropriate change in society that turns the original "different experiences" into discrimination. If discrimination were removed from society, different groups of people should experience this change differently. If instead they all experienced the change in the same way, it is hard to say, at least in my opinion, that there was ever "discrimination" in the first place.

Imagine the further complication to my fantasy if the privileged persons' parallel selves told of horrible acts of discrimination based on race. Could discrimination be said to be absent in the parallel world, or did it just get changed to some other kind of discrimination?

As one who is White and who would be considered privileged by some, I am acutely aware of how hollow-sounding a theoretical analysis of the type I have just given may appear to those on the front lines of social action. There is not much I can do about that, of course. I can only add that my intended audience are those analysts who use statistical models to estimate race effects and from them try to deduce the effects of racial discrimination. My purpose is to dissuade these analysts from using such casual interpretations of their analyses.

Race and Causes Together?

The point about discrimination being a "statistical interaction" between a (potential) change in society and racial categories of people is just a special case of a role that I think is very important for the use of race variables in analyses. Racial categories are hardly homogeneous, and treating them as such is what defines stereotyping. Yet, racial categories do capture some important phenomena that pervade many societies throughout the world. For this reason, in my opinion, the study of statistical interactions of causal variables with racial categories is a useful activity. Consider, for example, educational studies. Reading programs that are more effective for some groups of students than others are not as useful, in a general sense, as those programs whose effects are powerful throughout society. The same can be said in other domains such as medical treatments.

Whether or not racial categories are useful for finding programs that are not properly targeted for large groups of students is an empirical question. As long as wide differences in educational achievement exist between different racial/ethnic groups I am sure that checking for the interactions of program effects with race variables is both productive and easy. As I have told many a graduate student when I taught in the Graduate School of Education at Berkeley, "Please check the interactions with both gender and race of your favorite educational programs. These are two easily obtained variables and, if you find interactions with race or gender, that will tell you very interesting things about your educational program, no matter how well thought-out and implemented you think it is."

BIASED TESTS, RACE, AND CAUSE

In this final section I want to briefly integrate some of the ideas that have been put forward here in an example that combines racial categories and causes—the study of biased tests.

Claims that tests are racially (and otherwise) biased are made every day. As far as I can tell these are mostly based on the main effect of race when examining test scores. That is, racial/ethnic groups differ in their average test scores, sometimes by very large amounts—as much as one standard deviation. This "main effect of race" is not limited to one or two tests or to tests of particular formats such as multiple choice or essay. They are to be found in many tests, some would say in virtually every test.

Having been heavily involved in the study of item and test bias (Holland and Wainer 1993) I have long ago rejected the view that a simple difference in mean scores on tests or items for different groups of examinees implies that the test or items are biased. The differences in test scores between racial and ethnic groups replicate across so many tests and types of tests that either all tests are biased or this definition makes no sense. I accept the latter rather than the former view. This is based on seeing, first hand, the extreme care that goes into the development of tests for serious uses. Indeed, the century-old application of scientific principles to test development has weeded out many sources of test bias and has made the constructs that the tests are intended to measure and the uses and consequences of the tests the paramount factors in the design and construction of modern tests.

In 1986–1987 several of us at ETS (reported in Hackett et al. 1987) developed four specially constructed "experimental" sections of a real test used for admission to a particular graduate-level course of study. We did this in order to study the effects of using item statistics to manipulate the difference in average scores between Black and White test takers. Our immediate interest was in a procedure associated with the "Golden Rule law suit settlement" (McAllister 1993). We wanted to see what effect this procedure would have on the reliability and validity of the resulting tests.

The Golden Rule procedure attempted to minimize the score differences between Black and White test takers by choosing only those test questions that minimized the performance difference between these two groups. In our study we did this but we also developed, in addition, sections of the test that maximized these differences in performance. Furthermore, we had, for comparison, other examples of the same section types for the test that had been developed in the usual professional way for this real graduate-level testing program.

The view of the proponents of the Golden Rule procedure was that by reducing the difference in the average scores of Black and White test takers, test bias was being reduced. My opinion on this is based on the observation that the performance by examinees on individual test questions varies due to many factors. In my opinion, all that the Golden Rule procedure did was to choose that subset of test items on which Black test takers performed on average somewhat higher than usual and, simultaneously, White test takers performed on average somewhat lower than usual. From my perspective both of the specially constructed types of test were biased in a sense that is clear, consequential, and as it turned out, entirely undetectable by those who only look at the words in the test booklet to assess the bias of a test.

My position is that arguments about test bias are just so many empty words unless one has examples of real tests that are biased in clearly specified ways. It is hard to say much that is useful about biased tests unless we have real examples of them for study and analysis. So the point of view that I will take here is that the two types of experimental sections were biased in favor of different groups of examinees. Some were biased in favor of Black test takers and some were biased in favor of White test takers.

Of course, following ETS test fairness rules, our experimental sections were never used in actual operational tests that affect examinee scores. They were tested on real examinee populations but in such a way that they did not affect their reported scores. This study allow us to see if biased tests can be built to real test specifications, and, if so, how tests that are really biased behave. This work is reported in detail in Hackett et al. (1987), so I will only use a few aspects of that report to show how, in this instance, race and a causal variable worked together to give information that otherwise could not be obtained.

We used good test questions to construct our test sections. They had passed many different kinds of reviews (including those for the purpose of identifying possibly biased or "insensitive" questions) by different people and had met the usual criteria of standard statistical analyses. These were not newly developed test questions, but those that had been evaluated along the lines that serious testing programs use to produce serious tests. They were all multiple-choice questions, they all had very defensible right answers, and there was no evidence that they elicited unusual testing behavior from examinees. In my opinion, no teacher-made test in any school or university in any subject has ever been scrutinized as well as our test questions had been.

We selected two question types, Sentence Completion from the verbal dimension and Problem Solving from the quantitative dimension. These were both question types that had been used for years in the testing program in which we did our experiment. We did not introduce anything novel into the actual questions used in our study. Instead, we exploited the natural variation that occurs in actual test questions in terms of the performance on them by real examinees. Based on their pretest statistics, we grouped these questions into those that favored White examinees more than average, and those that favored Black examinees more than average. It must be clearly stated that we simply used the proportion of examinees getting each question correct as our measure of whether an item "favored" White or Black examinees. Furthermore, because of the large White-Black difference in overall performance on this nationally administered test, White examinees always averaged higher than Black examinees on each test question (i.e., the "main effect of race" mentioned earlier). Our choice of labeling of an item as biased against White or Black examinees was really a matter of how much higher the White examinees scored on it than did the Black examinees. Those questions with the smallest White/Black differences were interpreted as questions that "favored" Black examinees and those with the largest differences were interpreted as questions that "favored" White examinees. Our purpose in choosing test questions in this way was to manipulate the average score differences between White and Black examinees on the experimental test sections. This purpose was to insure that the resulting tests really did have a consequence for differences in the scores of Black and White examinees.

Our first requirement of the experienced test developers who constructed our biased sections was that they build them to meet both the content and statistical specifications that are required of any such sections for the real test. This came first because we wanted real tests not pseudo tests. Next came the biasing through the final choice of test questions using the pretest statistics as described above. As a final check, once the tests were printed we had several independent reviewers go over the sections that we had created to see if they could detect which ones were which, and they could not.

Suffice it to say we achieved all our goals. All of the test sections we had specially constructed met the content and statistical specifications for those sections. The test sections that were designed to maximize the White-Black difference in mean performance (the White-biased sections) did exactly that and the sections designed to minimize this difference (the Black-biased sections) were successful as well. Thus, we were able to create tests that varied the White-Black difference in predictable ways. In this sense, we created biased tests that were both (a) indistinguishable from the usual sections that are routinely constructed for this test and (b) that were biased in ways that could have had an impact on real scores had they been used to report real scores. They were not used, of course, in this way.

Return now to the discussion of the first parts of this chapter. What was the causal variable in this study? What we did was to arrange it so that randomly selected examinees in an operational test administration were exposed to either the White-biased sections or the Black-biased sections in a part of the operational test that did not count for their score. In addition to our special test sections, examinees also could have been randomized to one of three comparable Sentence Completion (SC) sections and to one of six Problem Solving (PS) sections. These had been constructed to meet the very same test specifications that our special test sections had been designed to meet (but not the bias, of course). These comparable sections are our control sections because they are just ordinary sections of the test developed to meet the specifications of those test sections, PS or SC. In the analysis given here, I present only the average scores over all the several control sections because they are very similar relative to the other differences that interest us.

Thus, the causal variable is the "bias type" of the section that an examinee responded to. Race will also play a role because in studying test bias we are interested in the interaction of "bias type" and race.

Table 5.1 summarizes the results of the study, emphasizing the basic messages rather than the many other relevant details that are given in Hackett et al. (1987).

The values in table 5.1 are average "formula scores," the usual raw score computed for these sections. The SC and PS sections are quite different in terms of numbers of questions and difficulty so that it is not useful to

Table 5.1. Average Section Scores for Black and White Test Takers by Subject and Type of Bias (White, Black, or Control Sections)

Subject	*Section Type*	*Black Test Takers*	*White Test Takers*
Problem Solving	Black-biased	7.2	10.4
	White-biased	4.3	10.6
	Control Average	5.5	10.1
Sentence Completion	Black-biased	10.7	12.4
	White-biased	8.6	14.3
	Control Average	9.8	13.1

compare the values across the two subjects. In case the reader is concerned that these score changes are not large enough to make a difference, I report that the standard deviation of the control sections for PS was 4.3 and for SC it was 4.4. Thus the differences between the mean scores on the Black- and White-biased sections for a given group was as large as two-thirds of a standard deviation—that is, for Black test takers on the PS sections.

I think there are three messages of table 5.1. The first is the obvious one that for this test, like many others, there is a noticeable main effect of race; that is, regardless of the type of bias used to construct the tests, White test takers score higher on average than Black test takers. Secondly, we were able to impact the scores of Black and White examinees in predictable ways using these specially constructed test sections. White scores go up (relative to the controls) for the White-biased sections and Black scores go up (relative to the controls) for the Black-biased sections.

Thirdly, and what is even more interesting to me, is that the two subjects (SC or PS) seem to behave in different ways in how the bias works. For the Problem Solving sections, the scores of White examinees are not influenced very much by the manipulation of bias type, but those of Black examinees are. However, for the Sentence Completion sections we seem to have a case of robbing Peter to pay Paul. In this case, when White scores go up, Black scores go down; and when Black scores go up, White scores go down. It could well be argued that in the PS sections the manipulation did, in fact, reduce bias for the Black test takers. But this is harder to argue for the SC sections, where some sort of "exchange" took place. In my opinion, this difference in the effect of biased tests on the scores of examinees of different races is an important point to understand with further research. Is it specific to different content areas, or question types or are there other factors involved? These are questions that can be studied and they can inform notions of test bias in ways that go well beyond the usual speculations of question wording, and such.

Once one has examples of tests that are really biased for and against different groups (rather than examples of tests that are called biased due to their main effect of race) we can begin their scientific study with the ultimate aim of understanding how to make real tests as fair as they can be.

CONCLUSION

Race is not a causal variable and attributing cause to race is merely confusing and unhelpful in an area where scientific study is already difficult. The useful causal role of race is its ability to reveal varying effects of interventions on different parts of a diverse population. In the study of test bias, it is crucial to study the interaction of race with tests developed to have different types of bias, rather than to call the main effect of race on a single test evidence of its bias for or against different groups of examinees.

6

Swimming Upstream

Theory and Methodology in Race Research

Quincy Thomas Stewart

Race is perhaps the most salient representation of inequality in the Western world. The persistent, significant racial disparities in education, earnings, wealth, health, mortality, and other indicators of social well-being confirm this assertion (Blau 2003; Conley 1999; Grodsky and Pager 2001; Hayward and Heron 1999; McCall 2001; Oliver and Shapiro 1995; Williams 1999). Over the past century countless scholars analyzed the aforementioned racial outcome disparities in an effort to find the source(s) of racial inequality—the mechanisms of racial privilege. Recent research suggests that a variety of countervailing factors such as genetics (Bamshad 2005; Burchard et al. 2003; Karter 2003), hidden racism (Bobo, Kluegel, and Smith 1997; Bonilla-Silva 2003), cognitive skills (Farkas and Vicknair 1996; Neal and Johnson 1996; O'Neill 1990) and an oppositional culture among minorities (Fryer and Torelli 2005; Ogbu and Davis 2003) contribute to the observed racial outcome disparities.

In quantitative research on race, where conclusions on the source(s) of racial inequality enlist mathematical objectivity as a shroud, the debate on the factors responsible for racial inequality remains highly contested. Quantitative articles on racial inequality are often followed by critical commentary on the *other* factors responsible for the racial outcome disparities under consideration (see Cancio, Evans and Maume 1996). These ongoing quantitative debates on racial inequality, though, revolve around a conventional, regression-based methodology that is used to identify the source(s) of inequality. This methodology employs individual- and community-level variable-based data to identify the source(s) of racial disparities in a particular outcome. A social scientist studying mortality, for example, models racial disparities in dying (i.e., the dependent variable) as a function of education, occupation, age, wealth, and many other "independent" variables known to covary with mortality (Collins and Williams 1999; Gornick et al. 1996; Menchik 1993; Rogers 1992). The goal of this generic analysis is the isolation of the variable set that *explains* racial mortality disparities—the source(s) of inequality.

In what follows, I show that two regression-based quantitative techniques used to identify the factor(s) responsible for racial outcome disparities—variable and comparative analysis—overlook the interactive processes that create and maintain racial inequality. Schwalbe et al. (2000) noted that "[to] explain inequality requires attention to the [interactive] processes that produce and perpetuate it" (420). Research on race must recognize that observed racial inequalities are the culmination of countless—and often modest—social interactions where actors' characteristics are translated into opportunities and rewards (Bonilla-Silva 1997; Emirbayer 1997; Reskin 2003; Schwalbe et al. 2000; Tilly 1998; West and Fenstermaker 1995). Quantitative research on race largely overlooks the interactive processes behind racial inequality and, as a result, is hampered two dilemmas: (1) interpreting variables that explain the race effect as the source of racial outcome disparities, and (2) interpreting the unique characteristics of outliers as the keys to racial uplift. These issues have received little attention (Bonilla-Silva [1997], Bonilla-Silva and Baiocchi [2001], Reskin [2003], and Zuberi [2000] partially address these issues). I critically analyze these issues and advance the idea that research on race can overcome them by critically analyzing social interactions both within institutions and across social institutions.

In this chapter, I use a literary analysis technique—an allegory—to generate a framework that highlights the concept of race and, consequently, the limitations of the conventional quantitative research methods.[1] The allegory centers on two swim teams that race in a river each week. The meets are structured such that one team swims downstream and the other swims upstream. These structured interactions—competitive swim meets—that result in swim times represent the social interactions and unequal outcomes that occur in modern society. Hence, an analysis of the allegory promises to shed light on race in general, and the methods used to study racial inequality in particular.

BACKGROUND

A review of recent quantitative research reveals two predominant techniques of identifying the source(s) of racial inequality. Blumer (1969) defined the first method, variable analysis, as "the scheme of sociological analysis which seeks to reduce human group life to variables and their relations" (127; see also Abbot [1999] and Emirbayer [1997]). Indeed, there are many statistical methods used in the variable analytic tradition. Emirbayer (1997) wrote that variable analysts "employ a variety of quantitative methods . . . including multiple regression, factor analysis, and event history approaches" (286). Regardless of the method, though, variable analyses of race aim to identify the factors that reduce the coefficient on the race variable, or explain the "race effect." In variable analysis, we interpret the independent variables that explain the race effect as the source of racial disparities in an outcome (Reskin 2003).

The second technique used to identify the source(s) of racial inequality is comparative analysis. In comparative analyses, scholars compare two or more similar groups to identify the factor(s) responsible for group disparities in success/failure. The most popular examples of the method are comparisons of West Indian immigrants and African Americans (Dodoo 1997; Katende 1994; Sowell 1978, 1983; Waters 1999). These type of analyses seek to pinpoint the variable set that distinguishes more successful West Indians from less successful African Americans, and, subsequently, interpret this variable set as the source(s) of racial inequality—the mechanisms for racial uplift.

While variable and comparative analyses of race pursue the variable set responsible for racial outcome disparities, recent research locates the source of inequality in everyday social interactions (Reskin 2003; Schwalbe et al. 2000; Tilly 1998). Emirbayer (1997, 292), for example, noted that defining inequality "as a matter of variations in the possession of 'human capital' or other goods" is in error. He writes, "Unfolding [social] transactions, not preconstituted attributes, are . . . what most effectively explain equality and inequality" (Emirbayer 1997, 293). In line with Emirbayer, West and Fenstermaker (1995) wrote: "[R]ace is not simply an individual characteristic or trait but something that is accomplished in interaction with others" (23). Thus, recent research suggests that racial inequality is created in countless social interactions taking place at various levels (e.g., organizational) and locations in society. These interactions represent the social space where actors' characteristics, such as race, are converted into rewards and opportunities—that are often modest in size—and, in turn, observed racial inequalities are created and maintained.

The conventional practice of modeling racial outcome disparities strictly focuses on the identification of explanatory factors—factors that covary with racial disparities in a specific outcome. This practice does not recognize or analyze the multitude of social interactions that create and maintain racial inequality (Abbot 1999; Blumer 1969; Emirbayer 1997). For this reason, Tilly (1998) wrote:

> [I]ndividualistic analyses of inequality have all the attractions of neoclassical economics . . . confronted with unequal outcomes, their user searches the

> past for individual differences in skill, knowledge . . . that must explain differences in rewards. These analyses fail, however, to the extent that essential causal business takes place not inside individual heads but within *social relations* among persons and sets of persons. That extent is, I claim, very large (33; emphasis added).

Quantitative research on race must unveil the interactive processes that create racial inequality to identify the source(s) of inequality and, in turn, advise policy designed to alleviate existing racial outcome disparities. I now turn to the allegory of the swim meet to shed new light on the limitations of conventional quantitative research on race and develop a research program to identify the source(s) of racial inequality.

THE ALLEGORY OF THE SWIM MEET

The Allegory

There is an ongoing series of swim meets between two groups, the pros and cons. Each week the groups meet at a river to swim a uniform distance. Swimmers in each group are competing for the best time. An individual's status in the group, though, is related to his/her ability to beat competitors in the opposing group. Thus, swimmers in both groups want to post a better time than his/her teammates and the swimmers on the opposing team.

To conduct each swim meet match, officials place random swimmers from each group at opposite ends of a section of a river. The competitors begin swimming at the sound of a gun, pass each other swimming in opposite directions, then are timed as each passes his/her respective finish line. It is the swim meet tradition that one group of competitors—the pros—always swims downstream, and the other group—the cons—always swims upstream. This tradition began as it represented each team swimming toward their village. Swim meet officials initially presumed that these conditions were just and fair for each group.

Officials conducted the meets for several years in a variety of rivers of different speeds. Statistics indicate that pros swimmers have won every competition. In many of the meets, the officials noted that a few cons, swimming upstream, had better times than their competitors in the pros. They also noted, however, that the average time of the pros was significantly shorter than the cons average swim time in every meet. These events piqued officials' interest in the cons repeated failure and led them to hypothesize that the swim meet structure does affect swim times. As a result, officials asked scholars to estimate the river speed at a recent meet and identify the factors responsible for group time disparities. They intend to use this information to equalize the meets.

Officials provided scholars with data on a recent swim meet [k] where swimmers raced a uniform distance, *D*. The data contains the time [T_{ik}] for each swimmer [i], and information on a vector of characteristics [X_{ik}] that is argued to independently influence swim speed—the characteristics covary with times within/across groups. Officials inform scholars that characteristics (i.e., X_{ik}) were influenced by conditions faced in previous meets [$V_{j<k}$], and were normally distributed with mean μ, and variance σ among both groups prior to all swim meets [i.e., $\mu_0(pros) = \mu_0(cons)$ and $\sigma_0(pros) = \sigma_0(cons)$].[2] Altogether, the officials provide data on group membership [G_i], swim times at meet k [T_{ik}], the distance of the meet [D], and the characteristic vector for each swimmer at meet k [X_{ik}].

MODELING GROUP DIFFERENCE

The allegory presents the problem of finding the source of group disparities. Below, I present a general theoretical solution to locating the source of group disparities. Then, I analyze two simple solutions using the general theoretical solution as a frame.

The General Solution

The source of group swim time disparities is swimming in different directions (i.e., the swim meet structure). Before the swim meets, the characteristics that influence swim times [X_{i0}] were normally distributed with equal means and variances in both populations. The structure of the swim meets led to group disparities in these factors and swim times. Thus, the analysis of group swim time disparities begins with recognizing the motivating role of the swim meet structure.

After recognizing the importance of the swim meet structure, we turn to the characteristics (i.e., factors) that influence swim times. Swim times are a function of the characteristics vector that, in turn, is a function of previous conditions faced. Characteristics, then, are the product of countless prior interactions between swimmers and rivers—river speed facilitated/impeded swimmers, and swimmers reacted. We write this functional relationship as:

$$X_{ik} = f\,(\theta_{i(j<k)}, V_{j<k}) \tag{1}$$

where X_{ik} is the characteristics vector for individual *i* in swim meet *k*, $V_{j<k}$ is a vector of previous environmental conditions, and $\theta_{i(j<k)}$ is a vector of swimmers' reactions to prior conditions. Group disparities in characteristics, then, are a product of prior conditions (e.g., swimming upstream) and reactions.

To solve the allegorical problem, we build on Eq. 1 to create a general model of swim times. The general model of swim times is

$$T_{ik} = f(X_{ik}\,(u_{i(j<k)}, V_{j<k}), V_k, \theta_{ik}) \tag{2}$$

where T_{ik} is the time of individual i in swim meet k, X_{ik} is the characteristic vector for individual i in swim meet k (a function of prior conditions and reactions), V_k is the speed of river k, and θ_{ik} refers to the reaction of individual i to conditions in river k. Swimmers times, then, are a function of current characteristics, current/previous conditions, and current/previous reactions.

Two Simple Models

The general model of swim times (Eq. 2) is missing several key pieces of information. There are two ways, however, that we can use this information to estimate river speed and identify the sources of swim-time disparities. The first solution is to simplify the general model (i.e., variable analysis), while the second is to analyze the within-group disparities (i.e., comparative analysis).

For variable analysis, we assume that swimmers uniformly respond to environmental conditions [$\theta_{ik} = c$], and that swimmers' characteristic vectors are not related to the previous conditions [$X_{ik} \neq f\,(\theta_{i(j<k)}, V_{j<k})$]. The second assumption implies that disparities in characteristics are the product of unobserved exogenous factors—not the structure of the *current* swim meet. A swimmer's time, then, is a function of an independent set of characteristics and river speed (Eq. 3).

$$T_{ik} = f(X_{ik}, V_k) \tag{3}$$

We estimate this model by incorporating an error term and using regression.[3] We write

$$T_{ik} = \alpha_0 + \beta_0 \cdot G_i + \sum_{j=1}^{J} \gamma_{0l}\, X_{ijk} + e_{ik} \tag{4}$$

where G_i is a dummy variable for cons group membership (upstream), X_{ijk} refers to characteristic j for person i in river k, and e_{ik} is the error term. In this formulation, the β_0 parameter is the unstandardized estimate of river speed and the γ-parameters highlight the factors that are responsible for group swim-time disparities.[4]

Albeit simple and easy to interpret, the variable analytic solution does not account for current characteristics'—and swim times'—dependence on prior conditions and reactions. If prior conditions or reactions are positively correlated with current characteristics (e.g., characteristics increase by swimming downstream), then we would underestimate river speed. The variable analytic solution, then, is not likely to produce unbiased estimates of river speed.[5]

In contrast to variable analysis, the comparative analytic solution focuses on within-group variation in swim times. We assume that variation in the characteristic vector $[X_{ik}]$ is largely a function of swimmers' reactions to prior conditions [e.g., $\Theta_{k-m}, \ldots \Theta_{k-1}$], and that no cons swimmers would win in a *fast* river (i.e., current river speed is inconsequential)—the second assumption justifies the focus on within-group variance in swim time. Given these assumptions, we need only identify the characteristic(s) that distinguish successful cons swimmers [X^*_{ik}, where $X^*_{ik} \subset X_{ik}$]. We do this by running a within-group regression to identify the factors that covary with swimming success. And since we do not have reaction data, we hypothesize that a specific reaction (e.g., working harder) to prior conditions is the source of within-group variation in characteristics and times.

Like variable analysis, this solution does not account for current characteristics' dependence on prior conditions and reactions. The solution gives primacy to current characteristics and unobserved—hypothetical—reactions to prior conditions. The solution also assumes that the unique characteristics of outliers are the source of disparities. Indeed, current characteristics are related to success. However, current characteristics are related to prior conditions, reactions, and chance as well. The disregard for other factors (e.g., prior conditions) in the model is inaccurate and biased.

Summary: Modeling Group Difference

The general model of swim-time disparities suggests three steps to identify the source of group disparities. Scholars should: (1) recognize the significance of the swim meet structure, (2) analyze the impact of prior conditions and reactions on characteristics, and (3) analyze the covariance between characteristics and swim times while accounting for prior conditions and reactions. The aforementioned simple solutions do not embrace these three steps. They fail to recognize the significance of the swim meet structure as well as the nuanced role of prior conditions/reactions in creating swim-time disparities. While the second solution is more problematic than the first (i.e., stricter assumptions), both solutions fail to see beyond the current characteristic vector.

RACIAL RIVERS

The General Model

The parallels between the allegory and race appear in table 6.1. The first parallel is between the swim meet structure and racial ideology. Here, racial

Table 6.1. Corollaries between Allegory and Race

Allegory		*Interpretive Meaning*
1) Swim Meet	→	1) Competition for Social Status and Resources
2) Rivers	→	2) Institutions
3) Structure of Swim Meet	→	3) Racial Classification/Structure
4) Swimming Upstream	→	4) Confronting Racial Discrimination
5) Swimming Downstream	→	5) Receiving Racial Privilege
6) Swim Times	→	6) Social Outcomes
7) Swim Time Disparities	→	7) Racial Disparities in Outcomes
8) Reactions to Environmental Conditions	→	8) Reactions to Racial Treatment
9) Relationship between Current and Prior Characteristics	→	9) Relationship between Racial Disparities across Institutional Contexts

ideology refers to the belief that a person's racial classification covaries with his/her abilities, character, and culture (Drake 1987; Graves 2001). The swim meets are analogous to social interactions. The ideology of race, then, structures countless social interactions in a variety of institutions (i.e., rivers) operating at different levels and locations in society. Racial treatment[6] refers to the use of race—in addition to other characteristics—in the social interaction space (i.e., mechanism) where characteristics are converted into opportunities and rewards. The reactions of swimmers in the allegory represent actors' reactions to perceived racial treatment.[7] And the end product of countless social interactions structured by racial ideology is observed racial outcome disparities.

The parallels between the swim meet allegory and race highlight a general interactive model[8] of racial inequality. This model suggests that racial outcome disparities are created in countless social interactions taking place in various locations and levels in society with the general form shown in Figure 6.1.[9] As in the allegory, the model indicates that the racial ideology structures everyday social interactions. The first place this ideology structures the generic interaction, k, is in the treatment function, Λ_{ik}. The treatment function is based on racial bias/nonbias $[V_{ik}]$ toward individual i in interaction k and the characteristics vector $[X_{ik}]$. Here, the treatment function indicates whether a person $[i]$ is treated impartially or with bias.

After the treatment, a person perceives the treatment $[P_{ik}]$ as just/unjust based on past experiences and comparisons with similar others.[10] If an actor perceives unjust treatment (i.e., discrimination), he/she may use an adaptive coping response $[\Theta_{ik}]$—or reaction—to offset the related negative outcome. This adaptive coping response can vary from seeking social support to exercising to drinking, and, subsequently, lead to various outcomes $[X_{ik+1}]$.[11] If a person perceives just treatment, then the outcome vector is

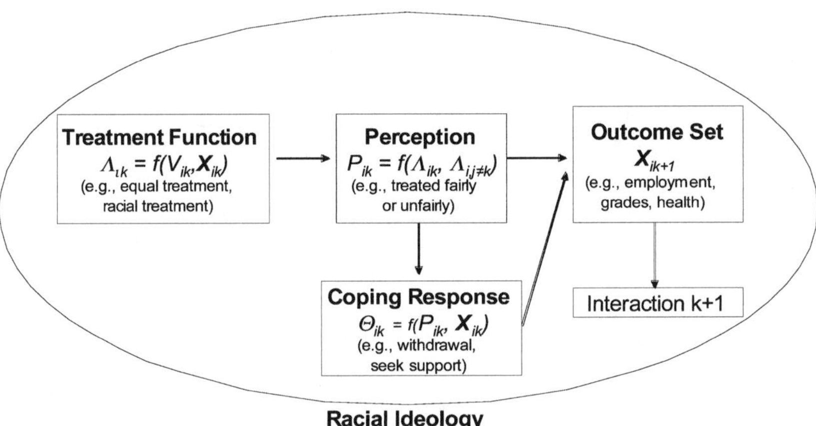

Figure 6.1. General Interactive Model of Racial Inequality: Interaction *k*

largely determined by the treatment function [Λ_k] (represented by a line between perception and outcomes in figure 6.1).

The interactive model of racial inequality in figure 6.1 embraces the lessons learned from the swim meet allegory. The model situates each interaction in the larger racial ideology (lesson 1). This model also highlights the importance of prior treatment and reactions on group characteristics/outcomes (lesson 2). Lastly, the model indicates that current social interactions are related to characteristics, *and* prior conditions and reactions (lesson 3).[12]

Two Simple Solutions

As in the allegory, there are two simple solutions one can use to locate the source(s) of racial outcome disparities: variable and comparative analysis. Variable analyses examine the covariation between race, several variables of theoretical import, and an outcome variable. They most often take the form

$$y_i = \beta_0 + \beta_1 \cdot R_i + \sum_{j=2}^{J} \beta_j \cdot C_{ij} + e_i \tag{5}$$

where y_i refers to an outcome variable, R_i refers to the race dummy variable for person i, C_{ij} refers to characteristic j for individual i, and e_i is an error term. The goal of variable analyses of racial inequality is to identify the variable set that reduces the race coefficient [β_i]—the race effect. We interpret the variable set that reduces the race effect as the source(s) of inequality and the residual race effect as a sign of equality/inequality (Reskin 2003).[13]

Unfortunately, the conventional variable analytic model of racial inequality strictly focuses on the covariation between *current* characteristics and outcomes—not unfair treatment, perceptions, or coping responses (i.e., the interactive process). Given that this model overlooks the relationship between current characteristics and prior conditions/reactions, scholars are left to speculate about: (1) the source of the residual race effect (e.g., skills, racism), and (2) the role of other independent variables in the social interaction (e.g., factors employers use in hiring and wage determination).

An example of variable analytic speculation can be seen in research on racial wage inequality. Recent research indicates that controlling for background factors (e.g., years of education), work experience, and cognitive skills (as measured by the Armed Forces Qualifying Test) reduces the Black-White wage disparity to insignificance (Farkas and Vicknair 1996; Neal and Johnson 1996; O'Neill 1990). This work is often cited as evidence of race neutrality in the American labor market (D'Souza 1995a; Herrnstein and Murray 1994). The flaw of this popular interpretation lies in ignoring the complex social interactions that create racial wage inequality. More specifically, conventional wage analyses assume that employers use various measures of skill (e.g., education, work experience) and other productivity indices to determine the wage for an employee.[14] Social scientists, consequently, control for various productivity-related factors argued to be related to earnings disparities. This technique yields an unbiased estimate of the average racial wage disparity in several categorical dimensions—the residual race coefficient. It does *not*, however, assess any of the actions that are essential to concluding that racism exists or does not exist in the American labor market—racial treatment by employers and coping responses of actors.

Like variable analysis, comparative analysis is often used to identify the source(s) of racial outcome disparities. The focus of comparative analyses, however, is the variable set that distinguishes successful minority actors from the unsuccessful mass. In comparative analysis, we assume that the distinct characteristics of successful actors—and the related hypothetical reactions—are the means for racial uplift (i.e., the source(s) of inequality). Sowell (1978), for example, used comparative analysis to identify the characteristic(s) that distinguish West Indian success, and, by default, the source(s) of native-born Blacks' low social outcomes. Similarly, Lieberson (1980) used comparative analysis to pinpoint the characteristics that distinguished the high social mobility of Southern, Central, and Eastern European immigrants and the source(s) of low social mobility among Blacks in the early twentieth century. Although comparative analytic research often fails to find *the* characteristic(s) that explains racial inequality (Lieberson 1980; Roediger 1993; Waters 1999), several popular scholars claim to have identified the essential traits that distinguish successful minority (or immigrant) groups and point to family structure, culture, and motivation as the primary culprits (McWhorter 2000; Ogbu 1974, 1978, 1983, 1987, 1990; Sowell 1978).

A critical issue with comparative analysis is that it often overlooks the dependence of current characteristics on prior treatment and reactions. As mentioned previously, the divergent outcomes of any two groups are related to variation in prior interactions. Waters's (1999) research supports this assertion—and is an exception in comparative analytic research. In her analysis of West Indians and African Americans, she found that Black immigrants' background shaped their work orientation (i.e., willingness to accept lower wages) and perceptions of racism. These differences led to disparities in employment rates and slight differences in interpersonal relations with coworkers. Thus, Waters's research reveals that the prior social interactions of Black immigrants and natives are related to the divergent group characteristics and interactions.

QUANTITATIVE METHODOLOGY AND RACE RESEARCH

For more than a century, scholars and policy makers alike have turned to quantitative research on race to locate the source(s) of racial inequality. The previous discussion highlights the limitations of two analytic techniques used in this body of research. In particular, the literary analysis highlights that identifying the source(s) of racial inequality by using the variables that explain the race effect in variable analytic models or by using the unique characteristics of outliers in comparative analytic models is in error. The analysis also revealed three lessons for scholars who aim to locate the source(s) of racial outcome disparities. Namely, future quantitative research on race should: (1) recognize the significance of the larger racial ideology; (2) assess the impact of prior treatment and reactions on group characteristics—the relationship between prior interactions across social institutions; and (3) analyze the relationship between current characteristics, reactions, and outcomes while accounting for prior interactions. This three-pronged research strategy is tantamount to a theoretical shift from variable-based models of difference to an interactive model of racial inequality.

At first take, these three lessons do not seem radically different from existing research on race. Indeed, there is a considerable amount of qualitative and sociohistorical research that highlights the relevance of the existing racial ideology, and the nuanced aspects of social interactions that create and maintain observed racial outcome disparities (Higginbotham 1978; Oliver and Shapiro 1995; Royster 2003; Waters 1999; Williams 1944). Much of this work, though, is subject to the limitations of qualitative and sociohistorical research; that is to say one cannot easily generalize the results or estimate the social significance of a particular interaction. These are the two benefits of quantitative research and reasons for their wide appeal among scholars and policy makers.

Thus, the question remains: *What do these three lessons mean for existing and future quantitative research on race?* Interestingly, the lessons suggest that prior quantitative research on racial inequality using variable and comparative analysis is not invalid. Rather, the conventional interpretation of prior quantitative research on race is flawed. Previous variable analytic research, for example, often uses multiple regression to identify the source(s) of racial inequality. Although interpreting the results of conventional variable analyses as the source of racial inequality is flawed, one can interpret the model as a standardization. In other words, the race effect in previous research is an estimate of the average racial outcome disparity between actors in similar categories. This type of interpretation of variable-based analyses reframes the results as standardized racial differences in a particular context rather than the source(s) of racial outcome disparities.

Although one can reinterpret much of the existing quantitative research on racial difference, there must be a theoretical shift in future quantitative research if we aim to locate the source(s) of racial inequality. On the basis of the aforementioned three lessons and the interactive model of racial inequality, I suggest a research program with two foci. First, *quantitative research on race must examine racial treatment in American institutions*. There are a few increasingly popular ways that scholars can examine racial treatment: (1) audit and vignette studies, (2) natural experiments, and (3) mixed-method research. Audit and vignette studies involve sending pairs of individuals (auditors) or records depicting individuals (vignettes) with different racial backgrounds who have the same characteristics otherwise (e.g., education, experience) into a particular interaction (e.g., applying for a job, mental health diagnosis). Social scientists then analyze the data to see whether persons from a particular racial group are treated differently in the interaction of interest (Bendick, Brown, and Wall 1999; Heckman and Siegelman 1993; Loring and Powell 1988; Pager 2003; Yinger 1993). These types of studies are increasingly popular in research on race, but the existing work largely centers on racial treatment in housing, employment, and health care. Future audit and vignette research should expand to include more social dimensions, cases, and information to further highlight the nature of social interactions in American institutions.

Natural experiments, on the other hand, involve using spatial/temporal variation in policies or environmental conditions as explanatory variables in variable analytic models (Marini and Singer 1988, 387–88). These types of studies allow scholars to assess the extent to which variation in a particular policy or condition—the mechanism—is related to racial disparities in a particular outcome (Bansak and Raphael 2001; Clay 1998). Unfortunately, natural experiments are quite limited because scholars can only analyze the factor(s) that vary across geographic, political, and temporal space.

Lastly, mixed-methods research designs are well suited to analyzing racial treatment in a particular domain. Mixed-methods studies have the benefits of unveiling the interactive processes inherent in racial inequality while empirically highlighting the degree to which this process affects outcomes. Oliver and Shapiro's (1995) research on racial disparities in wealth, for example, used historical policy data, qualitative data, and quantitative panel data to shed light on how racial treatment—social policies in particular—helped create and maintain the current significant racial disparities in wealth.

As for the second focus, *future research on race must analyze the role of perceptions and coping responses in determining racial inequality*. Two methods that scholars can use to examine perceptions and coping responses are: (1) survey research on perceived discrimination, and (2) social psychological experiments. Recent survey research consistently shows that people who perceive high levels of discrimination have poor health outcomes (Kessler et al. 1999; Mossakowski 2004; Schulz et al. 2000; Williams 1999). Unfortunately, this result, and the growing body of survey research on the topic, is limited to medical sociology. Future research on perceptions and coping responses can build on this literature by analyzing perceived discrimination in an array of institutional contexts and myriad coping responses. The aim of this expansion is to shed light on the role of actors' perceptions and coping responses in creating racial disparities in an array of outcomes.

Social psychological experiments also promise a better understanding of the role of perceptions and coping responses in racial inequality. Steele's (2003) research on stereotype threat is a great example of how perceptions of inequality influence performance. This work, however, has been limited to controlled settings revolving around cognitive or physical ability. Future research in this area should expand to shed light on how perceptions and coping responses affect performance/habits for other outcomes such as teenage fertility and health.

The two proposed research foci underscore the need for quantitative research on race that unveils the process through which racial classification becomes observed inequality. Future research, however, must also reveal the connectedness of social interactions—racial treatment, perceptions, and coping responses—across time and social space. More specifically, future research should examine how the tenor of social interactions in one institution (e.g., education) at a particular time are either reinforced or weakened by the tone of social interactions in another institution (e.g., labor force)—or the same institution at a later time. Feedback effects in economic models of statistical discrimination offer one example of the covariation of interactions across institutions. These models suggest that minority students invest less in schooling in response to perceived discrimination in labor force outcomes (Blau and Ferber 1987; Loury 1995; Darity 1982; Darity and Myers 1998; Gould 1992). Thus, social interactions in the labor force and educational settings may jointly operate to increase racial outcome disparities (e.g., wages). Another example of research on the connectedness of social interactions across time and space is seen in Waters's (1999) research on West Indians and African Americans. As mentioned previously, this work highlighted how Black immigrants' prior interactions (e.g., growing up in a predominantly Black developing country) affected their work orientation (i.e., willingness to accept lower wages) and perceptions of racial treatment. This research further underscores the need to account for the role of prior interactions in shaping the character and consequences of the social interactions of that appeal to scholars. Future research in the aforementioned areas should expand beyond the labor force and immigrants to include a broad array of populations and a variety of institutions (e.g., familial, health care, and residential).

CONCLUSION

The goal of this chapter is to highlight that modern social scientific discussions on racial inequality are largely constrained by a variable-based perspective that readily leads to debates about Sen's (1992) original question, "Equality of what?" These debates become circular as scholars contest observed inequalities in a particular outcome with ethical claims of equality in another outcome (e.g., meritocracy, education). This debate leads to an endless pursuit of the variable set that explains the race effect. A shift in our theoretical perspective from variable-based to interactive leads to a shift in the focus of quantitative race research from "equality of what?" to "how do social interactions create and maintain observed racial inequalities?" By focusing on the creation and maintenance of racial inequality through a series of social interactions, participants in the current debate on "equality of what?" will be better equipped to test various theories on the source(s) of racial inequality. And, what is more important, research on race will take a large step forward in our goal of understanding and eradicating racial inequality.

NOTES

1. This type of literary technique often involves limitations. The allegory of the swim meet is limited in that it does not capture the historical dynamics of race. Specifically, the structure of the swim meets in the allegory is not attributable to a specific group. The ideology of race, on the other hand, was a purposive development by a specific group to increase Western trade and capitalist expansion, and sat-

isfy the demand for labor in the New World (Drake 1987; Graves 2001; Williams 1944). The fact that the swim meet structure was not a purposive event designed to undermine one group's performance does not limit the perspective gained for racial research. The allegory provides an accurate representation of the observed racial realities that social scientists aim to understand. Furthermore, the allegory provides an alternative frame through which I will critique recent racial research, and propose a program for future work on race.

2. To simplify the model, I assume that the factors that influence swim speed operate and develop independently to effect swim time in river *k*.

3. I specify a linear model only for ease of explanation. One can model this relationship as non-linear by specifying the parameters in another way. The purpose of this exercise, however, is not to hypothesize about the linear form of the model. Rather, the intent is to highlight the complexity in estimating river speed and adjusted swim times.

4. Specifically, β0 is the residual difference between the groups that is not related to the vector of characteristics. To estimate river speed we divide the uniform distance swam in each of the meets, *D*, by our parameter estimate

$$\hat{V}_k = \frac{\hat{\beta}_0}{D}$$

If we satisfy the assumptions of ordinary least squares estimation procedure, and our own modeling assumptions, then the above equation is an unbiased estimate of the river speed.

5. The role of reactions to environmental conditions is extremely important in models of group difference. We know that divergent environmental conditions are a determinant of group difference. Reactions to these conditions are often the mediating determinants of group difference. There exists an abundance of social psychological research on coping that theoretically and empirically supports this interactive model (Edwards 1992; Menaghan and Merves 1984; Nelson and Sutton 1990; Thoits 1995).

6. I will use the term "racial treatment" to refer to both racial discrimination and racial privilege.

7. The coping, distributive justice, and relative deprivation literature all address the response to stress/unjust treatment. For evidence on various types of reactions to stress/unjust treatment see Kawakami and Dion (1992), Jasso and Resh (2002), Mark and Folger (1984), Menaghan and Merves (1984), Nelson and Sutton (1990), Smith and Ortiz (2002), Thoits (1995), Tougas and Beaton (2002), Vanneman and Pettigrew (1972), and Walker and Mann (1987).

8. See Emirbayer (1997), Schwalbe et al. (2000), Tilly (1998), and West and Fenstermaker (1995) for a more complete discussion of interactive/relational theories of inequality.

9. This general model is a simple form of the cybernetic theory of coping model found in the medical sociology literature. See Edwards (1992), Menaghan and Merves (1984), Nelson and Sutton (1990), and Thoits (1995) for a more complete discussion of this model.

10. The perception of personal treatment is identical to the fairness evaluations that are widely discussed in the distributive justice and relative deprivation literature (Jasso and Resh 2002; Stewart 2006).

11. See Kramer (1993), Latack (1986), Lazarus and Folkman (1984), Nelson and Sutton (1990), and Pearlin and Schooler (1978) for empirical research on coping.

12. The fact that the current racially structured interaction is a function of prior interactions is seen in two places in figure 6.1. The first place is in the treatment function. Here, treatment [Λ_{ik}] is a function of characteristics [X_{ik}] and racial bias [V_{ik}]. Since interactions are cumulative, the characteristics of individual i are a product of previous interactions. The second place that prior interactions are seen in figure 6.1 are in perceptions [P_{ik}] and coping responses [Θ_{ik}].

13. See Blau and Ferber (1987), Farkas and Vicknair (1996), Neal and Johnson (1996), and O'Neill (1990) for examples of interpreting the residual race coefficient. Also see Bonilla-Silva (1997, 471) and Zuberi (2001a, chap. 7) for a discussion of interpreting residual race coefficients.

14. Arrow (1973) wrote of analyzing wage disparities:

> The fact that different groups of workers . . . receive different wages invites the explanation that the different groups must differ according to some characteristic valued on the market. In standard economic theory, we think first of all of differences in productivity. (3)

Here, Arrow expressed the general theory that employers use measures of particular characteristics—related to productivity—in wage determination.

7

Deracializing Social Statistics

Problems in the Quantification of Race

Tukufu Zuberi

> This study should seek to ascertain by the most approved methods of social measurement. . . .
>
> —W. E. B. Du Bois, "The Study of The Negro Problems" (1899)

In scholarly circles, demographic and statistical interpretation of racial differences has taken on an almost sacred quality. As a result, demographers and other scholars have forgotten—or perhaps have never realized—that the social concept of race affects *how* we interpret quantitative representations of racial reality. Moreover, many quantitative studies of racial differences fail to place race within a social context, thus allowing the faulty assumption that the existence of race relations could be benign.

In the beginning of this century, empirical social scientists took a eugenic perspective toward race. Du Bois was an exception to the accepted view about race among empirical social scientists. Du Bois was of the opinion that the best minds should study the problem of race according to the best methods. He thought that statistical analysis could help us gain a concrete understanding of the social status of the African American population. He formulated the first empirical refutation of eugenic and social Darwinist thought. After conducting an empirical study of African American life in a modern city in *The Philadelphia Negro*, Du Bois illustrated how *biological notions of African inferiority were grounded only in ideology.* However, Du Bois's contribution has been ignored by most sociologists, and its theoretical significance to understanding modern society continues to be underplayed. This chapter demonstrates the theoretical significance of Du

Bois's tradition of scholarship on our understanding of racial statistics, particularly his contributions to the understanding of quantitative data in societies where race is an "essential" variable.[1] Unfortunately, among social statisticians, including demographers there has developed an implicit tendency to accept the underlying logic of racial reasoning. In part the statistical logic of justifying racial stratification has resulted from a lack of critical theory among social statisticians, and a tendency to avoid reflexive discourse with statisticians in general and with other areas of the social sciences, such as African and African Diaspora studies in particular. This chapter describes the scientific birth of racial reasoning in statistical analysis, what I have learned from reading statistics and practicing demography, and how this shapes a new logic for the quantitative study of racial stratification that has developed between Du Bois's *Philadelphia Negro* and the reflexive discourse among statisticians.

BIRTH OF SOCIAL STATISTICS

Francis Galton was a key intellectual power behind the modern statistical revolution in the social sciences (Stigler 1986, chapter 8; Kevles 1985, chapter 1). His imaginative ideas are the conceptual foundation of eugenic thought and inspired much of the early work in social statistics. Galton's research in *Hereditary Genius* (1892), *English Men of Science* (1874), and *Natural Inheritance* (1889) all suggested that genius and success are inherited and that this process could be measured statistically.

Galton used statistical analysis to make general statements regarding the superiority of different classes within England and of the European-origin race, statements that were consistent with his eugenic agenda. In the 1892 edition of *Hereditary Genius* he outlined that "the natural ability of which this book mainly treats, is such as a modern European possesses in a much greater average share than men of the lower races. There is nothing either in the history of domestic animals or in that of evolution to make us doubt that a race of sane men may be formed, who shall be as much superior mentally and morally to the modern European, as the modern European is to the lowest of the Negro races" (27). While this statement may be considered insignificant in the context of Galton's overall statistical contribution, it is fundamental in understanding the direction and purpose of his causal explanations, and placing Du Bois's empirical response in a historical context (Zuberi 2000).

In 1875, Galton wrote an article, "Statistics by Intercomparison, with Remarks on the Law of Frequency of Error," that suggested that measurement of two values—the median and the quartile—was sufficient to characterize or compare populations. For Galton this meant different populations could be represented in a bell curve of all populations.

In 1885, Francis Ysidro Edgeworth (1845–1926) developed a test to ascertain whether different populations existed within the bell curve (Edgeworth 1885). Edgeworth's test adapted the bell curve to assess the "significance" of differences between the subpopulations. He used Galton's 1875 formulation as a vehicle to employ classical statistical theory in understanding social statistics.

In 1889, Pearson met W. F. R. Weldon, the chair of Zoology at University College, London. Weldon was attempting to adapt Galton's methods to the study of evolution in wild populations. Weldon turned to Pearson with a series of questions to which Pearson responded in a series of papers known as *Contributions to the Mathematical Theory of Evolution.* Published between 1894 and 1916, the series was retitled *Mathematical Contributions to the Theory of Evolution,* after the second in what became a series of about nineteen papers.[2] Pearson's elaboration of Edgeworth's theorems advanced correlation theory into the main of social statistics.[3] In Pearson's third and fourth papers of the *Mathematical Contribution to the Theory of Evolution*—"Regression, Heredity and Panmixa" and "On the Probable Errors of Frequency Constants and on the Influence of Random Selection on Variation and Correlation" (which he coauthored with L. N. G. Filon)—he provided a basic formula for estimating the correlation coefficient and a test of its accuracy.

In 1897, George Udny Yule provided the conceptual and statistical expression that completed Galton's project to apply statistics to the study of society.[4] Yule was one of the first social statisticians to demonstrate the relationship between regression and least squares estimates. Yule was exceptional in that his application of statistics focused on causation in social sciences. Yule extended the application of regression in one of the first regression analyses of poverty. Interestingly, Yule's analysis provided support for the conservative position advocated by Malthus at the beginning of the century (Yule 1899; Stigler 1986, 355–57). He argued that providing income relief outside the poorhouse increased the number of people on relief. By 1920, his approach to multiple correlation and regression predominated in social science research.

Social statistics took another intellectual leap when Ronald A. Fisher published *Statistical Methods for Research Workers* in 1925, and *The Design of Experiments* in 1935. Both books had a tremendous impact on the teaching and practice of statistics. His work clarified the distinction between a sample statistic and population value, and he emphasized the derivation of exact distributions for hypotheses testing. He is also credited with introducing the modern experimental design and statistical methods to social sciences. These innovations remain as the basis of social statistics.

CAUSAL REASONING AS RACIAL REASONING

The experimental notion of causal inference is the implicit guide in the selection of observations in quasi-experimental research and in the model selection, design, and statistical analysis of nonexperimental data from sample surveys and samples from census data. Most researchers, however, do not appear to appreciate the consequences of adopting the experimental model as a guide in the design, collection, analysis, and interpretation of social science data. Most social scientists use experimental language when interpreting empirical results, thereby entailing a commitment to the experimental mode of analysis introduced by Fisher (Holland 1986; Cox 1992; Sobel 1995; Smith 1990). I am intentionally explicit in this section so that I can present the fundamental elements of the causal process in statistical modeling.

Because most social science researchers study causal effects for the purpose of making inferences about the effects of manipulations to which groups of individuals in a population have been or might be exposed, causes are only things that can, in theory, be manipulated or altered. This recognition forces us to consider the individuals or units we study and our ability to alter or treat these individuals. This type of clarity is essential yet absent in most policy-oriented social research. In most policy research, decisions to manipulate the real world often depend on social researchers' causal inferences. A lack of clarity in the statistical analysis of racial processes has contributed in great measure to the confusion about how to resolve issues of racial stratification.

Cultural studies in anthropology, history, literary criticism, sociology, philosophy, and African studies have questioned and criticized the concept of race. Statisticians are in the process of an important discussion on the issue of using attributes like race in social statistics (See Holland 1986; Cox 1992; Sobel 1995; Rosenbaum 1984). This discussion has not focused on the issue of the conceptualization of race. It nevertheless places a considerable theoretical burden on social statisticians who use race as a variable in their statistical analysis to predict social outcomes. Most social statisticians have not yet integrated the latest statistical research in their statistical analysis of race.

Statistical populations consist of observed measures of some characteristic; yet no observational record can capture completely what it is to be a human being. Researchers employ observational records to define abstract concepts like race. The researchers or the subject (as in self-administered surveys or censuses) can make the observation; however, the researchers and the purpose of their study determine the meaning of the record. This is how empirical research reifies race. If we have records of racial classification, the population of races rather than the population of persons is open to statistical investigation; yet in social statistics it is always a mistake to think of a population of races as a genetic population. A population of races in this sense is a statistical concept based on a politically constructed measure. Deriving a statistical model of social relationships requires an elaborate theory that states explicitly and in detail the variables in the system, how these variables are causally interrelated, the functional form of their relationships, and the statistical quality and traits of the error terms. Once we have this theoretical model, we can estimate a regression model.[5] Rarely, however, does social science research provide the level of theoretical detail necessary to derive a statistical model in this manner.

The alternative is a data-driven process. To derive a statistical model from data we assume the model is a black box and "test" it against our empirical results. Both the theory- and data-driven statistical models attempt to provide a parsimonious and generalizable account for the phenomenon under investigation. Statistical models attempt to provide a rigorous basis—rooted in abstract statistical theory—for determining when a causal relationship exists between two or more variables in a model. However, unless we start with prior knowledge about the causal relationship, the calculation of the regression equation refers to a regression model and its system of equations, not to the "real" world the model purports to empirically define!

The language of causation originates in the experimental framework of modeling causal inference (Holland 1986; Cox 1992; Sobel 1995; Rosenbaum 1984). Statistically, causation has a particular meaning. Measuring the effects of causes is done in the context of another cause, hence **X** causes **Z** relative to some other cause that includes everything but **X**. In the context of causal inference each individual in the population must be potentially exposable to any of the causes. And, as the statistician Paul Holland notes, "the schooling a student receives can be a cause, in our sense, of the student's performance on a test, whereas the student's race or gender cannot" (Holland 1986, 946; also see Holland, chapter 5 in this volume). For example, being an African American should not be understood as the cause of a student's performance on a test, despite the fact that being African American can be a very reliable basis for predicting test performance. The logic of causal inference itself should give every nonpartisan scholar reason to avoid flamboyant rhetoric about the genetic-based cognitive causes for racial and gender stratification.

Race and gender as unalterable characteristics of individuals are inappropriate variables for inferential statistical analysis (see Holland, chapter 5 in this volume). Statisticians are beginning to question and criticize the use of such attributes—unalterable properties of individuals—in inferential statistical models (see Holland, chapter 5 in this volume; Cox 1992; Rosenbaum 1984; Sobel 1994, 1995). Most social statisticians, however, continue to treat race and sex as an individual attribute in their inferential models. *Statistical models that present race as a cause are really statements of association between the racial classification and a predictor or explanatory variable across individuals in a population. To treat these models as causal or inferential is a form of racial reasoning.*

FROM CAUSATION TO ASSOCIATION AS AN ASPECT OF DERACIALIZED STATISTICS

I suggest that we reconsider the notion of causation in the study of race. It may be better to interpret these impacts of race as the association of racial stratification on an individual's mortality outcome. In this context the attenuation of the race variable that occurred via the introduction of wealth into Menchik's (1993) model would imply the way that race interacts with wealth in its association with mortality.

Association may not prove causation; however, it may provide the basis for support of a causal theory. Association is evidence of causation when it is buttressed with other knowledge and supporting evidence. When we discuss the "effect of race" we should be more mindful of the larger world in which the path to success or failure is routinely influenced by other contingencies or circumstances.

CONCLUSION

Some will argue that causal models are the best way for social scientists to make public policy statements. They will say that statistic models used in this way allow us to elaborate on how and what produces particular effects. This may all be true, but human knowledge is uncertain and imperfect and it is not clear how statistical models contribute to this uncertainty (Freedman 1987). Interpreting the results of a causal inference is validated by an underlying causal theory. If the theory is rejected, the interpretations have no foundation. Decision makers may like causal models that appear to support their position on important questions, but it is the continued misuse of the statistical models by scholars that gives the process scientific credibility.

Some will argue that the causal language used by many social scientists is not reflective of an unarticulated causal model but is simply the careless use of language. However, this tendency has significant implications for how results are interpreted in policy circles and within the professional discursive mode.

Race, or more specifically the process of racialization, may be the stimulus for how other individuals respond or interact with persons so characterized. The examination of discrimination and prejudice provide a solution to the trap of racial reasoning. One example of such research is the study of racial attitudes (see Bobo and Smith 1998). Du Bois was aware of this process and gave it direct attention in his work. Another example of research of this process is found in the economic study of statistical racism and the demographic study of environmental racism.[6] The causal factors in statistical racism are discriminatory practices by employers not the races of the people involved. The causal factors in environmental racism are discriminatory practices by institutions in determining the location of hazardous wastes cites.

The solutions to the problem in the analysis of unalterable characteristics like race and gender in inferential statistics requires a shift in perspective. We should describe race and gender as events that represent the acquisition of the attributes for each individual. Thus, being classified one way or another might have a particular impact. As our understanding of what race or gender means changes, so too does our statistical analysis.

The National Liberation movements to decolonize Africa, Asia, and Latin America, the civil rights movement to deracialize civic society in the United States, and the antiapartheid movement in South Africa all questioned the Eurocentric division of humanity. We would benefit by continuing to question the racialization of identity. Using racialized census, survey, or other social data is not in and of itself problematic. But the racialization of data is an artifact of both the struggles to preserve and to destroy racial stratification. Before the data can be deracialized we must deracialize the social circumstances that created race. Statistical research can go beyond racial reasoning if we dare to apply the methods to the data appropriately.

NOTES

1. For a more extensive examination of the social statistical analysis in *The Philadelphia Negro: A Social Study* see my paper on this classic community study (McDaniel 1998; Zuberi 2004).

2. The long series of memoirs entitled *Mathematical Contributions to the Theory of Evolution* was reissued by the Trustees of Biometrika in 1948 in a single volume. The selected papers consist of articles published in the *Philosophical Transactions of the Royal Society*, in the Drapers' Company Research Memoirs, and in *Philosophical Magazine*. Most of these papers cover Pearson's *Mathematical Contribution to the Theory of Evolution* series. The article published in *Philosophical Magazine*, "On the Criterion That a Given System of Deviations from the Probable in the Case of a Correlated System of Variables Is Such That It Can Be Reasonably Supposed to Have Arisen from Random Sampling," presents the first derivation of the distribution referred to as the chi-square. The chi-square test, a goodness-of-fit test, is considered Pearson's most significant contribution to statistical theory. In this work Pearson greatly expanded social statistics. He also expanded on Edgeworth's

significance test by measuring difference in terms of standard deviations. See: Pearson (1948), Stigler (1986).

3. Pearson's correlation coefficient, **r**, continues to be the most commonly used measure of correlation. When people use the term "correlation" without any other specification this is what they mean.

4. Yule's paper "On the Theory of Correlation" reconciled the theory of correlation with the method of least squares from the traditional theory of errors. See Yule (1897) and Stigler (1986, 348–58) for an excellent discussion of the importance of this paper for social statistics. Linking least squares and regression made the developments in simplifying the solutions of normal equations and the calculation of the probable errors of coefficients by astronomers and geodesists available to regression analysis among social statisticians.

5. I use the term "regression" in a broad sense to include logistic regression, regression analysis, regression analysis of survival data, ordinary least-squares regression, and so on.

6. It is important to distinguish between the "statistical" reasoning by an employer, and the statistical reasoning discussed in this chapter that focuses on social scientists engaged in a very different sort of statistical reasoning from that of an employer. The econometric "theory" of statistical racism maintains that racial preference of an employer for a "White" job candidate over a "Black" job candidate who is not known to differ in other respects might stem from the employer's previous statistical experience with the two groups (Phelps 1972). This analysis has been extended to the examination of the impact of affirmative action on employer beliefs and worker productivity (see Lundberg 1991; Coate and Loury 1993).

According to my argument, statistical racism is a difficult process to examine. An employer's assessment of the expected productivity of employees in less-favored groups may be wrong in a way that a longitudinal study could effectively demonstrate; however, such a study is still prohibitively expensive. We might argue that an employer's perspective is invalid because it does not incorporate certain systemic mechanisms of other types of prejudice, such as the effect of higher rewards themselves on the productivity of employees in a less-favored "race."

The analysis of environmental racism examines whether facilities for treatment, storage, and disposal of hazardous wastes are located disproportionately in communities of the less-favored race (See Bullard 1990; Anderton et al. 1994). While the study of statistical racism focuses on intentional prejudice and the study of environmental racism has focused on dumping prejudice, both depend on inequitable distributions as evidence of intentional prejudice.

IV

INTERPRETING THE PROBLEM

8

Anything but Racism

How Sociologists Limit the Significance of Racism

Eduardo Bonilla-Silva and Gianpaolo Baiocchi

Mainstream sociological currents on race have historically followed Whites' racial "common sense."[1] Thus, well before Wilson published his immensely popular *The Declining Significance of Race* (1978), Whites had expressed in interviews and surveys that they did not believe racism was a significant fact of life in America, that the plight of minorities was their own doing, and that it was Whites who were suffering from "reverse discrimination," a view already captured in interviews conducted by Bob Blauner in 1968 for his *Black Lives, White Lives* (1989).[2] This chapter argues that sociologists have followed, rather than enlightened or challenged, Whites' racial common sense (McKee 1993; Lyman 1994), as we examine and criticize the methods mainstream sociologists have used to validate Whites' racial common sense on racial matters in the post–civil rights era. While we leave to others the detailed examination of the mathematical and statistical logic used by sociologists to justify the racial status quo (Zuberi 2001a), in this chapter we discuss five ways in which sociology helps maintain Whites' declining of significance thesis. While our choice of areas is neither exhaustive nor our discussion completely thorough, we believe it offers a fair rendering of the status quo and will serve as an important first step in a long overdue conversation in our discipline.[3]

Our contention is that mainstream sociology has observed racial matters with an inadequate racial theorization, and, hence, has not "seen" the significance of racial stratification in America. The earliest moment in this racial theorization (1920s–1950) assumed racism would go away naturally as industrialization and/or modernity advanced or as rational actors brought the market logic to bear in interracial interactions (Becker 1957).[4] This version of the theory became untenable in the tumultuous 1960s and alternative interpretations emerged, such as Blauner's internal colonialism approach or the institutional racism perspective,[5] forcing mainstream sociology to revise its racial theory. Racism came to be defined as a set of erratic beliefs that may lead racist actors to develop "attitudes" (prejudice) against the group(s) they conceive as inferior, which may ultimately lead them to "act" (discriminate) against the stereotyped group(s).

With minor adjustments, this is how mainstream sociology conceives of racism today.[6] Unlike the earliest noninterventionist stance, the modern-day approach has a clear social policy: educate the racists, who tend to be concentrated in the South and among members of the working class (Adorno 1950; Lipset 1996), and racism will be eradicated. Although the new version includes the notion that racism is more than just ideas, it is still bounds the problem ideologically and assumes that it is ultimately something that we could manage via education or therapy.

These two moments in the theorization of racism have functioned as a "discursive formation" (Foucault 1972) and have kept a more structural (or institutional) view on racism at bay as an explanation for "racial" outcomes. By failing to grasp racism as a structural phenomenon, racism has therefore been regarded as (1) a disease afflicting certain individuals, (2) a phenomenon that does not affect the social body and its institutions, and (3) a social problem that has to be analyzed "clinically," that is, by separating the "good" versus the "bad" apples in the population through surveys on racial attitudes (Wetherell and Potter 1992; Sniderman and Piazza 1993).

In our review of the state of sociology today, we consider the ways in which sociologists still minimize the structural features of racism as we consider research in a number of substantive areas. First, we discuss how the attitudinal research that shows tremendous levels of "racial progress" reflects, more than anything else, a new racial ideology that protects the post–civil rights racial order. Second, we discuss some of the limitations of various demographic indices to assess post–civil rights racial matters. Third, we examine how mainstream social scientists have "seen" minority cultures, portraying them as pathological while hiding the centrality of racially based networks. And fourth, we briefly tackle how the manner in which social scientists report their results tends to distort the significance of racial stratification.

Our goals in this chapter are sociological as well as political. We challenge the tactics sociologists have used to minimize the significance of racism in explaining minorities' plight, bring to the fore the need for a radical reform on how they conduct research on racial matters, and warn of the dangers of continuing to do business as usual without taking into consideration new patterns of racial inequality. More generally, we hope to force a conversation on the myriad ways in which racial considerations shade the way we do sociology, exposing the facade of objectivity and neutrality of mainstream sociologists while hoping to enthuse other sociologists to join in the criticism from the interstices of the sociological house to produce a more democratic, useful, and politically engaged discipline.

THERE AIN'T NO PARADOX OF WHITES' RACIAL ATTITUDES, JACK! A CRITIQUE OF MAINSTREAM SURVEYS ON RACIAL ATTITUDES

Guided by a weak theory that regarded racism as a problem of individual pathology (e.g., affecting workers with an "authoritarian personality"), sociologists examined Whites' racial attitudes in the post–civil rights America. Predictably they found that racism appeared to be declining in significance. An early group of analysts described the change in Whites' racial attitudes as "revolutionary" (Hyman and Sheatsley 1964).[7] Although many researchers have continued endorsing this interpretation of Whites' racial attitudes (Firebaugh and Davis 1988; Sniderman and Piazza 1993; Lipset 1996), nuanced arguments have emerged from other quarters on aversive racism (Dovidio and Gaertner 2000), symbolic racism (Sears 1988), and social dominance (Sidanius 1989). Nevertheless, one of the most successful books on post–civil rights' Whites attitudes (Schuman et al. 1997) has advanced the new consensus among *mainstream*[8] survey researchers: the idea that there is a paradox in Whites' racial attitudes. The paradox, according to Schuman et al. (1997), lies in the observation that Whites support the principles of integration (e.g., agree with equal opportunity for jobs, etc.) but oppose programs to implement[9] these goals (e.g., affirmative action, etc.), a view long defended by certain researchers (Campbell and Schuman 1968). In its most current iteration, the view defended is that "[w]e are dealing with a fundamental transformation of social norms and with the issue of what this transformation means at the individual level" (Schuman et al. 1997, 306).

Because the normative climate in post–civil rights era has delegitimized the public expression[10] of racially based feelings and viewpoints, however, surveys on racial attitudes have become less meaningful to assess racial practices and have become like multiple-choice exams where respondents work hard to choose the "right" answers. For instance, although a variety of data suggests racial considerations are central to Whites' residential choices (Farley et al. 1994; Emerson et al. 2001), over 90 percent of them state in surveys that they have no problem with the idea of Blacks moving into their neighborhoods. Similarly, even though about 80 percent of Whites claim not to have problems if a member of their family brings a

Black for dinner (Schuman et al. 1997), research shows that very few Whites (less than 10 percent) can legitimately claim the proverbial "Some of my best friends are Blacks" and that Whites rarely fraternize with Blacks (Jackman and Crane 1986).

Notwithstanding that most research on Whites' racial attitudes is based on survey data, we believe it is time to rely more on data gathered from in-depth interviews and mixed-research designs.[11] Conceptually, the focus ought to be on the examination of Whites' racial ideology, and ideology, racial or not, is produced and reproduced in communicative interaction (see Bonilla-Silva 2001). Hence, although surveys are useful instruments to gather *general* information on actors' views, they are severely limited tools for examining how people explain, justify, rationalize, and articulate racial viewpoints. After all, people do not express their positions and emotions about racial issues by answering "yes" and "no" or "strongly agree" and "strongly disagree" to questions. Instead, they express their ideological positions in talk and text. Despite the gallant effort of many survey researchers to produce methodologically correct questionnaires, survey questions still restrict the free-flow of ideas and unnecessarily constrain the range of possible answers for respondents.

Of more import yet is survey researchers' insistence on using questions developed in the 1950s and 1960s to assess changes in racial tolerance. This strategy is predicated on the highly questionable assumption that "racism" (what we label here racial ideology) does not change over time. If instead one regards racial ideology as in fact changing, survey researchers' reliance on questions developed to tackle issues from the Jim Crow era will produce an artificial image of progress and miss most of Whites' contemporary racial nightmares. The "paradox" of Whites' racial attitudes is the product of the methodology and the conceptual apparatus used to examine post–civil rights "racism" (racial ideology). Today most Whites reject the old Jim Crow racial tenets in public discourse,[12] yet endorse new ones that help maintain contemporary White supremacy. Rather than a paradox, this is the post–civil rights way in which most Whites defend the racial status quo (Brooks 1990; Bonilla-Silva 2001).

IF THE INDEX DOESN'T FIT, YOU MUST ACQUIT: HOW INDICES THAT DO NOT MEAN MUCH HELP SUPPORT WHITES' RACIAL COMMON SENSE

Another important strategy to produce what Alphonso Pinkney (1984) has labeled as "the myth of black progress" is relying on traditional demographic indices to assess the status of racial minorities. For example, if the goal of researchers is presenting a felicitous image of Blacks (or other minority groups) in the post–civil rights era, they can rely on the index of occupational dissimilarity, or present data on life expectancy, or even use traditional indices to measure residential segregation and compare them to those of the 1940s and 1950s (Farley and Frey 1994). Although many of these indices are used as if they were sophisticated measures, the reality is otherwise, as they essentially rely on "simple numerical and percentage comparisons of the numbers and proportions of persons in each race/ethnicity group in a population" (Murdock and Ellis 1991, 152). Relying on these indices as the last word is very problematic because the issues presumably grasped by these indices have changed substantially, making them less useful and *valid*, in the sociological sense (Carmines and Zeller 1979).

One example is the index of occupational dissimilarity. After occupations are transformed into values using Duncan's socioeconomic index (SEI), the dissimilarity index is computed based on the following formula:

$$D = 100 \times S\tfrac{1}{2}\ wi\text{-}bi\tfrac{1}{2} / 2$$

"where *i* denotes the *i*'th category of [an occupational] distribution, and *wi* and *bi* denote the proportions of Whites and Blacks, respectively, in the category" (Fossett and Seibert 1997, 202; see also Murdock and Ellis 1991). The numerical value of the index can be interpreted as "the minimum percentage of one group (either one) that must change [occupational] categories to make its relative frequency distributions identical to that for the other group" (Fossett and Seibert 1997, 202). Hence, its interpretation is straightforward: the higher the index the more occupational status convergence among the groups being compared (see Farley 1984, 47).

The problems with this index are multiple and many of them have been discussed by social demographers (see Fossett and Seibert 1997). For example, because D is not "symmetrically distributed around the point of equality," it is possible for D to distort totally a situation (203). This means that it is possible to produce false negative (or positive) outlooks on occupational status differences between compared groups if one relies on this index. Another problem with this index is that it is usually computed using few census job categories (12 to 13 categories) which has been shown to underestimate occupational inequality—as compared to when one uses broad occupational categories (513 categories)—by as much as 28 percent (236). Lastly, this index has been used to indicate large changes in *relative* values while ignoring huge differences in *absolute* ones. This was clearly explained by Blalock (1979):

> [If blacks have been excluded from a profession such as actuaries forever and increase their representation from] 2 to 12, there is a sixfold increase! Suppose this is compared with a white increase of, say, 3,000 to 4,000, a one-third

> increase. The blacks are obviously gaining ground through this increase of ten actuaries as compared with a thousand whites! (116)

For example, Featherman and Hauser (1978) argued that Blacks had a higher "relative upward shifts in current occupational status than did whites" and used that finding to suggest structural arguments were inaccurate. Hence, they concluded, "stratification has grown more universalistic" and "more rational" (225–26). In truth, Whites' status improved from a score of 39.5 to 42.59 while Blacks improved from 17.7 to 25.76, with Blacks clearly remaining significantly behind Whites. Unfortunately, the reliance of sociologists on this index blinds them from truly looking at occupational differences as they materialize in real jobs. The index becomes a fetish and little analysis is done on how Blacks and Whites fare in similar occupations; on why it is that if this index has shown tremendous progress, the income differential between Blacks and Whites has not decreased accordingly.

Some early works in the discipline, interestingly enough, avoided these problems. Reuter in his *The American Race Problem: A Study of the Negro* (1938) analyzed the job structure of Blacks and Whites using traditional indicators (labor force participation, occupational representation, etc.) but also included data on how inequality operated in various jobs such as those in the agricultural sector. In Harris's 1926 study of the Black population in Minneapolis, he analyzed the macro- and microdeterminants of Blacks' depressed economic conditions in a manner that is seldom surpassed even by today's standards (see Darity 1982; Cherry 2001). Drake and Cayton's *Black Metropolis* (1993 [1945]) makes use of statistical indicators in interesting ways. While they did make use of some demographic techniques, they warned us of the importance of the interconnection between physical segregation and related processes that made up "the color line." The book contains significant descriptions and ethnographic examination of these processes, including the informal networks that maintained physical segregation, and the types of substantive segregation that took place *even when there was physical proximity between groups*. Importantly, Drake and Cayton are critical of positions that equate physical contact with substantive integration, calling it "doubtful, however, whether [such contact can] play a dominant part in shifting the line of color" (1993, 126). They also call for attention to the context of these racial contacts, warning that in reality, "[s]uch contacts do little to create goodwill among White people, but they do leave a residue of resentment among Negroes" (1993, 126).

With the advent of computing power since the 1950s, and principally in the 1970s and 1980s, studies of segregation have relied on ever more sophisticated models based on various indices and statistical techniques (Duncan and Duncan 1955; Farley 1984; Massey and Denton 1985). Many students of urban segregation, however, have ignored the insights of Drake and Cayton and have simplistically relied on, and even fetishize, indices of physical separation, that is, regard physical proximity as a proxy of substantive integration.[13]

Here we propose something different and quite heretical from the point of view of mainstream sociology, namely that such indices may not mean much by themselves and need to be complemented with other types of studies and indicators for them to acquire significant meaning. Dissimilarity indices are derived from Duncan and Duncan (1955) and are permutations of the formula offered above. The index measuring evenness, which is the one usually discussed in analyses of residential segregation, is

$$D = 1/2 (\Sigma [bi/b - wi/w])$$

where b_i and w_i are the numbers of Black and White persons living in an area i, and b and w are the total numbers of Blacks and Whites in the city, respectively.

Scholars have pointed to the problem of unmeasured segregation because of the scale of census tracts (James and Taeuber 1985). In recent times, urban theorists have also pointed to types of physical segregation that are not visible through this metric, such as gated communities, which have been becoming more common in recent years with the economic restructuring of cities (Graham and Marvin 2001). More fundamentally, however, we suggest that "racial contacts" *do not* mean substantive integration, since there are significant forms of racism compatible with "physical closeness." The apparent "integration" some scholars have noted in some settings (Farley and Frey 1994) may have to do with poverty and falling incomes of poor Whites, or simply the restructuring of urban space.

This index belies a weak theorization of racism, as it reduces it to a phenomenon of physical separation. A stronger theorization of racism—one that understands its structural features—necessarily calls into question racial practices, such as those that deny access to resources, in *different* types of separateness (physical and social). This would require more comprehensive approaches that include ethnographic and systematic within-tract studies of socio-spatial interaction between racial groups. The studies carried out by DeSena (1994) highlighting the role of informal networks in maintaining residential segregation are examples of what needs to be done. Statistical approaches can be useful too. Alba et al. (2000b), for instance, in studying the types of "more integrated" neighborhoods that middle-class Blacks live in found that they tended to be lower-middle-class neighborhoods, with the class standing of Whites in the neighborhood being significantly lower than that of Blacks in it. While some of these neighborhoods may appear to be integrating according to various segregation indices, a closer look shows that Blacks still pay a significant "penalty," a fact obscured by aggregate indices.[14]

THE CHILDREN OF SÁNCHEZ IN THE INNER CITY: ECHOES OF THE CULTURE OF POVERTY IN RECENT SOCIAL CAPITAL APPROACHES

Another way of minimizing the effects of racial stratification is by portraying the effects of poverty as the causes of poverty; specifically, by focusing on the "culture of the natives" as the problem. While it is Oscar Lewis (1968) who is credited with making the "culture of poverty" argument, and Patrick Moynihan with making it part of the broader discourse on the poor, the argument dates farther back. The notion that the cultural inadequacy of "natives" is what holds them back in America is already present in the functionalism of the Chicago School that decried the lack of work values and cooperation within the city's slums (Zorbaugh 1929). The "culture of poverty" refers to the values and behaviors of the poor that keep them poor from generation to generation. The culture of poverty had a number of components: lack of participation by the poor in major institutions; awareness of, but not living by middle-class values such as stable marriages; low levels of community organization; absence of childhood as an extended period; and feelings of marginality, helplessness, lack of ambition, and inferiority (Lewis 1968, 189–92). While these arguments were originally developed in the context of the urban poor in the "third world" and were vigorously contested (Eckstein 1977), culture-of-poverty arguments became particularly influential in the 1960s and 1970s.

While the culture of poverty thesis has fallen out of fashion and most scholars today distance themselves from explicitly supporting it, the crux of the thesis still exerts significant influence: the culture of the poor (and generally non-White poor) is inadequate for modern society and is the primary reason responsible for their social pathology. A historical analysis of studies of Black family life in the *Journal of Marriage and the Family*, for instance, showed that culture-of-poverty arguments were the single dominant analytic lens through which it was seen (Demos 1990). The understanding of underclass ways of life as pathological and causing the reproduction of poverty itself continues to be a central idea in social policy circles and among scholars, and it has deviated little from the original culture-of-poverty language in some quarters (Murray 1999). Myriad studies in the areas of education, health, and social welfare implicitly hold up "pathological" minorities to the yardstick of mythical middle-class values: ambition, trust, and "believing in the system."

The idea that inner-city minorities perpetuate their own situation through self-defeating cultural values and practices—such as crime, lack of trust, lack of family values and role models, remains starkly influential. It is implicit in Wilson's description of the "tangle of pathology" that besets the underclass; for Wilson, the departure of middle-class Blacks from the inner city contributes to a lack of role models and proper values and contributes to the deviant behaviors that perpetuate poverty (Wilson 1987). In *Code of the Street,* Anderson (1999) differentiates between "decent" and "street" families that negotiate the unpredictability, violence, and poverty of the inner city. "Decent" and "street" are differing responses, based on whether they have regard for middle-class values, societal institutions, and the law. The "code of the street" is depicted as a deep pathology that emerges from experiencing exclusion from the wider social world; it is a culture of alienation, disrespect for the law, selfishness and mistrust, pathological family structures, and lack of self-respect (1999, 32).

The intellectual legacy of the culture of poverty thesis can be seen in the recent boom in social capital studies. Whereas the culture of poverty focused on the failings of the pathological culture of the poor, social capital focuses on the other side of the coin: it idealizes a kind of community life in which virtuous citizens take care of each other and enforce community norms. In the view currently in vogue, social capital refers to collective stocks of "trust, norms, and networks" in certain communities (Putnam 2001). Communities that have such stocks of "social capital" are ones in which people work together, and buffer the effects of inequality or social need through community action. Social capital in this view has been used to explain a number of outcomes, such as health outcomes (Hawe and Shiell 2000), violence prevention (Kennedy, Kawachi, and Prothrow-Stith 1998), school achievement (Valenzuela and Dornbusch 1994), adolescent behavior and juvenile delinquency, and others. This perspective, which minimizes the insights of network analysts who have studied social networks as something to which individuals have differential access (Portes 1998; Smith 1998; Stanton-Salazar and Dornbusch 1995; Waldinger 1995), also minimizes structural inequalities. Whereas culture-of-poverty arguments implied certain kinds of interventions in the inner city, however, social capital implies a scaling back of all government intervention (Muntaner et al. 2000).

Portes (1998) has pointed to the lack of precision in social capital arguments, and the slippage between its use as an individual attribute and as a collective attribute. Others have pointed out the circular nature of social capital arguments when referring to communities—communities that have "good social capital" are successful communities because they have "good social capital." Well-functioning communities, the argument goes, possess this collective good that is equally available to all. In these communities, concerned citizens become involved in solving collective problems and enforcing norms. In the context of economic inequality and the rollback of the welfare state, communities that possess social capital are believed to be able to buffer negative impacts. Therefore, much of the current discussion on public policy and poverty has now turned to the question of how to generate bonds of trust in these deficient communities, because it is the lack of social capital—and not structured inequalities—that accounts for undesirable outcomes.

From our vantage viewpoint, the missing link in social capital theory is the following: in societies in which resources are distributed partly along racial lines, social networks (social capital) will also be racialized. Social networks and norms of social behavior are often mobilized to defend racial exclusion in a racialized society. Blee's (2001) study of women in White supremacist movements found the women to be involved in the life of their community, and found them to be recruited *through* social networks. Similarly, DeSena (1994) discusses the role of community women in gate-keeping and maintaining the homogeneity of certain White neighborhoods, while Waldinger (1995) discusses how social capital in ethnically based job networks helps exclude other ethnic groups. Second, individuals in a racialized society do not have equal access to networks, and networks themselves are racialized. Disadvantaged youths, for example, experience differential access to networks along racial lines, and African Americans suffer labor market disadvantages by virtue of segregated networks (Smith 1998).

Third, the assumption that social capital leads to certain virtuous norms of behavior is both untenable and confusing of causes and effects. The vision that a community in which there is civic involvement is one in which crime and deviant behaviors are inhibited and it is possible to "walk outside at night" (Portes 1998, 3) commits the same error that culture-of-poverty arguments make: it is not possible to abstract norms or cultural values from the context in which they exist and assign them causal status without seriously confounding causes and effects. More importantly, it is not possible to explain deviance or crime as a result of lack of participation or trust in a community that then spirals to perpetuate a community's poor standing. Rather, such behaviors take place in definite social contexts marked by inequality and structured along racial lines. To think otherwise and attempt to explain these outcomes by lack of social capital, a culture of poverty, or another mechanism that obfuscates structural inequalities is to seriously minimize the impact of racism.

WHEN REPORTED FINDINGS REPRODUCE RACIALIZED READINGS OF READINGS

The way most sociologists report results and structure their statistical analyses reproduces racialized readings of the world. Sociologists routinely fail to explain that the "race effect" presented in their findings is the outcome of "racism" or "racial stratification." This leads their audiences to interpret "race effect" findings as embodying truly *racial* effects. ("There must be something wrong with Blacks if they are three times as likely to participate in crime!") Therefore, reporting results on crime, marriage arrangements, or a host of other matters without properly informing the public of the myriad ways in which racial stratification is at the core of these findings helps support racist readings of Black-White inequality (Dumm 1993).

One example of this problematic way of reporting findings is Christopher Jencks's work on the fixity of the Black-White test-scores gap (1972). However, he and his colleagues still claim that, "Neither differences between the schools that Blacks and whites attend nor differences in their socioeconomic status suffice to explain why Blacks learn less than whites with similar initial skills" (Phillips et al. 1998, 257). Furthermore, the same authors claim they controlled for "fixed effects" (1998, 255) (racial/socioeconomic mix, per-pupil expenditure, and curriculum) and thus suggest the net gap may be a pure "race effect." What is lacking in their analysis and data is "controlling for" a school's differential impact on its Black and White students (e.g., school tracking, school differential treatment by teachers and school administrators, etc.) *within* the school. Failing to acknowledge that children in "integrated" schools have radically different experiences helps Jencks and his audience believe that the Black-White test score gap is a "race effect" rather than a "racism effect."

An example of this "it is class not race" strategy appeared in 2000 in the pages of the *American Sociological Review*. In a paper entitled, "The Significance of Socioeconomic Status in Explaining the Racial Gap in Chronic Health Conditions" (Hayward et al. 2000), the authors seek to disentangle the "race" from the "class" effect in chronic health conditions between Blacks and Whites. After showing that the "race effect" remains, net of education and health behaviors, the authors introduce the magic bullet of "class" (socioeconomic status) and find that, "Of the 10 health conditions for which Blacks and Whites differ significantly in terms of incidence, the race effect is reduced to nonsignificance for 7 conditions after measures of socioeconomic circumstances are included" (925). Hence, they are dismissive of work that suggests racism is central to explain Black-White health differences (Williams 1997), and point out that, "these differences are rooted in the fundamental social conditions of life" (Hayward et al. 2000, 927).

The problem with their argument—and the statistical strategy that it entails—is that *class is not independent of race* (these authors did not even bother to check for multicollinearity). Even Erik O. Wright, probably the most renowned American academic Marxist, acknowledges in his *Class Counts* that Blacks are exceedingly overrepresented in the working and underclass categories and states that, "By a large margin, the American working class now predominantly consists of women and racial minorities"

(1997, 69. See also Horton et al. 2000). Hence, Wright points out that "race therefore seems to have a bigger overall effect on access to privileged class locations than does gender" (69).[15] Even the authors of the article in question admit, "blacks and whites are differentially channeled into socioeconomic circumstances over the life cycle in a way that deprives blacks of good health relative to whites" (Hayward 2000 et al., 927).

Our argument here on the thorny race versus class debate is not that race is more important than class. What we want to point out is that if race—and racial stratification—shapes everything in the social system, the debate should not be over whether it is race or class that affect Blacks' (or Whites') life chances. Instead, we believe the debate should be about specifying what are the independent and combined effects of these two forms of social stratification on social actors?

Researchers of segregation sometimes also separate racially structured patterns from racial structures, in effect "controlling for" supposed nonracial factors and diminishing the impact of racism. For instance, a group of scholars have defended the position that it is the presence of economic factors that solely explain segregation, a position largely discredited by counterevidence (Clark 1992; Galster 1988; Massey and Fischer 1999). Other scholars have argued that Whites' neighborhood preferences that seem like "racial" choices are not so. Specifically, Harris (1999a, 2001) has argued that race is a "proxy" used by Whites to choose neighborhoods that are better served by the state, have better schools, lower crime rates, higher property value, and so on. The implicit theory that informs Harris's approach is that racial factors are *independent* from nonracial factors and, therefore, that it is possible to assume nonracial factors account for segregation. Most research on contemporary racial matters, however, has documented that discussions on crime, schools, government, etc. are highly racialized (Kinder and Sanders 1996; Bonilla-Silva 2001; Emerson et al. 2001).

CONCLUSION

We are not the first ones to challenge the sociological project regarding race (Ladner 1972; Mckee 1993; Lyman 1994) or even the methods sociologists use to investigate racial matters (Stanfield and Dennis 1993). What we hoped to have shown in this chapter is that (1) mainstream sociology is fundamentally connected to Whites' common sense on racial matters and (2) that the theory, methodologies, research strategies, and even writing style used by mainstream sociologists in the post–civil rights era bolster Whites' "declining significance of race" thesis.

To make our case we examined some of the ways in which sociology contributes to the reproduction of Whites' contemporary racial common sense. First, since the mainstream theory of racism conceives of it as irrational "ideas" that individuals hold, attitudinal research has been at the core of the "race relations research agenda." We argue this is misguided because it fails to understand how racial ideologies work in the post–civil rights era. Second, we examined two widely used demographic indices (index of occupational and residential dissimilarity) and pointed out their limitations. Overall, we suggested these indices are less appropriate to study how racism affects the U.S. racial policy today. Third, we argued that work on the culture of minorities is still often bounded by "culture-of-poverty" concerns, which shades the way mainstream sociologists interpret the plight of poor minority communities, including new work on social capital. And fourth, we argued that the way analysts report their findings and their reliance on the statistical technique of "controlling for" helps reproduce racialized readings of reality.

If this is the state of affairs, what can be done? We believe demographers, ethnographers, and social psychologists need to continue trying to measure inequality, observing social life and surveying Americans on their "racial attitudes." But we urge sociologists to undertake a number of steps to correct the dominant biases of our discipline. First and foremost, sociology must engage in a serious debate on its dominant theories of race and racism. Continuing to endorse weak theories—or paying lip service to, for example, the social constructionist approach—will no longer do the trick. Although one of the authors has proposed a particular theorization (Bonilla-Silva 1997; Bonilla-Silva 2001), we believe the discipline at large would be much better off if any serious structural or institutional theorization replaces the dominant theorization. Second, we urge demographers to incorporate historical and ethnographic concerns in their attempts at gauging how race affects the social landscape. This will lead to mixed research designs and new methodologies, such as the ethno-survey developed by Massey to measure immigration, and implementing the insight of ethnographers on the manifestation of "everyday racisms" (Eliasoph 1999; DeSena 1994). In our quest for these research methodologies, as we have shown, we are fortunate in our discipline to have pioneering models that provide us with rich insight: the work of Drake and Cayton, Du Bois, and others. For instance, a typical summary table in *Black Metropolis*, in addition to providing some statistical measures, compares segregation in Chicago with that of the American South along *thirty* different dimensions including the social definition of children of mixed marriages, patterns of office-holding, access to professional associations, and ability to enter theaters and restaurants (Drake and Cayton 1993, 331).

Third, we challenge sociologists not to reify methods, indices, or strategies as if "racism" and its manifestations can be studied "one way." Rather than struggling to be "methodologically correct," we ought to struggle to accurately report how racial stratification affects those at the "bottom of the well" as well as those drinking the clean water at the top of the well. This will force social analysts to seriously think about how to examine racial matters rather than jumping into research with prefabricated formulations and data sets. And fourth, the myth of objectivity and neutrality espoused by mainstream sociologists needs to be exposed. On this, the methodological observations of analysts as different as Mills (1959), Myrdal (1944), and Gouldner (1961) ought to suffice. Taking as a given that all knowledge has a political foundation, we urge sociologists to explicitly join in the more complex project of challenging the racial common sense and racial structures in the post–civil rights era.

NOTES

1. This is not a new trend. Robert E. Park (1950) argued that race contacts went through "race cycles" that ended in racial assimilation.
2. See also Caditz (1976).
3. The authors, along with Hayward Horton, are working on a book manuscript on the various ways in which social scientists have diminished the importance of racism, tentatively titled *Anything but Racism: How Social Scientists Limit the Significance of Racism*.
4. Interestingly, as in all discursive fields, there are always alternatives. In *Caste and Class in a Southern Town* (1957), John Dollard developed a holistic and materialist analysis of racism.
5. See chapter 2 of Bonilla-Silva (2001).
6. Despite the theoretical break of the "racial formation" perspective (Omi and Winant 1986; 1994) this perspective runs the risk of being co-opted as it focuses too much on the *ideological* aspects of racism as well as on the "racial projects" of certain elites. See Bonilla-Silva (2001).
7. See also chapter 9 in Brink and Harris (1963).
8. We wish to separate them from radical survey research, such as carried out by Jackman (1994).
9. The more sanguine interpretation assumes that even this opposition has nothing to do with race (see Sniderman and Piazza 1993; Lipset 1996).
10. Although survey researchers believe surveys are private forums, surveys have become public forms of communication and, thus, less reliable means to assess people's views on sensitive matters.
11. For instance, the methods already used by Du Bois (1899) could be used as a model.
12. Social scientists have very little systematic data on what Whites believe and say about minorities in private, though anecdotal and ethnographic research suggests many Whites have a double racial life. (Cose 1993; Otis-Graham 1995).
13. A clear example are the patterns of segregation in Brazil. Brazilian Blacks on the whole have many more apparent racial contacts than U.S. Blacks (Telles 1995),

but are much worse off in terms of income differences and labor market position, child mortality, and life expectancy, among other indicators (Lovell 1999).

14. Similar cases could be made about how indices of residential segregation or health do not tell the full story (index of residential dissimilarity) or flat out distort the racial picture (life expectancy). We explore these in the book manuscript.

15. The position we take here is distinct from Wright's, however. See his perspective on race in *Classes* (1985), particularly pp. 96–98.

9

Experiments in Black and White

Power and Privilege in Experimental Methodology

Carla Goar

This chapter examines the way that White privilege manifests itself in social methods and, in particular, in experimental methodology. In the past, social science methodology asserted that anyone with adequate training could engage in nonbiased observations required for successful data collection and coding. This idea has been contested by methodologists in both the ethnographic and statistical arenas (see Harding 1991, 1993; McCorkel and Myers 2003; Zuberi 2001a) but has gone relatively unchallenged in experimental research. This chapter suggests that, as in the case of both survey and ethnographic analysis, White privilege has seeped its way into experimental methodology. The chapter begins by examining White privilege and the way it has been challenged in certain research areas while remaining undisputed in experimental research. The chapter then examines the ways that race has been used in past social experiments and moves forward to discuss current experimental scholarship on race. Finally, a discussion focuses on the lack of experimental scholarship in the area of race and the failure to recognize research positionality, suggesting that this serves as a mask for color-blind racism.

WHITE PRIVILEGE AND METHODOLOGY

White privilege refers to the special advantages or benefits afforded to White persons and withheld from certain others or all others in societies characterized by White supremacy (Jensen 2005). Mills (1997) defines

White supremacy as a "political, economic, and cultural system in which Whites overwhelmingly control power and material resources, conscious and unconscious ideas of White supremacy are widespread, and relations of White dominance and non-White subordination are daily reenacted across a broad array of institutional and social settings" (37). Included in this domination is scientific inquiry, the process of objectively gathering information through observation, the creation of a question, the construction of a plausible explanation or hypothesis, and the test of the hypothesis. This domination is characterized by silent and invisible conceptualizations that fail to identify the ways that inquiry is impacted by current political, economic, and cultural systems. Indeed, it has long been assumed that when strict adherence to proper methodological procedure is followed, the inquiry process can be relied upon to be objective and value free.

These ideas have been challenged by researchers in the areas of ethnography and statistics. Born out of ethnographic feminist methods, standpoint theory calls for a recognition that all human beliefs—including scientific ones—are socially situated (Harding 1998, 1991; McCorkle and Myers 2003). That is, they reflect the historical, sociological, and cultural conventions of a particular era. This perspective acknowledges that research is impacted by broader social relations at every stage—inception of a question, design of a study, collection of data, interpretation of finding. Claiming that science is constrained by structure and ideology, Harding (1998) argues that current objectification standards fail to fully consider the full spectrum of social desires, interests, contents, and agendas.

In the area of statistics, Zuberi (2001a) suggests that there is a connection between the development of the idea of race and the origins of social statistics. He argues that the beginning of racial categorizing required a measure of social difference and that the groundbreaking work of Galton and Pearson was developed in part to meet the need to racially differentiate (2001a). He argues that the logic of statistical measurements of race is strongly connected to a period's ideology and that those ideologies guide the interpretation of data. For example, the use of statistics during the late nineteenth-century eugenics movement reflected the society's overt commitment to categorizations of racial superiority and inferiority. This suggests that inquiry is not objective and value free, but reflects the ideology of the times.

The researchers above would argue that the values and assumptions associated with ideology could not be eradicated with strict adherence to methodological procedure and that within the context of White supremacy, these values and assumptions tend to benefit White individuals. Experimental researchers, however, have been relatively silent not only in dealing with the idea of White supremacy, but also in study of race itself. Recent studies indict social psychological experiments for their lack of scholarship on race, particularly beyond the domain of in-group/out-group studies and other intergroup activity (Hunt et al. 2000; Morawski 1997).

Experimental methodology offers many advantages for the study of social life: the ability to retain high levels of control, to isolate particular variables, to test causality, and to replicate findings (Blalock and Blalock 1968; Babbie 1998). By design, researchers are able to create conditions that observe how one factor brings about a change in a second factor. Using random assignment, controlled conditions, and the establishment and comparison of treatment groups, experiments show causality. That is, the researcher can determine what (if any) effect in one variable was due to the treatment of another. This sharp focus gives experiments a narrow, highly specified quality and a logical rigor that is difficult to achieve in other social science methods. Because of this, the experiment has long been praised as failsafe, a tool that is as strong or weak as the design upon which it is based. However, the very attributes that give the experiment its logical rigor (randomization and control) may also contribute to its racial blindness. The nonreflective emphasis on control and randomization may serve to mask the ways that White privilege operates within experiments. Though current research (what little there is) is careful when considering race, this was not always the case. Past research highlights the way that ideology impacts inquiry.

EARLY EXPERIMENTS

In the late nineteenth and early twentieth centuries, scholars used measurements to justify racial inequality. For instance, the procedures that Francis Galton[1] and Karl Pearson developed helped establish the precedent for statistics of significance—the measurement of dissimilarity. These methodological contributions were especially important in the fields of education and psychology and laid the groundwork for experimental study (Guthrie 1998; Besag 1981). This new science[2] set the stage for early studies that attempted to measure the intellectual differences between people.

In 1916, psychologist George Ferguson claimed that physical characteristics were strongly linked to personality traits: "The color of the skin and the crookedness of the hair are only outward signs of many far deeper differences, including . . . temperament, disposition, character, instincts, customs, emotional traits" (3). Claiming that the average Black IQ was 25 points below that of the average White IQ (75 vs.100), he justified this position with scientific evidence pointing to "a lack of foresight . . . small power of serious initiative . . . and deficient ambitions" in Blacks, which translated into lower academic performance, adding:

> The Negro's intellectual deficiency is registered in the retardation percentages of the schools as well as in mental tests. And in view of all the evidence it does not seem possible to raise the scholastic attainment of the Negro to an equality with that of the white. It is probable that no expenditure of time or of

money would accomplish this end, since education cannot create mental power, but can only develop that which is innate (Ferguson 1916, 125).

In an effort to test Ferguson's ideas, Crane (1923) designed an experiment to detect a causal link between Black immorality and defective inhibition. In this study, a heavy block of wood was raised high over the subject's hand. The subject, having been assured that the block would be stopped before making contact with his hand, was instructed not to move it when the block fell. Crane, unable to find significant differences in hand movement between Black and White subjects did report the following as significant: during the experiment, White subjects seemed relaxed and curious, "looking about the room, examining the apparatus, and testing their assumptions concerning its functions with a stream of questions. . . . All such behavior among the blacks was conspicuous by its absence. Apparently the idea of inspecting the apparatus never entered their heads" (15). Though the experiment failed to show any difference between White and Black behavior, Crane tried to find other evidence to maintain bigotry, attributing their failure to question the investigation as proof that "in those vocational pursuits which involve great sensory shocks and strains not unaccompanied by danger the black man should prove more efficient than the white" (18).

Other studies show the impact of the period's ideology on experiments. Bache (1895) examined the reaction time (conducted using a magneto-electric physiological apparatus) exhibited by White, Black, and Native American subjects. He found that "superior" races had higher reaction times than those of "inferior" races: Whites showed fastest reaction, followed by Blacks and Native Americans. Bache posited that the Native American reaction time was not as high as the Black time because Black Americans tended to have a greater mixture of White blood than the Native group. Another experiment in reaction time showed significant racial differences in reaction times and sensory traits (Sengupta 1944). The author claimed that these differences affected social production, explaining why some societies produced artisans who excelled in wood carving and weaving (due to fineness of touch) or fierce warriors (due to ability to endure pain) while others did not.[3] A study by McGraw (1931) compared White and Black babies (ages two to eleven months) and found White babies superior to Black ones in terms of developmental age, developmental quotient, and percentage of successful reactions. Based on these experimental findings, he stated that "even with very young subjects, when environmental factors are minimized, the same type and approximately the same degree of superiority is evidences on the part of the White subjects as that found among older groups" (98).

Besag (1981) argues that, contrary to claims of experimental objectivity, these studies reflected the racial ideology of their day. That past ideology was open about racial hierarchies of intellect and worth becomes clear as we read through past studies. What is not as clear, however, is whether or how racial ideology is reflected in current experimental methodology.

CURRENT EXPERIMENTS

In response to an article indicting social psychology (and experimental methodology, in particular) for its silence on issues of race, there has been concern at the lack of scholarship in the area. As a result, some research is moving toward the increased use of race in analysis. Much of these recent studies tend to focus on group identity and group interest. For example, a study by Lowery et al. (2006) focuses on White attitudes toward affirmative action. In this experiment, White participants are primed to focus either on in-group (White) interests or on potential Black gain where White interests would not be affected. Group members who were primed to focus on Black gain were more supportive of affirmative action than participants who were primed to focus on White interests. An experiment by Philippot and Yabar (2005) indicates that, when subjects were exposed to anxiety, they were more likely to attribute stereotypical beliefs to members of racial out-groups than to members of their own group. Barthelow et al. (2006) examined how alcohol affected the racial self-regulation of White subjects. This experiment suggests that the careful control respondents usually employ in dealing with racial situations may become weakened when subjects use alcohol. Powell et al. (2005) found that when subjects are primed to think about racial inequality in terms of White privilege instead of Black disadvantage, White racial identification decreases and subjects are better able to avoid the negative psychological implications of inequality and prejudicial attitudes.

Other recent experimental work focuses on ways to create, isolate, and measure processes such as authority, legitimacy, and prestige. An experiment by Goar and Sell (2005) examines whether changes in task perception might affect the way that power and prestige operate in small, mixed-race groups. Findings show that White advantage can be masked, creating opportunity for all group members to participate more equitably. Biernat and Kobrynowicz (1997) show that while low general competency standards are set for low status individuals (Black vs. White), high-ability standards are simultaneously set. That is, it may be easier for devalued individuals to meet low standards, but they must work harder to prove that their performance is based on ability.

Other recent work examines the idea of stereotypic threat—the threat of being negatively stereotyped and of perhaps confirming the stereotype—that may be elicited in certain domains (i.e., testing situations). Steele and

Aronson's (1995, experiment 4) seminal study demonstrated that the idea of stereotypic threat depressed the academic performance of African American students on a standardized test. Asking African American students to identify their race on a demographic information sheet before completing a portion of the verbal GRE was a strong enough prime to depress the students' scores. Black students in that condition scored lower than both White and African American participants who did not indicate their race prior to the test (an interesting note here was that White students who completed the demographic information sheet by identifying their racial background performed better than the Black students in the same group, suggesting some type of stereotypic advantage). Aronson et al. (1999, experiment 2) found that White participants who read that Asians outperform Whites in the area of math scored lower on a test of mathematical ability than when this information was not provided. This test supports Steele's idea that when the stereotype about a group's lower intellectual ability is activated, the intellectual performance of those group members can be affected. In an interesting twist, Wheeler et al. (2001, experiment 2) found that non–African American students for whom the African American stereotype was activated performed lower on a standardized math test than students who were not primed, suggesting that stereotypic threat exists not only as a threat mechanism but also by activating behavioral instances of stereotypic traits.

LACK OF EXPERIMENTAL RACE SCHOLARSHIP

Though the number of sociologists who utilize experiments is small, the relative absence of experimental race scholarship in social psychology is curious. It is doubtful that this reflects an attitude of casualness or disregard toward the topic. There are practical reasons why studies of race in experimental social psychology are rare. First, it is possible that some experimenters have shunned studies of race because of the inability to generalize their findings to an actual population defined within a particular space and time. Generalization, however, is always relative to a particular inquiry. Lucas (2003) notes that one must determine generalizability based on the particular question being asked. Not all populations are defined at particular points in time. Questions such as "Under what conditions is stereotyping decreased?" and "What techniques tend to foster cooperation instead of competition in diverse work groups?" are not questions that pertain to a defined place and time. Instead, these questions focus on testing theoretical principles that apply to many different places and points in time.

Second, most experiments use undergraduate students as subjects, and students of color are underrepresented at the university level. And third, experimental methodology assumes that differences between subjects are controlled through randomization (in classical experiments, the assignment of subjects to experimental and control groups by randomization is the primary means of controlling for biases in how the two groups may respond to the independent variable) so that variations due to race would be equally disseminated throughout all conditions (Blalock and Blalock 1968; Babbie 1998). The concept of *ceteris paribus* or "all other things being equal," for example, is fundamental to the causal nature of the experiment in that it rules out factors (including race) that may interfere with a specific causal relationship (Babbie 1998). Moreover, Hunt et al. (2000) suggest that studies of race have been overlooked in social psychology due to the assumption of race/ethnic similarity, the idea that "basic social psychological processes and theories apply equally well to various racial and ethnic groups (353). Though much empirical evidence fails to support this notion and few social psychologists would agree with the idea that race is not important, Hunt et al. argue that the scarcity of studies in race reinforce the idea of race neutrality.

Race neutrality serves not only to restrict our knowledge of racial groups by assuming that different groups of people experience things the same way or that a method's randomness will disperse differences in such a way that they cancel each other out, but also to maintain current racial ideology. When explained in terms of race neutrality, the absence of race scholarship can easily be attributed to benign neglect: the unintended lack of consideration due to oversight or inconvenience. However, this chapter suggests that ideas such as neutrality and normality are characteristic of present racial ideology. Though not as pronounced and blatant as the ideology of early scholars, the silent domination to which Mills refers may be as pervasive as the old.

FAILURE TO ACKNOWLEDGE RESEARCH POSITIONALITY

Race similarity is more insidious than underrepresented undergraduates, reliance on randomization, and benign neglect. The idea of race neutrality serves to restrict our knowledge of racial groups. One aspect of this neutrality that evades critical inspection concerns the race of the experimenter. Armed with control and randomization, experimenters are taught that strict adherence to the scientific method will result in objective and bias-free findings *regardless of the race of the investigator*. The race of the experimenter is seen as irrelevant. Yet, as many social psychological studies suggest, race is an important status characteristic that affects the way individuals perceive social phenomena (Goar and Sell 2005; Harlow 2003; Brezina and Winder 2003). To suggest that individuals who possess different ascribed statuses may observe things differently is certainly in line with the literature, but violates the basic premise of objectivity: that trained empiricists be capable of removing all personal and subjective understanding as they proceed with research endeavors.

Because social psychological experimental methodology has historically deflected attention away from critically assessing the ways that the race of the researcher might affect findings (Hunt et al. 2000), examples of published studies examining this have been difficult to find. Morawski's (1997) meta-analysis reports that over 100 experimental studies focused on race in the last seventy-five years. Of those studies, 90 percent failed to mention the race of the investigator. Of those that did, the race of the researcher was viewed as a specific variable that affected the response activity of subjects. These studies tended to be in the psychology discipline and indicated that subjects often change their behavior based on their perception of the researcher's race (Annis and Corenblum 1986; Cukor-Avila and Guy 2001). For example, Danso and Esses (2001) examined whether White college students' test performance was impacted by the race of the experimenter who proctored an exam. The results show that the experimenter's race did matter—students whose test was administered by a Black experimenter scored significantly higher than students whose test was administered by a White experimenter. Again, however, the scrutiny is focused upon the subjects' reaction to racial stimuli.

The literature in other areas of social science tends also to focus solely on subjects' response to race. For example, survey and questionnaire studies show that the race of the interviewer is significant when assessing subjects' responses to topics such as education (Hatchett and Schuman 1975–1976), military protest (Schuman and Converse 1971), civil rights (Rambo 1969; Campbell 1981), voting behavior and political attitudes (Anderson, Silver, and Abramson 1988; Finkel, Guterbock, and Borg 1989), marketing research (Hyman 1954), and information processing (Davis and Silver 2003). In fact, Davis (1997a) claims that the race of researcher effect is so strong that it can speciously weaken or strengthen observed relationships between variables and become a significant source of nonrandom measurement error. Again, however, when the above-mentioned studies consider "race of the researcher effect," they refer to the effect of race on subjects and subjects' responses and not on the impact that a researcher's race might have on the project. The race of the researcher is treated as standard and neutral.

This lack of critical examination is found also in experimental methodology. Sociological experiments that focus on race (Goar and Sell 2005; Biernat and Kobrynowicz 1997; Steele and Aronson 1995; Webster and Driskell 1978) inform us of ways that race is activated in small groups, but fail to adequately address the ways that the practices and resources of the prevailing culture (and the experimenter's position in that culture) inform the experiment. Armed with the principles of control and randomization, experimenters claim that their method resides safely outside the realm of contaminants. Only after Black Americans made gains in education after the Civil Rights movement and joined the ranks of experimenters did the issue of the race of the experimenter receive critical attention (Morawski 1997, 2005). Black experimenters were among the first to produce a critical analysis and design an experiment to measure the affect of the experimenter's race (Bond 1927; Canady 1936) that suggested that the race of the experimenter does affect his or her perceptions and comprehension. (It is not surprising that such knowledge would come from experimenters who also hold the status of racialized other. Perhaps their non-White position required additional steps to acquire neutrality).

EXPERIMENTS, WHITE SUPREMACY, AND COLOR-BLIND RACISM

Morawski (1997) argues that experimenters hold a "dual model of persons: at least when the experimenter is White, the race of experimenter is held to be unrelated to his or her cognitions, whereas the race of the subject is held to possibly affect his or her cognitions" (15). She argues that the notion of experimental objectivity is so strong because it claims to maximize standardization and ideology. This concern echoes the unease of other methodologists who are critical of the scientific assumption of objectivity, arguing that research is affected by broader social relations.

Mills (1997) argues that, under White supremacy, a vital part of the research strategy is to promote, normalize, and objectify science. This influences what problems are identified as scientific and worthy of study, how hypotheses and research designs are selected, and how data is collected and analyzed. Mills refers to these hidden conceptualizations that fail to identify cultural assumptions of inquiry as a "self- and social shielding from racial realities that is underwritten by the official social epistemology" (45). This suggests there is little impartiality in scientific neutrality. Proctor, describing the central importance of neutrality to the research process, suggests that it has not produced unbiased knowledge but rather served as "myth, mask, shield, and sword" to those who hide behind its standard (1991, 262). It is through this normal, value-free, apolitical inquiry process that dominant groups can define agendas and hypotheses, and ultimately gain the information and explanations needed to advance their interests.

Bonilla-Silva (2001) describes these new racial practices as color-blind racism: collective, multidimensional, normalized, and hegemonic. This ideology is maintained by a racialized social system that hierarchically places the social desires, interests, contents, and agendas of one social group over another, "creating the social relations among races" (37). The race placed at the top of the hierarchy enjoys social, physical, and psychological advantages that groups occupying lower positions do not. These systemic advantages and disadvantages are attributed to merit and deservedness, which results in the deracializing of people, incidents, and events. The color blindness that results from this new racism considers cultural differences irrelevant and racial disparities a result of individual deservedness.

In the area of experimental methodology, this type of color blindness is especially insidious. Hidden behind the last bastion of social science objectivity, the color-blind doctrine assumes that race is an individual attribute that should be of no consequence, resulting in a failure to recognize it as an essential and feasible area of study. Color-blind racism also affects one's authority to make knowledge claims, depending on the race of the researcher and the race of the subject. Far from being neutral, the current production of research occurs within a wider field of social relations that is characterized by the agendas, interests, and values of the dominant group. By failing to seriously consider race, current experimental methodology reifies the interests of the prevailing culture by reflecting color-blind racism and supports the deracialization of inquiry.

NOTES

1. Galton was the founder of the international Society of Eugenics that promoted the idea of racial improvement through selective mating and sterilization (Guthrie 1998).
2. This "scientific racism" was used to justify and protect the exploitation of a disadvantaged group so that the advantaged group could reap social, economic, and political rewards (Marshall 1993; Tucker 1984).
3. Subsequent experiments show that there is no consistent or significant racial difference in reaction times (Livesay and Louttit 1950; Bluhm and Kennedy 1965).

10

"The End of Racism" as the New Doxa

New Strategies for Researching Race

Charles A. Gallagher

Never before in U.S. history has an honest and frank discussion about racism or racial inequality and its causes been so difficult to broach. Although Hurricane Katrina punctured the myth that racism and abject poverty were social ills of the past, the political hand wringing and the promise of rebirth has already retreated from center stage. The lack of dialogue concerning racism and poverty in America was reflected in Louisiana governor Kathleen Babineaux Blanco's depressing observation that "the harsh reality is that for many people in Washington, Katrina is yesterday's problem." The reason for the silence on the state of race relations in America is that a majority of Whites (and some racial minorities) have embraced the view that we are now a color-blind nation (Bonilla-Silva 2003; Brown et al. 2003; Gallagher 2003b, 2006a). It is not that these individuals are blind to color. Color matters and plays a major role in how most Whites structure their lives, from selecting a neighborhood, mapping a route through an urban area, what they watch on television, or the message conveyed to their children about which groups are acceptable dating partners. What is a radical break from the past is the belief that racial discrimination and racism are no longer an obstacle to upward social mobility. As the majority of Whites now see it, race has mutated from a social hierarchy that allocates resources and shapes life chances to one that is nothing more than a cultural identity. The shift from race being understood by Whites as an unequal power relation to a benign cultural marker has dire implications for those studying race. In this chapter I identify three epistemological and methodological concerns researchers must now navigate when they research how Whites understand, frame, and reflect on race relations, racial inequality, and White privilege in the United States. The first challenge requires researchers to reframe their research questions and background assumptions in light of the changing views Whites now hold regarding race relations and what role race is perceived to play in allocating resources or shaping life chances. It is no longer enough, as Bonilla-Silva (2001) points out in his discussion on measuring racial attitudes, to only "ask questions developed in the 1940s, 1950s and 1960s." While these data can be valuable for a number of reasons, Whites' perceptions of race have changed dramatically in the past twenty years. Second is the ever widening chasm between the narrative of racial equality a majority of Whites now espouse and quality of life indicators that point to continued and in some areas growing, race-based inequalities. Finally there is the social baggage that researchers on White privilege bring to the research project itself. I argue that the subject position one occupies, in concert with the distorted view many White respondents have about race relations, can shade, if not outright bias, research on White racial attitudes. I close with nine factors those doing research on Whites' perceptions about race and race relations should consider before they undertake their research projects.

THE NEW DOXA, OR THE "ILLUSION OF INCLUSION"

Those who research race and racism in the United States are now faced with the daunting task of attempting to accurately measure the racial attitudes of the dominant group in an era where an overwhelming majority of Whites now believe, as conservative social critic Dinesh D'Souza argues, that "The End of Racism" (to quote the title of his book [1995a]) has been achieved. The new doxa, or commonsense understanding, of race held by most Whites is the belief that we are a color-blind nation (Pierce 2003; DiTomaso et al. 2003; Gallagher 2006a, 2004, 2003b; Bonilla-Silva 2001).

Many Whites acknowledge that individual and institutional discrimination directed toward racial minorities continues to exist and these past and present practices explain relative socioeconomic group inequalities. This group, a relative minority of Whites in the United States, knows that institutional racism, prejudice, and discrimination continue to shape the life chances of racial minorities. Still another sizable part of the White population realizes that discrimination is still prevalent but nonetheless maintains the fiction of color blindness because embracing such a stance provides them with the means to preserve, justify, and reproduce White privilege. I would however argue that a majority of Whites occupy a social location that is characterized by racial isolation, a distorted and fanciful view about America's opportunity structure, and the cognitive dissonance that accompanies holding a deep belief that the United States is a meritocracy on one hand and the in-your-face racism demonstrated by Hurricane Katrina (to name just one example) on the other. These Whites, a clear majority in the United States, live in suburbs that are almost entirely White. Many of these households comprise the 7 million households who live in gated communities that are all White. Their children attend public schools or private schools that are almost entirely White. Their neighbors are White. They attend religious services in a house of worship that is nearly all White. The close friends invited over for dinner on a regular basis are all White. In addition this group comes to know non-White America primarily through para-social interactions or an understanding of the racial "other" that comes almost exclusively from television where they can choose mainly between a relatively narrow range of stereotypes—criminals, athletes, or the all-American success story. In this White bubble, where employment opportunities are abundant, public schooling translates into upward mobility, property values appreciate, and crime is typically not a concern, it becomes quite easy for Whites to project this version of what America is like on the rest of the nation. Since race is not an issue for Whites in this environment and non-Whites appear to be making gains as measured by depictions of racial minorities in television advertisements and token representations in key government posts and corporate America, then racism must be a thing of the past. The social isolation Whites experience in the suburbs and the distorted view of race relations that accompanies being surrounded only by people who look, feel, and act in similar fashion normalize White privilege while making the prerogatives of this group invisible.

This color-blind account of America holds that since it is now illegal to deny individuals access to jobs, housing, or public accommodations because of one's skin color, factors *other than* racism or discrimination must explain socioeconomic disparities between racial groups. Framed within the context of neoliberal ideology where the imperatives of the market have rid society of the irrationality of racism, color blindness allows members of the dominant group to view racial inequality as the result of cultural pathologies internalized by racial minorities. With complete disregard for the historical or contemporary racist practices that reproduce and racialize inequality, Whites are able to argue on nonracist grounds that Blacks and other racial minorities are the "cultural architects of their own disadvantage" (Bobo and Smith 1998, 212). This color-blind perspective that equality of opportunity is now normative is constructed and reinforced through depictions of racial equality in the media. The handsome, upper-middle-class, integrated, racial utopia that is now a staple in advertisements, situation comedies, dramas, or movies is for most White Americans an utterly unremarkable event (Giroux 2003; Gallagher 2006b). If one were to rely on the mass media as a reflection of contemporary race relations one would come to think that the multimillionaire Black or Latino next door is now the norm, not the exception.

This new racial logic explains away racial inequality by coupling the deeply held conviction that America is a meritocracy with the neoliberal belief that the impersonal, nondiscriminatory, rational mechanisms of the market are the means by which individuals or groups are sorted within the socioeconomic pecking order. The resulting fusion of neoliberalism and a belief in racial equality is a color-blind perspective of U.S. race relations that allows Whites to embrace what I call an "illusion of inclusion" (Gallagher 2006b) where ability, luck, pluck, and bootstrapping, not skin color, discrimination, or institutional barriers determine life chances.

Not only does the color-blind "illusion of inclusion" maintain and protect White privilege by denying contemporary racist practices, but also the long-term effect of such a perspective is that it cements these distorted accounts of racial equality for future generations. According the U.S. Census Bureau, almost 64 percent of the U.S. population was under the age of forty-four in 2000 (U.S. Census Bureau 2000). The 180 million White Americans within this category have had very little firsthand knowledge of the Civil Rights movement or the caste system that until quite recently defined this country. Even for the oldest Whites in this population (born around 1956) their racial reference point is more likely to have been *The Cosby Show* or an unending stream of Black-White buddy movies rather than any real-world events depicting racial turmoil or unrest. The *Lethal Weapon* movie franchise that spanned four movies and eleven years (1987 to 1998) was the most successful in the color-blind, postrace entertainment genre. Not only did this series present a reality where interracial relationships were the norm and the color line had been erased, but it accomplished this feat by creating a psychologically damaged White character, Sergeant Martin Riggs (played by Mel Gibson), who is made whole again by the actions of a Black sergeant, Roger Murtaugh (played by Danny Glover), and his family, who adopt this kind, yet psychotic White man. Rodney King, the LA riots, the OJ trial, and the aftereffects of Katrina have become fleeting, distant blips in the march toward the neoliberal color-blind racial nirvana many Whites honestly believe we now inhabit. Martin Luther King Jr.'s dream of racial equality in 1963 has not yet come to pass if quality-of-life indicators are a proxy for racial equality, but for a majority of Whites today that dream equal opportunity and racial parity is now a reality. As a reactionary ideological anchor, "the end of racism" sophistry can only operate as America's trope of racial equality if one buys into an "illusion of inclusion" where equal opportunity is normative. What is accomplished by presenting a leveled-playing-field argument is both the maintenance of White privilege and the deeply held belief by a majority of Whites that racism no longer shapes life chances. This is the new starting point race scholars must acknowledge and address when they go into the field to interview or conduct surveys. What is most problematic is that a majority of Whites, at least the ones I have interviewed over the years, truly believe that the United States has finally ended its relationship with its racist past. The next generation has written a new narrative where America is a color-blind nation. If we have, however, arrived at the end of racism in the United States, the terminus is only in the minds of the majority of Whites, not in the material conditions or life chances that face a disproportionate number of racial minorities today.

The new commonsense notion of racial equality creates a self-serving script for the dominant group where at a visceral and cognitive level the color-blind view of race relations is, as Bourdieu (1990) explains how doxa shapes reality, "beyond question." We start the research enterprise on race with a majority of the White population believing all things are equal, a dilemma that is similar to astronomers addressing the Flat Earth Society or biologists presenting how environmental pressures shape natural selection to adherents of Intelligent Design. We can no longer continue to ask questions crafted for cohorts that had church bombings, poll taxes, and lynchings as their cultural and racial reference point, just as we cannot use questions that do not take into account the fact of color blindness.

OUR SURVEY SAYS

As evident in a number of recent national polls, a majority of Whites have constructed a view of America's opportunity structure where race no longer plays a significant role in allocating resources or shaping life chances. What is important to note is how Whites perceive the opportunity structure to be and the actual differences that exist between the opportunities afforded Whites and Blacks. A 2002 Gallup Poll found that 81 percent of Whites felt that Black children had "as good a chance" as White children to get a quality education (Mason 2003). It strains credibility that parents in the overwhelmingly White suburban neighborhoods believe that America's mostly urban, Black and brown children are receiving the same quality education as their own children. A Gallup Poll conducted for AARP and released in 2004 found that a majority, 61 percent of non-Hispanic Whites, responded that "blacks have equal job opportunities as whites" (Gallup 2004). Among those with a high school degree or less (the majority of White Americans in the United States) the number who believe there is now equality in the labor market went up to 71 percent of non-Hispanic Whites (Gallup 2004). A 2003 Gallup Poll asked if the goals of the civil rights movement have been achieved. Among non-Hispanic Whites 56 percent said all or most of the goals of the civil rights movement had been achieved. Again, it is hard to reconcile these perceptions of achieved goals when we examine the quality-of-life indicators by race. In almost every category—unemployment, incarceration, home ownership, college attendance, wealth, and infant mortality—racial disparities between White, Black, and brown populations exist. Equality of opportunity (a false assertion in itself) has somehow become synonymous with equality of results. A whopping 82 percent of White Americans now say they have a close personal friend who is not White (Mazzuca 2004), although 50 percent of all White Americans work in environments that are all or mostly White. Doing the math, for 82 percent of Whites to have a Black or brown close personal friend, every single Black and brown American would have to have about three very close White friends. In an exercise I have done in my class for the past decade I asked my students to list their three best friends. My students' responses are the mirror opposite of the findings in the above Gallup Poll. Typically almost all my Black and White students have three "best" friends who are the same race. A record 70 percent of Whites in a 2003 Gallup Poll said they "generally approve" of marriages between Blacks and Whites (Ludwig 2004a), although this group is one of the least likely among all possible racial pairings to marry. Ethnographic accounts however, of what transpires when Whites cross the color line in romance tell a much more complicated and hostile account than the approval ratings national polls would suggest (Dalmage 2000; Childs 2005).

Given that there is a serious disconnect between the responses Whites provide researchers with when they are surveyed about abstract racial matters and the objective, concrete ways that race shapes almost every facet of how Whites act and organize their lives, race researchers need to question the face validity of such survey data. What questions do we need to ask, given that most Whites no longer see racial inequality as being a significant obstacle to upward mobility? How do we engage our respondents in such a way that we are able to move beyond socially appropriate answers and distorted sound bites to research that addresses more complicated structural accounts of racial inequality?

FROM SURVEY DISTORTIONS TO INTERVIEWS

A color-blind perspective of race relations also has implications for how White researchers position themselves in the research they conduct. It may be assumed that since the researcher and respondents are White and the focus of the interviews are about what whiteness means, then the social biography and location of the researcher need not be scrutinized as critically as, for example, a Black researcher interviewing Korean grocers in a Black neighborhood or a self-identified Jewish researcher interviewing members of the Christian Identity Movement. The legitimacy of one's role in the research process may be questioned, but because race and racial divisions are so central to how we structure every aspect of our lives, the belief in a common perspective or narrative of whiteness may guide research assumptions and the interaction between respondent and researcher.

One may be, as I initially was when I started my research, lulled into the belief that the 200 million Whites in the United States share a common cultural thread or a similar lived experience because they are the dominant racial group. While the majority of Whites enjoy many privileges relative to members of other racial groups, this shared privilege does not mean one can minimize the need to critically access where one's social location, political orientation, and attitudes on race fit into the research project.

Not only did I imagine myself having access to Whites because I was White but much of the literature on qualitative methods suggests ascribed status should guide, at least in part, who one is able to study. John and Lyn Lofland (1984), while cautioning researchers not to overemphasize the ascribed status of the interviewer, post this warning in their widely used qualitative methods textbook:

> If you are black, studying Ku Klux Klan members and sympathizers will probably not be feasible. Nor are you likely to reach the desired "intimate familiarity" if you are male and attempting to study a radical lesbian group.

Providing an overview of how social location influences what researchers see and do not see John H. Stanfield II (1994b) argues, "only those researchers emerging from the life worlds of their 'subjects' can be adequate interpreters of such experiences." As a White researcher studying Whites I saw myself being situated squarely within the insider doctrine, which "holds that insiders have monopolistic or privileged access to knowledge of a group" (Baca Zinn 1979). While inscribing myself within these interviews as a racial insider I was also able to maintain the role as the "objective" outsider. This methodological legerdemain could be maintained simply by embracing the neutral techniques of qualitative methods outlined in textbooks that define the field. I could embrace the role of detached dispassionate researcher-outsider with access to knowledge "accessible only to nonmembers of those groups" (Baca Zinn 1979) while simultaneously being an insider because of my color.

However, being an insider because of one's race does not mute or erase other social locations that serve to deny access or create misunderstood or biased interviews with those from the same racial background. Nor does perceiving or defining oneself as an outsider allow one to claim one's research is value free. Skin color does not necessarily allow one to automatically pass into and have access to individuals or communities because of shared ascribed characteristics.

"Being White," like being a member in any social group has a host of contradictory, symbolic, and situationally specific meanings. As a Northerner raised in a working-class section of a big city who now lives in the South, being White did not provide me with automatic access to the Whites I interviewed in rural southeast Georgia. My whiteness did not smooth over differences based on my age or gender that I encountered in my interviews. My Yankee dialect and professor status with "big city" university affiliation made me a cultural outsider. The perception that I am Jewish, and the racial confusion many have concerning this category painted me as the "other" among a number of older White men I interviewed. In a focus group interview with a number of older, Southern, rural, White males a respondent stopped mid-interview and exclaimed "Why, ya a Jew-boy, ain't ya." It is unclear how this influenced my interview, but it was clear that I was viewed as a religious (possibly racial) outsider. Southerners have explained to me that I may be viewed as White, but when I interview Whites in the rural South I will still be an outsider. In these scenarios, as a cultural and/or racial outsider, I had to consider how my perceived characteristics shaped my interviews with individuals who viewed me as an interloper.

Many Whites feel at ease expressing their racism to other Whites they do not know because they believe their skin color makes them kindred spirits in racism or at least sympathetic to the "white experience" (Myers 1993). White researchers examining the meaning Whites attach to their race are cognizant of this, either explicitly capitalizing on their whiteness to gain access to and rapport with respondents or, perhaps more dangerously, tacitly believing their whiteness unburdens them from examining their own racial biography. One's whiteness becomes a form of methodological capital researchers can use to question Whites about the meaning they attach to their race.

Perceiving oneself as a White insider and interrogating whiteness from the outside as a researcher creates a number of methodological and ethical questions. Do I have immediate access to White respondents simply because I am White and my questions were about "being White"? Am I automatically an insider because of my skin color? Is the potential for tension, misunderstanding, or lack of rapport minimized because race is so central to how we structure our lives that the whiteness shared by researcher and respondent transcends other social markers? Is it possible to be manipulated into reproducing racist stereotypes of Whites, particularly working-class Whites, by asking questions about race and race relations that use the language and ideology of White victimology constructed, circulated, and endorsed by neoconservatives, the media, and survey research?

To what extent does the "objective interviewer" stance taken by many researchers allow White respondents to validate and justify the existing racial hierarchy that privileges Whites while simultaneously allowing these respondents to claim they are now at a social and economic disadvantage because of their skin color? The ethical and moral implications for those working in White studies are clear. Asking questions that decontextualize and treat whiteness as normative or existing outside of the established racial hierarchy makes the researcher complicit in valorizing and creating a narrative of whiteness that unburdens researcher and informant from the responsibility of challenging White racism and White privilege.

A number of overlapping and interrelated concerns emerged in my research that led me to question whether I was engaged in antiracist scholarship or if the questions I asked were reproducing a variation on what Stuart Hall calls "inferential racism." Hall argues that how we represent or frame the idea of race "whether 'factual' or 'fictional' which have racist premises and propositions inscribed in them as a set of unquestioned assumptions . . . enable racist statements to be formulated without ever bringing into awareness the racist predicates on which the statements are grounded" (Hall 1981). Hall's "inferential racism" is a critique of how the media normalizes racist ideology through various representations of race. Hall's examination of the pernicious effects of how the media maintains and reproduces racial hierarchy could just as easily serve as a warning to researchers to question how their research normalizes whiteness by relying on the "unquestioned assumptions" about racial identity construction, racism, or the dominant belief that Whites do not think of their whiteness or their race in relation to other racial groups.

Many of my White respondents would often frame their own racial identity based on information about race that was factually incorrect. Respondents routinely double- and triple-counted the Black and Asian population in the United States (Gallagher 2003a; Alba et al. 2005), dismissed contemporary racism as an occurrence of the past, and saw the workforce as significantly biased against Whites. As an academic committed to antiracist research it became unclear if I was conducting the "normal science" of a racist paradigm or was engaging in inferential racism by allowing my respondents' beliefs to go unchecked. Since I did not explain to my respondents that Whites make up about 75 percent of the U.S. population, was I confirming and lending academic legitimacy to their anxious and fearful version of U.S. race relations and White victimology? Is it possible that among those I interviewed whiteness emerged as identity under attack or unfairly maligned that was now in need of academic attention? This concern was made clear to me when I explained to an older secretary that I was examining the meaning Whites attach to their race. She snapped at me, "Good, it's about time somebody studied us." Whites, she believed, had been ignored in the contemporary discussion of race relations. Was I condoning racism or encouraging White supremacy by validating a view of race and power relations that was largely fictive? By not challenging these reactionary versions of White identity construction the chance to engage in direct antiracist action was not only lost but responses that might have generated counternarratives or created a crisis of whiteness could not emerge or be explored.

I also want to suggest that there is an inherent danger in claiming insider status because researchers and respondents are both White. Henry Giroux (1998) reminds us that racial categories exist and shape the lives of people differently within existing inequalities of power and wealth. These inequalities exist as much within racial categories as they do between them. The recent scholarship on the cultural meaning of "white trash" is yet another way Whites have been sorted along a socioeconomic continuum by academics (Wray and Newitz 1997; Hartigan 2005). When I first started asking questions in my focus groups and interviews I had, at least in part due to my sampling frame, leveled the within-group differences that existed among my respondents. The internal variation that exists in the way 200 million Whites in the United States understand, mark, and articulate their race does however create formidable research challenges. The unquestioned assumption of White invisibility, that Whites view themselves as colorless or, as Richard Dyer (1997) agues, having no content or, as Alastair Bonnett (1997) puts it, existing outside of the political and economic forces that seem to shape other racialized identities, is a metanarrative that should be resisted. In my interactions with Whites throughout the country, how individuals came to understand, ignore, or validate their whiteness varied enormously within and between city and suburb as well as within each region of the United States (see Hartigan 1997, 2005). Class, geography, education, political ideology, sexuality, religion, age, gender, local culture—all these influences shaped the construction of whiteness for my respondents as much as they did for me as an interviewer.

The "social geography of race," to borrow Ruth Frankenberg's phrase, varies in real and idiosyncratic ways (1993). Researchers studying whiteness and the various meanings, expressions, and emotions Whites attach to their race need to reexamine the insider/outsider dilemma that arises when studying something as slippery as racial identity construction. Being White may be a necessary condition to gain access and trust with some White respondents, but being White is not, in and of itself, sufficient. Other aspects of one's social identity that pose a greater threat or suspicion among respondents may negate access or rapport based on skin color. I was reminded of my White-as-"outsider" status among Whites when an elderly, working-class Italian American I had been building rapport with in Philadelphia was told by a neighbor I was a graduate student. This seventy-year-old high school dropout and numbers (illegal lottery) runner no longer viewed me as just a "young White guy" from the neighborhood. Recently in Georgia I was talking with an older woman at a yard sale and she asked me, "What country are you from?" "Pennsylvania" did not appear to be a satisfactory answer. My olive skin color, dark hair, and brown eyes have cast me, at least by some Southerners, as the generic, racially ambiguous foreign "other." I was not clear if this woman thought I was White, but I was left pondering how her view of my racial identity might unfold, influence, and shape the outcome in an interview about how she defined or understood her whiteness.

I also want to suggest that researchers examining whiteness can be unintentionally (or intentionally) manipulated into racism by embracing a set of the "commonsense" assumptions about White racial attitudes that guide their research. Henry Giroux's work on how whiteness is reproduced and normalized is instructive. A counterhegemonic narrative that provides a cultural space for whiteness to be "renegotiated as a productive force in a politics of difference linked to a racial democratic project" (1998, 109) should be as central to White studies as the inclination to demonstrate that White identity construction is based only on, as David Roediger (1994) puts it, "what one isn't and on whom one can hold back."

Finally I want to suggest the whole enterprise of White studies and the rush to critique whiteness as a sociohistorical category results in an essentialized and ultimately racist discourse (Andersen 2003; Doane 2003). While whiteness is understood as a socially constructed category, the internal variation within this category is often leveled. Without acknowledging how culture, politics, geography, ideology, and economics come together to produce numerous versions of whiteness, researchers will continue to frame and define whiteness monolithically. Just as we might cringe in a classroom when a student starts a conversation by stating that "all blacks do this . . ." or "gays always seem to . . ." we should be as careful not to accept the political construction that whiteness is culturally or ideologically monolithic. Without critically examining how the questions we ask as researcher reshape the meaning of race, whiteness can be reconstituted and rearticulated and the essentialist beliefs that undergird the idea of race go unchallenged.

RESEARCHING WHITENESS AS ANTIRACIST PROJECT

In almost all of my focus groups I asked or respondents offered their views on affirmative action. Respondents who had been reticent throughout the focus group discussion suddenly came to life, arguing forcefully about the need for, or more often, the inherent unfairness of, affirmative action. In many interviews this topic was a turning point. Many Whites took the opportunity to articulate a narrative of their whiteness that was based on victimization (Gallagher 1997, 2003, 2005). This conversation often led to a discussion about welfare, multiculturalism, and downward economic mobility because the labor marked now preferred Blacks and Asians to Whites. The laments, outrages, and pent-up guilt about this topic were a fascinating, sociologically rich, and deeply troubling exchange.

What if, after these issues had been exhausted, I had asked my focus groups to consider another scenario? What if they were provided with a number of social facts about the relative social standing of Whites compared to other racial groups in the United States? How might Whites define themselves if it was demonstrated that racial discrimination in the labor market is unquestionably still a sorting mechanism that privileges Whites, that Whites are twice as likely as Blacks to graduate from college, that the face of welfare in the United States is White, that almost every socioeconomic measure, from infant mortality to home ownership rates to the accumulation of wealth favors Whites over Blacks, Latinos, or many Asian groups?

If the belief that Whites are losing out to Blacks or Asians was refuted in the interview and Whites had a chance to articulate an identity that could not be based on victimology, what would that White racial identity look like? Would there or could there be a White racial identity that was not merely, as Cornel West suggests, "a politically constructed category parasitic on blackness" (1993)? While critical of my own research for bracketing a narrative of whiteness within a reactionary and conservative framework, Henry Giroux (1998) asks how, as antiracist researchers and educators, we might provide:

> The conditions for students to address not only how their "whiteness" functions in society as a marker of privilege and power, but also how it can be used as a condition for expanding the ideological and material realities of democratic public life. (108)

The conditions required to think ourselves out of an oppositional understanding of whiteness means breaking the racial template that seduces researchers into asking questions that do nothing more than reproduce a "commonsense," neoconservative definition of whiteness and race relations that is based on Whites' perceived marginalization. Those who wish to "abolish the White race" or define whiteness *only* as a source of power all Whites universally and equally share levels the social, political, and economic differences among Whites while creating a simple racial dichotomy that is easily and routinely manipulated politically (Ignatiev and Garvey 1996).

Data does not "speak for itself" nor does our data "emerge" in a vacuum. Who we are influences the questions we ask, the responses we get, and in turn the scholarship we produce, which is reproduced by yet another cohort of graduate students. Some of this scholarship finds its way into *Newsweek*, the *Wall Street Journal*, or as a discussion topic on Rush Limbaugh or Hannity and Colmes, where it becomes part of the new doxa—our collective understanding of race relations. A White male in a focus group reminded me of this trickle-down understanding of race relations. He insisted that Rodney King was a threat to the police officers that savagely beat him because he kept moving when he was on the ground. If you want to know what is really going on, he told the group "You gotta watch Rush [Limbaugh]." There is no shortage of right-wing radio shows or neoconservative entertainment that passes as news (for example, Fox News and Bill O'Reilly) that maintain the fiction that the "end of racism" is upon us.

Unfortunately the counternarratives that might challenge the existing racial status quo go, in large part, unexplored. A colleague from a working-class background who was familiar with my work told me the focus of my project was to demonstrate that working-class Whites are racist. I would, as others had done before, paint a portrait of working-class Whites as racists. This was not my intention, although his prediction was fairly accurate. I was steered toward one version of whiteness that had been framed by the narrow, binary ways in which many researchers choose to explore racial identity construction and accepting the script that has been provided to my respondents.

BEYOND WHITE ESSENTIALISM

An agitated White male in focus group, typical of many I interviewed, complained that Whites are the new minority group in the United States. Talking about the treatment of Blacks, Mike explained to me:

> It's not like they're discriminated against anymore, it's like the majority is now the minority because we are the ones being discriminated against because we are boxed in. We can't have anything for ourselves anymore that says exclusively White or anything like that. But everyone else can. You know what I mean.

Throughout my research, White respondents generally embraced the belief that the U.S. class system was fair and equitable. Most respondents argued that individuals who delay gratification, work hard, and follow the rules would succeed, irrespective of color (Gallagher 2005; 2003; 1999). Many White respondents felt the leveled playing field argument has rendered affirmative action policies a form of reverse discrimination and source of resentment. Jennifer Hochschild (1995) calls this "whites' quandary." "Whites are more sure that discrimination is not a problem," that Blacks can succeed, that self-reliance pays off, that Blacks now "control their own fate" *and* Whites feel that their life chances have eroded. This is how my respondents are able to define themselves as victims; as the above quote from Mike explains, it is Whites who are "now the minority." Like the White stories I heard in my interviews, the Whites' victim perspective can be added to the ever-growing list of those situations, attitudes, or injustices that make up the "White experience."

Mike, like many other young Whites from modest backgrounds, defined himself as the racial "Other." Mike views himself as someone lacking agency in a world where he is marginalized because of his race. This perception of victimization and belief that many Whites are now the racial "other" lends itself to the development of defensive strategies based on an essentialist understanding of whiteness. What, many of my respondents asked me, would Blacks do if we wore "It's a white thing . . . you wouldn't understand" T-shirts? My point here is not to examine if Whites can be the subaltern, the racial outsider in a White society or the other "other." My question concerns the shift from a racial identity that is invisible to one made explicit and how this process may essentialize whiteness. Michael Omi and Howard Winant (1994) explain that a racial project can be defined as racist if and only if it creates or reproduces structures of domination based on essentialist categories of race. While ostensibly concerned with social justice and racial equality it is unclear the extent to which White studies, as a racial project, can embrace an antiessentialist epistemology or methodology.

Much of the work being done in White studies embraces an essentialist standpoint in two ways. First, by allowing a narrative of whiteness to emerge that has been molded by a reactionary political and cultural climate that has a vested interest in defending the racial status quo, we might then challenge the tendency for White respondents to validate and justify White privilege by inverting the questions we ask so respondents are forced to think of the structural advantages they receive because of their skin color. How might a White informant respond to the question that requires them to consider how a fifty-year-old, white-collar Black or Asian woman might view their whiteness? Do we ask questions that challenge our respondents to think about race as a political category, or do we reproduce, normalize, and continue to make whiteness invisible by uncritically validating the version of whiteness we expect to hear? There is also the concern, as Margaret Andersen so eloquently puts it, that the study of whiteness itself results in "people of color becoming invisible once again as Whites become the center of attention" (Andersen 2003, 31). Those studying White racial attitudes are in the position to explore counternarratives of racial identity construction that imply that Whites have agency in how they wish to define themselves and how they might take responsibility, or at least a fuller understanding of racial privilege in the United States. This becomes a greater challenge as Whites increasingly come to view the opportunity structure in the United States as being color-blind.

WHITE LIES: NEW STARTING POINTS FOR STUDYING WHITE RACIAL ATTITUDES

Listed below are several factors that should be taken into account when conducting research on White racial attitudes.

1. *There is NO White privilege.* Most Whites reject the idea that their skin color privileges them in any material way. The general view held by most Whites is that White privilege is a perk of the past. Almost half of all adult Whites (46 percent) believe that "society" treats Whites no better than Blacks (Gallup 2004) and a majority of Whites (61 percent) believe Whites have equal employment opportunities compared to Blacks.

2. *The United States is a meritocracy.* How can we as researchers ask questions about racial hierarchy if the racial privileges that maintain and reproduce inequality are dismissed or denied? Enter the field with the understanding that most Whites now believe we live in a meritocratic, color-blind society. This is the ideological starting point for a majority of Whites. How might this knowledge about Whites' perceptions of the opportunity structure shape the questions you ask about racial inequality or their reflections on racism?

3. *The front-stage socially appropriate answer.* A majority of Whites provide a socially acceptable answer to questions concerning race. These responses may not accurately reflect their beliefs. A literature exists describing how Whites talk when they are around other like-minded Whites, but you are unlikely to get those types of candid answers in your interviews. What does it mean for the validity of your research when Whites try to appease the interviewer or have internalized the socially appropriate script concerning race relations?

4. *Racism is always in past tense.* Any White guilt about the inherent unfairness of slavery, Jim Crow, and systemic institutional racism that has defined almost all of American history is, for the most part, entirely gone. Enter the field with the understanding that a majority feel that the civil rights movement addressed racial inequality and that Whites today feel they should not have to pay for what other Whites did generations ago. What does it mean for the research project if one's respondents enter a conversation where racial equality is perceived to be the norm and any suggestion of White privilege is treated with scorn?

5. *If Oprah can make it . . .* Start your project with the understanding that a neoliberal orientation, where the non-discriminatory invisible hand of

the market rather than government policies, is viewed by most Whites as the appropriate and fair way to rectify any lingering racial inequalities. How do we get beyond the rather stock assertion by most Whites that today anyone can make it in the United States, regardless of skin color? How might we challenge the assertion that upward mobility and equal opportunity are no longer linked to race?

6. *The media is the medium through which Whites know racial minorities.* The knowledge most Whites have of racial minorities is not based on one-on-one interactions or close personal friendships but through depictions of these groups in the mass media. What does it mean that Whites can speak so easily about Black and brown America when they share little, if any, social space with members of these groups. What is the impact on race research when the knowledge most Whites have of racial minorities is restricted to representations of these groups on television?

7. *I'm not racist, some of my best . . .* Most Whites believe they are not racist. How, then, do we measure racism within this population if language used about race is highly guarded and censored?

8. *A color-blind United States allows you to choose your destiny.* Most Whites believe racial minorities on the socioeconomic margins are, to borrow Lawrence Bobo's phrase, "the architects of their own disadvantage." The mind-set is that our prisons, ghettoes, and barrios look as they do because individuals make a conscious choice to be there. Within the color-blind neoliberal framework, one chooses failure just as one embraces success. Does our research challenge this new doxa, and perhaps more importantly, how does the race research we do reproduce this narrative?

9. *Ivory tower myopia.* Imagine those White researchers raised in a middle- to upper-middle-class White environment who went to a prestigious undergraduate institution and received their PhD from one of the big research schools. It is likely that along the way to tenure, this group's window into the lives of the working class and/or racial minorities (if one ever did exist) slowly closed. This group is privy to racial inequality and racism by reading other upper-middle-class researchers' reflections on race and poverty. The human exchanges this group has with racial minorities on the economic margins are cash exchanges at supermarkets and retail outlets and, for those higher up in the socioeconomic queue, interactions with maids, nannies, and gardeners. It is likely that everyone with the inner circle of friends within this group has at least a college education. In other words, members of this group inhabit an upper-middle-class, white-collar, typically segregated, white bubble. How might the survey questions we write or the ethnographies we conduct be influenced by or own class experiences, the privileged social status professor's occupy, and the particular social milieu in which White middle-class professors reside?

11

White Ethnographers on the Experiences of African American Men

Then and Now

Alford A. Young Jr.

It is not without some degree of irony that ethnography, the branch of sociology most associated with debate and discussion about the significance of intimacy and rapport between the researcher and those being researched, is also the branch of the discipline in which many of the classic and most highly regarded studies of African Americans have been produced by White American or White European (hereafter referred to as White) sociologists. Indeed, the past four decades have comprised a period of extensive exploration by these scholars of the social organization and cultural fabric of African American communities and the Black men who reside in them (Hannerz 1969; Liebow 1967; Rainwater 1970; Schulz 1969; Stack 1974; and Suttles 1968).[1]

While exposing a broad intellectual, political, and civic community to the lifestyles and mores of marginalized people, the earliest of the work produced in the 1960s aimed to explain how urban-based, low-income African American men were culturally similar, yet also culturally distinct, from what had, in actuality, been a nebulous notion of an American mainstream society. Indeed, although much of this work emphasized cultural difference as rooted in structural circumstances such as diminished local job markets and anemic social environments, a lingering point of emphasis was on the differences between impoverished African American men and the so-called rest of us.

While the proliferation of this scholarship has ebbed and flowed since the breakthrough moment of the 1960s, the 1990s brought forth a period of its extraordinary reemergence. The scholarship produced during the

1990s is distinctive in that it emerged soon after the term "underclass" was proliferated as an identifier of the urban African American and Latino poor. Much of the more prominent work in the 1990s, while produced in what many might consider to be a more socially and economically turbulent time for urban-based African Americans, argued much more strongly about the cultural similarities between those African Americans caught in despair and malaise and those who were argued to comprise "mainstream" America. Hence, if the urban ethnography of the 1960s reflected an initial period of intense and curious exploration of the Black American urban landscape by White scholars, in the 1990s that scholarship was rooted in a national condition of intense anxiety about the presumably extreme threat to the American social order that such people represented.

In this chapter I comment on the politics of cultural analysis as they pertain to ethnography conducted across the Black-White color line. I will first explore some central works produced by White scholars in the 1960s and then consider work produced in the 1990s. My point of emphasis will be on the kinds of cultural analytical frameworks forwarded in some of the most prominent works of these periods, and the particular kinds of intellectual politics that emerged precisely because the work was produced by White ethnographers. I conclude with some comparative assessment of the cultural analytical and intellectual political projects of both periods, and a discussion of what this comparative framing offers for some critical considerations of the implications of ethnographic analysis of African American men by White scholars.

THE LOGIC OF THE WHITE ETHNOGRAPHIC GAZE IN THE 1960s

During the1960s urban ethnography served as a site for the production of intense and elaborate research, analysis, and argument about the cultural dynamics shaping the lives of low-income African Americans. A slew of research initiatives brought forth the notion that there existed a durable, visible, and needy population of Americans who lived lifestyles in severe contrast with middle-class America. The prosperity and vibrancy of the American economy in the early 1960s buttressed the blossoming idea that, if understood and addressed assertively, poverty could be obliterated, or at least managed effectively, in American society (Hodgson 1976; O'Connor 2001).

Social research in the pre-1960s era asserted that Black Americans generally desired the accouterments of the good life—secure employment, decent housing, and family stability. Accordingly, the research produced during that era elucidated the relevant issues, means, and mechanisms for African

Americans to achieve these desires. Hence, under the pretense that the social problems afflicting African Americans, especially those residing in disadvantaged urban communities, could be fixed once they were best understood, the 1960s-era research agenda turned to detailed considerations of people who seemed divorced from the American Dream. Moreover, the involvement of White ethnographic researchers during the 1960s helped to firmly situate the ethnography of African American urban life within mainstream of sociology as well as mainstream American public policy and scholarly discussion.

Investigations of the cultural dimensions of African American life were presumed to be the means by which White ethnographers could gain some purchase on this agenda. The calling of that day was to make sense of what appeared to outside observers to be extreme (but also, in some cases, rather subtle) differences in the behaviors of such people when compared against a constructed middle-class normative referent. Of course, some of this behavior was considered fatalistic. Accordingly, one of the key issues of concern for urban ethnographers was how such behavior could be transformed so that urban, low-income African Americans could better attain the good life that they, and other Americans, so deeply desired.

Behavior became a logical point of emphasis for these researchers as the urban American landscape became populated with underemployed and unemployed African American men whose idleness was reflected by their congregating in highly visible public spaces (i.e., parks, vacant lots, etc.) and on street corners. If such men were not visibly idle in the midst of occupying public space, they presumably were involved in gangs and illicit activity, and that was, simply enough, taken to be inappropriate behavior. Of course, serious discussion of behavior had to be rooted in an interpretive foundation, and the terms that provided this foundation were those that constituted the core lexicon of mid-twentieth-century cultural analysis in sociology; norms, values, and attitudes.

Norms, or the creeds employed by people to regulate and sanction their behavior, became one area of intense preoccupation in this field of research because it seemed that low-income African Americans abided by normative systems that differed from what was construed as the standard in American life. The same concern became manifested around values, which are the creeds and principles that people embody or aspire to achieve. After all, if people seemingly behaved so differently then the presumption was that they adhered to a value system in their everyday lives that differed from, if not contrasted fully with, that adhered to by many other Americans. Along these lines, attitudes were taken to be those dispositions, feelings, and expressions that demonstrated fatalism, futility, or frustration on the part of urban, low-income African Americans to achieve the highly desired good life in America.

The fact that the nascent cultural sociology of the mid-twentieth century relied so extensively upon these terms, and the social processes and dynamics associated with them, meant that a robust and salient vocabulary was in place to decipher what seemingly was so culturally distinct and different about Black Americans living in urban despair from so-called mainstream America.[2] Of course, without there being much serious investigation study of the cultural dimensions of the American middle class in the 1960s, there was no strong empirical legitimacy for advancing any definitive arguments in support of this normative referent.[3] Yet, the mandate to intimately explore the seemingly exotic and unfamiliar terrain of low-income African American men in the urban sphere compelled researchers to draw comparisons between that domain and one that was construed as the normative in mainstream America.[4] In fact, this turn in the 1960s was dramatic precisely because it drew so much attention from White scholars.

In the 1960s many ethnographers began employing the term "subculture" as scaffolding for discussion of the presumably unique and different lower-income African American normative, value, and attitudinal systems (as well as those of other ethic groups and social classes falling below that of the American middle class). An account of how the emphasis on subculture emerged in this research tradition can be found in Lee Rainwater's classic work, *Behind Ghetto Walls: Black Family Life in a Federal Slum* (1970), which was based on a study of family dynamics of residents in the Pruitt-Igoe public housing development in St. Louis. There he argued that by the early 1960s social science had adopted a consistent and robust notion of lower-class subculture. This notion was created and sustained in ethnographic studies of European-American ethnic enclaves in urban areas (Gans 1962; Suttles 1968; Whyte 1943) as well as by studies and commentaries about lower-income Americans from a broad range of racial and ethnic backgrounds (Berger 1960; Bordua 1961; Cloward and Ohlin 1960; Cohen and Hodges 1963; Coser 1965; Gans 1969; Miller 1958; Rodman 1963).

White ethnographers advanced the idea that subcultures were created by members of subordinate social groups contending with the difficulty of achieving the goals and desires that the larger social system considered legitimate (Abrahams 1964; Hannerz 1969; Liebow 1967; Riessman 1962; Schulz 1969). These goals and desires either were beyond the means of members of the lower echelon group to achieve, or not attainable in the ways that they were for those in more privileged positions (Rodman 1963).

An ultimately more pejorative point of reference in the debates and discussions of lower-class subculture, and one that had strong ethnic overtones, was the culture-of-poverty thesis associated with the work of anthropologist Oscar Lewis (1959, 1961, 1966). Lewis coined the term "culture of poverty," and expounded upon it through studies of Hispanic and Mexican families in neighborhoods in the United States and Mexico. However, he said much less, and also something a little different, about the culture of poverty than has usually been attributed to him. He did imply the relevance of structural conditions in affecting how poor people responded to their situation and how those conditions affected their prospects for escaping poverty. Whether he was read accurately or not, his work sparked extensive discussion about the relationship between poverty and culture.[5] More importantly, it solidified social scientific and popular conceptions of the power of cultural forces for determining the social outcomes of those living in poverty, and this was maintained aside from whatever durable qualities were assigned to external or structural factors.

The penetrating criticisms of the culture-of-poverty thesis emanating from liberal intellectual and policy circles did not prevent it from impacting the content and forms of 1960s-era urban ethnography and that which followed. Since that time, urban ethnographers have rejected certain aspects of the culture-of-poverty thesis, endorsed other aspects, and grappled to specify and refine that which could not easily be handled in one of the first two ways. The rejection appears most vividly in the explicit inclusion of structural effects in its analysis. The most crucial one was the absence of stable and substantive employment prospects for urban-based, low-income African American men. Not only did the leading ethnographies of the 1960s make specific claims about how good work prospects were essential for changing anything in the cultural milieu of the Black urban poor, but they also directly tied the cultural developments in these communities to the absence of adequate work (Hannerz 1969; Liebow 1967; Rainwater 1970).

Despite the attention given to structural factors, however, a major point of emphasis in this work was on drawing distinctions between low-income Black and middle-class White Americans along various barometers of culture. For example, Lee Rainwater argued that low-income Black Americans embraced unique cultural orientations and practices precisely because of the structural constraints they faced. Those orientations and practices included the development of a dramatic public persona that blinded outside observers from detecting any insecurity or discomfort that disadvantaged people might experience from encounters in mainstream America, and a heightened sense of suspicion, caution, or self-awareness in navigating the tumultuous public spaces of low-income, urban neighborhoods. This kind of vision of low-income African Americans was not very distant from that cultivated by adherents to the culture-of-poverty thesis. Hence, significant aspects of the cultural analysis promoted by White ethnographers in the 1960s were far from a complete break with that line of thinking.

Another example of this effort was provided by Eliot Liebow in his classic monograph, *Tally's Corner: A Study of Negro Streetcorner Men* (1967). This work examined the activities and outlooks of a group of African American men who congregated on a Washington, D.C., street corner. In attempting to dissect the distinct values, norms, and attitudes of these men, Liebow, much like Rainwater, stated that their value system was consistent with that of mainstream America. However, their norms differed to the extent that their experience in poverty necessitated that the men interact and make use of public space in ways that differ from those who comprised mainstream America. Liebow argued that one such way in which interaction took place was for the purpose of allowing the men to demonstrate and promote their moral worth to others. The street corner was a relevant platform for such demonstrations because its inhabitants had no secure access to employment sectors or highly regarded social statuses that could otherwise affirm their moral worth. The mild exotic flavor of Liebow's work becomes apparent, then, in that although he argued that the men in his study shared the basic value system of mainstream America, he also said that their attitudes, norms, and behavior took on vastly contrasting forms, as evident by their conduct in public space.[6]

Indeed, a major theoretical emphasis of much of the ethnography produced in the 1960s by White scholars was how low-income African Americans shared the American value system but were otherwise culturally distinct from White Americans. Those distinctions were explained by making reference to norms and attitudes. The argument put forth in this research was that structural constraint, best exemplified by limited employment prospects, prevented low-income Black Americans from realizing their values, thus provoking their adaptation of norms, attitudes, and behaviors that contrasted with those fostered and upheld in mainstream America.

In some cases, however, White ethnographers of the 1960s did not always restrict their arguments about the cultural distinctiveness of low-income African Americans to norms, values, and attitudes. There also were queries about whether this population produced cultural patterns that escaped classification by these terms and that also could be regarded as even more autonomous from mainstream America. Perhaps the most comprehensive investigation along these lines was produced by Swedish anthropologist Ulf Hannerz. In his book *Soulside* (1969) he devoted considerable attention to a discussion of "soul," a common term used in the 1960s and 1970s to refer to general attitudes and styles of expression by Black Americans (144–58).

Hannerz's purpose in exploring this term was to investigate its potential implications for affirming a coherent definition of urban-based African American subculture. However, his writing revealed deep insecurity about what to make of the term as a referent for some definitive quality or aspect of African American urban life. Hannerz argued throughout much of *Soulside* that culture is a public property, and that its constitutive elements usually were available for anyone to take possession of and employ for his or her own purposes. Yet he was intrigued and puzzled about Black Americans, who seemed to him (and many other outsiders as well) to have a cultural repertoire that was not so easily transferable or adoptable. Many of these attributes, which included an easy-going but colorful expressive style and bodily comportment, were captured by the concept of soul.[7]

Hannerz ultimately pursued his query into his book without providing an analytically precise solution to it. This effort is similar to Eliot Liebow's, where he attempted to discern African American male violent expression as an element of a shadow culture (1967, 212–15) because this behavior escapes interpretation within his own configuration of the norms/values/attitude terminology. Hence, shadow culture became a residual concept for locating behavior that stands outside of the mainstream. Moments like those provided by Hannerz and Liebow show that despite some efforts to the contrary, vivid claims were made in this 1960s-era ethnography about the cultural distinctiveness of low-income Black Americans. Perhaps theirs is the clearest demonstration of how the social character of African American men was depicted in that work.

Street Culture and the Public Persona of Black Men

In trying to make sense of moments of cultural continuity and difference, White ethnographers of low-income, urban-based African American men centered much of their empirical considerations on public behavior. In discussions of how low-income African American men dealt with the issues, individuals, and circumstances that comprised their everyday lives, their public persona got construed as consisting of highly expressive styles of public engagement, including talking loud, being aggressive, or interacting in overtly sensational ways such that others would not detect any weakness in one's character. Indeed, 1960s-era ethnographic considerations of the street culture of low-income African American men became a primary means of asserting the cultural distinctiveness of poor Black Americans. In promoting this vision, many ethnographers regarded African American men to be locked into a fatalistic outlook on the social world.

The emphasis on fatalism in the lives of poor Black men in 1960s-era ethnography was abrupt and dramatic. Concepts like anomic street culture (Rainwater 1970) were used to shed light on how low-income communities differed so much from more affluent ones in terms of the potential for violence and the absence of social and institutional buffers from physical, economic, and emotional threat. Rainwater argued that an anomic street culture caused people to function in unique and sometimes aggressive ways in order to survive their social environment. This discussion of culture still was directly tied to structural forces and factors, with the latter being regarded as the critical context for affecting any kind of positive change in people's lives, yet the behavior itself was now the point of intrigue and excitement. More importantly, it was the common point of analysis for the empirical emphases of this and other work of this period.

For instance, Eliot Liebow showed how feelings of defeat and deficiency are managed on the street corner as the men do things to elevate their public image among their peers (e.g., animated interaction with their children, for whom they otherwise cannot provide much material support) and reduce the emotional turmoil in their lives. He argued that much of what these men did on the street corner helped them to present a positive public persona as compensation for the personal and family-based problems they encountered. This argument about the utility of the street corner for engineering social conduct brought forth an additional perspective to Rainwater's discussion of the anomic quality of the streets in low-income urban areas. Both demonstrated the relevance of public space in the lives of Black American men. Yet, both also drew attention to the ways in which public space was related to some problematic aspects of their lives.

Hannerz, as well, delivered an argument about the utility of the street corner as a site for meaning making (1969, 52, 116–17). In this case, the street corner was explained as the domain whereby men came together to discuss their everyday experiences so that they could inform and reinforce each other about what it meant to be an African American man interfacing with individuals (i.e., police officers) and institutions (public aid agencies, employers, or employment training programs) that were embedded in the social organizational arrangements of low-income urban life.

The intense preoccupation with the public persona of low-income African American men in 1960s-era ethnography provided ample grounds for readers to conceive of such people as unlike mainstream Americans. Although there were efforts to offer cultural analyses that, at times, challenged notions of cultural difference, the ways in which such men's behavior was interpreted left a strong impression that these men simply were out of sync with the cultural fabric of American society. That vision allowed for exoticism to endure as part of the legacy of the 1960s urban ethnography produced by the most prominent White scholars.

The Cultural, Political, and Intellectual Legacy of the White Ethnographic Project of the 1960s

While some arguments by White urban ethnographers claimed that the cultural analysis of Black Americans should not be construed as the study of a social group apart or detached from the cultural fabric of mainstream America, the empirical emphases of much of this work did portray these individuals as culturally distinct from, if not altogether in contrast with, the imaginary construction of the mainstream. The intellectual politics emanating from this period of research, then, centered on the means and mechanisms necessary for greater inclusion of low-income Black Americans in American society. Achieving this end meant eradicating any defeatist, fatalistic, and profligate tendencies that were believed to comprise the cultural parameters of lower-income African American urban life. Prior to the process of eradication, however, was the effort of 1960s-era ethnographers to illustrate these tendencies in a vivid and thorough manner.

As has been the case for the majority of the scholarship produced in American higher educational institutions, this research was intended for audiences comprised of White Americans. More specifically, the aim was to remedy the plight of low-income, urban-based Black Americans with a liberal interventionist logic. Hence, it was not at all surprising that this research would appropriate an assimilationist ethic in fostering the notion that normative and attitudinal adjustments were in order for such Black Americans to function more effectively in the American social order. Of course, many of the arguments substantiated the idea that difference emerged by way of socioeconomic exclusion. The logic was that if economic opportunities were brought to these people, then they would undergo cultural transformations—that is, shifts in their behavioral, normative, and attitudinal systems—that would position them more like other Americans. While these debates constituted a crucial part of the ethnographic intellectual project of the 1960s, a very different one emerged as a result of White ethnographic pursuits in the 1990s.[8]

THE LOGIC OF THE WHITE ETHNOGRAPHIC GAZE OF THE 1990s

The 1980s was a period of sweeping public exposure to and rapid acceptance of the concept of the underclass. This term was used in social scientific inquiry and policy circles to designate a segment of the urban poor as a criminally inclined, violence-prone, and culturally deficient group of individuals who were locked in an inescapable web of economic deprivation and pathology. The underclass was made up of the most immobile and socially isolated of these urban dwellers. They had the fewest prospects for upward mobility and they experienced little sustained interaction with those in more mobile positions. Hence, they were understood to be the most immobile and socially isolated of the urban poor (Aponte 1990; Wilson 1987).

The term was a lightning rod for generating public attention to the urban poor, and not necessarily in an ultimately constructive manner. In essence, this term was used as an identifier of behavior and public demeanor (Auletta 1982). The personal characteristics and images that most often emerge around the use of the term are violence, aggression, and extreme idleness. The reemergence of a substantive ethnographic emphasis on African American communities occurred shortly after the introduction of this concept, and both Black and White scholars pursed such research under the aegis of exploring the social organizational and cultural dynamics of the underclass (Anderson 1989, 1990, and 1999; Billson 1996; Bourgois 1995; Majors and Billson 1992). Accordingly, the first wave of urban ethnography in the age of the underclass involved the employment of this term as a core descriptive device for the populations under study.[9] Moreover, much like the case with liberal social scientists in the 1960s, this perspective on culture allowed many liberal urban ethnographers to embrace aspects of the underclass thesis, even if not as wholly as many conservatives did.

While preoccupation with the term "underclass" endured from some time into the 1980s and 1990s, much of the prominent urban ethnography produced by White ethnographic scholars by the middle of the 1990s actually strove to highlight the commonalities of lower-income African American men and women with majority constituencies in American society. In essence, the objective was to exhibit certain forms of cultural similarity even in the midst of sometimes acknowledging points of difference. In a move that seemingly followed from the efforts of sociologists to criticize or abandon all together use of the term "underclass" (Wilson 1991; Gans 1995), these ethnographers attempted to frame a different image of the African American urban poor. The emerging image rested in a more intensive quest to depict individuals who often were too easily cast into the category "underclass" as more culturally similar rather than different from mainstream America.

In working toward that end, these scholars dispensed with trying to define low-income African Americans as members of a subculture or an alternative culture and instead posited that when critical investigations probed below the surface of publicly visible behavior, these people functioned as cultural agents in much the same way as did others. Moreover, many of these scholars argued that the most effective way to deliver this message was to adopt what they believed was a more illustrative or journalistic style of writing (Duneier 1992, 1999; Newman 1999). Hence, some of this ethnography appeared as straightforward reporting without extensive incorporation of social and cultural theory. The idea was to explicate the common everyday experiences of the kind of African Americans considered to be in the underclass with such depth and detail that a readership that had no more than limited exposure to this population could lucidly embrace a new vision of them. That vision was more sanitized and less exotic than what was offered by the underclass depiction.

A second approach was to write about men who did not fit the underclass depiction, but who lived near or among those classified as such. The men who were the focus on this kind of ethnography projected an alternative image of urban-based African American men, either by their social outlook or behaviors. In most cases, this was indicated by their consistent maintenance of formal employment (Duneier 1992; Lamont 2000; Wacquant 2004).

Finally, some ethnographies of this period offered cultural analyses of men who, by virtue of their income status and association with public places and street corners, seemingly fit the definition of the underclass, but through the respective analyses were found to be much more similar in social outlook and functioning to mainstream America than is conveyed by that label (Duneier 1999; Wacquant 2004).

In the course of producing two ethnographies, Mitchell Duneier strove to achieve some degree of each of these objectives. In *Slim's Table: Race, Respectability and Masculinity* (1992), Duneier captured the views and attitudes of a group of mature, working-class African American men. These men worked in blue-collar occupational sectors. Duneier conversed with them while they took lunch at a public cafeteria in the Chicago-based neighborhood in which they worked. His encounters and interactions with them demonstrated that they upheld intense commitments to going to work, providing for their families, and leading what many would construe as good and proper lives. They did so while living in communities that contain the kinds of people that are not regarded by many outsiders as willing to live such lives (e.g., the underclass).

By intention, *Slim's Table* was a highly illustrative rather than interpretive account. Instead of engaging a deep and penetrating analysis of the worldviews or other cultural properties embraced by these men, Duneier posited that the pattern of their everyday lives and the moral judgments that they make about the world in which they live affirms there is more to African American men than the depiction of the morally flawed, angry, threatening, and fatalistic underclass constituency. Hence, rather than engage contemporary cultural theory, Duneier's effort was to provide an empirically rich alternative portrait.

The empirical findings in Michelle Lamont's *The Dignity of Working Men* (2000), bear some similarity to those in Duneier's book. In her work, Lamont presents an image of working-class African American men as morally equivalent in their social outlooks and dispositions to other blue-collar and white-collar men in American society. The book is based upon a comparative analysis of how Black American, White American, French, and French immigrant men develop and apply conceptions of moral worth and value. Among other findings, Lamont argued that African American men hold particular views about multiculturalism and social diversity that differ from the views of more socioeconomically privileged people. A key claim here about working-class Black American men is that discourses abounding in academia and other privileged circles about racial inequality, social justice, multiculturalism, and other related concepts do not resonate with them in the ways that they do for people who are in those milieus. This occurs for these men despite the fact that such discourses are very much about race, social opportunity, and other matters that concern the situation of working-class African American men.

Rather than embrace that discourse as it unfolded in more privileged settings, these men draw from their own life experiences to formulate conceptions of the moral worth of individuals and ideas about fairness and justice in American life. In essence, the professed value of interracial contact and exposure that is a cornerstone of multiculturalism in more privileged spheres is of minimal interest to such working-class men, as they are more focused on achieving economic security and enhancing their social opportunities. Thus, they negate attending to philosophical principles in order to focus on more tangible desires and interests.

Ultimately, Lamont maintains a cultural theoretical agenda that is not the concern of Duneier. That is, the analytical emphasis in this work is that the men in her book (African Americans as well as the others) construe symbolic boundaries that elucidate values and beliefs that they adhere to and embrace, but that also create distance between them and those values and beliefs that they reject. However, those values and beliefs often still become attached to them by people in other social groups (i.e., people of different racial or class standings). Although they differ in the socioeconomic class categories that they consider in their work, the commonality between Lamont and Duneier is that both have produced works that speak about types of African American men who have been omitted from the public eye in the underclass debate.

In doing so, both convey the idea that such men develop moral perspectives and outlooks in the same ways that other people do (even if the content of such perspectives and outlooks may differ). Hence, rather than render portraits of Black men as different from those in the so-called mainstream, both ethnographers aimed to demystify African American men by positing that they operate as cultural agents in the same ways as other people do. Furthermore, both ethnographers aimed to tell stories about these men to audiences that appear to be socially distant and, thus, unfamiliar to them. Hence, the portraits of these men that emerge would not surprise those who have regular contact with or exposure to them. For instance, the attitudes and behaviors discussed in these works are commonly understood by many Black Americans to be representative of the kinds of men belonging to these class categories (Kelley 1997). Yet for a distant readership that has been inundated with images of the underclass for the past two decades, these portrayals deliver rather new depictions of African American men.

A work that also appears to have been written for audiences unfamiliar with socioeconomically disadvantaged people is Katherine Newman's *No Shame in My Game* (1999). This work is based on the experiences and outlooks of employees in a fast-food restaurant located in a depressed urban community. Newman's objective is to tell a story about what it means to go to work in an employment sector that many gainfully employed people regard as irrelevant when it comes to garnering significant financial remuneration. Much of the argument in this work is that the African American and Latino employees at "Burger Barn," the pseudonym for the restaurant where the study was launched, go to work simply because they imagine that such work can lead them to a better future.

Newman documents the trials and tribulations of some "Burger Barn" employees as they strive to maintain balance and security in their lives. Hence, life experiences and family circumstances of the people in her book position them as quite similar to those who have been labeled as underclass. As meaningless as employment in the fast-food industry might be for those in more secure and rewarding occupational arenas, it is quite meaningful for people who otherwise see no prospects for advancing their lives. Newman argued that the pursuit of and commitment to such work is an indication of the degree to which these people are conscientious, calculating, rational, and disciplined in their approach toward the future.

Like Duneier in his first book, Newman aims to provide a rather transparent story to a distant public that is unfamiliar with the kinds of people explored in the account. The Burger Barn scenario is a familiar one for many inner-city residents who, amid everyday living with violent-prone, unemployed, and unstable people, also know that there exist people who work hard at garnering whatever resources they can from the lower-tier work that is available in their communities, and in doing so plan their everyday lives with care and meticulousness. For those who readily accept the underclass thesis, however, *No Shame in My Game* offers a stark alternative. Moreover, like Duneier, Newman embraces the journalistic approach and asserts that urban ethnography is made richer by committing to provide elaborate stories about its subjects that are not encumbered by excessive academic jargon. Hence, while Lamont maintains some analytical objectives that extend far beyond the mandate of the journalistic approach (e.g., her efforts concerning theorizing symbolic boundary construction and maintenance), her empirical contributions serve the same end as these two works in providing information that is new to its targeted audience while familiar to people like those in the study.

Together, these works illustrate how much people who are in or close to populations that have been viewed as hypermarginal and nearly incorrigible in their moral deficiencies actually approach everyday life with the convictions, interests, and perspectives that parallel, if not fully resemble, those considered to be mainstream. The work aims not to portray Black Americans as culturally inferior or problematic, but as people who are as culturally complete and complex as other Americans. Thus, these works provide evidence that amid African American–populated urban communities riddled with violence, drug dependency, and despair there exist many people who function like those whose daily lives involve no confrontation with such social forces and pressures.

Unlike Duneier's first book and Lamont's, Katherine Newman's work focused more directly on people who have been traditionally classified as underclass. In Mitch Duneier's second book, *Sidewalk* (1999), he does the same. Here he penetrates the social world of street corner vendors in the Greenwich Village section of New York City in order to examine how they manage and regulate public space, and how they promote images of themselves in a public arena where they face the prospects of either being easily ignored or immediately regarded in the disdainful manners by which many people react to such "street-oriented" people.

Unlike the men in *Slim's Table*, the individuals in this book are on the periphery of the world of work. As they spend a considerable amount of their lives on public streets, they must find ways of handling private issues and concerns (such as relieving themselves, resolving personal conflicts and tensions, treating injuries and illnesses, or finding a meal) in the public domain, where their actions are highly visible to others. Yet, in acknowledging and exploring these circumstances Duneier also advances claims about the entrepreneurial spirit and commitment to survival that these men exemplify. He portrays them as rational, forward-thinking people who strive to achieve a sense of material and emotional security. Duneier discusses how passersby on the street corners where these men and women sell their wares, or just hang out, may often feel insecure or threatened by their presence. Yet, the sidewalk inhabitants do not dwell on their effect upon such people as much as they commit to trying to achieve as much normality and consistency as they can in their everyday lives.

Rather than restricting his analysis to a description and interpretation of public behavior, Duneier brings to surface the thoughts and feelings of these street corner vendors about what it means to spend so much of their lives in a public venue. This analytical perspective allows Duneier to position subjectivity into his work in a more thorough and immediate way than did Elliot Liebow. Liebow tended to present his own vision of what street corner behavior meant for the men in his study. His interpretations of peer interactions, involvements with children, and encounters with women (who were often the mothers of those children) often overshadowed any focus on the thoughts of the men. Duneier, by contrast, puts their thoughts in the foreground so that readers acquire a more vivid sense of how the people in his work react and respond to the unique way in which they live as public figures. In doing so, the decidedly transparent delivery of this image of Black masculinity in *Slim's Table* is rendered slightly more complex in *Sidewalk*. Accordingly, *Sidewalk* is analytically parallel to Lamont's work, as each reflects an effort to theorize rather than report.

In fact, in producing *Sidewalk* Duneier has aimed to live up to a critical challenge that he posited in chapter 9 of *Slim's Table*. There he argued that highly stereotypical images of Black Americans (and men in particular) have been intensively promoted in ethnography and the media. In that chapter, entitled, "The Stereotype of Blacks in Sociology and Journalism," he stated that this image consists of a one-sided depiction of these men as ghetto-affected such that in their behavior, social outlook, demeanor, and opinions they are made to appear as distinct and different from so-called mainstream Americans. He further proclaims that even liberal-minded ethnographic scholarship has offered an image of African American men that would be unacceptable if such an image was attached to White ethnic groups (1992, p. 140).

Duneier argued that this depiction results from an underlying conviction of a sense of moral innocence by liberal-minded ethnographers who have pursued their research out of a sincere and salient interest in contributing to the social advancement of low-income African American men (1992, 137–45). In essence, this results in portraits of these men that reify the anomic street culture and the dramatic African American male persona that was brought to life in the 1960s. To counter the continuation of this limiting, if not altogether untrue, depiction of African American men, the ethnographic tradition had to turn to more mundane, but also more consistently reflective, dimensions of the lives of these men. *Sidewalk* serves as Duneier's effort to counter the problem that he defined in *Slim's Table*. Both the argument presented in the first book and the evidence delivered in this second one comprise rather strong moves to reposition how the academic lens had been focused on low-income African American men.

One final work considered here ventured, in a nuanced way, into the low-income sphere of the African American community, like Newman and Duneier in his second book, but reflected a theoretical mandate much like Lamont's. That work, authored by Loïc Waquant, is *Body and Soul: Notebooks of an Apprentice Boxer* (2004). In this work Wacquant meets the challenge offered by Mitch Duneier to advance beyond presentations of the dramatic African American man in the public domain.[10] Yet, ironically, he does so by examining men who engage in the craft of boxing. This sport stands in the minds of many as the activity that best illustrates the kind of intense competition, violence, physicality, and hypermasculinity that is often associated with low-income African American men. A major goal for Wacquant in this book, as he has asserted quite consistently in response to others readings of the work (Wacquant 2005a, 2005b) is to shift the gaze away from African American men in urban blight and onto his own body as he immerses himself into the social world of the pugilist. In the course of doing so, however, his work ultimately helps to resituate the image of the African American men who are the far majority of his gym-mates during his years of involvement with a South Side boxing gymnasium in Chicago. He achieves this end by positing that African American men who engage in this sport are most successful at it as a result of having to function in the kind of orderly and disciplined manner that is rarely associated with life in urban depressed regions.

Those traits are evident in the training regiments and actual boxing matches, as well as in the caution and care men must take with their bodies when outside of the training facility or boxing arena. Hence, while telling a story about himself, Wacquant also explains that the African American male, at least those who participate in boxing, actually reflect many of the most valued principles and traits in a modern American social world that promotes (if not always abides by) the values of hard work and discipline. Accordingly, even though the site for Wacquant's work is a relatively unusual place in terms of the terrain that most people navigate in their daily lives (and in many ways exotic in its own right), he entered into it to produce an account that promotes normality as a trait that urban-based, low-income African American men can embrace.

In essence, then, the prominent works of White ethnographers of the 1990s reflected one or more of a series of tendencies. They either provided empirical information expressly targeted to a distant and presumably uninformed audience (Duneier 1992; Lamont 2000; Newman 1999), created a more diverse portrait of urban-based African American men by investigating men who did not easily fit the description of the underclass (Duneier 1992; Lamont 2000; Wacquant 2004), or peered into the lives of the kind of low-income African American men (and sometimes women) who would be defined as underclass in order to create a different image and reading of them (Duneier 1999; Wacquant 2004). Despite the sometimes strong differences in style and emphasis between the ethnographic products of Wacquant, Duneier, Newman, and Lamont, they come together in reflecting a particular moment of 1990s-era cultural analysis. They aim to foreground low-income and working-class African American men as culturally similar to those classified as mainstream Americans. The effort to forward such a vision in the immediate post-underclass intellectual climate is a radical turn in comparison to the claims made by 1960s-era ethnographers, who more often held steadfast to some demarcation of these people as culturally distinct. The implications of the claims of the 1990s-era scholars will now be explored in greater depth.

The Cultural Political and Intellectual Legacy of the White Ethnographic Project of the 1990s

Those who are intimately familiar with the African American urban poor may be struck by how straightforward the findings are in some of the urban ethnography produced by 1990s-era White scholars. This body of work was not always designed to offer novel empirical insight to those who live among, or in close proximity to, this population. However, I maintain that the point for much of this work is not to deliver such insight, but rather to more explicitly convey to people who now are farther removed from this constituency (geographically as well as cognitively) than they have been for many decades what is commonsense knowledge of low-income Black Americans and about how they engage their everyday lives. While White ethnographers were conducting their studies and publishing their findings, scholars in another subfield of sociology, social demography, were making clear exactly how wide and severe the geographical and, by implication, social divide between Black and White Americans had become (Farley 1984, 1996; Farley and Allen 1987; Massey and Denton 1993).

Unlike the 1960s, when large numbers of White Americans still had some experience with living in what is today known as the inner city, the notion of the underclass emerged as White Americans fled the urban core of many American cities. This meant that increasing numbers of White Americans would have to learn whatever they desired to about the experiences and plight of low-income Black Americans from the media or from academic research-based publications. It also meant that such learning would commence from a position of considerable ignorance about low-income African Americans except for the myriad images of the underclass that were disseminated throughout that period. The social context of racial distancing in America, then, facilitated the kind of agenda that emerged for White ethnographers who studied Black Americans in the 1990s.

White ethnographers of African American men in the 1990s share with their counterparts of the 1960s a desire to translate an understanding of a particular kind of social experience to a less-informed but curious audience. The difference is that rather than highlighting cultural and social differences (i.e., "this is why these people seemingly behave differently in comparison to us even if, along some points of analytical consideration, they may not be") the more recent work foregrounds particular aspects of cultural sameness (i.e., "these people behave very much like us, they just have fewer resources, and thus, less social options and opportunities to choose from, than we do").

CONCLUSION

Aside from the extensive proliferation of ethnography on the urban African American experience by White scholars, the periods of the 1960s and the 1990s stand out because of the two very different agendas associated with each. While much of the work of the 1960s aimed to highlight, investigate, and interpret the presumed social difference of African American men and so-called mainstream Americans, that of the 1990s aimed to stress cultural and social commonalities. An ironic feature of each period is that *differences* were acknowledged in the 1960s, when integration had emerged as a prominent societal mandate (although that mandate was never fully realized, and not very much promoted, by either Black or White Americans by the decade's end) while *commonalities* were stressed in the 1990s, a period when the lexicon of underclass alluded to extreme social and cultural differences between many Black and White Americans. White ethnographers were able to promote this agenda in the respective periods of time because they were uniquely positioned to serve as less partisan message bearers to academic and civic audiences precisely because they were not Black Americans.[11]

All scholarship is shaped by social and political contexts. A pivotal social context concerning the work produced by White ethnographers on African American men is that their outsider status afforded them great potential to function as impartial conveyors of information to a distant audience. This circumstance has more to do with the ways in which an audience receives such work than the efforts or intention of the authors, but the point remains nonetheless. Accordingly, when taking into account that the broader sociopolitical climate of the 1990s, when such work was produced, was much more conservative than that of the 1960s, issues of social and political context mattered in particular ways for audience reception as much as for scholarly production. That being said, it has also been clearly demonstrated by researchers that many Americans are less preoccupied with, attentive to, or tolerant of representations of American society as systematically racist (Bobo et al. 1997; Doane and Bonilla-Silva 2003; Sears et al. 2000). Hence, some of the consequences of White ethnographic exploration of the urban-based, low-income African American experience is that this work informs a constituency that racism matters in ways that are not as easily dismissed (or immediately regarded as ideologically loaded and biased) as is sometimes the case with the work of African American scholars. Thus, in some of the work of White ethnographers robust and complex models of cultural analysis did not come to the surface precisely because the intention of such work has been to more explicitly to inform constituencies that have minimal means of apprehending the normality of such African Americans.

What also matters contemporarily in terms of the relevance of social and political context is that the higher educational landscape is riddled with debate about the degree to which clear access remains for people of color and the socioeconomically disadvantaged (Orfield and Miller 1998). A consequence of demographic shifts that diminish the presence of low-income African Americans in this milieu is that scholarship takes on the role of providing insight about these people's lives at the expense of much sustained interaction with them. This provides a venue for White scholars to address and inform these audiences with information that conveys what for low-income African Americans is virtually commonsense logic about who they are and how they live their lives. The great irony is that fairly straightforward and direct arguments get constituted as significant breakthroughs precisely because there exists less familiarity with this population on the part of audiences for such work. The agenda for more far-reaching and daring cultural analysis is, in essence, put on hold so that the readership of such scholarship can reconcile with the more basic task of understanding better the everydayness of low-income African American people.

If that agenda can be pursued in the future, it will be beneficial for it to take the form of comparative cultural analyses that allow the study of low-income African American men to shed insight and understanding about the American social condition, rather than just being depicted as a problematic group within America. That is, cultural models, paradigms, and interpretations must be built from analyses of the experiences of low-income African Americans that are not restricted to social problem solving or to illustrating the everyday realities of their lives. Rather such analyses must lead to enhancing and refining the modern vocabulary of cultural analysis that, in addition to the traditional words such as *norms, values, attitudes,* and *behaviors,* includes such concepts as agency, *structuration, habitus,* and others that comprise the modern project of cultural analysis. A richer and fuller understanding of what each of these terms means in and for American society, and the world at large, can only be achieved by elevating the African American urban poor to the analytical landscape that other groups share so that rather than these people being viewed as a special social problem case, they acquire full recognition as informers of the human experience and condition. Perhaps this will constitute an ethnographic project of the twenty-first century. If so, and if White and Black scholars fully engage that project, the discipline of sociology can only stand to benefit.

NOTES

1. Historians of social science have debated the various causal factors leading to the production of this scholarship, but one point of common understanding is that

vastly increased private and governmental funding for research in urban poverty in the 1960s was a key catalyst for this unfolding (O'Connor 2001). Thus, it was with public sector, foundation, and federal government attention and support that large numbers of White scholars began pouring into low-income, urban-based, African American neighborhoods in order to uncover and document the cultural properties and social dynamics of Black Americans.

2. The proliferation of a more theoretically expansive and sophisticated pursuit of meaning making would comprise a later period of cultural sociology. Thus, these terms, which may appear to be rather trite concepts when assessed in the context of contemporary research and theory in cultural analysis, became the central concepts for such analysis in 1960s-era urban ethnography. Indeed, a watershed moment that constituted the turn toward a more theoretically and conceptually broad cultural analysis was the publication of Clifford Geertz's *The Interpretations of Culture* (1973). This work paved the way for cultural sociological investigations of meaning making, the social factors relevant to the formation of individual and collective belief systems, and the interconnection of beliefs and actions. These issues were central to the agenda for cultural sociology in the following decades (Bourdieu 1990; Giddens 1984; Swidler and Arditi 1994; Wuthnow 1987; Wuthnow and Witten 1988; Zerubavel 1997).

3. In the 1950s sociologists produced a series of works during a moment of provocative cultural criticism. These works argued that homogenization and complacency were emerging phenomena in a society that had become overwhelmed by technology and the rationalization impulses that were attributes of an advanced industrial social order fueled by modern capitalism (Marcuse 1964; Mills 1959; Riesman 1950). This work was not produced from ethnographic data, but was more theoretically centered commentary. Little attention was paid to Black Americans in this work, so that the arguments about the emerging homogeneity of American culture were constructed without any sense of whether, and if so, how African Americans were situated within it. This exclusion also helped position African Americans outside of most conceptions of normative referents in American society, and in the discipline of sociology in particular. Consequently, rather than being investigated through a more balanced comparative lens, research on Black Americans was pursued in the 1960s with such people essentially predetermined to be a nonnormative group.

4. A significant part of the rational for the emphasis on the presumably problematic state of cultural difference between White and Black Americans can be attributed to American sociology's early twentieth-century preoccupation with the cultural and social assimilation of African Americans into American society (see McKee 1993). The assimilationist logic reigned supreme in much of the mid-twentieth-century social analysis concerning Black Americans. An elaborate account of how this logic applied to studies of African American men is found in Young (2004).

5. Lewis presented a number of tenets in explaining the culture of poverty. First, despair and hopelessness were argued to develop from the realizations of inability to get ahead in life (or to achieve the values and goals maintained in the larger society). Apathy, hostility, and suspicion comprised the general state of psychological being for those immersed in the culture of poverty. Children were explained as psychologically unprepared to take advantage of changing conditions or increased op-

portunities if any were to come their way. Adults in the culture of poverty were seen as lacking the ability to effectively participate and integrate into mainstream institutions. They also were perceived as incapable of organizing for their own behalf. Finally, adults also were viewed as being minimally engaged with their children due to the adults' preoccupation with the problems of being poor.

Essentially, the culture-of-poverty thesis argued that the behavior and values of the poor led to an enclosed, self-perpetuating, and intergenerational world of dependence. Unfortunately, although Lewis argued that structural contexts such as employment opportunities were critical factors in the proliferation of poverty, he said little about precisely how the structural context mattered and how it intersected with culture. This helped the emphasis on culture as an all encompassing, generative force that leads to the reproduction of poverty to reign supreme in reactions to his work and elaborations on his ideas by other scholars.

6. Liebow's excursion into a discussion of shadow culture demonstrates that despite his claims about a shared value system in his effort to delineate cultural differences between low-income African Americans and those regarded as mainstream he also was compelled to question the degree to which such value systems were shared.

7. A key underlying factor in the ethnographic pursuit of lower-income African Americans during this era was the intrigue over what was perceived to be potentially extreme differences in the cultural repertoires of Black and White Americans. Some of this intrigue was reflected in their manner of speaking, styles of bodily expression, and basic attitudes toward life that Charles Keil articulated is his book, *Urban Blues* (1966). Indeed, by the 1960s, many people began to regard African American expressiveness as "cool." That expressiveness became all the more acceptable in an American social landscape where different forms of expression and public demeanor began to draw popular attention.

8. At the time of the production of this research, some African American scholars whole-heartedly rejected the legitimacy of thinking about Black Americans as having to adopt the cultural fabric of White America (Ladner 1973). The critical challenges offered by African Americans to the scholarship produced about them in the 1960s was sustained by a later generation of African American scholarly critique of that period of research (Kelley 1997; Scott 1997). This new effort has posed a robust challenge to some scholars' quest to ascertain a durable and comprehensive conception of African American urban or low-income subculture. These contributions resemble those of anthropologist Charles Valentine (1968), who first argued that much of the 1960s era ethnography stood on faulty grounds as it contained a vastly underdeveloped emphasis on social structure as well as an absence of comparative analysis.

9. Bourgois's work is not treated in this chapter more systematically because, although he fits the definition employed here of a White ethnographer, his study focused on Latinos more so than African Americans.

10. I maintain that Wacquant's claims about African American boxers stand as an example of the counterimage of such men that Duneier called for in chapter 9 of *Slim's Table*, despite the fact that both Wacquant and Duneier have asserted that the other has not been consistently committed to advancing such a counterimage (Wacquant 2002; Duneier 2002).

11. I stand in sympathy with much of the 1990s ethnographic project as I, too, have aimed to produce scholarship that challenges the underclass thesis that circumscribes much public perception of low-income African American men (Young 1999, 2000, 2004, 2006). One difference between my efforts and those of some White ethnographers is that I aim to direct my work at (sometimes quite esoteric) issues of meaning making that are at the core of cultural and social theory rather than catering to a more journalistic style of writing. A second difference, which distinguishes me from all of the 1990s-era White ethnographers, is that in the course of presenting lectures and in general conversation about this work, I have been implicitly and explicitly labeled as an impartial commentator because as an African American male I present a more compassionate, rather than intensely critical, portrait of such people.

V

DIMENSIONS OF SEGREGATION AND INEQUALITY TYPICALLY MISSED

12

Indices of Racial Residential Segregation

A Critical Review and Redirection

Brent Berry

No single methodological orientation or measure can quantify segregation because it is a multilevel concept. Segregation is in one sense the lack of social contact between status groups due to structured opportunities and spatial mismatch (Grimes 1993). But it is also unequal sharing of a broader range of social activities, relationships, and identities that fortify different forms of separateness between groups that may be in contact (e.g., DeSena 1990; Grimes 1993; Fisher and Hartman 1995; Zuberi 2001a). Thus, both the quantity and quality of contact, or lack thereof, as experienced and felt by different group members are elements of segregation.

The most common measures of segregation provide only a trace of this broader conception. For example, the index of dissimilarity is the degree to which two groups are spread evenly among neighborhoods in a metropolitan area. The index is typically interpreted as the percentage of Blacks (or other minority group) needing to move to achieve an "even" residential pattern—one where every neighborhood replicates the racial composition of the entire metropolitan area. It varies between 0 and 1.0, with the number of minority members moving expressed as the proportion of the number that would have to move under conditions of maximum segregation (Jakubs 1979).[1] For example, if a neighborhood is 20 percent Black, but a city is only 10 percent Black, then achieving an even residential pattern for the city requires half of the Blacks in such neighborhoods to move elsewhere.

In this chapter I first discuss three limitations of segregation indices—they equate proximity with contact, they are cross-sectional, and they discount the distinctiveness of cities when used in comparative studies. Second, I advocate for an expanded conceptual view of segregation as a multidimensional form of separateness defined by macro-, meso-, and micro-boundaries. Segregation indices speak only to the "hard" macro-level territorial boundaries approximated by census tracts. Other meso-level boundaries within neighborhoods influence intergroup contact through spatial, temporal, and organizational means. Micro-level situational and predispositional boundaries also influence the quantity and quality of contact. Third, I conclude by offering a range of approaches for measuring segregation. Rather than abandoning conventional indices, I argue that they are valuable tools in the toolbox of segregation researchers when used in a more restricted way.

THREE PROBLEMS WITH SEGREGATION INDICES

I focus on three problematic assumptions with segregation indices, using the index of dissimilarity as an example (henceforth, the index).[2] First, the index relies on weak inferences linking spatial proximity to contact because it is not based on contact per se. Second, the index for a particular city is a cross-sectional indicator that does not use any information on migration or metropolitan change over time. Third, the index's frequent use in nationally comparative studies eschews the distinctive histories and features of individual cities and the groups that live there.[3] These limitations apply not just to the index of dissimilarity, but to all of the common segregation indices.

Proximity Does Not Equal Contact

The value of segregation indices for gauging race relations depends on the extent to which physical proximity is associated with positive intergroup contact. The contact hypothesis has generated widespread debate because it assumes that "social relations are inevitably correlated with spatial relations . . . physical distances are, or seem to be, the indexes of social distances" (Park 1926; see also Powers and Ellison 1995 and Sigelman et al. 1996). Not long after Park's work, Drake and Cayton (1993) began to document the role of informal social networks and routine processes of social exclusion on intergroup contact *even when there was physical proximity between groups*. They were critical of positions that equated physical contact with substantive integration, calling it "doubtful, however, whether [such contact can] play a dominant part in shifting the line of color." (1993, 126). They also called for attention to the context of these racial contacts, warning that, in reality, "[s]uch contacts do little to create goodwill among White people, but they do leave a residue of resentment among Negroes"(1993, 126).

Despite criticism of the contact hypothesis, the measurement of segregation has been dominated by indices of physical separation that regard proximity as a proxy of substantive integration. None of the measures examine the nature of physical barriers, interaction within communities (Grannis 1998), or the cultural and symbolic boundaries of meaning internalized within individual actors (Alexander 1988, 312). Weak theorizations that equate proximity with social closeness miss the ways that racism can maintain separateness in diverse situations. For example, Brazilian Blacks on the whole have many more apparent racial contacts than U.S. Blacks, but are much worse off in terms of income differences, labor market position, child mortality, and life expectancy (Telles 1992). Proximity provides only a weak opportunity structure for meaningful contact because the quality of contact depends on the details of environments and actors' interpretations of one another. Important contextual factors in a particular social arena include the level of contact, the formality of contact, status differences, group ties, familiarity, mutual respect for and membership in social institutions, shared symbolic understanding of the situation, and similar access to resources. In some cases, proximity per se may deter social integration by exposing minorities to more diverse forms of racism. Thus, "racial contacts" *do not* necessarily mean substantive integration, since there are significant forms of racism and exclusion compatible with "physical closeness" (Bonilla-Silva et al. 2004; Fine and Weis 1998).

The Index Is Cross-Sectional

Segregation indices are cross-sectional measures of the departure of an observed pattern of settlement at one point in time (e.g., tract-level census data in 2000) from an *idealized* pattern of "evenness" rather than from an *observed* pattern of settlement at an earlier time (e.g., 1970). This distinction is important because underlying processes may re-create segregation in different ways but not change the calculated value of the index. For example, the index of dissimilarity for the city of Detroit has remained between 0.83 and 0.85 since 1960 despite dramatic shifts in population and activity that have effectively reconfigured segregation over this period. In other cities, integration that some scholars have implied from modestly declining spatial measures may have as much to do with poverty and falling incomes of poor Whites, or simply the restructuring of urban space through gentrification (see e.g., Farley and Frey 1994; Fischer et al. 2004; Logan et al. 2004). Changes over time in the concentration of a city's population, activity, and job distribution are not controlled for in segregation indices.

As Carmines and Zeller (1979) have observed, the index does not account for the expansion-based processes of resettlement and urban growth underlying patterns of segregation emerging since the 1950s. Incentives for "White flight" in the 1960s may have been substantially different from those in the 1990s, but segregation measures cannot convey differences in the perceived push and pull factors of individuals in those two periods. Before the rapid sprawling of metropolitan areas, segregation was largely maintained through processes of contestation within existing urban territories (Lieberson 1980). Beginning in the 1950s, "in-place" segregation has been gradually replaced by segregation through metropolitan expansion and White flight to new communities. Index values for many cities between 1960 and 2000 have remained stable and high, silent to their internal reconfiguration through processes of migration, suburbanization, and boundary creation over that period.

Interpreting cross-sectional measures over time is unclear unless the unit of analysis (cities and metro areas) remains constant or is appropriately controlled for in the analysis (James and Taeuber 1985). Otherwise, interpretations are ambiguous because changes in the spatial layout of cities and their population (their "morphology") are confounded with the calculated values of the index. An appropriate longitudinal measure of segregation would need to "difference" change over time to internally account for cities as they were in the past.

Without some accounting for changes in the underlying processes that produce segregation values, the indices' usefulness is diminished and sometimes may be misleading. Pinkney (1984) argues that a "myth of black progress" has been reinforced by relying on traditional demographic indices to assess the status of racial minorities. He argues that comparing indices of residential segregation today to those of the 1950s without such accounting presents a felicitous image of Blacks (or other minority groups) in the post–civil rights era because reported declines in segregation may be due to changes independent of race relations.

Intermetropolitan Comparisons Discount Intracity Change and Uniqueness

A number of studies compare segregation indices across cities (e.g., Frey and Myers 2005). Comparing indices across cities discounts the uniqueness of each area. The consequence is that the index fails to capture details of segregation within and across neighborhoods; rather, it is used to compare different cities at one point in time. Each city or metropolitan area has unique histories of racial migration, built environments, size, and overall level of diversity. For these reasons, it is difficult to fairly compare different cities. Because most of the population movement between censuses is within a city or metropolitan area, intrametropolitan analyses over time provide a better opportunity for understanding the dynamics of segregation.

For example, it is difficult to compare segregation between many Southern and Northern industrial cities because African Americans in Southern cities have traditionally lived as much in the rural areas as in the urban centers. Likewise, recently emerging large cities like Phoenix, Orlando, or Tampa are substantially more likely to have gated communities and cul-de-sac neighborhoods than the grid-patterns of Detroit, Chicago, and Newark. Thus, the distinctive historical patterns of population (e.g., rural Blacks in the South) and recent differences in the development of the residential environments (e.g., cul-de-sacs, gated communities) compromise cross-national comparisons.

THE MULTILEVEL BOUNDARIES OF SEGREGATION

An expanded conception of segregation encompasses both spatial-opportunity distance (e.g., living in different neighborhoods) and social-psychological distance (e.g., avoidance, denying close relationships, selective membership, shared identities and language). Segregation indices limit their focus to racial contacts that are presumed to flow from proximity. However, feelings of trust, familiarity, and the confidence that others would help in the event of trouble require some agreed sense of togetherness, but not necessarily a close relationship. An integrated community exists when such resources are equally distributed both within and between groups. Conversely, a segregated community can be described by the absence of these characteristics and processes.

Boundaries are a rich tool for describing this expanded conception of segregation (Emirbayer 1997; Pellow 1996). Boundaries separate "us" from "them" by regulating the distribution of social and symbolic resources (Lamont and Molnar 2002). Individuals, groups, and organizations actively harness their social and symbolic resources to do "boundary work." To varying degrees, boundaries in place today retain the historical imprint of boundary work in the past, so historical perspectives are important.

At least three levels of boundaries describe segregation. The "macro-level" refers to residential boundaries across communities (e.g., living in different neighborhoods). These territorial boundaries prevent groups from being physically close. Conventional segregation indices gauge the extent to which groups are physically close, or share these macro-boundaries. Ideally, a stronger theorization of segregation in the macro tradition goes beyond basic territorial boundaries to emphasize structural (physical and social) and institutional features that deny access to symbolic and social resources (Lamont and Molnar 2002).

"Meso-level" boundaries account for segregation within communities, whereby different racial/ethnic groups may live in the same neighborhood but seldom make contact due to temporal, spatial, and organizational boundaries. Rather than precluding contact, these boundaries minimize the likelihood of contact under equal status, cooperative, and personal bases (Allport 1954). These boundaries can be both in-place in the environment, or erected in situations to avoid intergroup contact.

"Micro-level boundaries manifest themselves in situations based on contextual information and predispositional schemas. At this level, actors are in physical proximity and even making superficial contact, but seldom share social and symbolic resources in the form of close ties or mutual feelings of membership or identification. While macro- and meso-boundaries are tied to a setting (e.g., the neighborhood), micro-boundaries follow individuals across contexts. A strong theorization of micro-boundaries emphasizes the situational and predispositional factors of routine racial practices, paying close attention to how actors read, interpret, and respond to group differences. Micro-boundaries are both (1) situational responses to immediate verbal and nonverbal cues that deter interaction and identification, and (2) predispositional, responses to intangible psychological characteristics, such as schemas or scripts that are either preexisting or revealed upon engagement. These schemas or scripts brought to a given situation reflect the culmination of an actor's social and cognitive development. However, actors are not automatons driven by these internal scripts alone. They also creatively interpret their environments.

IMPROVED SEGREGATION INDICES AND ALTERNATE APPROACHES

Different methodological approaches help reveal which boundaries of segregation are operating in a setting. Approaches focusing on macro-level boundaries include segregation indices and careful study of how physical features of neighborhoods and built environments limit intergroup contact. Approaches focusing on the meso- and micro-level boundaries of segregation seek to reveal the scripts, schemas, and space-time arrangements within neighborhoods that underlie segregation when groups are proximate.

Retooling Existing Segregation Indices

Existing segregation indices can be used in a more restricted way that better reflects the weaknesses described above. First, comparisons of the index across many cities should be discouraged in favor of within-city comparisons over time. Second, researchers should interpret measures of segregation relative to past settlement patterns. The index is currently interpreted as the proportion of one group that would have to relocate to achieve "evenness." This simple interpretation does not provide much practical knowledge of how to undo segregation because it has no factual basis on real data about population change over time or spatial properties of metropolitan areas. A more policy-relevant measure of residential segregation would be longitudinal, answering a question like "What would be the value of the index had a historically realistic process happened instead of what actually happened?"

Using existing indices to answer such a counterfactual question requires turning attention to the processes that changed settlement patterns within cities between time points. For example, "What would be the value of the index had Whites moved at the same rates as Blacks between 1950 and 1990?" This use of the index allows for the proposal and testing of counterfactual scenarios consisting of *processes* of settlement that might have occurred if suburban growth and/or migration patterns were different. The answer to this question is found by projecting the past to the present by applying processes derived from past information. Analysts would compare real index values with those computed under a counterfactual scenario. Such a shift in emphasis allows scholars to focus on conveying hypothesized *processes* of population migration and redistribution from one census to the next. For example, comparing real to simulated segregation indices can give insight into how residential segregation remained high despite tremendous metropolitan expansion and suburban growth since 1950. A window into what processes change or maintain residential segregation is more informative than static snapshots. Furthermore, the interpretations are more policy relevant, as they address causes of residential segregation.

Scholars have begun to use simulation approaches to answer counterfactual questions about metropolitan change over time (Epstein and Axtell 1996; Robinson 1981). Simulating requires the analyst to evolve the residential locations of a synthetic population based on actual tract-level data to a hypothetical metropolitan distribution ten years later. The migration reassignments are made probabilistically according to hypothesized reasons for migration and loosely constrained by known parameters of the overall population in the future. The set of hypotheses that yield a simulated population closest to the actual observed distribution are likely to identify the most important macro-level processes.

This approach is superior for focusing on processes of intermetropolitan change, the dynamics of segregation within cities, emphasizing historical data, emphasizing structural/institutional/ecological causes, and the policy relevance of the conclusions. Comparing simulated to actual indices doesn't focus on any particular group moving, but points to the role of institutional decisions and structural changes in influencing migration (e.g., urban planning and development priorities, mortgage lending practices, job restructuring). Disadvantages of this approach are that modeling is data and computation intensive and the hypothetical process must be specified using a small set of probabilistic rules.

Physical Features within Communities

Residential segregation arises not only from physical distance per se, but from physical environmental barriers, such as the absence of small, residential streets that connect different neighborhoods and promote pedestrian traffic. Grannis (1998) found that physical features that bridge communities, such as tertiary streets, are stronger predictors of contact than mere proximity. Specifically, he argues that the presence of "tertiary streets" (those with one lane on each side and no divider, which are designed to promote pedestrian traffic) connecting "t-communities" (in which every household is reachable from every other household by using only tertiary streets) better predicts racial composition than spatial proximity. This approach adds to what we know from indices of residential segregation by showing that "segregated networks of neighborly relations [can] emerge from segregated networks of residential streets" (1530). An extension of Grannis's approach would examine smaller physical features such as sidewalks, which are also thought to promote integration (Jacobs 1961; Duneier 1999).

Segregation Indices of Interracial Couples and Households

A good indicator of an integrated neighborhood may be its extent of *interracial households* and *interracial couples*. The extent of racially mixed households in a census tract is in some ways superior to simple group proportions (the basis of convention indices) because within household diversity reflects direct social contact and intention to co-reside. People who choose to co-reside, whether for romantic or instrumental reasons, are much more likely to have social contact that is equal status, cooperative, and personal (Allport 1954). Furthermore, interracial couples are probably more likely to choose a place to live that they perceive to be more welcoming in terms of racial boundary crossing.

A new index based on this idea would represent a contact-based alternative to the index of dissimilarity. The first simple index is the neighborhood (e.g., tract) mean of intergroup contact through marriage relative to what is expected:

$$\text{Mean of Contact} = 1/N\ (\Sigma\ \text{actual}_i/\text{expected}_i)$$

where $actual_i$ is the rate of intergroup marriages in neighborhood i . . . N, while $expected_i$ is the rate of intergroup marriages if there were a random assortment based on population proportions in the neighborhood. A second "evenness" measure of contact through intermarriage is:

$$\text{Evenness of Contact} = 1/2\ (\Sigma\ |actual_i/Actual - expected_i/Expected|)$$

where Actual and Expected are the real and expected rates of intergroup marriage for the entire city. Unfortunately, except for the 1970 census data, tract-level data about the rates of interracial households or couples are not available to researchers.[4]

Indices of Friendship Segregation

As with interracial marriage, friendship segregation is a desirable measure because it reflects contact. Friendship has received less attention, but may be one of the best gauges of race relations because it is a less formal and less permanent relationship than either marriage or residential segregation (Berry 2006; Quillian and Campbell 2003). While census data make it possible to examine interracial marriage and household composition, no data to my knowledge permits estimation of interracial friendship segregation at smaller levels of geography.

APPROACHES FOCUSING ON MESO- AND MICRO-BOUNDARIES

A number of scholars have investigated the meso- and micro-boundaries that influence the amount and quality of intergroup contact (e.g., Drake and Cayton 1993; Jacobs 1961; Anderson 1990, 1999; DeSena 1990, 1994; Duneier 1999; Lamont 1999; Klinenberg 2002). Like foundational work by scholars from the Chicago school of community studies, this body of work examines social and symbolic boundaries via labeling and categorization (Erikson 1966; Suttles 1968). Several approaches can give a closer look at how residents use their residential environments and negotiate boundaries within them. For example, DeSena (1990) used in-depth interviews and personal observations to examine the formal and informal strategies used by residents of Greenpoint, Brooklyn, to maintain non-Hispanic White neighborhoods against an influx of visible minorities. Anderson (1999) studied how Black residents in poor neighborhoods of Philadelphia come to make distinctions between the "decent" and "street" people with whom they have contact. Fine and Weis (1998) discuss how poor Whites are hypervigilant of borders as a way of maintaining one of the last areas they believe they can control: the domestic front.

I will briefly review these approaches.

Systematic Social Observation (SSO)

SSO has been used to examine whether visible physical and social disorder in neighborhoods is correlated with crime, violence, and health. It can be used to quantify the physical conditions and social interactions within neighborhoods, providing a perspective of that environment that is independent of residents' perceptions, provides quantifiable data, and can be replicated (Sampson and Raudenbush 1999; Ross and Mirowsky 2001). Within communities, SSO is useful for measuring the spatial, temporal, organizational (meso-level), and situation (micro-level) boundaries that community members are either unaware of or unwilling to discuss in face-to-face interviews or focus groups. For instance, systematic observation of public corridors, social contact areas, and flows within the community might gauge the suitability and appeal of public spaces, revealing the subtle physical features and routine patterns of interaction that residents take for granted but that affect the degree of social integration. To assess the potential racial/ethnic patterning of usage, one could systematically observe shared laundry rooms, swimming pools, or playgrounds within a community to see if distinct groups time their usage of facilities to maintain social distance. In this vein, Clack et al. (2005) studied racial interaction in lunchrooms. Another possibility would be to observe apartment building lobbies or other shared spaces to obtain objective counts of different facial expressions, clothing styles, and systematic racial differences in the use of space (e.g., stairs vs. elevator). Such boundaries might correlate with, and help explain, more direct measures of segregation, such as the extent of interracial friendships, marriages, and shared feelings of membership. SSO is limited for (1) not directly considering residents' viewpoints, (2) potentially misinterpreting observable behavior that may play a beneficial role within the community, and (3) being obtrusive by observing public spaces without permission (Raudenbush and Sampson 1999).

Survey Interviews

Surveys of residents in a community can help depict the micro- and meso-boundaries of segregation. Micro-level boundaries can be studied with survey questions about the interests, values, and beliefs of residents about intergroup contact. The meso-level boundaries can also be studied with creative survey items. *Inventories of the organizations* residents belong to, descriptions of *competing interests*, and the *timing* and location of activities can also be systematically recorded with surveys. Surveys can also give insight into why people live in some neighborhoods but not others. Survey data is one of the only sources for estimating the actual levels of cross-ethnic engagement and shared feelings of membership in a neighborhood that may appear to be semi-integrated. A substantial literature on interracial friendship has used survey data to determine if opportunity for contact in schools has translated into intergroup friendship (Quillian and Campbell 2003).

Unfortunately, some respondents will not honestly describe their own experiences, motives, and thoughts (Nisbett and Wilson 1977). Respondents are often motivated to avoid telling what they perceive to be the truth; as DeSena (1990, 30) puts it, "Respondents know the socially desirable answers to questions on race and ethnic relations." Nevertheless, face-to-face interviews can capture how people consciously (and openly) perceive, describe, and make sense of their lives, and might yield invaluable insight into the meso- and micro-level boundaries that SSO and broader statistical measures cannot.

Feeling thermometers. These are questions that measure affinity or repulsion to other groups present in their neighborhood. As mentioned earlier, however, most people are wary about responding to such questions in a "politically correct" manner. Asking residents how warm they feel toward Blacks, Whites, Arabs, and other ethnic groups may miss covert feelings of racial animosity. *Hypothetical vignettes* are a more sensitive technique for gauging distrust or prejudice toward particular groups (Moreland and Beach 1992).

Organizational inventories. Asking community members to fill in an inventory of the organizations they belong to both inside and outside the neighborhood may reveal the racial "mismatch" in the use of public/private schools, hospitals, sports leagues, country clubs, churches, and other community groups (as well as occupation/place of employment). In addition, the researcher could randomly select a few respondents of each prominent racial/ethnic group in the community and ask them to elaborate on why they joined the organizations they did and whether they perceive those organizations as "integrated."

Competing interests. Residents could be asked to rate the relative importance of a series of competing interests as they relate to hindering or encouraging interracial ties. The particular interests might be derived from a standardized list or adapted to the community under study (e.g., a list might be generated or modified during preliminary focus groups). Competing interests that may affect the degree of racial/ethnic social integration include: a busy family life, a busy work or school life, different activity interests, different values, and so on. Such a measure would begin to assess the relative importance of an array of micro-level boundaries.

Cognitive mapping. Map drawing is one way to discover subjective definitions of "neighborhood" and patterns of interaction. To measure spatial boundaries, one could use various map-based measures. For instance, residents might be shown a map of their city sector, and first asked to draw their "neighborhood." After defining their neighborhood geographically, residents would be asked to draw the path(s) that they usually take to work, the grocery store, and other activities inside and outside the neighborhood. They would describe their mode of transportation and typical social interactions along those paths. As for the time-use measure, if enough observations were gathered, one could begin to assess any racial/ethnic differences in the usage of space that may contribute to social segregation.

Boundary crossers. What groups would be more aware of the boundaries needed to foster interracial social ties than interracial couples and members of interracial households? A study delving into the trials and tribulations of this exceptional population would highlight many of the boundaries preventing segregation and convey through personal biographies ways of overcoming them.

Demographic mismatch in semi-integrated communities. The semi-integrated neighborhoods that middle-class Blacks live in tend to be lower–middle-class neighborhoods, with the class standing of Whites in the neighborhood being significantly lower than that of Blacks in it (Alba et al. 2000a). While some of these neighborhoods may appear to be integrating according to various segregation indices, a closer look shows that Blacks still pay a significant "penalty" of demographic mismatch, a fact obscured by aggregate indices. Other aggregate indices also distort the racial picture (e.g., racial differences in life expectancy largely reflect differences in infant mortality rather than poor health behaviors or violence of adulthood). This demographic mismatch in "semi-integrated" neighborhoods should be considered in conjunction with simple segregation indices when interpreting the likelihood of contact.

NOTES

1. The index of dissimilarity measures departure from evenness by taking the weighted deviation of every neighborhood's minority proportion from the metropolitan area's minority proportion, and expressing this quantity as a proportion of its theoretical maximum (James and Taeuber 1985; Massey and Denton 1993). The equation is

$$D = 1/2 \left(\Sigma \mid bi/b - wi/w \mid \right)$$

where bi and wi are the number of Black and White persons living in an area i, and b and w are the total number of Blacks and Whites in the city, respectively.

2. Several studies have critically debated the statistical qualities of segregation indices (Cortese et al. 1976; Grannis 2002; James and Taeuber 1985).

3. This is not an exhaustive list of problems. See Duncan and Duncan (1955), Cortese et al. (1976), and Jakubs (1979) for discussion of the statistical problems with segregation measures.

4. Personal communication with John Iceland, U.S. Census Bureau (May 2004), and Douglas Massey, Princeton University (December 2005).

13

Qui Bono?

Explaining—or Defending—Winners and Losers in the Competition for Educational Achievement

Walter R. Allen, Susan A. Suh, Gloria González, and Joshua Yang

Who benefits under the current system of education? Who are the winners and losers—and why—in terms of educational achievement? California's economic success was built on a well-educated workforce; therefore, the current crisis of public education compromises the state's future economic viability. Due to declining state funding and failing schools, we must ask, "Where will California find tomorrow's highly skilled workforce?" A troubling paradox is Latino and African Americans represent an increasing fraction of California's youth population, and they are denied educational opportunities that fully prepare them to contribute to the state's economic prosperity (Allen et al. 2002). This pattern of Black and Latino school-age populations denied equal educational opportunities is common across the United States (Kozol 2005). Equally common are research studies and popular discourse that attribute racial gaps in educational achievement to individual or group shortcomings but ignore systemic inequities by race/ethnicity in educational opportunity (Feagin 2006).

The history of research shows persistent racial gaps in educational attainment, yet despite the voluminous research into the reasons for racial gaps, we still do not fully understand the many factors that shape student success at multiple levels of the education pipeline. Moreover, a significant body of work promotes, directly or indirectly, theoretical explanations of the racial achievement gap that are biased, racist, and ultimately dehumanizing (Horvat and O'Connor 2006). The emphasis on analyzing large statistical data sets risks dehumanizing disadvantaged students by ignoring the complex experiences that influence educational attainment.

We begin with the assumption that social science research is not—nor should it be—value neutral. In contrast to the canon that guides most methodological and statistical studies of educational achievement, our starting point for dialogue is the call to arms of several Black social scientists during the revolutionary 1970s. These scholars articulated a new vision of social science research with the central goal of empowerment for Black (and other marginalized) communities. In the process, new tools, theories, and approaches for social inquiry were created (Billingsley 1968; Hill 1972; Ladner 1973; Marable 1983). We are also indebted to Zuberi's recent work *Thicker Than Blood: How Racial Statistics Lie* (2001a), which provides an alternative perspective on intersections between race, educational achievement, and methodology. We are critical of research that does not emphasize theory and methodology since, failing to place statistical patterns in broader sociohistorical context, such quantitative methods-driven research often reproduces unchallenged racist theories and methodologies (Waters 1973; Zuberi 2001a). In this chapter, we present an alternate methodological approach to examining educational achievement among racially marginalized groups. This approach seeks a better fit between theory and methodology and more accurately identifies the processes underlying educational achievement among students of color.

PURPOSE

The purpose of this chapter is threefold: (1) provide a critical summary of theoretical and methodological pitfalls in educational research literature; (2) offer alternative perspectives and approaches; and (3) present a case study that emphasizes experiences of students of color in context, and in their own voices. The questions that guide this chapter are:

- In general, how are statistics used to explain educational inequities across racial groups? What sorts of conclusions are drawn from extant research?
- What are the limitations of methods commonly used to explore how race affects educational processes? To what extent do conventional statistical approaches reify, reproduce, and validate race, ethnic, class, and/or gender disparities in educational achievement?
- Given the literature's pervasive "race blindness," can statistics allow us to explore how deeply race affects educational processes and simultaneously encourage research that forefronts the humanity of individuals and groups?

Project CHOICES has as its goal the identification of the factors and processes related to the educational and occupational success of minority students in California. Our study's focus is on ten schools in Los Angeles; this chapter reports data from one of those schools. We use not only empirical results from the study, but also lessons from its methodological conceptualization and implementation as a novel approach to research on education and race, intending to improve educational outcomes for students of color. In the next section, we provide a brief overview of selected research on educational attainment and achievement that highlights racial disparities, but provide very different conclusions and prescriptions for what to do about it.

CRITIQUE OF EDUCATION STATISTICS

The sizable extant literature examining high school academic outcomes and experiences can be categorized into three research foci: *individual factors* (commitment to academics, impact of family—especially parental, personal aspirations and fears, impact of peers, role of religion and beliefs); *organizational factors* (resources of school, school management policies); and larger, overarching *social structural factors* (how and why resource allotments vary across and within schools, across and within different racial, ethnic, class, and gender groups). The approach to examining educational attainment and achievement is linked to theoretical underpinnings, research methods, and the implications or conclusions drawn. The history of educational attainment research comprises traditional ("value-free") theoretical models—a perspective that asserts as a possibility (and in fact an imperative) an absolute knowledge, free of encumbering moral or value judgments or biases in the conceptualization, implementation, and analysis of research. This tradition tends to divorce academic pursuits (general knowledge acquisition) from social, moral, or even human responsibility at the outset. The approach is justified as the only legitimate means to discover true patterns of social phenomena.

However noble this pursuit may appear, Zuberi (2001a) reminds us "[c]urrent statistical methodologies were developed as part of the eugenics movement and continue to reflect the racist ideologies that gave rise to them" (x). Because of the dishonorable beginnings of using race in statistics, he cautions us to be wary of disassociating racial statistics from eradicating racial stratification, for that will lead us to uphold status quo inequality, even if perhaps unintentionally. Traditional research eschews the goals of group empowerment, accountability, and value to disenfranchised communities,[1] even as it calls attention to these communities' deficits. As a result, many studies using educational statistics have been problematic. In addition to contributing little to social justice, such studies actually often reaffirm or confirm (explicitly or implicitly) racist ideas that objectify and caricature communities of color. Although our critique begins half a century ago, unfortunately, this research tradition is also very much present in the recent literature (Carter 2005).

Early work in education was the first social science to rely heavily on statistics, and pioneered "objective" and "scientific" disparaging of Blacks (Jencks 1972; Herrnstein and Murray 1994). This research claimed to empirically demonstrate innate biological and intellectual inferiority of Blacks. Scholars who traced these historical developments challenged the flawed perspectives of Blacks as subhuman or inferior (Du Bois 1939; McKee 1993; Zuberi 2001a).[2] Following the inferiority model built on the "Social Darwinism" of White racial supremacy, sociologists continue to use a "refined" attainment model to explain the inferiority of Blacks.

IQ Controversy

Jencks (1972) examines the effect of family and schooling in America. His major finding concludes that the number of years a person spends in school has little effect upon later occupation and income attainment. He discusses "the hereditary/environment controversy" and tries to assess the relative importance of genes, family background, social class, and race in determining test scores. Jencks argues that the main determinants of occupational and income success are due to factors such as "inherited" intelligence and family background.

Taylor (1980) criticizes Jencks's use of selected modeling, arguing the analysis, path analysis, does not allow for systematic removal of alternate causal models since Jencks does not "test for" or eliminate causal models that could be "implausible or false" (456). Although Jencks briefly mentions the pitfalls of path analysis, he does not offer or examine alternative models. Moreover, Taylor argues, the literature that discusses clear steps for eliminating alternative models is never mentioned[3] and the variables Jencks uses have a hierarchal ordering, "IQ score in school (X_5) can affect later occupation (X_8), but the latter cannot possibly affect the former." As a result of this hierarchical order, many important variables are not included in the analysis, variables that "did not lend themselves easily to a nice hierarchical ordering" (456).

The path analysis restrictions of interval measurement, linearity, additivity, and variable ordering together *underestimate* the effects of various factors upon occupational and income inequality in American society, particularly the effects of education (Taylor 1980). Jencks failed to include many important independent variables and made no systematic attempt to assess the effects of school quality, school prestige, grades, peer-group pressures, extracurricular activities, how much a person actually learned in school, and a host of other potentially important variables. Finally, Taylor points out that Jencks ignores important literature on the structural effects of school context (e.g., Davis 1966; Nelson 1972).

Like Jencks (1972), Herrnstein and Murray (1994) improperly consider the effects of inherited intelligence on schooling. *The Bell Curve* argues that individual intelligence, measured by IQ test scores, is accurate in predicting problematic citizens. The authors analyze the National Longitudinal Study of Youth (NLSY) to observe IQ effects in order to clear "away some of the mystery that has surrounded the nation's most serious problems" (118). This longitudinal data sampled youth ages fourteen to twenty-two in 1979, and Herrnstein and Murray use the 1980 Armed Forces Qualifying Test (AFQT) administered to the NLSY sample as the measure of intelligence, that is, respondents' IQ.

The Bell Curve uses logistic multivariate regression analysis to estimate correlates of variation in White NLSY respondents' IQs. The authors are interested in explaining how 1980 AFQT scores predict whether a respondent was poor, a high school dropout, unemployed, unmarried, an unwed mother, on welfare, a neglectful mother, or a criminal in the next decade. For these analyses, the authors only examined *White, non-Latino* respondents concluding that AFQT scores better predicted problematic situations than parents' socioeconomic status.

The Bell Curve has been highly criticized for its methodological faults and errors (Fischer et al. 1996; Taylor 1973). Fischer et al. (1996) critique and analyze Herrnstein and Murray's assertions, methods, statistical analysis, and conclusions. To test the assertions, Fischer et al. "accepted Herrnstein and Murray's evidence, their measure of intelligence, and their basic methodology and then reexamined their results" (92). Fischer et al. discover *The Bell Curve's* findings contain critical errors—missing information, lack of reliability, and omitted variable bias. By correcting these statistical errors, Fischer et al. show that coming from a disadvantaged home was nearly as important a risk factor for poverty as it was for a low AFQT score.

Inequality is a social construct resulting from historical acts, and is not fated by nature. Rather, it is an individual's social environment and the group's sociohistorical circumstances that largely influence outcomes (Feagin 2006). Fischer et al. (1996) argue that the psychometric paradigm, the measurement of mental traits (e.g., speed and precision of mental processing), does not measure native intelligence. Rather, the psychometric paradigm measures exposure to instruction versus practical skills, social acuity, and self-discipline. Scores on intelligence tests are determined by social background, and not the inverse—intelligence does not determine social background. Thus, the psychometric approach is a better measure of social background, and not native intelligence, since it measures factors such as quality and quantity of schooling.

Research on the test-score gap between Blacks and Whites (Jencks and Phillips 1998) concludes that the gap plays a much larger role in explaining racial disparities in educational attainment and income than previously realized. Second, many common explanations for the test-score gap, including racial disparities in family income, school resources, and innate ability, did not seem to be as important as their proponents claimed (vi). Phillips et al. (1998) find that African Americans start to fall behind Whites before the first grade and various environmental background factors (e.g., parents' education, childrearing practices, and the schools mothers attended) contribute to this test-score disparity. Certainly racial differences in school opportunities and resources also play a critical role (Kozol 2005).

Status Attainment and the Wisconsin School of Social Stratification

A long-standing explanation of educational attainment differences comes from the social stratification literature treating educational attainment as a social psychological process devoid of historical and social contexts. Educational attainment is seen as dependent primarily on parental occupation and position in the social hierarchy (Sewell et al. 1969). University of Wisconsin researchers developed a model of educational attainment utilizing a data set on the state's White high school seniors in 1957 (Sewell et al. 1969; Sewell and Hauser 1972; Sewell and Hauser 1980). It emphasized family background as the dominant factor in determining individual educational attainment. As the Wisconsin School was developing its status attainment model, the Coleman Report concluded family background was a stronger predictor of academic achievement than school environment (Coleman 1966). The concurrent release of these studies emphasized the importance of family background, especially parental education, on educational attainment and pushed school influences to the background.

The educational attainment model by the Wisconsin School was extended to adult socioeconomic status by other researchers at the University of Wisconsin. Early work emphasized the influence of family background on occupational attainment (Featherman 1971). Elaborating Blau and Duncan's (1967) seminal model of educational attainment, father's occupational prestige was found to have the greatest impact on the occupational attainment of White men in metropolitan areas sampled for the analysis. Featherman and Hauser's (1976) replication of Blau and Duncan's Occupational Changes in a Generation (OCG) study over a decade later further refined the occupational status model. They argued that schooling had become a more significant determinant of occupational status than family background, especially for Black men, and found "little support" in their findings to suggest that achievement should be cast in terms that emphasize "racist tendencies, whether de jure or of de facto, to the neglect of other tendencies in the allocation of statuses" (649).

The legacy of the status attainment model and the Coleman Report is still apparent in contemporary studies of status attainment. Analyzing trends in educational attainment through the 1980s, Mare (1995) recognizes that school success is not equal across all populations. He attributes the difference in the quantity and quality of schooling among students primarily to "the advantages or disadvantages that their parents confer on them throughout childhood" (155). Reflecting the influence of the Wisconsin Model, Mare posits that parental education level predicts educational attainment and attributes racial/ethnic differences in attainment to differences in family socioeconomic status.

The status attainment model has been aligned with an explanatory ideology that results in victim blaming. The Moynihan Report (1965) typifies the ideological argument made with traditional status attainment models: Black families are inferior to White families and are held responsible, even blamed, for successive generations of underachievement. An ideology that characterizes Black families as inferior does not recognize their strengths (Hill 1972) and ignores schools' considerable influence over educational attainment. Far too many contemporary approaches to educational research do not adequately examine the effects of school context.

The status attainment model has methodological and statistical problems that call into question its usefulness for explaining the racial gap in educational attainment. First, the students in the original Wisconsin sample were racially homogenous, White high school seniors. The educational attainment process described should not be assumed to apply to racial minority groups. The statistical models used to derive the status attainment model assume a linear relationship between aspirations and educational attainment, for both Whites and non-Whites. Research has shown, however, that the path from educational aspirations to actual attainment has greater impediments for racial minorities than Whites (Horvat and O'Connor 2006; Stanton-Salazar 2001; Taylor 1973). This further calls into question the validity of the methodological and statistical assumptions made in constructing and applying the status attainment model.

The most contested aspect of the Wisconsin model is that neighborhood and school contexts make no great contribution to educational outcomes (Sewell and Armer 1966). In combination with the findings of the Coleman Report (1966), this finding has stirred considerable debate over the relative importance of school and neighborhood contexts on educational attainment. Persell (1977) has argued that focusing on individuals and their strengths or deficiencies, instead of examining the social contexts that constrain individuals, is problematic. Teacher expectations of a student's academic performance, for example, can act as a self-fulfilling prophecy and affect student achievement (Rosenthal and Jacobson 1968). Expecting more of a student can raise achievement while expecting less can cause lower achievement. As a result, teacher racial bias toward minority students can have negative effects on their achievement (Ferguson 1998). Other school factors such as curriculum, school communal organization, and governance have been proposed as critical elements to equitably distribute student learning with regard to race and class (Bryk et al. 1993; Horvat and O'Connor 2006). Dismissing the impact of school context on educational outcomes is a severe conceptual oversight in status attainment models. Nevertheless, emphasis on non-racialized family background and inherited qualities has been tremendously influential outside of the social stratification literature as well.

ALTERNATIVE THEORIES AND METHODS

Researchers must closely monitor and avoid racist assumptions at the beginning, implementation, and analysis stages of any research project, especially one that uses statistics at its core. According to Zuberi (2001a), two specific areas require special attention. Beyond the standard research limitations, ignoring the intersection of race and methodology can result in two common errors. "Race" can be used as both an attribute to describe a person (e.g., an African American student who gets poor grades at school) and as a "causal factor" that mistakes the classification as the *cause* of an actual individual or biological attribute (e.g., being "African American" makes a student get poor grades). As Zuberi puts it, "An individual trait like race cannot determine another trait of the individual" (95); rather, race can only be used to describe associations that point to racial stratification. Further, he notes that many scholars tend to confuse "causal effect" ("effect of a factor on a given response variable") and "causal theory" ("how and why the effect operates") (125), giving little thought to the latter; thus racist explanations are implied for observed patterns.

Zuberi urges for more thoughtful reflection in the use of racial concepts in research, thereby aligning with Myrdal's contention that social science research focused on race is infused with biases. In *An American Dilemma,* Myrdal (1944) argues that though "objective" truth is the standard for obtaining knowledge in the social sciences, full objectivity can never be reached. Social scientists are part of the culture that holds racial biases, and thus are never entirely free from those biases in their research. In order to minimize it, Myrdal urges social scientists to reflect on and make explicit the values and judgments brought to their work. This is essential for the ultimate task of working toward practical research intended to guide public policy.

Du Bois (1899), who conducted the nation's first social science survey in *The Philadelphia Negro: A Social Study*, is an exemplar of the approach Myrdal advocates. Du Bois emphasized the need to join theory with empirically driven research, grounded in statistics and historical analysis. It is clear in the formulation of the work that Du Bois does not dismiss the tremendous power of racism to circumscribe the lives of Blacks in Philadelphia. For instance, Du Bois links the high illiteracy rate among Blacks with limited, inferior educational opportunities[4] and the distortion of generalized statistics when age and gender are not controlled. Furthermore, Black families have logical reasons for keeping their children out of school, reasons directly related to racism and limited economic opportunities. Poor Blacks need their children to work for income, and many do not see the value in their children going to school because so few occupations open to Blacks require formal education (96).

Fortunately, some recent studies point to racially aware and responsible ways of doing research. In contrast to Ogbu's 2003 study,[5] Stanton-Salazar (2001), Fordham (1996), and Carter (2005) use ethnographic methods to reach very different outcomes and conclusions about reasons for educational achievement (and underachievement) among disempowered urban Mexican American and African American youth. Stanton-Salazar examines the "social support networks and help-seeking experiences of low-income Mexican-origin adolescents from immigrant families" (3). His critical framework incorporates the micro- (personal understandings), meso- (social networks, institutions), and macro- (political economy, subculture) levels of engagement. From the first, then, Stanton-Salazar situates low student academic success and engagement as a problem that occurs on multiple social levels and not just on the individual psychology/preparedness level. He utilizes social network data, personal interviews, and statistical analyses of survey data.

Similarly, Fordham's ethnographic study of Black high school students attending an urban magnet school does not simply focus on individual effort, but situates individuals in the contexts where they are both a part and a product. Data were collected via formal and informal interviews, survey questionnaires, documents, participant observation, and talking with peers and nonfamilial adults. She situates these students in the "second emancipation" (1960–1986) of Black Americans, a period that led to both opportunities (under integrationist ideology adopted by both White and Black America) and subtle limitations. Thus, Fordham concludes, both underachievers and high achievers have "reasons for their madness," pointing directly to larger forces at work and simultaneous agency and will on the part of the students and the choices they make. Underachievers view the school route to success as undesirable, given the high cultural costs they must pay (e.g., loss or repudiation of Black identity, some level of acceptance of

White dominance, and distancing from Black community), while high achievers choose this path as the only way to contradict beliefs of Black inferiority and personal advancement.

Likewise, Lewis's (2003) ethnographic study of the reproduction of racial meaning and inequality in elementary schools takes a multiple data collection and analysis approach. Lewis prioritizes differing school contexts in order to capture the reality of race as product and process:

> Although much educational research has looked at race in relation to gaps in achievement, differences in discipline patterns, or disparities in test scores, these numbers do not capture the reality of race as a product of schooling, as part of the process of schooling. When studies ask why Black children and White children achieve differently, they fail to ask what it means to be Black or White in different contexts. (3–4)

Over one year, Lewis (2003) conducted site participant observations in and outside the classroom, conducted formal and informal interviews, and collected school site documents. Lewis studied three elementary schools—a Black and Latino urban school, a White suburban school, and a bicultural or non-White school (Latino students at a Spanish-immersion program) (8–10). As a result, Lewis's comparison of three school sites and various data collection methods provide a means of investigating racial meaning and racial inequality across differing sites and contexts. By examining the contexts of students' schooling, Lewis finds "the curriculum (expressed and hidden) teach[es] many racial lessons, but schools and school personnel serve as a location and means for interracial interaction and as a means of both affirming and challenging previous racial attitudes and understandings" (4). Thus, the school and its personnel play a role in the production of race and as a race-making institution.

A recent study of achievement outcomes among racial and ethnic minority students challenges cultural explanations for differences in educational achievement. Carter (2005) interrogates the widely accepted idea that Black and Latino youth underperform in school in order to avoid "acting White." Students report differential treatment by teachers when they do not fit the dominant cultural ideal's concerning dress and demeanor. As a result, teachers often ignore very intelligent students because they do not conform to external or interactional styles valued by teachers (Carter 2005). Carter writes, "As gatekeepers, teachers enforce a stratified system, rewarding those students who embrace the 'right' cultural signals, habits and styles" (69). Carter reminds us that in this society, schools are racialized contexts where White, middle-class culture is privileged. In these school settings, African American and Latino cultures were devalued and equated with academic failure. As a result, students of color who embraced or signified Black or

Latino cultural markers (e.g., speech, clothing, hairstyles, mannerisms) were automatically categorized and treated as poor students (read "bad" people). African American students experience teacher-student interactions that are less than ideal, experience school as nonsupportive, and experience problematic relationships with teachers who have low expectations of them and their classmates (Carter 2005).

The evidence of extreme racial/ethnic disparities in school achievement across California and the United States is clear and indisputable. However, debate swirls over the source of these differences. One school of researchers attributes these differences to individual and cultural factors. In this view, African Americans and Latinos lag behind Whites and Asian Americans because of individual failings. A contrasting school of researchers attribute these differences to systematic discrimination and factors that disadvantage Latinos and Blacks, while privileging Whites and Asian Americans to some degree. More research is needed to unpack the black box of complex, interrelated factors and processes that produce race/ethnic inequities in school achievement.

CHOICES: EXAMINING EDUCATIONAL SUCCESS AND ASPIRATIONS AMONG CALIFORNIA HIGH SCHOOL STUDENTS

We now share results from Project CHOICES, an in-depth study of race/ethnic inequities in school achievement across a select set of California high schools. Our study was multimethod, using data from large-scale government statistics, high school profiles, and focus group interviews. The goal of this research was to compare and contrast the variable pictures of race, ethnicity, and school achievement presented by various methodological approaches. It is presented here as an example of how an innovative research approach and methodology can provide a new understanding of racial/ethnic differences in educational attainment.

CHOICES Part I: Conception of Project—People, Aims, and Objectives

Project CHOICES was developed to examine historically low college-going and graduation rates among Latino and African American students. The overall goal was to identify key factors and processes related to ethnic minority students' academic success. We used a multimethod design to explore the academic experiences, college access, and support networks of high school juniors and seniors. Qualitative and quantitative data from high school students, teachers, counselors, and parents were used to construct a more complex perspective of the social and institutional challenges facing Black and Latino students who aspire to attend college.

Data were collected from September 2001 through June 2002 across ten public high school sites in Los Angeles County. Focus groups were conducted with students, parents, counselors, and teachers about various aspects of academics and the college-going process, including college preparation, academic preparation, college advising, parental involvement, and classroom experiences. Survey data were used to broadly contextualize and supplement students' qualitative responses. Incorporating students' demographic information and general impressions of their quality of education allows a point of reference from which to interpret student experiences and outcomes. In total, 496 juniors and seniors, 51 parents of juniors and seniors, 31 high school counselors, and 48 high school teachers participated in the study.

CHOICES Part II: Applying Traditional Methods—Aggregate Data Site Description

Quantitative data were used in the study to loosely contextualize participants' qualitative responses. Survey data such as demographic information, background characteristics, and general impressions of college access provide a reference point from which to interpret participants' in-depth responses to open-ended questions. Findings from quantitative data analysis for one case site in particular, Central Senior High,[6] will be used to demonstrate how a novel methodological approach can provide a richer, more comprehensive description of the educational experiences of minority students.

The total school enrollment for Central Senior High is 2,867. The majority of students at Central Senior High are African American (75 percent) followed by Latinos (24 percent). Sixty percent of Central Senior High students are eligible for free and reduced-price meals, while only 47 percent of the state's students are eligible. Similarly, 25 percent of students qualify for CalWORKS (formerly AFDC) compared to the state average of 11 percent. The average class size at Central Senior High is two larger than the state average and there are ten students per computer compared to the state average of six (CDE 2002a, 2002b, 2002c, 2002d).

The teaching staff differs drastically from the state average by race/ethnicity as well as credentialing. Sixty percent of teachers (N = 77) are African American, while California's 306,940 teachers are only 5 percent African American (CDE 2002a, 2002b, 2002c, 2002d). Only 29 percent of Central's teachers are White, while 74 percent of California teachers are White. Fewer teachers at Central Senior High are fully credentialed (65 percent) compared to the state average (86 percent).

The picture of Central Senior High presented by the aggregate statistics is one of an underresourced school. In stark contrast to expectations based on other measures, however, the percentages of graduating students completing University of California (UC) and California State University (CSU) requirements by race/ethnicity are impressive (table 13.1). Of 389 graduates at Central Senior High, 216 African Americans (69 percent) and 40 Latinos (56 percent) are UC-eligible. By contrast, compared statewide this is true for only 25 percent of African American and 22 percent of Latino high school graduates. Eligibility rates for African Americans and Latinos at Central Senior High are also at odds with the substantial underrepresentation of both groups in California's higher education institutions (California Postsecondary Education Commission 2002; University of California 2004). Instead of overlooking or dismissing the UC and CSU eligibility numbers as statistical anomalies, it is apparent that aggregate statistical data for Central Senior High do not tell the complete story of the situation within the school. Data from the school narrative and focus groups play an integral role in revealing the processes by which a

Table 13.1. Twelfth Grade Graduates Completing All Courses Required for UC and/or CSU Entrance by Race/Ethnicity, California Department of Education, 2001–2002

	Central Senior High		*California State Total*	
	Graduates	*Graduates with UC/CSU*	*Graduates*	*Graduates with UC/CSU*
African American	311	216 (69.5%)	23,453	5,929 (25.3%)
American Indian or Alaska Native	2	0 (0.0%)	3,034	688 (22.7%)
Asian	3	3 (100.0%)	35,624	20,441 (57.4%)
Filipino	0	0 (0.0%)	10,311	4,491 (43.6%)
Latino	71	40 (56.3%)	109,043	23,750 (21.8%)
Pacific Islander	1	1 (100.0%)	2,271	599 (26.4%)
White	1	0 (0.0%)	140,440	56,370 (40.1%)
Multiple or No Response	0	0 (0.0%)	1,743	408 (23.4%)
Total Grade 12 Graduates	389	260 (66.8%)	325,919	112,676 (34.6%)

disproportionate number of these urban, low-income Black and Latino students become eligible for higher education.

CHOICES Part III: Extending Aggregate Statistics—Case Site Narrative and Focus Group Analysis

The community of Central High School is predominantly African American, with a large percentage of families in poverty and fewer high school graduates compared to the national average.[7] African Americans constitute nearly three-quarters of the community (72 percent) and Latinos one-fourth (23 percent). The percentage of high school and college graduates in the community (74 percent and 20 percent, respectively) is lower than national averages (80 percent and 24 percent, respectively). The median family income in 2000 was $40,805, with 17 percent of families and 21 percent of individuals living below the poverty level.

California Department of Education (CDE) and census data would lead one to conclude that both Central High School and the surrounding community are resource-poor. Traditional educational attainment models suggest that students from a resource-poor community have low levels of achievement and college preparation. Yet data on Central High School graduates show the school is preparing students for college far better than one would expect given low school and community resource levels as determined through aggregate district-level data. Our institutional questionnaire asked school representatives to review CDE data on their schools and also asked more in-depth questions about school characteristics, curriculum, teaching personnel, academic counseling, parental involvement, facilities, and any school partnerships.

For example, we learn at Central High School there are three computer resource centers and a total of 500 computers for students to use (student-computer ratio 5.6 to 1), much higher than the CDE aggregate data show and comparable to the state average of 6 to 1. Although the library seems small with holdings of 12,000 books, several copies of the current year UC and CSU catalogs were made available to students, as well an annual subscription to the *Los Angeles Times*. Moreover, Central High maintained several partnerships with colleges from the community through university levels (University of California–Los Angeles Career-Based Opportunities Program; California State University–Los Angeles ACCESS Program; Southwest Community College; and Los Angeles Community College).

Qualitative research methods were used to complement the aggregate data identified. We present two key reasons why Central students are doing "better than expected": a highly dedicated and active group of counselors, and the abundance of outreach programs targeting and involved with Central High School to increase exposure to college.

Recipe for Success, First Ingredient: Committed Counselors

Despite facing numerous obstacles to successful interactions with students, counselors at Central employ a balanced counseling philosophy that addresses "academic, career, and psychosocial" needs with each successive grade in hopes of achieving continued student development over four years. One counselor takes two hours of her own time (5:30 p.m. to 7:30 p.m.) to set up meetings with parents one night a month because, as she says, "of my commitment." The college counselor puts up stars in the school every year, honoring individuals who go to college. In particular, the availability of a full-time college counselor as a point of reference and source of motivation to go to college is seen as critical by the academic counselors.

The efforts of counselors are not lost on students. Students interviewed consistently recognized the role of counselors in influencing and motivating them to prepare for college. For example, one student, Becka,[8] reported that she was "very satisfied" with both academic counseling and college-related information received at school:

> Ever since I have attended this school . . . my counselor . . . and others, they influenced me to um, to consider what I was going to do once I exit high school because before to be honest, I never really gave it any thought, but they influenced me and encouraged me to take courses that are challenging and rigorous, that will look good on applications so that people can say well yes, this is a well rounded young woman.

Support and motivation, however, will only take a student so far. Counselors not only provide support, but also are actively involved in increasing the likelihood of their students to go to college. As one counselor says, "I think almost all the right mechanisms are in place" for student success, and students report that counselors are providing them with opportunities to succeed, as in the comment by Oleg, an African American male student below.

> Yeah, I went to [another high school] before I went, came to Central, and they, they really, really didn't motivate anybody, well, especially, you know, the minorities to go to college. They kind of put you down, and that was really contrary to what, what was at Central, where you have like [the college counselor] and my counselor . . . helping you out and, you know, really putting you in the right classes and getting you to take tests and, you know, just make you, helping you to succeed.

In Oleg's case, the counselors not only encouraged him to go to college—an experience far different from what he received at his previous school as a minority—but also placed him in the appropriate classes and informed him of the right tests to be able to succeed. On his student questionnaire,

Oleg responded he expects to take over ten AP classes before graduating high school, and the two main sources of college information for him were the school counselor and the Internet. A counselor who recognized Dave's potential turned what he intended to be a routine change of classes into a step toward better college preparation.

> I went to my counselor just to change my chemistry class and she dragged me in to talk about my grades last year, 'cause they were really good. And then she ended up putting me into AP classes and I actually didn't really know she did that cause I just needed a chem class. So I looked at it and I was like, "AP, I'll try it" so now I don't regret her putting me in AP classes.

Despite numerous barriers to achieving their counseling goals, counselors at Central High School exhibit both a philosophical and practical commitment to preparing as many students as possible for college. The routine pattern is to extend themselves beyond what they are required to do. They not only provide intangible support and motivation, but also actively place their students in positions to go to college. Students report that counselors place them in all the right classes—sometimes unbeknown to them—in order to improve their chances of attending college.

RECIPE FOR SUCCESS, SECOND INGREDIENT: PROGRAMS FOR COLLEGE GOING

Central High School is affiliated with numerous programs geared toward increasing the number of minority students in higher education. Programs include UCLA's Career-Based Outreach Program and Early Academic Outreach Program, Young Black Scholars, Volunteers of America Upward Bound, and college representatives from local universities who make regular visits to the Central High School campus.

One role of these programs is to shape students' career aspirations. Sheila, a Latina who will pursue a business degree at UC Berkeley, said of her involvement in Students for a Better Tomorrow, a mentorship program with successful graduates of the school district,

> And people used to put [the mentors] down, some of them were in gangs, some of them, you know, used to be drug addicts, and they're like, you know how we overcame this? And they started telling us. And that's what motivated me to continue business actually, and to pursue an education at Berkeley.

For Sheila, Students for a Better Tomorrow provided exposure to successful individuals, but also to people who came from her school district, who faced life circumstances like her own. They were not merely successful adults; she also saw a foreshadowing of what she could attain from people who had grown up in her community. Although an A student, Sheila benefits tremendously from exposure to this program because her parents have little to no experience preparing for, applying to, and attending college.

Outreach programs expose students to college-going-related activities and peer networks that act as a positive influence on students' plans and preparation for college. Dez, a male student of multiple ancestry (African American, American Indian, Hawaiian, and Cuban) remarked:

> I don't really have any friends that influenced me to go to college except the ones I guess that I have gone to college courses classes with. I'm also in Upward Bound so when we go to different colleges I meet new friends and I guess that's in a way they influence me to go to college. But my immediate friends here at Central don't really influence me at all.

Dez is one example of a student who, without an extracurricular program, may not have had the peer support necessary to accomplish his college-going goals. He later mentions that at the high school he attended before Central, he had friends who influenced him to go to college, but this was no longer the case at Central; thus, he needed Upward Bound as a source of positive peer influence. Such support is even more necessary for students who come from families with little to no experience in the college-going process, as is true for Dez, whose mother has a high school education (father's is unknown).

More than any external program, however, the Central High School college center was clearly the most influential noncurricular influence on students' college-going goals and preparation. The college center is open all day and can be visited during nutrition, lunch, class sessions, and after school. There are peer college counselors every period. It is the foci of all college activity at Central High: College representatives are based there; college outreach programs such as Upward Bound work through the college center; the college center hosts the annual college fair and arranges field trips to local universities; and the college counselor is informative and motivational. Students explain how the college center has been a source of information and inspiration:

> like you can come [to the college center]. You always see somebody from like UCLA or a college to help you. So it's very useful.

> I would say that the college center does help because [the college counselor] has told me things I didn't know about college, how to prepare for it and like sometimes [I'm] scared about what college is gonna be like. She tells me it's going to be okay and stuff like that, so yeah the college center does help.

> As soon as I came to the college center [the college counselor] immediately reminded me of my mother. As in, she was making sure I handled all my business and handled all my important tasks so that I could go ahead and get to college and succeed.

Taken together, the strong counseling core and abundance of outreach programs are key factors increasing the preparation of students from an apparently resource-poor school for higher education. The committed counseling staff and large number of outreach programs in the school are critical for students not accounted for in standard measures of student educational attainment. The use of the case study approach and qualitative methodology complement aggregate statistics to produce a more complete picture of student learning experiences.

CONCLUSION

"Qui Bono—who benefits from the current educational system?" is our question in this chapter. We recognize and challenge a status quo that perpetuates inequality. Traditional educational statistics have played a crucial role in rationalizing and justifying this status quo. Here we propose alternative research approaches to better understand and to change this status quo. By approaching research with a mind toward racial justice, interpretations of research findings, then, regardless of the methodology employed, do not reify racial groups as static "things" that produce "causal effects." Rather, our CHOICES research project emphasized as a goal the eradication of racial stratification and the "humanizing" of aggregate data so often used in empirical studies of educational attainment across racial groups. From this aim, we chose a mixed methodology approach of qualitative and quantitative data at various levels and from different constituents to provide a clearer understanding of the mechanisms that lead to disparate rates of college-going among racial/ethnic minority students. The example of Central High School presented above shows how mixed methodologies can help to explain anomalies in aggregate data, in this case, a resource-poor school and community that produced relatively high rates of college-eligible graduates. However, this approach can also be used to better understand the status quo. Traditional approaches to educational attainment research have been unable to address the question "Qui Bono?"—who *benefits* from the current organization of the education system? As a clearer, more complete understanding of the factors inhibiting the path of minority students to higher education results, real progress toward closing the gap in racial/ethnic college-going rates can be made.

Complementing state- and school-level data, qualitative data expand the number of variables researchers take into consideration when addressing educational inequities. Beyond the typical variables used in regression and other quantitative analyses, qualitative data bring to light other processes that otherwise go unexamined. Not only does the number of variables increase, but also the range of factors considered is expanded. Specifically, it provides space for individual experiences and interpersonal processes to inform analyses. These experiences and processes show the range of factors that contribute to commonly used statistical measures. We also are reminded that processes summarized in single measures are not uniform. Instead, a rich set of factors, relationships, and processes underlie mean statistical measures. To "unpack" and to "interrogate" this complexity is to "humanize" statistics.

This is not to say, however, that the range of factors and interactions makes generalizability and prediction unattainable. When placed in context, the larger set of factors and interactions being considered makes logical sense. The result is not an innumerable series of atomized experiences that makes no useful empirical contribution to scientific generalization and prediction. Instead, what we achieve is a wider range of possible processes and explanations that need and deserve closer examination.

Postscript and Policy Implications

We tell a "feel good" story about Central High School that could have been written by a Hollywood playwright. It is a Horatio Alger story of first rank, in the finest tradition of the treasured American Dream of triumph over all obstacles. Poor Black and brown students from a failing, inner-city high school beat the odds to not only set but also achieve high academic goals. As the narrative goes, these "deserving poor" resisted the lures of the ghetto and barrio, rose above bad culture and broken families to achieve academically. Surely as a result, they would go on to secure the success that is the birthright of any and all in America who display the requisite work ethic, discipline, sacrifice, and intellect.

Unfortunately the subsequent "backstory" is not nearly so favorable or uplifting. Since we gathered these data, the public higher education landscape in California (and across the nation) has shifted dramatically. Affirmative action, or race-based admissions, having successfully opened the doors of higher education for Blacks, Latinos, Asians, and White women, fell into public disfavor. In California, Proposition 209 prohibited consideration of race in college admissions with devastating results. The ensuing years have seen precipitous declines in the enrollments of Black and Latino students in the flagship University of California system, as well as in the California State

University system. For example, the University of California–Los Angeles's fall 2006 entering class of over 4,500 students included only 96 African American students. Black students, who represent 12 percent of all high school graduates in the state, were a mere 3.2 percent of total fall 2006 admits to the University of California (Comeaux and Watford 2006). These dismal numbers signal a failure of the promise of *Brown v. Topeka Board of Education* and the Civil Rights movement.

As Hurtado et al. (1999) remind us, educational outcomes are very much influenced by a combination of personal, institutional, *and* contextual factors. Previously, affirmative action helped to level the playing field, encouraging high aspirations and rewarding academic striving among Central High School's Black and brown graduates. Whereas before the University of California–Berkeley and the University of California–Los Angeles admitted significant numbers of the school's graduates—as many as ten or fifteen some years—the majority of whom were successful in college and in careers, under the new regime, a rare few Central High School graduates were admitted to University of California campuses (Comeaux and Watford 2006; Laird 2005). The Central High School students, teachers, or parents did not change; what changed was the sociopolitical, legal context in which they were forced to operate.

We conclude with the sad story of a public higher education system and a correctional system in California that represents the fruits of racial apartheid. In the prisons Blacks and Latinos are overrepresented, far exceeding their proportion of the state population. In the universities, Blacks and Latinos are dramatically underrepresented, present in proportions far below their share of the state population. What remains is for the future to be written. Will this state, this nation, rise to the higher ideals of equality, liberty, and opportunity or sink to the baser instincts of exploitation, degradation, and blocked opportunities? In this writing of our future, for better or worse, will reside the hopes of many American Dreams, carrying with it the promise or failure of a nation.

NOTES

1. Waters (1973) mentions an interesting way to make social scientists usefully accountable to Black communities, and to challenge existing "White social science" projects: create research "watch dogs." He cites the Community Research Review Committee in Boston (now defunct), a group of Black social scientists who screened research proposals to study local Black communities, to pay attention to what kind of research was funded, by whom, carried out by whom, what findings came out of it, and how and why it was disseminated, in order to be able to intervene at any stage of the research process (p. 206–7).

2. For direct responses to earliest racist claims about Black intelligence, see Du Bois (1903), Ballard (1973), and Woodson (1933).

3. Cited by Taylor (1980); Blalock 1962, 1964, 1968, 1971; Heise 1969; Simon 1957.

4. Public schools were historically segregated by race, with few or no public high schools that Blacks could attend. Black teachers were relegated to teaching only at these few (and inferior) all-Black student schools.

5. Ogbu focuses on Black "community factors" that negatively affect Black students' educational achievement.

6. "Central High School" is a pseudonym for one of the urban high schools we studied.

7. The community is defined as the area contained in the same zip code as Central High School. Data were gathered from the 2000 census (www.census.gov).

8. Student names are pseudonyms.

14

Critical Demography and the Measurement of Racism

A Reproduction of Wealth, Status, and Power

Hayward Derrick Horton and Lori Latrice Sykes

Racism continues to be a major, if not the most salient, component of the American social structure. Yet despite its historical and contemporary influence on social institutions, population processes, and population policy, conventional demographers have tended to avoid racism as a topic of scholarly research. It is maintained that one impediment to the use of the concept as a variable in demographic analyses is the problem of measurement. Accordingly, the purpose of the research note reported in this chapter is to employ Critical Demography to facilitate the development of measures of racism relative to wealth, status, and power in the United States. Specifically, the following questions are addressed: (1) How is racism measured relative to wealth, status, and power in the United States? (2) Based upon these measures, how has racism changed over time? and (3) What are the theoretical implications of the measure of racism in the study of sociology, demography, and the social sciences in general?

RACISM AND THE MEASUREMENT OF RACIAL DIFFERENTIALS

Demography is not alone in its avoidance of racism as a topic, let alone variable, of analysis. Mainstream sociology has likewise tended to avoid the issue, as evidenced in the publication of articles in the *American Sociological Review*, the *American Journal of Sociology*, and *Social Forces*. However, what has emerged in both disciplines is a tradition of the measurement and analysis of racial differentials. The classic work of Otis Dudley Duncan (1968) set the standard for this approach. Essentially, the logic behind

Duncan's measure of "the cost of being black" is: once you have controlled for the array of variables that logically function as plausible alternative explanations, the net effect for the race variable is in essence a measure of racial discrimination.

Despite the obvious problem of not knowing if the next variable to be included might in fact make race statistically insignificant in a multivariate model, this has yet to be the case. Arguments on the declining significance of race not withstanding, there have been no studies to date that have been able to eliminate the statistical significance of race in multivariate models—even in the face of a multitude of social and demographic controls. However, what has changed is the interpretation of the effect of race in these models. There has been a subtle, but noticeable, attempt to attribute the remaining differential to cultural differences between Blacks and Whites. Ironically enough, this trend represents a return to the "blaming the victim" paradigm that predated Duncan's original work (Ryan 1972).

Since Duncan (1968), there have been a number of attempts to measure and/or assess racial differentials (Daymont and Kaufman 1979; Beggs et al. 1997; Bendick et al. 1999). A disproportionate amount of this work has been done by sociologists and psychologists who focus on the attitudes of Whites toward Blacks (Chin 1986; Dyer et al. 1989; Sidanius 1989; Gilbert 1998). In fact, in some cases, social psychological measures of racism itself have been attempted (Kleinpenning and Hagendoorn 1993). However, while this type of micro-level approach has some inherent value, it is maintained here that it misses the very nature of the social structure. Not only does racism at the macro-level impact micro-level attitudes on race, but it also functions independently of those individual level manifestations. In other words, given the structural nature and origin of racism, it can exist despite the relative decline of such at the micro-level. It is for this reason that not only is racial prejudice distinct from racism, the former is neither necessary nor sufficient to infer or indicate the presence of the latter. In practical terms, this means that in contemporary America, racism can continue to be a major force in determining racial inequality although the majority of dominant group members may not themselves be racist. But they don't have to be. The racism embedded into the heart of the social structure is on autopilot. Therefore, the first task toward the effective utilization of racism as a variable of analysis is to properly operationalize the concept. It is to this task that this chapter now turns.

OPERATIONALIZING RACISM

Since the introduction of the term by Ture and Hamilton (1992), racism has been defined in myriad ways. However, it is maintained here that prior definitions have not facilitated the operationalization of the concept so as to be amenable to measurement and analysis. Conversely, Horton's (forthcoming) definition that was introduced in the context of the Critical Demography paradigm is deemed the appropriate exception to this general rule:

> Racism is a multi-level and multi-dimensional system of dominant group oppression that scapegoats the race and/or ethnicity of one or more subordinate groups.

The implications of the use of this operationalization of racism are clear. First, any measure of racism must include models that encapsulate racism's role at both the macro and micro levels—at a minimum.[1] Second, because of the complexity and depth of racism in American society, it has many empirical manifestations. Thus, not only is the measure of racism likely to vary by context, within each there are likely to be multiple indicators of the phenomenon. Third, racism is a variable rather than a constant. That means it is subject to change over time. Accordingly, to properly measure racism, models must be used that capture the multilevel and multidimensional aspects of the concept while simultaneously accommodating the element of change.

Racism and the Emphasis on Wealth, Status, and Power

An acknowledgment of the structural basis of racism necessitates a reconsideration of racial differentials in wealth, status, and power. These are in fact the valued resources that dominant groups in any society struggle to maintain for themselves and to exclude from others. In the United States, there are clear indicators of each that provide the basis for the measurement of racism.

Racism and Wealth

The clearest indicator of the impact of racism on wealth is the distribution of the latter by race. Arguably the best example of this phenomenon is the level of racial inequality in home ownership and housing values. Racism in mortgage lending is well documented. Horton (1992) demonstrates that racial differentials in home ownership persisted even in the face of a broad range of social and demographic variables. Horton and Thomas (1998) find significant race-class interactions in their study of race and housing values. In fact, class actually exacerbated the race effect on housing values. In other words, despite the ongoing argument of class superceding race in its effect on lifestyle, middle-class Blacks were found to be at a greater disadvantage relative to middle-class Whites than working-class Blacks to their White counterparts in terms of housing values (Horton and Thomas 1998). Hence, it is argued here that it is quite appropriate to use housing values as a proxy for wealth on both historical and empirical grounds.

Racism and Status

Education, occupation, and income are defensibly the best indicators of racism and its effects on social status in the United States. Since Blau and Duncan's (1967) classic, *The American Occupational Structure*, sociologists have acknowledged the role that racial discrimination plays in impeding, if not eliminating altogether in some cases, the chances of improvements in socioeconomic status for Blacks. And where there has been a broad acknowledgment of an improvement in the likelihoods of Black achievement in these areas (Wilson 1978), there has yet to be any evidence that would suggest that Blacks have gained parity with Whites in education, occupation, and income (Horton et al. 2000). In fact, recent findings from the 2000 census show that the racial differential in income was practically unchanged over the 1990–2000 decade. Again, following the logic introduced by Duncan (1968), in a multivariate framework, the net effect for these variables are proxies for micro-level indicators of racism.

Racism and Power

Max Weber defined power as the ability to realize one's goals irrespective of the resistance of others. In contemporary America, the most visible manifestation of the power to maintain racial advantage is segregation. In contemporary research, the emphasis has tended to be confined to the area of residential segregation (Massey and Denton 1993; Emerson et al. 2001). However, Lieberson (1980) documented the process by which the dominant group in the United States eliminates subordinate groups from competition in education and income as well. This is a macro-level process and is perpetrated and perpetuated on the basis of race (Lieberson 1980). Accordingly, it is reasonable to argue that segregation measures across a broad range of social and economic indicators function as proxies for macro-level measures of the use of power to achieve racist goals, that is, macro-level indicators of racism.

DATA AND METHODS

The data employed in this study are the 1980 and 1990 Integrated Public Use Micro-Data Series (IPUMS) from the U.S. Bureau of the Census and the Minnesota Historical Census Project. The IPUMS data are well suited for this study because they allow for the inclusion of characteristics at the level of standard metropolitan statistical area (SMSA) and individual household. Moreover, IPUMS allows for the inclusion of a relatively large subsample of minority populations (in this case, Blacks). It should be noted that the data are cumulated so as to facilitate the assessment of change over time (Firebaugh 1997). The Ns for Blacks and Whites respectively are 277,780 and 2,581,676.

Combining Changing-Parameter and Hierarchical Linear Models

A unique feature of this study is the combination of changing-parameter models (Firebaugh 1997) with hierarchical linear modeling (Bryk and Raudenbush 1992). To our knowledge, there have been no prior studies to combine these two approaches. However from the standpoint of measuring racism, this combination is quite logical. In the case of hierarchical linear models, the rationale for the application is straightforward. The very definition of racism employed here requires that multilevel analysis be employed in its measurement. The inclusion of the changing-parameter model approach is necessary to assess the extent to which racism has changed over time. The resulting changing-parameter/hierarchical linear "hybrid" model is represented as follows:

$$E(Y_{ij}) = \alpha + \gamma D_{yr} + X_{ij}\beta + X_{ij}D_{yr}\delta$$

$X_{ij}D_{yr}$ represents the interaction term, which in essence measures the change in the predictor variables. For the sake of parsimony and clarity of interpretation, the use of interaction effects will be limited to the race-year interaction. It should be noted that cross-level interactions will be considered in subsequent analyses.

Operationalization of Variables

There are three dependent variables in this analysis: income, education, and housing values. All of the three are measured at the interval level. Income and housing values are logged.

The measures of racism are MSA-level variables. To create these variables, individual-level data for Blacks and Whites were aggregated. The index of dissimilarity was used to measure Black-White segregation in the areas of housing, educational attainment (college level), and social class position (middle class). In each instance, the index shows the level of movement that would have to occur between two or more groups to achieve complete integration.

Table 14.1. Descriptive Statistics for Whites and Blacks on Select Social and Demographic Indicators, 1980–1990

	Whites	*Blacks*
Region	2.83	2.78
Housing Values	$93,866.50	$68,113.78
Age	48.64	45.98
Sex	1.53	1.56
Marital Status	0.69	0.47
Education	6.76	6.09
Income	$16,559.60	$11,102.13
Social Class Position	2.12	2.26
Employment Status	1.77	1.79
Region	2.63	2.61
Proportion Middle Class	0.19	0.17
Proportion in Professional Occupations	0.14	0.10
Proportion Homeowners	0.72	0.55
Proportion College Educated	0.39	0.28
Observations	2,581,676	277,780

The logic in assessing the validity of the macro-level measures of racism is straightforward. Following Duncan's approach let's assume that controlling for plausible alternative causal factors leaves a race effect that represents racism at the micro level. That being the case, then the inclusion of macro-level indicators for racism should have a measurable effect on the micro-level race variable. In fact, we argue that this is the clearest evidence that the macro-level measures and the micro-level measure are in fact measuring the same phenomenon.

Race is a dichotomy with the codes of 1 for Black and 0 for Whites.[2] Other dichotomies are female, 1990, married, college, and homeowner. Trichotomies are class (middle, working, and bottom) and employment status (employed, unemployed, not in the labor force). For both variables the last category listed is the reference category. South is the reference category for the region variable. Table 14.1 presents the descriptive statistics for the study.

RESULTS

Table 14.2 presents the multilevel analysis of educational inequality. Model one represents the baseline model and consists of the micro-level racism effect and the intercept only. This model shows the expected trend that Blacks tend to have lower levels of education than Whites. Model two incorporates the standard controls that sociologists and demographers tend to employ in studies of racial inequality. The inclusion of these vari-

Table 14.2. A Multilevel Analysis of Inequality on Education between Blacks and Whites across Metropolitan Statistical Areas, 1980–1990

	Model 1	*Model 2*	*Model 3*
Intercept	9.7873***	7.0610***	7.3423***
Black	−0.6991***	−0.6688***	0.5995***
Controls			
1990		0.3709***	0.1144***
Age		−0.02950***	−0.02240***
Female		0.07889***	0.1662***
Employed		0.8054***	0.5566***
Unemployed		0.09649***	0.1864***
West		0.5859***	0.3497***
Northeast		0.3825***	0.2701***
Midwest		0.2636***	0.1596***
Married		0.1780***	0.1449***
Measures of Racism			
Middle Class Segregation			0.2051***
Occupational Segregation			0.4765***
Housing Segregation			0.3080***
Educational Segregation			3.8979
Between MSA Variance	0.1336***	0.1027***	0.003695***
Within MSA Variance	3.9038***	3.2682***	2.3467***
Subjects	321	321	321
Observations	2,860,000	2,860,000	2,680,000
−2 Log Likelihood	12,010,744	11,502,556	9,902,397

*** Indicates that the coefficients are statistically significant.

ables does not eliminate the effect of micro-level racism. In fact, there is only a marginal (and arguably nonsignificant) change in the magnitude of the micro-racism effect.

However, such is not the case with the inclusion of the macro-level measures of racism. In fact, the findings are so dramatic that they may be appropriately termed, in a Mertonian sense, "serendipitous."

The effect for race reverses in direction. Equally dramatic is the magnitude of the switch. The race effect goes from a −.6688 to a +.9843. The interpretation provided here is that while Blacks in general tend to have lower overall levels of education than Whites, in a few MSAs a different pattern emerges. When levels of racial segregation in class, occupation, housing, and (most importantly) college education are insubstantial, Blacks actually experience levels of education that exceed that of Whites. This is indeed a significant finding because not only does it provide dramatic evidence of the effects of the measures of macro-level racism, but it likewise shows that there are "pockets of progressiveness" in the United States relative to educational attainment.

Table 14.3 presents the income inequality analysis. As before, model one represents the baseline model. It shows the predictable pattern of Blacks having lower levels of income than Whites. Model two includes the controls. It should be noted that after the introduction of the controls the race effect is reduced to −.3076 from an original figure of −.4161 in the baseline model. However, the introduction of the macro-level measures of racism reverses the macro-level racism effect to .1558. Taken at face value, this finding essentially means that in a few MSAs where the levels of racial segregation on the indicators in question are relatively low, Blacks tend to experience higher levels of income than Whites.

Once again, this finding heretofore has not been reported in prior research and adds further credence to the argument that these measures are in fact measuring racism as it relates to income.

Table 14.4 presents a multi-level analysis of inequality in housing values. The baseline model (model one) shows the expected differential of Blacks

Table 14.3. A Multilevel Analysis of Income Inequality between Blacks and Whites across Metropolitan Statistical Areas, 1980–1990

	Model 1	*Model 2*	*Model 3*
Intercept	9.3505***	7.9712***	8.2358***
Black	–0.4161***	–0.3076***	0.1558***
Controls			
1990		0.2934***	0.1750***
Age		0.02455***	0.02197***
Age^2		–0.00014***	–0.00010***
Female		–0.7471***	–0.6811***
Employed		1.0757***	1.0064***
Unemployed		0.3431***	0.3558***
West		0.09447***	0.05274***
Northeast		0.09407***	0.04996***
Midwest		0.03049***	–0.03023***
Married		–0.08940***	–0.1040***
Some College		0.4587***	0.3624***
Measures of Racism			
Middle Class Segregation			0.5190***
Occupational Segregation			0.1996***
Housing Segregation			0.2806***
Segregation in Education			0.5546***
Between MSA Variance	0.01983**	0.01132***	0.008422***
Within MSA Variance	1.2255***	0.8642***	0.8291***
Subjects	321	321	321
Observations	2,550,000	2,550,000	2,680,000
–2 Log Likelihood	**7,756,419**	**6,865,445**	**7,111,154**

*** Indicates that the coefficients are statistically significant.

Table 14.4. A Multilevel Analysis of Inequality in Housing Values between Blacks and Whites across Metropolitan Statistical Areas, 1980–1990

	Model 1	*Model 2*	*Model 3*
Intercept	11.0529***	10.1586***	9.9763***
Black	–0.3902***	–0.2787***	0.03945***
Controls			
1990		0.4900***	0.5427***
Age		0.000963***	0.01556***
Female		0.03661***	0.01129***
Employed		0.04091***	0.07961***
Unemployed		–0.07500***	–0.05213***
West		0.2986***	0.2643***
Northeast		0.4372***	0.4100***
Midwest		–0.03633***	–0.1371***
Married		0.2042***	0.1887***
Measures of Racism			
Middle Class Segregation			0.2900***
Occupational Segregation			0.09302***
Segregation in Education			0.4892***
Housing Segregation			0.1307
Between MSA Variance	0.1937***	0.1087***	0.1117***
Within MSA Variance	0.5773***	0.4801***	0.4791***
Subjects	321	321	321
Observations	1,890,000	1,890,000	1,600,000
–2 Log Likelihood	4,319,252	3,971,021	3,361,220

*** Indicates that the coefficients are statistically significant.

owning homes of lower value than Whites. Once controls are introduced (model 2) the effect is reduced but is still substantial (from −.3902 to −.2787). However, the introduction of the macro-level measures of racism reverses this effect again. The positive log-odds of .0395 indicate that in those MSAs where the macro-level effects of racism are relatively low, Blacks tend to have slightly higher levels of housing values. To reiterate, this serendipitous finding is clearly at odds with past studies and present assumptions. Moreover, it underscores the fact that racism is multilevel and multidimensional in nature.

Finally, table 14.5 presents the results of the multilevel changing-parameter model analyses. The educational inequality model shows that the trend of higher levels of education for Blacks than Whites in those MSAs with relatively low levels of macro-level racism was evident in 1980. That trend significantly increased by 1990. In short, in those MSAs, Blacks further extended their advantage over Whites in education over the decade. The income inequality model shows that Blacks trailed Whites in 1980, but improved modestly over the decade. The housing value model shows that

Table 14.5. Changing-Parameter Models for Blacks and Whites on Education, Income, and Housing Values, 1980–1990

	Education	*Income*	*Housing Values*
Intercept	6.0362***	7.7283***	9.9819***
Black	0.6243***	–0.09470***	–0.1117***
Black*1990	0.5664***	0.07164***	0.2120***
Controls			
1990	0.1946***	0.2527***	0.5254***
Age	–0.02311***	0.02347***	0.01570***
Age^2		-0.00011***	
Female	0.1744***	–0.7068***	0.01232***
Employed	0.5303***	0.9791***	0.07954***
Unemployed	0.1453***	0.3557***	–0.05264***
West	0.4413***	0.05739***	0.2653***
Northeast	0.3707***	0.07882***	0.4110***
Midwest	0.3052***	0.03174***	–0.1347***
Married	0.1685***	–0.1169***	0.1894***
Some College		0.5197***	
Measures of Racism			
Middle Class Segregation	0.1896***	0.5539***	0.2851***
Occupational Segregation	0.4622***	0.2048***	0.09306***
Housing Segregation	0.3973***	0.2767***	0.1383***
Segregation in Education	3.9014***	–0.3057***	0.4937***
Between MSA Variance	0.05427***	0.007225***	0.1115***
Within MSA Variance	2.3447***	0.7999***	0.4786***
Subjects	321	321	321
Observations	2,860,000	2,550,000	1,600,000
–2 Log Likelihood	10,552,873	6,668,355	3,359,270

*** Indicates that the coefficients are statistically significant.

Blacks improved relative to Whites over the decade on this measure. In short, the evidence shows that on every measure of inequality, Blacks experienced significant improvement relative to Whites between 1980 and 1990.

CONCLUSION

The purpose of this chapter was to employ the Critical Demography paradigm to facilitate the development of measures of racism. Using the definition of racism that was introduced by Horton (forthcoming), hierarchical linear models and changing-parameter models were used to assess the impact of macro-level measures of racism on micro-level race effects and to measure their respective effects over time. The analyses provided some surprising results. First, once the macro-level measures of racism were incorporated into the standard models of racial inequality, there were dramatic changes in the micro-level race effects relative to education, income, and housing values. Education showed the most dramatic change. Blacks went from having significantly lower levels of educational attainment to actually surpassing Whites in those MSAs where the levels of racial segregation in class, occupation, education, and housing were relatively low. The race effects on income and housing values were similar in direction though of lesser magnitude. In essence, in both cases the effects were reversed from the baseline model: once the macro-level effects for racism were controlled, Blacks exceeded Whites on income and housing values. These serendipitous results have not been found by prior research and represent a major step forward toward the understanding and reconceptualization of the meanings of race, racism, and racial inequality in contemporary America.

Moreover, the results of the analyses from the changing-parameter models showed that on all three measures of inequality there was improvement for Blacks over the decade. In the case of education, it was revealed that the unexpected higher Black than White effect in some MSAs actually was present in 1980. Ultimately, these results provide substantial support to the rationale of the inclusion of measures of racism in multilevel models of racial inequality.

While it is important to note that this study is preliminary, it is nevertheless appropriate to discuss some of its implications—there are several. First, MSAs can be identified and ranked based upon these macro-level measures of racism. This would be of benefit to researchers interested in the conditions that facilitate or inhibit the levels of racial inequality in society. From a policy perspective, knowing where the "pockets of progressiveness" are would be helpful in the further enhancement of the conditions that promote racial equality.

Another implication of the application of these measures of racism is to determine if and how the macro-level measures of racism vary across racial and ethnic groups. In other words, it has been long established that Blacks are the group that experiences the greatest degree of racial segregation across a number of dimensions. However, if there are MSAs where Blacks equal or exceed Whites on education or income, then it is logical to argue that there would be similar patterns when Asians and/or Latinos are so compared. Moreover, it would be possible to determine if there are certain MSAs that are more favorable to one minority as opposed to others. Past research would lead us to believe that the relative population size of the minority group in question is an important factor. However, prior research also provided no evidence to suggest the findings of this analysis. It is likely that there may be more "serendipity" to be found once we expand beyond the simple Black-White model.

In sum, Critical Demography facilitates a freedom of thought and scientific inquiry that is alien to its conventional counterpart. Measuring racism is but one example of the potential of this dynamic new paradigm. And while it is premature to state that the measures provided here are definitive, we believe that they represent a major step forward in the study of racial inequality in the fields of sociology and demography. One thing is unequivocal: whatever racism truly is, there is evidence here to support the argument that it is multilevel and multidimensional in nature. Moreover, we have demonstrated that it is possible to incorporate racism, race, and racial inequality in a single multivariate model. Consequently, we will continue to develop new measures and to introduce more refined and in some instances more complex (i.e., three-level and cross-level interaction) models to capture the dynamics of racism in American society. We welcome other scholars as we continue to expand the boundaries of Critical Demography and sociology as well.

NOTES

1. It should be noted that racism also functions at the medial level. In fact, one might argue that it is at this level where much, if not most, of the racism that impacts individuals exists. However, for the purpose of exposition, and as well as the developmental nature of the current analysis, only two levels of racism will be considered here. Most certainly, further development of the racism concept will incorporate the medial level in its conceptualization and measurement.

2. It should be noted that Hispanics and Asians are excluded from this analysis. The logic here is based upon lower levels of segregation for these groups (compared to Blacks). Future analyses and development of the measure of racism will include these groups.

15

As Racial Boundaries "Fade"

Racial Stratification and Interracial Marriage

Jenifer L. Bratter and Tukufu Zuberi

Over the past 400 years the racial demography of the United States population has undergone several shifts in racial composition, altering the potential for interracial contact and the landscape of racial relationships (Zuberi 2001a; McDaniel 1995a). Since the 1960s, increased international migration from Africa, Asia, the Caribbean, and Latin America; increasing marriages across racial lines; and subsequently a growing number of multiracial births have similarly altered the picture of potential interracial contact. These recent changes have been cast as harkening a "new era" of diversity. Several note, that while immigration has always shaped the ethnic character of the United States, these "new immigrants" are largely non-White and these new waves of immigration are more extensive than the wave from Europe (Gans 1999; Lee and Bean 2004; Gibson and Lennon 1999). What are the implications of these changes in diversity? According to the classic assimilation model, the changing distribution of group difference and thus the growing potential for intergroup contact will result in an increase in those contacts and in turn transform "race" from a marker of status to a neutral aspect of human difference, much like ethnicity (Alba and Nee 2002; Park 1967). However, this relationship presents an interesting conundrum—How can race become less relevant through a process by which race becomes more differentiated? How does race cease to segment human interactions when more individuals are faced with racial difference? Will racial boundaries fade from existence as racial diversity increases?

Prior to suggesting an answer, these questions are premised on the notion that increased racial diversity will necessarily narrow majority-minority social distance. In this chapter, we critique this assertion by extending the analysis beyond the purview of the assimilation model. From a racial stratification standpoint, the development of race and racial categories is based on allocations of power and privilege (Bonilla-Silva 1997; Mckee 1993; Bashi and McDaniel 1997; Cox 1948; Zuberi 2001b) and therefore is rooted in a hierarchical relationship between those who have access to resources and those for whom access is restricted. The empirical basis of race is reflected in how it stratifies life experience in several arenas (i.e., social and economic mobility, mental and physical health) (Williams and Harris-Reid 1999; Oliver and Shapiro 1995) and maintains meaning in social interactions (e.g., Timberlake 2000). In light of the varying ways race continues to matter, growing potential for contacts may have variable effects on actual relationships. Extending from this variation, increases in racial diversity and increases in racial differentiation may not necessarily narrow the social distance between majority and minority members, between Whites and non-Whites. In this chapter, we build on our prior work on associations between racial diversity and racial contact (see Bratter and Zuberi 2001) by exploring two issues. First, we focus on the most recent increases in diversity and their impact on the level of intermarriage occurring between various racial pairs. We also account for the impact of recent immigration by subdividing our analyses between a sample of the entire U.S. population and those who were born in the United States.

RACIAL DIVERSITY AND INTERRACIAL CONTACT: A NEEDED LENS OF RACIAL STRATIFICATION

We situate the study of racial composition and intergroup contact within a framework of racial stratification. We argue that racial stratification provides a useful framework to analyze these issues on two grounds. First, this framework explores the ways racialized social systems operate to reproduce racial hierarchies (see Bonilla-Silva 1997). In this sense, the reality of rising diversity, instead of doing away with race, may alter how race influences social interactions.

Second, changes in racial composition cannot be explored independent of social, historical, and legal realties of racial classification (Bashi and McDaniel 1997; McDaniel 1996; Zuberi 2001a), and therefore we cannot assume that race is a constant set of fixed mutually exclusive categories whose composition merely reflects a wide array of objective human differences. Recent changes in racial classification, including the recent implementation of multiple-race reporting on the 2000 census, indicate that increased racial diversity may serve to redraw the lines of race.

Third, it allows for a critical analysis of the role of whiteness in the study of racial contact (Doane and Bonilla-Silva 2003). Many studies of intermarriage focus on the rate of contact between White and non-White populations as indicators of racial social distance (Qian 1997). Low levels of intermarriage are explained in terms of cultural or structural barriers that inhibit interaction with a White majority (Hwang, Saenz, and Aguirre 1997; Cready and Saenz 1997). However, if "whiteness" is viewed as a form of racialized power instead of an individual attribute, the reality of individual contacts becomes more a reflection of social structural circumstances and less the evidence of individual proclivities that operate at random.

This position has received scant attention from the literature on the topic. Broadly, the studies on intermarriage emphasize two major themes. The first is how the landscape of American racial relationships is being transformed through a reduction of social distance between racial groups and the reduction of salience of ethnic and racial differences in social interactions (George and Yancey 2004). The second, which derives from analysis of stratification and educational assortative mating, is the progressive decline of importance of ascribed traits (i.e., race, ethnicity, religion) relative to the increasing importance of achieved traits (earned education, occupational status) in the selection of mates (Mare 1995; Kalmijn 1993; Qian 1997). The underlying assumption is that ascribed and achieved traits are independent constructs and that the meaning of one has no bearing on the other. However, several have shown that a model of status exchange, where the caste status is traded for the class status (Merton 1941) is more applicable for intermarriage between Whites and African Americans and some Hispanic groups, relative to what is observed for Asians. For example, the likelihood of having White spouses is less contingent on education for Asians than for Blacks or Hispanics indicating a pattern of status exchange for the latter groups (see Fu 2001; Kalmijn 1993, Qian 1997).

Explaining the linkage between race, status, and interracial interactions requires an attention to the existence of racial hierarchies that supersedes the individual's ability to act. Racial stratification, as an alternate model to study racial difference, highlights the role of racial hierarchies both in the classification (who is classified as "Black" vs. "White") and perpetuation of racial categories and the dynamics of racial change. Through the application of racial stratification, we can consider how the operationalization of race as a neutral construct as well as models that view interracial marriage as the natural outgrowth of racial diversity, inhibit a broader exploration of the changing and enduring nature of racial relationships.

RESEARCH GOALS

We have three research goals addressed by the analysis. We begin by revisiting changes in diversity and intergroup contact by exploring the impact of immigration on these shifts. Many of the forecasts of changing diversity reflect the influx of immigrants from Asian, Latin America, and Africa that affect the overall racial composition. Our first analysis, which examines changes among the U.S.-born, only compares this to all U.S. residents, to show racial diversity within a native-born context relative to what we would observe if the entire U.S. population was analyzed. From this, we then compare two most recent eras of increased intermarriage, the 1980s and the 1990s, with the corresponding changes in diversity for both the U.S.-born and the total population. The increase of intermarriage throughout the 1980s has been linked to several notions of the ways racial interactions are being restructured (e.g., reduced importance of ascribed traits, increased social proximity, increased assimilation).

We contend that many of these are premised on the notion that White–non-White distance will narrow as men and women have an increase in the number of potential mates of different groups. To test this assertion, we show the percent change in interracial marriage for several White–non-White pairs in both eras of increased diversity. Ultimately, this will show whether the most recent changes translate into even greater increases in interracial marriage. Finally, we explore these associations statistically. We present a simple regression analysis of each type of intermarriage (e.g., Black-White, Asian-White, and Hispanic-White) on the index of racial diversity (which measures the probability of interracial contact) to show the associations in 1980, 1990, and 2000. These associations show both the direction of the association as well as the degree to which de facto changes in intermarriage are actually explained by de facto changes in diversity.

Racial Compositional Changes in the Recent Era

Over the past four centuries racial compositional shifts have reorganized the relationships between racial groups (Zuberi 2001b). In the most recent era, these patterns are characterized by increases in racial diversity due largely to (1) the influx of immigration from Asia, Latin America, and Africa; (2) the rise of interracial marriage and concomitant rise of multiethnic/multiracial births; and (3) the growth of populations of color outpacing the growth of the non-Hispanic White "majority" population (Lee and Bean 2004; Gans 1999). The compositional shifts since 1980 recorded in the decennial census are shown in table 15.1, which reports the racial composition of U.S. population for all residents and then separately for those born in the United States. The patterns show that many of the shifts in racial composition are due to the addition of foreign-born residents. For example, although non-Hispanic Whites represent a decreasing share of the population, from nearly 80 percent in 1980 to slightly less 70 percent in 2000, this change is less drastic among the native born, where in 2000 non-Hispanic Whites represent 75 percent of the population. The growth of the Hispanic

Table 15.1. Racial Composition of U.S. Population, All Residents and Native Born

	All U.S. Residents			*Native-Born Residents Only*		
	1980	*1990*	*2000*	*1980*	*1990*	*2000*
NH White	79.60	75.72	69.09	81.61	79.68	75.00
NH Black	11.60	11.77	12.00	12.04	12.30	12.78
American Indian	0.63	0.76	0.74	0.66	0.81	0.82
Asian	1.56	2.79	3.70	0.66	1.00	1.31
Other/Two or More Races	0.09	0.10	1.95	0.06	0.08	1.70
Hispanic	6.53	8.87	12.52	4.96	6.13	8.39

Source: Integrated Public Use Microdata Sample, 1980–2000 (Ruggles 2002).

and Asian populations during this period is almost entirely a function of immigration. Although in absolute terms Hispanics have dislodged African Americans as the majority minority group, representing a larger share of the population (12.5 percent Hispanic vs. 12.0 percent non-Hispanic Black), this difference disappears once the focus is narrowed to the native born only. Proportionately, African Americans represent nearly 13 percent of the population in 2000, and Hispanics represent 8 percent in the same year. However, recent forecasts of a changing racial landscape emphasize that these populations are both likely to overtake the classic biracial Black-White divide as being the major racial division. Asians and Hispanics have larger growth rates, and thus the contributions of the second and third generation in the years to come will also affect the racial composition in the future. Edmonston, Lee, and Passel (2002) estimate that the single-origin Hispanic population will grow from 29.7 million in 2000 to 77.2 million in 2100 and the Asian population will grow from 9.5 million in 2000 to 55.8 million in 2100. These authors estimate growing numbers of intergroup contact in each decennial year, as Asians and Hispanics of multiple-origin persons represent an increasing share of the entire group (see 244–48).

The changes in racial composition do suggest an increase in the extent of racial contact opportunities. To capture the full potential of interracial contact opportunities, we show the levels of the racial index of diversity (see Zuberi 2001b for formula), which documents the probability that two randomly selected individuals will be of the same race. As the index approaches 1.00, the probability that two randomly selected individuals will be of different racial groups also grows. Figure 15.1 shows the racial index of diversity across 1980, 1990, and 2000, for the entire U.S. population as well as the native-born population only. While the increases have been substantial, from 0.4 to over 0.5, this strongly reflects the influence of recent immigration altering the racial composition. Examining these figures among the native-born population only, the trend of racial diversity and

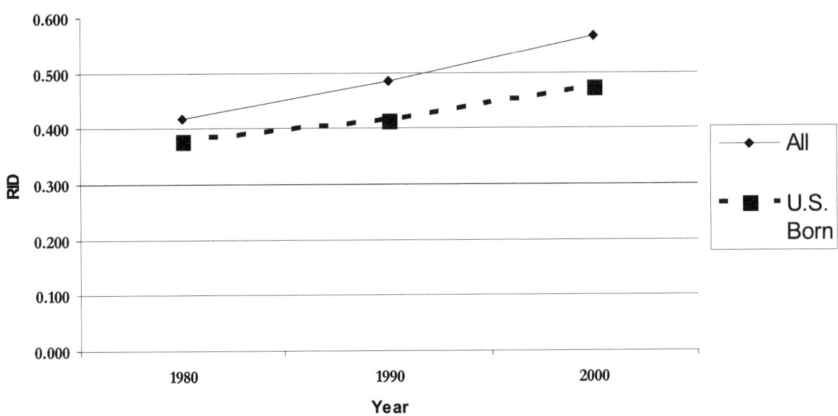

Figure 15.1. RID for the U.S., 1980–2000, by Nativity

potential for contact is much more subdued, indicating that among the native-born population the opportunities for interracial contact are lower than the full picture of racial composition would suggest but that increase in contact opportunities are present among the native born.

Implications for Racial Contact

These shifts in racial diversity have also coincided with massive changes in the ways race has organized relationships. During the twentieth century racial compositional changes have produced two disparate outcomes for the reality of cross-racial interaction. The first has been the increased potential of interracial contact and the increased opportunity to realize that potential. This path echoes expectations from an assimilation model of racial relationships where increased racial diversity, thus contact opportunities across racial lines, coincides with a withering away of racial difference insofar as it affects interracial contact. As interracial contacts increase, as evinced through increased interracial marriage, increased racial integration of populations of color with a White majority, and increased multiracial/multiethnic births, racial diversity can be seen as a mechanism of the declining importance race carries in social interactions (Alba and Nee 2002).

The second path is one of increased differentiation by race that has also produced increased potential for racialized conflict. This path suggests that changes will have very different impacts on different racial groups, particularly in how they engage with majority members (i.e., the non-Hispanic White population). While the demographic composition of the age, sex, and racial structure has always yielded some potential for interracial intermingling, the degree to which such potential has become a reality rests on a variety of factors. Rates of interracial marriage between various groups have been moderated by institutional arrangements, such as legal segregation or "Jim Crow," the legal bans on miscegenation, and the legal construction of a Black relative to a White identity (Williamson 1984; Lopez 1996). In addition, despite increasing diversity, there were several structural constraints to social interactions, most notably the degree of residential segregation experienced by the Black population following the mass exodus from the South to the North and the Midwest (Taeuber and Taeuber 1965; Massey and Denton 1993). This trend did not simply affect Black Americans, as "Black" Hispanics are also found to be relatively more segregated within nominally Black neighborhoods than other Hispanics (Massey and Denton 1985).

However, in light of diminishing institutional barriers since the 1960s and policy initiatives aimed at redressing racial inequality, some theorize that race presents less of a barrier in the modern era (Patterson 1997; Thernstrom and Thernstrom 1997). Several indexes of social distance, such as social attitudes, reveal that race is no longer the rift in relationships that it once was. Trends in attitudes regarding racial interactions from the most formal to the most intimate indicate that thinking about race has also changed in that levels of what has been called "traditional prejudice" have declined. Due to an increased social acceptance, interracial actions of all stripes as well as the absence of legal segregation and legal sanctions against miscegenation provide a context to make interracial interactions more available than was the case in the past. Buttressed by an increased institutional integration of African Americans within schools and occupations, men and women of different racial backgrounds also had an increased opportunity to meet each other. Further, the patterns observed in the 1980s, 1990s, and onward will be guided increasingly by cohorts of men and women who grew up during an era where such sanctions did not exist (Bobo 2001). Figure 15.2 shows the number of interracial couples, from 1980 to 2002, where at least one partner is White or Black. The top line demonstrates this pattern, as the number of marriages involving at least one White person or one Black person was enumerated as 651,000 in 1980 to 1.6 million in 2002. However, the overall trend seems to be driven more by the pairs of Whites and non-Blacks (e.g., Asians, Native Americans, Hispanics) than marriages involving one White spouse and one Black spouse. Black-White marriages represent roughly one-quarter of all interracial marriages involving one non-White partner and one White partner (Tabulation of CPS data) and though this is a sizable portion of interracial marriage, recently Asians, Hispanics, and Native Americans are reporting higher rates of intermarriage relative to African Americans (see Qian 1997). However, what is driving the increased propensity of contact that

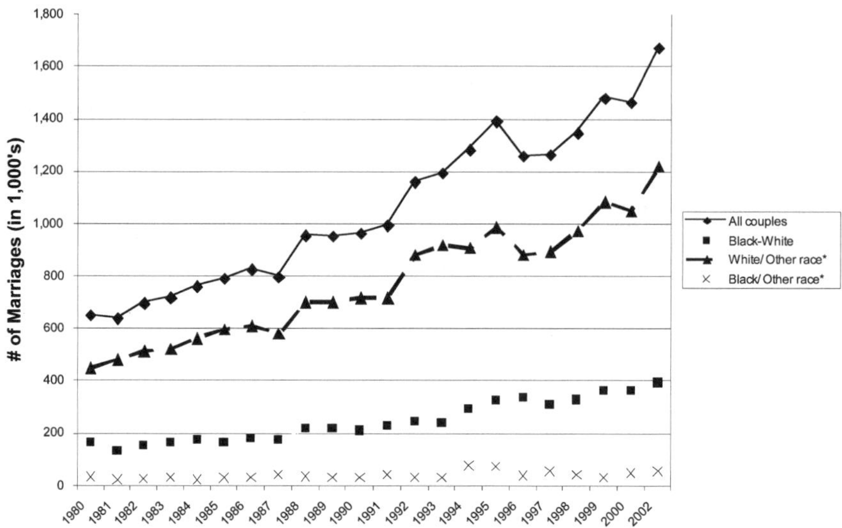

Figure 15.2. Number of Interracial Couples with at Least One White or Black Partner

occurs between some populations and not others? While a whole host of compositional influences such as age, sex, education composition, and local availability of mates in a local area play important roles (Hwang et al., 1997; Cready and Saenz 1997), accounting for these and several other conditions has not yet been able to fully account for the differences in propensity toward interracial marriage.

Several empirical accounts document the low levels of interracial marriage and intergroup interactions occurring between African American and Whites compared to other groups (Qian 1997; Jacobs and Labov 2003; Heaton and Jacobson 2000; Fu 2001). Here, what can be observed is that the growing contact is not necessarily a by-product of growing racial diversity and that racial contact opportunities will not render equal contacts for all groups. Recently several scholars have suggested that the most significant racial line to be crossed has shifted from being between Whites and non-Whites to existing between Blacks and non-Blacks (Gans 1999). The discussion of the variation in intergroup contact and its racialized consequences challenge the expectations of assimilation, and operate to support a path of continued racial stratification. The "emergence" of the Black–non-Black divide cannot occur without the folding of previously non-White groups into a category of socially constructed "whiteness." While this is framed as an emergence of a new dividing line, it reflects a barrier that has always been present as a consequence of the construction of race and its implications for the distribution of resources, identity, and social interactions.

This line has persistently placed certain individuals in opposing relationships to others (see Zuberi 2001a). This leads to the second outcome of increased diversity—that of growing differentiation.

Racial Contact and Racial Diversity

In order to assess this, we employ a measure that is not sensitive to compositional issues of group size, differences in the numbers of men or women, or the age structure. The Z index (see Schoen 1988 for formula) renders a scaled indicator of how much "marital attraction" occurs between two groups given the current degree of intergroup contact. The scale, ranging from 0.0 to 1.0, reports the total extent of intergroup contact as a proportion of the total contact occurring both within and between groups. Because this index is a symmetrical measure of contact between two groups, it improves on rates of intergroup contact that focus on the extent of out-marriage, or the degree that one population is marrying out of another, but do not account for the extent to which other populations are intermarrying. For example, interracial marriage statistics commonly report on the extent to which populations of color marry "out" of their respective racial group into a majority. However, few of these accounts report to what degree the majority (i.e., non-Hispanic Whites) marry "out" of their own group. In this sense, levels of Black and White homogamy are highly similar, though White homogamy has rarely if ever been identified as a product of social distance or of an inability for Whites to integrate into a multicultural majority experience.

In Figure 15.1, we show both the Racial Index of Diversity (RID) alongside the Z index from 1980 to 2000 computed for the native-born population only. The data we employ come from the Integrated Public Use Microdata Samples (Ruggles et al. 2004). In order to control for the influence of racial composition within different areas, particularly between rural and urban areas and impact on conduct, we restrict our analyses to the metropolitan samples. Similar to our previous work (Bratter and Zuberi 2001), we show that the degree of Black-White marital attraction is far lower than the degree of Asian-White, Hispanic-White, or Native American–White. However, within the most recent era of census (1990–2000), the only evident increase in marital attraction is between Blacks and Whites. All other groups experience a decrease in the level of marital attraction experienced with Whites.

Figure 15.1 reports the RID (shaded in gray) and the Z index figures for both the entire U.S. and native-born populations. We also present the analyses by region in order to account for regional differences in racial composition that affect interracial contact opportunities (Qian 1999). The figures reveal two compelling issues regarding racial contact. The first is that including foreign-born respondents seriously underestimates the extent of marital attraction occurring between Asians and Whites and Hispanics and Whites.

At every year, both regionally and nationally, the Z index for the U.S. born (listed in the right-hand panels) exceeds the marital attraction that occurs when all U.S. residents, regardless of nativity, are considered. This is to be expected, as foreign birth often impedes the process of marital assimilation because of cultural barriers—that is, linguistic isolation and spatial isolation in immigrant enclaves (Qian 1999; Hwang et al. 1997). However, this occurs in the midst of *greater* racial diversity not less. Regionally, the greatest degree of diversity is in the western and the southern United States. However, the greatest degree of marital attraction between Whites and Asians and Whites and Hispanics is in the midwestern United States. For Asian-White pairs, the Z index remains steady between 0.38 and 0.35 during 1990 and 2000 and for Hispanic-White pairs, the Z index is at 0.24 in 1990 and 2000. Therefore, levels of intergroup contact between Asians, Hispanics, and Whites are greatest in regions that have comparatively less diversity. Meanwhile, the Z indexes for Black-White and Native American–White pairs are greatest in areas with highest diversity, the western United States, a level of 0.05 for Black-White and 0.17 for Native American–Whites. Interestingly, these two estimates are less affected by including the foreign-born populations.

The results shown in the previous figure indicate that levels of racial diversity do not neatly translate into or correspond with levels of interracial contact. While this is somewhat due to the degree of diversity reflecting the inclusion of the foreign-born population, the patterns of U.S.-born persons in isolation (thus taking that foreign-born component out of the analysis) suggest that high diversity corresponds to high intermarriage for certain groups. Interestingly, the Z index is highest in regions where the minority group is proportionately less represented. Asians and Hispanics, even without the foreign born, have the highest numbers in western states, though this is the area of less intermarriage, despite higher contact opportunities.

Table 15.2 explores the rate of change between the RID and the Z during the 1980s (1980–1990) and the 1990s (1990–2000). Table 15.3 reports the percent increase (or decrease in the case of negative numbers) of the RID and the Z indexes. As the previous figures and table 15.2 indicate, levels of racial diversity have risen in both eras, but with a more expansive increase during the 1990s. Nationally, the RID rose 17 percent when considering the entire U.S. population and rose by 14 percent among the native born. Although diversity rose to a greater extent in the later decade, the percent changes in Z indicate interracial marriage increased more in the 1980s than in the 1990s. When observing the entire population, percent changes in Z indicate net decreases during the 1990s for every White–non-White pairing

Table 15.2. Racial Index of Diversity and Index of Marital Attraction, 1980 to 2000

	All U.S. Residents			*U.S. Born Residents*		
	1980	*1990*	*2000*	*1980*	*1990*	*2000*
Nation						
Index of Diversity	0.418	0.484	0.567	0.379	0.414	0.474
Black-White	0.009	0.016	0.022	0.008	0.015	0.021
Indian-White	0.095	0.133	0.116	0.095	0.136	0.122
Asian-White	0.101	0.090	0.071	0.146	0.182	0.191
Hispanic-White	0.095	0.100	0.083	0.129	0.154	0.158
Region						
North						
Index of Diversity	0.355	0.422	0.503	0.315	0.343	0.398
Black-White	0.012	0.023	0.023	0.011	0.025	0.024
Indian-White	0.029	0.079	0.092	0.027	0.091	0.136
Asian-White	0.073	0.059	0.048	0.222	0.316	0.248
Hispanic-White	0.078	0.096	0.084	0.095	0.120	0.125
Midwest						
Index of Diversity	0.275	0.306	0.368	0.257	0.278	0.315
Black-White	0.010	0.023	0.029	0.009	0.016	0.028
Indian-White	0.119	0.166	0.152	0.119	0.164	0.154
Asian-White	0.112	0.107	0.093	0.319	0.384	0.355
Hispanic-White	0.147	0.169	0.126	0.206	0.249	0.249
South						
Index of Diversity	0.496	0.536	0.607	0.468	0.489	0.537
Black-White	0.005	0.010	0.016	0.004	0.008	0.014
Indian-White	0.076	0.115	0.108	0.076	0.116	0.111
Asian-White	0.144	0.126	0.087	0.230	0.312	0.265
Hispanic-White	0.079	0.087	0.077	0.096	0.117	0.127
West						
Index of Diversity	0.518	0.610	0.681	0.443	0.494	0.563
Black-White	0.028	0.047	0.055	0.022	0.042	0.052
Indian-White	0.145	0.173	0.136	0.143	0.174	0.170
Asian-White	0.095	0.092	0.077	0.125	0.156	0.170
Hispanic-White	0.110	0.112	0.095	0.158	0.193	0.199

Source: 1980 1% PUMS (Metro sample), 1990 1% PUMS (Metro sample), 2000 1% PUMS. Collected with Integrated Public Use Microdata Samples (Ruggles, 2002).

except Blacks and Whites. While this undoubtedly reflects the inclusion of the foreign born, the percent changes among the U.S. born reveal increases in intermarriage across all pairs during the 1980s and either less extensive decreases during the 1990s or net decrease. From 1980 to 1990, the extent of intermarriage between Blacks and Whites rose 81 percent and then rose by only 41 percent from 1990 to 2000. The differences for Asian-White intermarriage are even more stark, as during the 1980s (from 1980–1990), the percent change in intermarriage was 24.5 percent; this lowered to only 4.7 percent in the 1990s. The degree of Hispanic-White intermarriage also increased by the 1980s, only to taper off to an increase of 2.8 percent in the 1990s. The extent of Native American–White marriage actually decreased during the 1990s by 10 percent.

Taking into account the regional differences in percent changes in the Z index, marital distance has narrowed to the greatest extent between Blacks and Whites. Despite the low rates of intermarriage in both eras, the percent change was positive in both time periods. The regions with the highest percent increases during the latter era were the Midwest and the South (71 percent and 76 percent respectively), followed by the West (increased by 24 percent), and the Northeast, which experienced a net decrease of intermarriage by 3.19 percent, after increasing by 120 percent. The comparatively low levels of percent change in Z for Asian-White and Hispanic-White marriage is reflected in the regional data. In the most recent era, Asian-White marital attraction has declined in every region, with the exception of the West, where the Z rose by 9 percent. This contrasts with what was achieved in a previous era, where the Z index rose by 24 percent during the 1980s.

As shown in table 15.3, Hispanic-White marital attraction increased in every region, with the exception of the Midwest where the index remained essentially the same from 1990 to 2000, declining by only –.04 percent. Among all the pairs, the Native American–White marital distance declined nationally by 10.29 percent, due to decreases in every region except the Northeast where the index rose by 49.65 percent. However, this is again dwarfed by the massive increase in intermarriage during the 1980s where the Z index more than doubled.

One clear pattern emerges throughout the trends of increases and decreases. The greatest increases occur for pairs with the lowest intermarriage rates (e.g., Blacks and Whites); meanwhile the least increase occurs for the pair with the greatest marital attraction (e.g., Asians and Hispanics). This strongly suggests that percent changes for Blacks may be exploiting the effects of a few marriages that result in what appears to be an increase of greater magnitude. These patterns suggest that marital attraction can only increase by so much during a ten-year period, at which point it either stabilizes or declines. This may indicate that race as a divider in the marriage market can only weaken so much, despite wholesale increases in the probability of racial contact represented through changes in racial diversity.

The Statistical Association between Diversity and Interracial Contact

The percent changes of table 15.2 show that increases in racial diversity do not necessarily result in a narrowing of marital distance between majority and minority persons. In some cases, these distances appeared to widen, suggesting that the connection between diversity and intermarriage may in

Table 15.3. **Percent Changes in RID and Z Index, Nationally and by Region**

	All U.S. Residents		U.S. Born Residents	
	1980–1990	1990–2000	1980–1990	1990–2000
Index of Diversity	13.66	17.20	9.17	14.56
Intermarriage Indexes				
Black-White	42.89	35.88	81.98	41.52
Indian-White	28.36	–13.23	42.36	–10.29
Asian-White	–12.50	–20.86	24.54	4.76
Hispanic-White	4.18	–16.31	19.61	2.89
Region				
North				
Index of Diversity	18.87	19.33	8.94	16.07
Intermarriage Indexes				
Black-White	95.08	–2.45	120.92	–3.19
Indian-White	169.16	16.68	236.59	49.65
Asian-White	–19.82	–17.28	42.40	–21.50
Hispanic-White	22.26	–12.06	27.02	4.19
Region				
Midwest				
Index of Diversity	11.30	20.22	7.99	13.22
Intermarriage Indexes				
Black-White	128.48	24.77	73.08	71.24
Indian-White	38.76	–8.11	38.40	–6.41
Asian-White	–4.21	–13.18	20.23	–7.42
Hispanic-White	15.00	–25.67	20.46	–0.04
Region				
South				
Index of Diversity	8.08	13.28	4.34	9.80
Intermarriage Indexes				
Black-White	108.55	65.90	105.47	76.88
Indian-White	51.49	–6.53	52.09	–4.33
Asian-White	–12.82	–31.12	19.98	–14.97
Hispanic-White	9.66	–10.89	22.27	8.28
Region				
West				
Index of Diversity	17.83	11.51	11.67	13.87
Intermarriage Indexes				
Black-White	68.43	18.19	88.26	24.07
Indian-White	19.65	–21.45	21.33	–1.84
Asian-White	–2.97	–16.77	24.37	9.40
Hispanic-White	1.88	–15.38	21.87	3.44

Source: 1980 1% PUMS (Metro sample), 1990 1% PUMS (Metro sample), 200 1% PUMS.

fact be negative, indicating that greater diversity yields greater differentiation and not greater proximity between races. In Table 15.3, we employ an ordinary least-squares regression of the marital attraction index (Z) on the racial diversity index.

In order to approximate these effects on a level that can approximate a marriage market and thus an arena where racial diversity may influence marriage activity, the data are further disaggregated to the level of state, instead of region. Several states were omitted from the analysis as the number of non-White persons was too low to produce a viable index. The degrees of freedom (df) are $n - 1$, or the number of states minus one for the parameter of the Index of Diversity that is in the model.

The results of table 15.3 suggest that the racial index of diversity is negatively associated with marital attraction in every case. For example, the index of diversity is negatively associated with marital attraction between Blacks and Whites in 1980, 1990, and 2000. In 1980, an increase in the index of diversity of 1 unit corresponds to a .09 decrease in the Z index of marital attraction between Blacks and Whites. In 1990, this relationship appears to be even stronger as the same 1-unit increase in diversity results in a decrease in marital attraction of 0.13 units of Z. In 2000, the slope is even more negative ($b = -.15$). A similar pattern emerges for the association between diversity and intermarriage and Native American–White marital attraction, where increases in racial index of diversity correspond to fairly substantial decreases in marital attraction. Racial diversity increases have the same impact on Hispanic-White marital attraction, where the racial index of diversity is negatively associated to the Z index in every year. Although similar relationships emerge for Asians, the nonsignificant F statistic reveals that we cannot be confident in the relationship between the independent and the dependent variable presented in the models. The racial index of diversity may not be a good predictor of marital attraction. The spatial proximity of racial groups does not automatically translate into racial attraction.

It is also worth noting that this relationship persists even after relative group size of the minority group is added to the model. Ancillary analyses (not shown) reveal that changes in Z index are insensitive to varying relative group size, which supports the conclusion that while group size may operate contextually, in that areas with smaller numbers a specific group will tend to have greater intermarriage among those persons, this association arises independent of what would be *expected* statistically.

CONCLUSION

Expanding Diversity, Declining Contact

Although the potential for interracial contact has risen substantially in the past twenty years, race continues to be highly relevant to the patterns of social contact. These results indicate that a racial stratification framework seems to provide a better explanation for our empirical results. Racial stratification purports that race is a system of relationships rather than attributes of individuals. Racial boundaries disappearing or "fading" as the title of this chapter suggests, is not a likely by-product of racial compositional shifts within a social context where race continues to exist. Rather, we ask how the structure of race remains in place, even in the midst of intermarriage. The analyses reveal the following findings: (1) that changing levels of diversity have translated into a greater potential for contact, and this is not just a function of the recent increase in immigration and thus the inclusion of the foreign born; (2) echoing prior studies on intermarriage, White–non-White marital attraction has not changed consistently across all racial groups (see Fu 2001); and (3) that White–non-White distance is not necessarily narrowing as a function of this rising diversity and rising contact opportunities. The negative association between the index of racial diversity and the White–non-White indexes of intermarriage indicate that the spatial pattern of intermarriage may be framed by the de facto racial composition but is not facilitated by it. Areas where racial diversity is at its highest, such as the southern and the western United States, do not hold on average the highest level of White–non-White intermarriage, regardless of the group of color under consideration or the year. The implication of this is that spatial proximity or closeness does not result in immediate integration. Spatial propinquity is a necessary condition of intermarriage (Peach 1980), but it is not a sufficient condition to promote or predict integration and interaction.

However, what is meant by integration? The recent increase in racial diversity and the forecasts that predict more of the same in the coming decades strongly suggest a fading racial order. A recent review by Lee and Bean (2004) posits that the biracial divide between Black and White that characterized the racial landscape for most of the twentieth century may be fading in favor of a structure that includes the recent immigrant groups of Asians and Hispanics. However, their experiences are markedly different from that of African Americans, given higher rates of intermarriage and greater fluidity of racial identity of multiracial children. This may bolster a new divide that is based on who is and is not Black instead of who is and is not White (see Gans 1999). Sanjek (1994) posits six different scenarios of how future changes in racial composition and intermarriage will affect racial relationships. One projection that seems to be gaining more currency among the current literature is "a transition from a White-Black racial order to a light-dark order in which Asians and some Hispanics align themselves with Whites" (117). However, if we still use the degree to which populations of color are interacting with Whites as a barometer of integration, the essential idea still underlies an expectation of more contemporary notions of racial assimilation, an asymmetrical expectation of groups becoming more like a prespecified "majority." Although the tenor of these expectations is a framework in which race can cease to operate as it has in the past, the application requires traditional ideas of race itself, a social construct that is evaluated relative to a standard (McDaniel 1995a).

Implications for Future Research

Future research should acknowledge the role of race as a system of relationships rather than an aggregate of individual attributes in order to fully explore the role of diversity in trends of interracial interaction. One way to achieve this is by exploring the ways race interacts with other social systems, such as class structure. While several studies have noted the ways individual educational attainment segments differ in the likelihood of interracial marriage (Qian 1997; Fu 2001; Kalmijn 1993), fewer have explored how the structure of racial differences in education, occupational status, or income alter the structure of opportunities for interracial interaction (see Cready and Saenz 1997; Heaton and Jacobson 2000). The inclusion of these measures indicates that independent of the individual's attainment, the larger structure of how wealth and opportunities are distributed impacts the structure of social associations (see Blau and Schwartz 1984). The expectation under a structural thesis would be that as class inequality between groups becomes narrow, the propensity toward associations based on sameness decreases in favor of intergroup associations. Although this thesis has been supported by some empirical accounts (Cready and Saenz 1997; Hwang, Aguirre, and Saenz 1997; Heaton and Jacobson 2000), race can hardly be deemed solely an indicator of class status, and accounting for de facto socioeconomic composition does not fully explain the persistence of homogamous norms or low levels of interracial marriage.

A related concern is the role of spatial organization and how it mediates the role of race. While increases in diversity, and thus residential integration, should facilitate narrowing the social distance between Whites and non-Whites, is this relationship a function of groups simply living closer together if racial composition is persistently conflated with neighborhood quality? Put another way, the White population persistently lives in higher-quality neighborhoods than populations of color, most notably African Americans (Massey and Denton 1993), and residential preferences for the "best-quality" neighborhood have often been phrased in terms of desired racial composition (Charles 2000; Emerson, Yancey, and Chai 2001; Timberlake 2000). The realities of class become apparent through the realities of spatial arrangements. Many accounts of residential segregation underscore the fact that African Americans are still living in highly segregated circumstances and poor-quality neighborhoods; meanwhile Asians and Hispanics are comparatively more able to spatially assimilate into White neighborhoods that are presumably of better quality. How this affects the structure of group relationships seems obvious, but few comment on how it perpetuates a structure of racialized relationships (Massey and Denton 1993).

Ultimately the future of race and racial contact is unclear. Scholars need to observe the existence of "race" and "racial constructs" as a persistence of systemic hierarchies instead of neutral characteristics that merely describe the population. If not, the future of a world where racial boundaries have faded into history will always be illusive.

VI

THE PRACTICE OF RACIAL RESEARCH

16

The Gospel of Feel-Good Sociology

Race Relations as Pseudoscience and the Decline in the Relevance of American Academic Sociology in the Twenty-First Century

John H. Stanfield II

THE COLORIZATION OF EPISTEMOLOGY AS THE CULTURAL HEGEMONY OF RACE

White like Black, blue, and green is a color, and logic does not appear and vaporize like unpolluted clear air on a sunny day. If we have learned anything of significance about human nature in the course of the past fifty or so years it is that race, that is the social and cultural meanings attached to real or imaginary phenotypical traits, is a most dehumanizing myth embedded in our deepest emotional beings (Stanfield 2006a) that taints every dominant and subordinated human being socialized into its pathology as a most grotesque ontological monster.

Therefore, rather than talking about White methods and White logic abstractly, we should talk about the way in which the cultural hegemony of race has as its dehumanizing ontological equipment the canny historical ability of perfectly correlating whiteness with invariable privileged pure goodness, while blackness and other colorizations of the human family real or imagined are perfectly associated with the dirt (Jordan 1968; Douglas 2002) that comes with the tainted lesser human qualities of those of the racialized underprivileged. So, it is not the color but the cultural hegemonic attributions given to color, be it genetic or imagined, that give whiteness, blackness, brownness, redness, and yellowness all the dehumanizing political meanings that function to create and sustain racialized orders of dehumanized human experiences, anchoring as well as creating and sustaining what becomes human character in race-centered societies (Stanfield 2006a).

And too, it is important to understand that logics of inquiries, that is, epistemologies, do not, as we are led to believe in positivistic scientific textbooks, exist divorced from the human lives that create the mental constructs that become our systems of ideas ("theories") and techniques of testing our ideas ("methods") about empirical realities. In this sense, there is a need to humanly ground, to contextualize, what is normally viewed as the reified mundane, rather sterile study of the epistemological roots of the sciences, especially the social sciences (Schwendinger 1974; Stanfield 1985a; 1985b; 1993).

This is a lesson in the history and philosophy of sciences, which we have begun to read about in more recent decades as the god-like quality of sciences have been found to have clay feet and, in other ways, human and therefore cultural, social, political, and economic origins and even functions (Rossitier 1982; Harding 2006). With this emerging more reflective mood in the history of science, the philosophy of science, and the sociology of knowledge, we are finding that nothing is untouched when it comes to understanding the human sources and functions of the production of scientific ideas. This is particularly the case when it comes to the production of social scientific ideas, since we find that such work has been much more closely tied to the cultural mirrors and social trends of the contexts in which social scientists are born, reared, and professionalized, and in which they produce the human products of epistemologies, theories, and methods (Stanfield 1985a).

It is within this reflective frame of reference regarding the human foundations of the production of epistemologies, theories, and applied methods about the social nature of human beings that we take leave from the usual conventional tour of the history of race relations research in American sociology and embark down the road of rather painful conversation about why it is that this subdiscipline has developed little beyond a self-serving ideology I prefer to call feel-good sociology of race-relations gospel, interchanged at times with the feel-good sociology of race-relations doctrine or ideology. In another place, I have called such pseudoscientific forms of reasoning about race the absurd assumptions and false optimism of the American sociology of race relations subdiscipline (Stanfield 1988).

A LITTLE LOOKING BACK

From the colonial roots of American society to the present, the uneasiness on the part of the dominant when it comes to the culturally plural nature of the colony and the nation that has emerged from it has been apparent in the tradition of avoiding dealing honestly with race questions in public policy and even in how we explore it as social scientists. There has yet to be an honest national public discussion about race in this country, and there is little hope there will be one soon. This is because it has been much more convenient for those in power to use race as a political football and as a way of sensationalizing issues such as crime than to develop safe public spaces to explore the phenomenon of race down to its deepest dehumanizing emotional roots, which social scientists have yet to even minutely uncover since it is too painful to do so.

The deep emotional roots of race are avoided by creating generations of Americans who either grow up naive about race if dominant or, if subordinate, grow up fearing talking about it at least openly (Stanfield 2006a). We are taught that nice people do not talk about race publicly. Only militants and radicals dare to do so, and of course such persons are viewed as marginals and as deviants from the norm of denial, silence, and muteness about race. This lack of coherent articulation subsequently reproduces the monster as the structure and content of everyday American life. Talking about race soberly is still grounds in this society for not getting a job, for not keeping a job, for being labeled as a troublemaker and one to be avoided at all costs, since the taint of public talking about race can be dangerously contagious.

It is, therefore, the deep emotional roots of race that make the discovery of race, either by a dominant or subordinate person, such a life-changing experience, very similar to a religious conversion experience at best and at worst to convulsive bursts of uncontrollable violence (Fanon 1965; Grier 1968).

At best, through generations Americans have tended to develop public ideologies to make race disappear or not be all that important or something that can be compartmentalized out of sight, out of mind, out of life. For much of the colonial period, the view that Blacks and Native Americans were savages made them easy to ignore since no doubt they did not have souls to Christianize (Jordan 1968). During the antebellum period, the antislavery movement split on the eve of the American Civil War when it became apparent that many abolitionists may have been opposed to slavery as a flourishing American institution but were quite comfortable with beliefs in African inferiority, which justified keeping Blacks in their lowly invisible places in this country or efforts to send them back to Africa (Douglass 2003).

While the melting-pot ideology emerged with a post–Civil War elite response to massive influxes of European immigrants, it was not meant to be for the recently freed African-descent slaves, and for the long free African descent population. In fact, since assimilation implied sexual unions, which would produce genetic hybrids in legalized family structures, the long establishment of laws against Black-White marriage in many states was certainly symbolic of the fact that assimilation was for

Whites only or for Blacks light enough to pass for White and then marry White (Kennedy 2003).

Instead of assimilation, it was expected for post–Civil War African-descent peoples to at best marginally "develop" in low-caste positions in the emerging industrial society. This is why Booker T. Washington's metaphor of five separate fingers on the hand about the natural segregation of the races, first articulated in the 1890s, resonated so well with an American White public which did not wish to deal with the realities of the presence of African-descent people in the United States. It is no wonder that Washington's epistemology of race in the new industrializing order would come to influence the first generation of feel-good sociological race-relations assumptions about the natural inferiority of Black people in an emerging professionalizing academic discipline called sociology. The natural segregation of Whites and Blacks, due to their presumed genetic and biological differences, made it essential to keep the races separate lest their conflicts disrupt the industrial order. Particularly, the views of planter sociologist Alfred Stone graced the earliest pages of the *American Journal of Sociology* in the early 1900s with this perspective (Schwendinger 1974; Stanfield 1982).

This feel-good sociological idea about the natural segregative order began to crumble with the advent of World War I and the mass migration of southern, African-descent people to northern cities. This mass migration coincided with the emergence of the University of Chicago School of Sociology and the movement of Robert E. Park, protégé of Booker T. Washington, from Tuskegee to Chicago. Under the tutelage of Robert E. Park and of his colleague Ernest Burgess, the entire paradigm of feel-good race-relations sociology shifted from the rural South outside the confines of professionalizing sociology in the North to the very core of this emerging discipline with an urban emphasis (Stanfield 1985b).

The good news that Park (1950) and Burgess spread with their conceptions of the city and of race relations was that after contact and conflict, populations such as Negroes would come to accommodate and then assimilate into a still segregated social order. Black assimilation became equated with middle-class status through the efforts of Park students, especially E. Franklin Frazier (1932), while lower classes were equated with lower-classness. This was good news, which was more declared by Park than empirically tested, and mimicked for generations by American sociologists influenced by the Chicago School of feel-good race relations. It could have come crashing down with the advent of the Civil Rights movements and race riots of the 1950s and 1960s, but by that time, sociology had become acceptable enough as an academic discipline for sociologists to be able to make proclamations, which adhered to the norms of their well-cloistered academic enterprise if not empirical reality. That is to say, one consequence of sociology becoming an insular academic discipline is that it became increasingly possible to build a career based upon promoting paradigms of race relations that did more to make everybody feel comfortable and optimistic than deal with the sobering aspects of race in post–World War II and now twenty-first-century America.

This was more than apparent in how the orthodox sociology community rushed to embrace William J. Wilson's (1978) *The Declining Significance of Race* in the late 1970s as evidence that the Civil Rights movement had ended racism. What mattered was for African-descent people to develop the social and cultural attributes to compete effectively. The embracing of Wilson's work was more the immortalizing of its title than a close reading of its contents, which did not really say what the title claimed. It became another ideological way to move away from seriously considering the persistent problem of race as a deep, multigenerational, emotional form of dehumanizing, with unconscious and semiconscious as well as conscious aspects, and to instead produce an evasive feel-good perspective. It would become a perspective—the declining significance of race, that is—that would prove so potent that it would even begin to influence race-relations sociology in South Africa. This was more than apparent at the 2006 International Sociology Association Meeting in Durban, during which time there were papers presented that attempted to demonstrate that class and/or gender were much more important experiences to explore than race in post-apartheid South Africa (reads as if apartheid has actually vaporized, similar to American Jim Crow in the 1970s) (Stanfield 2006c).

TWO OTHER WAYS TO GET AT THIS

There are two other ways of discussing feel-good race-relations sociology: through a discussion of science and pseudoscience, with the argument that feel-good race-relations sociology tends to be pseudoscience more than science, and also through discussing the political and career aspects of academic sociology: the promotion and endorsement of those sociologists who adhere to the norms of feel-good race-relations sociology as opposed to those who dare to discuss race and who find themselves being ignored, ridiculed, and discredited.

Science in its true form is a powerful way of interpreting realities, though it is not the only way. The reason we think that science is the only legitimate way to interpret realities is because science as a form of cultural and political hegemony reproduces dominance, like any from of autocracy, by labeling alternative perspectives as suspect, as being superstitious or inferior due to being dependent upon immeasurable factors, such as emotions and spirituality.

All ways of knowing relate to the ways in which the conceptual links up or does not link up with the empirical (Willer 1971). What makes science so powerful is that unlike, say, theocratic, mystical, and magical methods of interpreting realities, there is an attempt to test (methodological application) a system of concepts (theories) we construct in an empirical world, and when the test fails, we modify the conceptual system and retest and retest and retest. This is because science in its true form is the search for isomorphism, that is, the one-to-one fit between a conceptual system and what is being studied in the empirical world. Science as a way of knowing is also the quest for serendipity, the explanatory power of the theory across units of analysis and through time.

When there is an attempt to fit an empirical world into the conceptual system we have constructed, we are being theocratic rather than scientific. When there is an attempt to not have anything to do with empirical reality at all and instead stay on the conceptual level, even to the point that a false impression arises that there has been a test on the conceptual level without interfacing with the empirical, we have mysticism rather than science. When we attempt to just deal with the empirical level and completely ignore the conceptual, we are doing magic rather than science.

There are numerous examples in the history of sociological research of mystical, magical, and theocratic reasoning masquerading as scientific theory testing and theory building. Parsonian structural functionalism is an example of theocratic more than scientific reasoning. Marxian classless society is a mystical rather than an empirical concept in a corpus of otherwise empirically tested theoretical ideas. To employ survey or secondary data analysis with no explication of a derived conceptual framework is an example of magic in sociological research.

Theocratic and mystical reasoning masquerading as scientific reasoning are particularly deadly when it comes to the study of oppressed people such as White women, people of color, the poor, and the disabled. This is because historically speaking theocratic and mystical reasoning has often been used to legitimate the personal prejudices of the researcher who is more bent on confirming biases than working within the conditions of science in regards to the collection and analysis of reliable and valid data. This problem becomes even more serious when what the researcher has to say about the "problematic" attributes of the population under study resonates with the prejudices of the historically located general public.

In the general history of race in science literature, it is more than apparent that the production of ideas about inferior races came from researchers being mystical and theocratic in their theorizing by operating intentionally through taken-for-granted presumptions drawn from their prejudiced worldviews, even to the point of fudging and falsifying data to fit their beliefs (Gould 1996). Certainly the most contemporary example of this is the

Herrnstein and Murray bestseller *The Bell Curve* (1996), which though has a highly suspect methodology, conformed immensely to widespread public ideas about the cultural if not genetic inferiority of African Americans (Stanfield and Dennis 1995a, 1995b).

There are numerous cases of theocratic and mystical pseudoscience, which has served the purpose of generating feel-good race-relations sociology doctrines. The Park race cycle alluded to earlier is an example of a theocratic if not mystical form of pseudoscience, rather than a soundly tested empirically based theory (Lyman 1972). Nowhere in Park's writings did he develop a race-cycle theory and test it. If he had, it certainly would have been rejected and modified and further revised through the generations of sociologists who embraced it as a type of disciplinary gospel. I discussed this matter elsewhere, many years ago, about how it is that Park's race-cycle model was more congruent with his prejudices as a man who may have believed that Negroes should assimilate but within their own segregated institutions and communities (Stanfield 1985b). After all, it was Park who at one point told E. Franklin Frazier to take the freight elevator up to an American Sociological Society annual meeting not long before getting Frazier elected as the first African American president of the association, rather than make a fuss when the hotel elevator operator refused to take him up (Frazier 1945). Park's liberalism, steeped deeply in Booker T. Washington's view of "five fingers on the hand," only went as far as making sure that Blacks were fairly treated within the confines of a Jim Crow society (Stanfield 1985b; Cheeseboro 1999).

As progressive as Gunnar Myrdal's (1944) *American Dilemma* was and as influential as it was for generations as the holy script of post–World War II race-relations liberals, his American creed concept is very much an indulgence in mystical reasoning. In fact, it symbolizes a basic problem in liberal race-relations thinking even to this day, which views race from the standpoint of a moral contradiction in American democracy, an unfortunate deviation of norms in an otherwise lovely society of the free and equal, rather than the more gripping reality of how it is a historical cornerstone of a republic in which racial inequality is a central norm of power and privilege distribution.

The ideology of "the declining significance of race" of the post-1960s, which has become so much a part of the identity of American sociological study of race and its globalization, is as well very much a mystical if not theocratic pseudoscientific belief. It is convergent with other ideas that encourage reification of mystical beliefs in the study of racial inequality and racialized populations in the United States and abroad. The tendency to view race as a homogenous, quantifiable variable, rather than as a complex human experience of multiple identities with a vast range of heterogeneous cultural experiences both conscious and unconscious, within, outside, and across racialized categorical boxes, makes much of what gets published in major sociology journals and in book-length sociological studies quite divorced from the real experiences of racialized populations, be they dominant or subordinate.

The acceptance of such beliefs for publication and as credentials for tenure, and career awards says much again about the institutionalization of post-1960s sociology as a career that has decreasing relevance when it comes to explaining the intricacies of empirical realities such as the synchronism of race, gender, class, and cultural heterogeneity in the United States and in other nations.

The growing ability to do race-relations research, to become an expert without firsthand "field experiences" (let alone life experiences), is perhaps one of the reasons why so many policy makers turn to knowledge interpreters such as journalists and literary figures rather than sociologists for realistic assessments of race relations in the United States (Stanfield 1993). As much as academic sociologists are rightfully concerned about data reliability and validity issues, when it comes to the study of race, there is the persistent problem of irrelevance of the produced valid and reliable knowledge—except for building additional tiers of an academic career, which is why it is so easy to embrace the practice of being theocrats and mystics rather than scientists in the real meaning of the term (Stanfield 1999).

But to really be scientific in the study of race relations in the context of a society in which race is such an intergenerationally emotionally embedded, dehumanizing experience that taints and distorts the humanity of all is a dangerous thing to be. This is because truth telling in the study of race leads to asking uncomfortable questions not only about a population, an institution, a community, or a society, but also about ourselves as academics who are products of this race-drenched society. That is, when we dig down to the deep questions of what race is and how it is reproduced, we find that it is indeed a societal rather than a population-specific problem (Stanfield 2006a, 2006b). To be an American or to be here for a while is to be, with rare exception, both creators and victims of the dehumanizing monster of race. To discover that fact is a threat not only to the economic and political order of life in a race-based society such as the United States but to ourselves, to the fears we use habitually to stay away from those we dehumanize on a routine daily basis. As academics, to admit race as a form of mundane, everyday, multigenerational socialization potentially discredits the value-free claims of sociological and social-scientific knowledge production, which routinely ignores race altogether, categorizes and compartmentalizes it, or attempts to make it disappear by calling it something such as class or gender or pretending it does not exist at all.

Thus, it is no wonder that like a painkilling drug, we want feel-good sociological analyses of race relations as a reflection of historically specific public cultures, which demand feel-good race relations. It is no accident that in the historical rise of professional sociology in the United States over the past hundred or so years we find that academic sociology as an establishment has tended to anoint only those sociologists who tend to embrace and evangelize the feel-good race-relations gospel. This is apparent in two ways.

First, it is apparent in the selection of writings of sociologists who become immortalized as gods of the discipline. For instance, Charles Cooley (1909), who wrote about the moral obligations of Whites to eradicate racial injustices, tends to be remembered as the father of the concept of socialization, with no mention of his broader concerns for justice in the emerging Jim Crow era of his early twentieth-century days. As radical as C. Wright Mills was in his views about professional sociology, until the recent publications of his letters and autobiographical writings by his daughters (Mills and Mills 2000), we have known nothing about his views about race and the reasons why he preferred not to discuss race, for instance, in his classic *The Sociological Imagination*, published in the late 1950s, in the heat of the Civil Rights movement.

We have yet to read the more radical writings on race in America of E. Franklin Frazier (1927, 1945, 1962), Charles S. Johnson (Stanfield 1987), and William E. B. Du Bois, all sanitized in the University of Chicago's attempt to put their stamp on the history of African American sociologists: James Blackwell and Morris Janowitz's (1974), *Black Sociologists* (while ignoring women such as Anna Cooper and Ida B. Wells). We read in the Blackwell and Janowitz text about the conventional sociological perspectives of those chosen for textual inclusion, such as Frazier and Johnson, while ignoring, among other things, their common disillusionment with race in America as expressed in their last writings. There it became more than apparent that they saw that the new racially integrated society emerging in the 1950s and 1960s was not going to yield the equality they had assumed would happen with the court cases and civil rights policies that materialized in the last years of their lives and careers.

Particularly Frazier, in his last days in the early 1960s, would lash out at his generation of African American scholars of the 1930s–1950s, for their assimilation preoccupations, which may have allowed their dominant-group peers to feel comfortable around them but avoided telling the truth about the nature of race in the United States. What he said in his final (quasi-autobiographical) essay published after his death, "The Failure of the Negro Intellectual," is turning out to be prophetic for future generations of African American scholars, in a marginally desegregated academy, which continues to be reluctant to engage in sobering examinations about race and exploring ways to eradicate it from the baseline ontology of American life. The older we become, the more disillusioned we are bound to be, even at the height of cultural capital for those African American and other scholars of color who even in the midst of their material glory experience little sustained respect by many of their dominant peers. This is particularly seen when from time to time the blatant racism said to be of yesteryear raises its ugly head in the most tranquil places of American higher education. Such occasional reminders remind those of us with at least minimal consciousness that, regardless of our status, too many if not most of those of the other hue who are in dominant positions of control and those who look like us but conform to the prejudices of the dominant, we are nothing more at the end of the day than of the same categorical kindred as the faithful brothers and sisters who empty our office trash cans and clean the public bathrooms long after we have retired to our three-car-garage homes.

What has been at least equally tragic has been the long history of totally ignoring or relegating to careers in marginal institutions those American sociologists who have had the nerve to offer sobering accounts about race (Stanfield 1997). This is what happened to Anna Cooper, William E. B. Du Bois, Oliver Cox (Cheeseboro 1999), and Hubert Harrison. African American sociologists such as Lewis Jones (1962) were forced to have their writings about race and civil rights published outside the United States in the 1960s.

Even though Du Bois was only recently recognized finally by an ASA president as being a founder of American sociology, such recognition does not even begin to scrape the surface of understanding the profound influences Du Bois had in the crafting of professional sociology in both Europe and in the United States, influences that have been credited to others who liberally took his ideas without giving him deserving credit or who credited him while historians of sociology have tended to ignore such acknowledgments (such as the influence Du Bois had on Max Weber's conceptualization of ethnicity and Du Bois's founding of urban sociology in the United States).

In the 1970s, we witnessed the negative career consequences for Joyce Ladner (1973) and Wilbur Watson for daring to air the racism in the discipline. And while sociology feminized in the post-1970s, we still see major sociology departments reluctant to hire and promote African American women feminists.

We should also remember as the conclusion to this section that there are numerous White male and female sociologists as well as non-White male and female sociologists who have had, since the origins of sociology as an academic profession, their sobering ideas about race in America ignored, ridiculed, and discredited to such a point that their names are now hard to find in the annuals of the history of the discipline (Schwendinger 1974).

CONCLUSION

With all this said, the cultural currency of post-1970s sociologists of race who stress declining significance of race and color-blind arguments continues to increase, including among African-descent scholars in America who represent the post-1970s Black conservative if not right-wing elite (Sowell 1984, 1998; Loury 1995; Swain 1996, 2002, 2003; Patterson 1971, 1997, 1998; Carter 1991). Anointed as the best and the brightest, intellectuals of color and White neoliberal intellectuals who embrace the doctrines of colorblindness and the declining significance of race make prestigious academic careers for themselves even though it is apparent to even the casual observer that race is more than alive and well in America. Perched in their elite berths in academia, it has become a lucrative business for these sociologists and other scholars to point out the pathologies of Blacks and other people of color, especially Latinos, to affluent White and Black audiences who want to continue to feel good in a society that increasingly denies its moral and political responsibility for the gravely unfinished business of the civil rights struggles of the 1950s and 1960s and many decades before.

This is why as contemporary American sociology fiddles it is becoming more and more irrelevant except for academic career making. Through evading race, through discounting and ignoring and simply refusing to hire or retain scholars who tell it the way it is *scientifically*, the academic field continues to down-spiral, at least in terms of its use in exploring empirical worlds as they really are, particularly in a society going through such significant demographic changes.

The correlation between the persistent feel-good race-relations gospel of professional academic sociology and the decline of the discipline is due to the fact that the ideological doctrine is becoming increasingly unable to effectively grapple with the growing complexities of race in the United States and around the world (Stanfield 1997, 2006b). The binary (e.g., Black/White, dominant/minority) and the reified categorical thinking that undergirds so much sociological epistemology is too simplistic to deal effectively with the complexity of contemporary and emerging life worlds. The term "Black identity," for instance, has always been problematic historically in discussing American and transnational societal experiences since the subject of Black identity too often confuses race, ethnicity, and culture, three distinct though often overlapping human experiences. Black identity is even more complex now with the increasing cultural heterogeneity of African and Caribbean immigrants who are constructing identities outside conventional African American identity-formation processes. Moreover, we have those individuals who due to their proclaimed multiethnicity claim several rather than one or even two different ancestries and others who switch identities at will and walk on the borders of two or more identities. This matter of identities and multiple identities and slipping and sliding in and out of categories is even messier when we consider the demographic mosaic that goes well beyond the now obsolete White/Black binary of feel-good race-relations sociology. There is so much going on within and outside and across the racialized categorical boxes Americans have created in the history of nation building, and American sociologists continue to fail to comprehend it due to the simplistic ideological yearnings of feel-good race-relations doctrines.

The tendency to dabble in mundane American exceptionalism in treating racial issues as solely American rather than as global issues is another example of how inadequate feel-good race-relations sociology is for a much more interconnected world. In this respect, it is both amazing and disturbing how insular American race-relations sociology is as a topic of research and teaching. It remains rare to find a sociologist of race in the United States who understands racialized issues in other countries. And those who do have more than likely traveled to other countries to observe how race operates elsewhere. This is the reason why it is easy in the United States for scholars to indulge in such mystical and theocratic reasoning when addressing global issues. The Afro-centric perspective, which is very much an American paradigm and embraced by those who do not have a clue about the profound empirical complexities of continental African regions, societies, tribes, and classes, suffers seriously from such mystical romanticism. It is the same when it comes to American feminists, structural functionalists, and Marxists who attempt to apply their mystical and theocratic perspectives to African contexts and to other global regional contexts for that matter.

When it comes to South Africa, the African country most comparable to the United States, the American tendency to misname processes in one society that look like processes in another society, such as referring to Jim Crow in America as "apartheid," also comes from a lack of cross-national firsthand experiences. The waving of the magic wand that ends race due to national political policy changes is perhaps the most recent example of the overstepping of American feel-good race-relations doctrine (Stanfield 2006c).

While many of the American humanities disciplines are learning how to adapt to a world that is increasingly pluralistic in power and authority, sociology and the other American social sciences seem to be the most resistant to such realities. The response to demands for more representative curriculum in undergraduate and graduate education in sociology and in other social sciences has been to dig in heels and organize reactionary movements in the academy in an attempt to preserve the traditional and I should say false monocultural view of Western knowledge. Just what it will take for sociologists and other social scientists to begin to open their eyes and realize the world is dramatically changing is a burning question in need of a sobering answer if sociology and its kindred disciplines is not to become completely useless, enough to deepen their negative assessment in the academy as well as in the eyes of the general public, which has had a low sense of respect for academic sociology almost since its inception.

17

To Win the War

Racial Research and the Pioneer Fund

William H. Tucker

In December 1999 there was quite a stir in the social science corridors at many universities when a number of faculty members in psychology, sociology, and anthropology unexpectedly discovered in their mail an unsolicited copy of the "special abridged edition" of *Race, Evolution, and Behavior,* often accompanied by a card noting "compliments of J. Philippe Rushton," professor of psychology at the University of Western Ontario, the work's author. Discussion on various Internet Listservs quickly made clear that tens of thousands of other social scientists throughout the continent had been similarly selected as recipients of this unrequested gift; indeed, some faculty received multiple copies.

The tiny paperback—essentially a pamphlet—offered, in what the preface termed "a more popularly written style," Rushton's account of the origin of racial differences in behavior. According to Rushton (1999), from Arab explorers in the eighth century to European colonialists more than a millennium later, all the visitors to Africa had agreed on the nature of Blacks: they were like "'wild animals,'" naked, dirty, impoverished, the children often unaware of their father, but with "a natural sense of rhythm" and "oversized sex organs." Even "in the age of computers, fax machines, and the world wide web," Rushton observed, "getting a dial tone in many African cities is difficult." The IQ for "Blacks living in Africa is the lowest ever recorded," he noted, and "neglect and decay are seen everywhere in Africa and much of the West Indies" (10, 15, 17–18, 48).

As an explanation for this appalling condition of Blacks, Rushton's pamphlet proposed his "Out of Africa" theory—that although modern humans first appeared in Africa, a split took place 100,000 years ago between those groups that remained in their continent of origin and those who headed north. The migrants, eventually evolving into Whites and Asians, developed the larger brains and greater intelligence necessary to cope with the more "mentally demanding" tasks of "gathering and storing food, providing shelter, making clothes, and raising children during the long winters." These intellectual changes, however, were "balanced by slower rates of growth, lower levels of sex hormones, less aggression, and less sexual activity," with the consequence that non-African races came to enjoy longer lives and to develop greater ability for self-control, planning, complex social organization, rule following, altruism, and family stability. The resulting "genetically-organized group[s] of traits" reflected what Rushton termed a "basic law of evolution link[ing] reproductive strategy to intelligence and brain development. The less complex an animal's brain, the greater its reproductive output." Non-Africans thus tended to invest time and effort in the care of their children rather than "the pursuit of sexual thrills"; in comparison to Blacks, White and Asian men became, as Rushton succinctly put it, "'dads' rather than 'cads'" (1999, 85, 25–26, 89, 24).

When queried about this curious mailing, especially by those who suspected that the mailing lists of professional associations had been misused, Rushton posted the following reply on the Listserv of the Society for Personality and Social Psychology:

> I paid for the mailings from my research grant. There has been no misuse of any lists to my knowledge although perhaps some organizations are now trying to cover their asses for having sold their lists. Such is the power of vengeful political correctness that academics are scared of having other academics send them unpopular scientific views.

In addition to its extraordinarily pugnacious tone, this response seemed remarkable for another reason: what kind of granting agency would fund the distribution of thousands of copies of a book, especially in the absence of any expression of interest in it by the recipients?

The grant in this case came from the Pioneer Fund, an organization well known for its support of academics who find Blacks intellectually and morally less capable than Whites and Asians. Indeed, Pioneer continued to fund the mass distribution of Rushton's paperback after a disagreement with Transaction Press—which had published the original unabridged version of his work (Rushton 1995) but was horrified to find their name on the abridged and much more tendentious version without their review or consent (Horowitz 2000)—and forced him to destroy some 60,000 copies (reported in *Chronicle of Higher Education* 2000). Just six months later, 100,000 new copies of the same "special abridged edition" of *Race, Evolu-*

tion, and Behavior, now copyrighted in the author's name, were published by the Charles Darwin Research Institute, which had been founded by Rushton and used as an independent vehicle to channel Pioneer's funds directly to him.

This entire campaign, jointly conducted by Pioneer and Rushton, was clearly intended as a public relations effort, designed to influence the society's ongoing discussion of race. Not only was his paperback written in a breezy style containing no references, but on the first page it promised to address the public's concerns and to provide an explanation for their personal experience: "teachers in America know the races differ in school achievement. Policemen know the races differ in crime rates. And social workers know the races differ in rates of welfare dependency or getting infected with AIDS. They all wonder why" (9). Moreover, Rushton appeared at a press conference at Washington's National Press Club "to announce the publication of the new, for-the-public version of Rushton's academic treatise" (Charles Darwin Research Institute 2000), accompanied by three other Pioneer grantees, all outspoken proponents of Blacks' intellectual inferiority: philosopher Michael Levin, sociologist Robert Gordon, and Jared Taylor, the editor of *American Renaissance* and head of an identically named organization so extreme that it was denounced as "racist" even by Dinesh D'Souza (1995a, 396; 1995b), a Reagan conservative who has called for the elimination of all civil rights legislation (1995a, 545). The "Four Senior Researchers," according to the "embargoed" press release, recommended the "*New* Book [emphasis added] . . . on Genetic Races Differences in Crime and Intelligence," even though the identical paperback had been widely distributed half a year earlier and the unabridged version had been published half a decade earlier. In addition, on its website Rushton's Charles Darwin Research Institute announced frankly that the abridged version was published "in order to . . . actively promulgate" his claims "about race and human variation to media figures, interested general readers, citizen groups with interest in these topics, and students, by mass mailings of the booklet, putting it on the Internet and eventually perhaps by producing audio books and video tapes." And a tear-sheet in the back of the pamphlet offered bulk rates "for distribution to media figures, especially columnists who write about race issues." Like a William Morris agent seeking publicity for an entertainer, Pioneer was working to market Rushton to the media and public.

THE UNACKNOWLEDGED PAST

The Pioneer Fund is one of the most controversial foundations in the United States today. For the past thirty years, it has provided the resources for almost every social scientist who has concluded that Blacks are genetically less intelligent than Whites. Among the fund's grantees along with Rushton have been such well-known names as Arthur Jensen and William Shockley, as well as a number of lesser-known scientists who share the belief in Black intellectual inferiority. Pioneer has also provided resources for organizations specializing in legal challenges—like the Center for Individual Rights in Washington, D.C., which pursued the Hopwood case, striking down affirmative action in higher education in Texas, Louisiana, and Mississippi. Whenever criticized for its choice of grants or grantees, New York attorney Harry F. Weyher Jr., the fund's president from 1958 until his death in 2002, steadily maintained that Pioneer's "sole activity" has been to support "empirical research" of high quality, conducted only by the "top experts." Furthermore, according to Weyher, the fund "has never taken, and will never take, a position on any political . . . issue" (Weyher 1998, 1999a). In particular, Weyher defended Pioneer's founder, Wickliffe Preston Draper, as someone similarly interested only in promoting the advancement of science.

Taken at face value, Weyher's defense of the fund raises some important points. Is Pioneer in fact a courageous source of support for research too taboo or politically incorrect to enjoy funding from traditional sources? Or, as it was labeled by the journalist Charles Lane (1995), a keeper of the flame of scientific racism? Although Pioneer's little-known background is a very long story (see Tucker 2002), following are a few of the highlights revealed by archival records.

Wickliffe Preston Draper created Pioneer in 1937 and was the sole source of its funds until his death in 1972, when he left a substantial bequest on which the fund has operated ever since. Draper came of age during the teens and twenties, when eugenics was enjoying its heyday. Of particular importance, scientists and racists were frequent traveling companions at the time, the former perhaps distinguishable from the latter by their more technical training, but certainly not by any difference in their conclusions of "Nordic supremacy" or the social policies that they advocated as a consequence: opposition to political equality for Blacks and restriction of immigration from southern and eastern Europe. Draper's faith in this creed never wavered. Like a hippie still preaching flower power at the end of the century, or a McCarthyite still warning of Moscow's agents in Washington long after the demise of the Soviet Union, Draper would spend the rest of his life fixated in the zeitgeist of his youth, providing the resources for the use of science to transform racism into rational ideology, a tradition carried on after his death by the Pioneer Fund.

Indeed, at about the same time as he created Pioneer, Draper began his longtime and secretive support for a campaign to repatriate all Blacks in the United States to Africa—this campaign has been denied by Weyher but is amply documented by archival correspondence between Draper and Earnest Sevier Cox, the Klansman and ardent White supremacist who headed the effort. To Cox (1925), the removal of Blacks from the American continent was, in his own words, "a holy cause" (34). In his book *White America*, Cox (1923) described how all civilization was due to White superiority, and claimed that civilization had never survived "contact with the colored race." The only solution was the complete removal of all the "aggressive negroids," bent on revenge for their enslavement (237, 190). *White America* received little attention until Draper paid for the republication of 1,000 copies which were sent, unsolicited, with the compliments of the author, to every member of Congress and to legislators in Southern states.[1]

These two events—the distribution of Cox's and Rushton's writing—are bookends encompassing more than six decades of similar attempts employing Draper's money, both before and after his death in 1972, to influence public opinion by publishing material about race and sending it to influential groups. Prior to 1972, this process of publication and distribution was managed by members of Pioneer's board of directors with money that came directly from Draper's pocket; that is, these projects were not supported by official grants from the fund. After the founder's death, similar activities were conducted by the same people, but now supported by Pioneer with money that Draper left in Weyher's control.

During the civil rights era, Draper, Weyher, and a third Pioneer board member, John B. Trevor Jr.—three of the five members of the board altogether—worked behind the scenes organizing a group of scientists who not only received support from Draper for the publication and distribution of their writing in opposition to the Second Reconstruction, but enjoyed substantial, annual cash gifts from Draper "as a token of . . . appreciation of your scientific efforts during the past year." The work of these scientists too was distributed unsolicited to many thousands of recipients in mass mailings paid for by Draper.[2]

The most prominent scientist in this group was Henry Garrett, who, in addition to regular annual gifts, also received $50,000 ($214,000 adjusted for inflation) in Draper's will. Garrett was near the end of a lengthy professional career, in which he had been president of the American Psychological Association in 1946, the Eastern Psychological Association in 1944, and the Psychometric Society in 1943, a fellow of the American Association for the Advancement of Science, a member of the prestigious National Research Council, editor for a decade of the American Psychology Series, and chair of the Psychology Department at Columbia University for sixteen years before returning to his home state of Virginia in 1955.[3]

After the *Brown* decision, however, Garrett became a tireless polemicist for segregation, portraying Blacks as "savages"—the "blood brothers" of Africans, who lacked "towels, handkerchiefs and toilet paper"—and unfit for association with Whites (1961, 106). "No matter how low . . . an American white may be, his ancestors built the civilizations of Europe," Garrett declared, "and no matter how high . . . a Negro may be, his ancestors were (and his kinsmen still are) savages in an African jungle" (1962). Interviewed on a television program sponsored by the infamous Citizens' Councils, the leading defenders of segregation, Garrett told the viewing audience that the United States "is a European civilization, a white man's civilization . . . where the Negro is considered to be more or less guests."[4]

In late 1965, the affluent suburbs north and west of New York City were flooded with hundreds of thousands of copies of one of Garrett's pamphlets, "How Classroom Desegregation Will Work" (n.d.) published with Draper's money. The pamphlet predicted that integration would result in the spread of "Negroid culture," and the decline of "intellectual and cultural assets" through intermarriage. In "Breeding Down" (n.d.) yet another booklet distributed in huge numbers to teachers, Garrett explained that the Civil Rights movement's real strategy for Blacks to attain equality with their betters was to make Whites "Negroid" through "amalgamation." Interviewed by *Newsweek* as a result of the pamphlets, Garrett (1966) denied being a racist or hatemonger, observing, in dubious support of his demurral, that Blacks were "fine muscular animals when . . . not diseased . . . but when they're frustrated, they revert to primitive savages." Presumably, segregated schools would relieve Blacks from the discomfort of the former, so that Whites could be protected from the consequences of the latter. When Draper died in 1972, his place on Pioneer's board of directors was taken by Garrett, who only lived for another year himself.

Another recipient of Draper's generosity was Wesley Critz George, a retired professor of anatomy at the University of North Carolina and that state's leading defender of segregation even before the *Brown* decision. During the war, for example, he had written to a local White clergyman who had opened his church to Blacks, accusing the reverend of "furthering the work of the devil" by "aiding in the destruction of the white race" and "the civilization of America." Within three days of the Supreme Court's ruling, George had written to the governor of North Carolina, encouraging defiance and declaring that preservation of the public school system was not as important as "the protoplasmic integrity of the white race." In a subsequent pamphlet elegantly entitled "The Race Problem from the Standpoint of One Who Is Concerned with the Evils of Miscegenation," George (1955) opposed integration on the grounds that Blacks were "genetically unacceptable" and would "destroy our race and our civilization." Upon learning of George's opposition, Draper had Weyher write to the scientist, communicating Draper's interest in providing support for distribution of the pamphlet, and an unsolicited contribution would later follow.[5]

George also authored another work that enjoyed wide circulation in an effort again paid for by Draper and organized by Weyher: tens of thousands of free copies of *The Biology of the Race Problem* were distributed at the height of the Civil Rights movement. The crux of this report was George's review of evidence from a variety of physiological, psychological, and anthropological studies, all putatively demonstrating the innate intellectual inferiority of Blacks. To demonstrate the dangers of any social policy that would "convert the population of the United States into a mixed-blooded people," the professor of anatomy soberly described a study of crossbreeding among dogs, in which the poor, confused hybrid exhibited the drooping ears of its basset hound side but the excitable temperament of its German shepherd ancestry (1962, 77–78). Although the subsequent report bore only George's name as author, it was in many ways a collective project, supervised by Weyher, who circulated a preliminary draft to the group supported by Draper, including Garrett and a fellow Pioneer board member, all of whom then submitted their comments and corrections back to Pioneer's president to be passed along to George. Weyher also decided that there ought to be a foreword, much of which he himself then wrote. A grateful George actually wanted Weyher to sign his contribution, declaring that "few people have been more intimately or helpfully involved" with the project, but Weyher declined. In fact, Weyher even made decisions about the number of copies to be printed, monitored the costs of the process, and then provided instructions to the printer for the bulk distribution of copies. When the report was ready, Trevor proposed that it be distributed gratis to "all the leaders of the Western World, including the top hierarchy in government, state and federal, on through religion, law, industry, banking, education, the press, movies, TV-radio, etc."[6]

One other effort funded by Draper is particularly instructive in understanding the subsequent nature of the Pioneer Fund. In 1963 a group called the Coordinating Committee for Fundamental American Freedoms (CCFAF) was established as an initiative to discredit and defeat the Civil Rights Bill then being considered by Congress. During the next year, the CCFAF would become, according to the *Washington Post*, the "best-organized and best-financed lobby" (Clayton 1964) up to that time, far outspending any other single group attempting to influence legislation in 1964. Eighty percent of the CCFAF's budget came from the Mississippi Sovereignty Commission, essentially a state-level spying agency created to ferret out any deviations from segregationist orthodoxy. The contributions from the Commission were themselves private donations made to a "special fund," the contents of which were passed directly to the CCFAF. As the director of the Commission explained to a journalist, the money "represented donations from all over the United States and the Sovereignty Commission was merely the funneling agency."[7]

The records of the Commission, however, released in 1998 only after a thirty-year legal battle, indicate that, of the quarter-million dollars channeled to the CCFAF by the Sovereignty Commission, $215,000 ($1.25 million adjusted for inflation) arrived in the form of stock donations from an unnamed New Yorker, marked "fact and amount of the gift to be kept confidential." Only a handful of trusted insiders knew that they had been forwarded by Weyher from Draper's account at Morgan Guaranty.[8]

While this attempt to defeat the Civil Rights Bill was still in progress, Mississippi attorney John Satterfield, Weyher's contact in the state and, "the brains" of the CCFAF, according to one journalist (Winfrey 1964), submitted a proposal to the governor for a new, more ambitious organization, explaining that the same anonymous Northern donor had pledged $200,000 ($1.15 AFI) toward its creation, provided that the State of Mississippi would contribute a similar amount. Unlike the CCFAF, which was temporary and specific, having been created solely to oppose a single piece of legislation, the new organization was to be permanent and much broader in scope, designed to influence policy by convincing the public of "the completely different nature of Negro citizens and white citizens"; the nation had to be shown, according to Satterfield, that the plight of Blacks was not "due to environmental factors, particularly to mistreatment and 'discrimination,'" but to their own biological shortcomings. The CCFAF was "engaged in [a] battle," wrote Satterfield to the governor, but the new organization was necessary "to win the war."

Satterfield's proposal, developed in conjunction with others who had enjoyed Draper's financial support, included three components: "the base of the effort" was to be scientific documentation of racial differences, including "direct grants to educational institutions for . . . research projects"; work in areas other than "race differences" would be supported "insofar as they may be material to this basic problem." A public relations component would then circulate the results; a periodical "of our own," would be subsidized, though not published, by the new organization; and "fronts" would be created to distribute "more subtle writings, those which carry arguments *shaded* with our beliefs." Finally, the project's legal arm would "engage . . . in litigation and legislation."[9]

As evidence of his commitment to the project, Draper had Weyher forwarded stock valued at $50,000 ($288,000 AFI) to the Sovereignty Commission. The entire $200,000 in matching funds was quickly approved by the governor and included in the legislature's annual appropriation to the Sovereignty Commission but subsequently rescinded in the wake of national outrage over the murder of the three civil rights workers—Schwerner, Goodman, and Chaney—that occurred only weeks after receipt of Draper's latest display of generosity. In danger of becoming a pariah state, Mississippi was reluctant to begin another highly publicized effort at victim blaming. A year later, Satterfield returned to Weyher a check for the exact value of the stock. "Since no matching funds have been made available," wrote the Mississippi attorney to his friend in New York, "we have . . . concluded that these funds should not be utilized."

With their distribution of the writings by George, Garrett, and many others, Draper and his fellow Pioneer board members were the major financial and organizational resource behind the use of science in the struggle to maintain American apartheid. Yet at the same time the Pioneer Fund itself made only a few small official grants.[10] Like an accountant with two sets of books, only one of which was for public display, this dual system allowed Pioneer to portray itself as interested solely in assisting the pursuit of scientific knowledge.

FUND OR LOBBY

When Draper died a few years after Satterfield had returned his money, Weyher, who was left in control of a substantial portion of the estate and was pledged to carry out Draper's wishes, converted the Pioneer Fund into the project that his late client and mentor had intended to create in conjunction with the State of Mississippi. Pioneer includes all the components of the earlier proposal. Among other projects, it subsidizes, but does not publish, the *Mankind Quarterly*, a journal surreptitiously assisted by Draper during the civil rights era and, since the mid 1970s, edited by Pioneer grantee Roger Pearson, one of the most important figures in the postwar Nazi movement; throughout the four decades of its existence the *Quarterly* has consistently praised racism as a biological necessity, "an honored quality" essential to evolutionary development leading "healthy-minded people . . . to maintain a healthy reproductive distance" from other races in order to "maintain the integrity of the gene pool" (McGregor 1993, 426, 431).[11] Indeed, in addition to being the main, and perhaps the only, source of support for those scientists insistent that Blacks are genetically less intelligent than Whites, Pioneer has funded a number of organizations—the "fronts" called for in the Satterfield proposal—that distribute literature "shaded with our beliefs." The "Foundation for Human Understanding," for example, whose original directors included Garrett, bought 2,800 copies of Jensen's *Straight Talk about Mental Tests*, which argued that the decline in SAT scores was attributable to a decreased birthrate among the more capable "ethnic groups" (1981, 49) and sent them gratis to college presidents and admissions officers throughout the country.[12]

Although Pioneer's underlying agenda—as Satterfield so concisely put it, to convince the public of "the completely different nature of blacks and whites"—is thus undeniable, two important qualifications about its grants should be noted. First the fund's true purpose does not mean that none of its projects has been of genuine scientific interest. The well-known study of separated monozygotic twins conducted by Bouchard and his associates at the University of Minnesota (Bouchard et al. 1990), for example, has enjoyed Pioneer support, though even in this case the research has clearly played an instrumental role for the fund's agenda, concluding, as it has, that many traits have high heritability *within* groups. From Pioneer's point of view, such a result is a necessary (though hardly sufficient) element in the argument that differences *between* races are both genetic and immutable. As Satterfield's proposal observed, work in areas other than "race differences" would be supported "insofar as they may be material to this basic problem."

In addition, the existence of Pioneer's agenda does not suggest that every grantee necessarily shares it. Some recipients, like Pearson, not only desire to recreate racial segregation, but have devoted their lives to pursuit of that goal. Yet it is certainly possible that others may have no sympathy for such policies and wish merely to use Pioneer's money to advance their own research and their academic careers. Although ideological compatibility is thus not a prerequisite for obtaining support from Pioneer, scientific heresy would be fatal. The fund will provide assistance only to those researchers who can be relied on to produce the appropriate conclusions about heredity and race. Should someone like Rushton, however, undergo a sudden change of opinion about racial differences, his support from Pioneer would disappear faster than David Duke from the Apollo Theater.

Of course, it is difficult to draw the more charitable conclusion concerning their motivation for grantees like Rushton and others, who exhibit such missionary zeal in their attempts to persuade not only their scientific colleagues but also the larger public, and who appear as featured speakers before a group like American Renaissance, whose members are interested in "science" primarily as a source of rational justification for their desperate desire to reconstruct an American apartheid. Also supported by Pioneer, American Renaissance publishes excerpts from slave memoirs reminiscing over how much better life was under massa (Braun 1993), claims that there is no constitutional basis for extending the right to vote to Blacks (Francis 1995, 1999), and debates balkanization of the United States into separate ethno-states as a possible solution to racial problems (McCulloch 1995; Schiller 1995).

In any event, Pioneer certainly enjoys the right to support the researchers of their choice, as do scientists the right to accept that support. The rest of us should distinguish, however, between the desire to advance scientific knowledge and a lobbying effort for scientific racism. Thirty-seven years after its founder agreed to fund the Satterfield proposal, Pioneer is still the organization created "to win the war" against civil rights.

NOTES

1. Correspondence contained in the Earnest Sevier Cox papers (Special Collections Library, Duke University, Durham, North Carolina) indicates the lengthy rela-

tionship between Draper and Cox, in which the former provided anonymous financial backing for the latter's campaign to remove all Blacks from the United States. To further his campaign Cox recruited the infamous Mississippi senator Theodore Gilmore Bilbo, who, also with Draper's support, introduced the Greater Liberia Act in April 1939; the bill never made it out of committee.

2. Draper's estate papers, available at the Surrogate's Office, New York City, contain the list of gifts during the last three years of his life, a number of them provided to scientists who had opposed the *Brown* decision. One regular recipient of Draper's generosity was Wesley Critz George, whose archives, cited below, contain a letter from Weyher that accompanied each annual gift containing the "token of appreciation" language.

3. According to Andrew S. Winston (1998), Garrett requested an appointment in Virginia's psychology department, only to be rejected because of his views on race, but was then accepted by the education department, which was "pleased to have a person of such prestige."

4. Videotapes of *The Forum*, the regular interview program conducted by the Citizens' Councils, are available at the Mississippi Department of Archives and History; many of the featured interviewees were scientists supported by Draper.

5. The Wesley Critz George papers (archived at the Southern Historical Collection, University of North Carolina, Chapel Hill, North Carolina) document his obsession with keeping Blacks separate and unequal. Other scientists lent their authority to segregationist organizations; George actually led one, becoming president of the Patriots of North Carolina, the state's major opponent of school integration.

6. George prepared *The Biology of the Race Problem* in response to a request from an attorney for the governor of Alabama, hired "to represent him on racial litigation"; see "Alabama Orders Study of Races," *New York Times* (November 3, 1961), p. 1. When the State of Alabama, however, did not seem particularly interested in exploiting the work as part of the larger struggle against integration, correspondence in the George papers indicate that Weyher, Trevor, Citizens' Councils administrator William Simmons, and others supported by Draper arranged publication and distribution of the report.

7. The files of the Mississippi Sovereignty Commission (Mississippi Department of Archives and History) contain numerous memos listing contributors to the "special fund." In this well-organized campaign, checks, in amounts from $5 to $500, were first collected from their individual members by representatives of various business and professional associations—the Mississippi Bankers Association, the Bar Association, the Restaurant Association, the State Medical Association, Realtors, truckers, farm bureau organizations, and many others—who would then forward them to the Commission "to be credited to the special fund and not commingled with other funds." The executive director of the Bankers Association even circulated a memo to individual banks, "suggesting" a donation of $1 for every $100,000 of resources. These dedicated efforts, however, produced a total of less than $35,000 from donations within the state.

8. The stock arrived in three segments between July 1963 and January 1964, in each case accompanied by a telegram from a Morgan vice president, informing the Commission of an "anonymous gift" of stock from a client.

9. According to a letter from Satterfield in the Sovereignty Commission files, the plan had been drafted by three individuals, including Satterfield himself, all of

whose anti-integration efforts had been financially supported by Draper. The plan was headed "This Presentation Has Been Drawn to Illustrate How a Public Relations Program May Be Developed Which Would Inform the Public as to the Differences Between The Races."

10. While Draper was providing millions of dollars altogether to the campaign against the Second Reconstruction, Pioneer made only five acknowledged grants—a total of $103,000—which are detailed in Weyher 1999b.

11. "Alan McGregor" was one of numerous pseudonyms employed by Pearson to repeat, at regular intervals, his contention that racial prejudice was normal, natural, and necessary for evolutionary progress. Indeed, "McGregor" alone authored three articles in the *Mankind Quarterly* (1981, 1986, 1993), all of them insisting that interracial relationships were "abnormal patterns of behavior," and a "perversion" of natural instincts—like animals inappropriately attempting "to mate with animals of other breeds."

12. Pioneer's financial records, listing its yearly grants, are available from the Foundation Center, Washington, D.C. They can also be found on the website of the Institute for the Study of Academic Racism, www.ferris.edu/HTMLS/staff/webpages/site.cfm?LinkID=259&eventID=34

18

Being a Statistician Means Never Having to Say You're Certain

Oscar H. Gandy Jr.

While it is generally recognized that statisticians need not be burdened by the demands of certainty, especially when they are asked to draw inferences and arrive at conclusions on the basis of samples, they are nevertheless still called upon from time to time to be more precise than their resources will allow. Where professional standards and the weight of peer review may impose greater restraint upon the scholarly muse in the context of publication within elite journals, traditional scholarly caution and reserve often withers under the glare of public attention that the charge of racial discrimination often attracts. Indeed, we note that some of our colleagues and associates appear quite willing to throw caution to the wind in their haste to provide warnings, advice, and counsel about issues involving racial disparity. Journalists, public intellectuals, and expert witnesses increasingly rely on the tools of statistical analysis to buttress their claims, but as my examples will suggest, these interpreters of the gospel of chance are often unwilling, or unable, to avoid the sin of hubris (Gigerenzer et al. 1989).

Because I am a communications scholar, it is not surprising that I should focus most of my attention on the behavior of communications professionals—the journalists and their editors, who play such an important role in bringing public attention to bear on the problems that data and statistical analysis suggest might exist. But even though the practitioners of "precision journalism" (Meyer 2001) are ultimately responsible for most of the statistically based claims that we encounter in the news, they are not alone. Public intellectuals, and issue advocates more generally are very often the sources for the statistics and the interpretations that journalists and editorial writers pass on far too readily to their readers (Best 2001). Because the social problems that get defined in the press may ultimately be reified in the legislatures and in the courts, the ways in which the public testimony of experts is likely to mislead politicians, lawyers, judges, and juries ought not be ignored either (Faigman 1999).

This chapter examines a number of public issues that have been framed in racial terms with the aid of statistical data and analysis. In many cases, the selection of interpretive frames (Reese, Gandy, and Grant 2001) reflects strategic goals of the sort that Omi and Winant (1994) refer to as "racial projects," in that their "sponsors" hope to achieve a redistribution of wealth and other resources. In other cases, the interpretive frames that are selected reflect the anger and resentment of people who have grown tired of paying what they see as an unjust, but seemingly unavoidable "tax" on being Black (Armour 1997; Essed 1991). In still other circumstances, they reflect the view of people who have come to believe that Affirmative Action and other programs that institutionalize racial preference unjustly threaten the well-being of White males and their families (Kinder and Sanders 1996).

JOURNALISTS, DATABASES, AND THE FRAMING OF DISPARITY

The new precision journalists, on their own, or with the assistance of university researchers, have played an increasingly important role in keeping the problem of racial inequality on the national policy agenda. These reporters have, from time to time, produced a series of investigative articles that prominently feature analysis of statistical data that are said to reveal the nature and extent of racial discrimination in particular cities, and at the national level. They have been aided in their efforts by a professional organization, Investigative Reporters and Editors (IRE), that provides seminars, and publishes handbooks designed to teach journalists how to mine the wealth of data that exist in public records. The number of journalists who have turned toward statistics and away from pithy quotes has increased in part because journalism schools have begun to include courses in computer-assisted reporting in the curriculum (Garrison 1998; Houston 1999).

Unfortunately, in some cases it appears that those journalistic traditions that emphasize the importance of "personalizing" a story with a poignant example (Rucinski 1992) result in readers gaining a false impression of the base rates and distributions of particular risks that the journalists seek to describe (Zillman and Brosius 2000). It is clear, however, that journalists and editors continue to be warned about the ways in which statistics can be used to mislead the public (Best 2001; Cohn 1989; Mauro 1992).

Armed with these resources, investigative reporters have assumed the role of traditional muckrakers, and have published stories that have been crafted with the goal of provoking outrage, and hopefully, mobilizing sustainable political activism on the part of their target audiences (Protess et al. 1991). The topics that investigative journalists choose to pursue reflect the operation of several constraints, including the availability of data, and "commonsense" professional standards about newsworthiness, as well as the potential value of particular stories as contributions to their professional reputations and career trajectories.

Variation in the distribution of story types over time suggests that journalists may also have to meet a more demanding evidentiary standard when they seek to characterize some particular disparities as the product of racial discrimination, rather than bad luck, or some rather complicated causal process (Gandy 1996; Gandy et al. 1997). Investigative journalists have written stories about racial disparities in the delivery of health care, education, and social services, as well as stories that focus explicitly on discrimination in employment: hiring, compensation, and safety on the job. More recently, these stories have begun to include the use of geographic information systems to uncover the spatial character of discrimination.

Banks and mortgage lenders have been among the most popular targets of journalistic zeal. Dozens of investigative series have charged local financial institutions with discriminating against African American and Hispanic applicants seeking to acquire or improve their homes. Some of these stories have been treated as major news events at the national level, and have subsequently been followed up and duplicated with stories at the local level. The publication of similar stories across the nation serves to mark the place of the issue on the national policy agenda (Baumgartner and Jones 1993). We noted, for example, that within one day of the release of a study of racial disparity in mortgage lending by the Federal Reserve Board in 1991, 92 percent of the major newspapers in the United States published at least one article on the issue (Goshorn and Gandy 1995).

Unfortunately, many of the earliest published stories on discrimination in mortgage markets relied upon quite crude statistical analyses that were offered in support of the charge of redlining, or racially motivated geographic discrimination. A common analytical approach, limited in part by the data that were generally available, focused on comparisons across census tracts. Analyses reported in several cities indicated that more mortgages per thousand households had been approved in "White" neighborhoods, than in "Black" neighborhoods. On occasion, reporters gained access to the records of individual lenders, and in those stories, lending-rate comparisons reflected the differences in the number of applications that had been made. In only a few isolated cases were reporters able to gain access to individual case records that would support an analysis of the broad array of factors that influence lending, and if included in the analysis, might explain racial disparities in approval rates (Leven and Sykuta 1994).

Another popular target of database journalists has been the criminal justice system. Investigative series have presented what they felt was compelling statistical evidence of racial discrimination in the granting of plea bargains, convictions, and sentence length. Of course, it was investigative journalists who helped to put the problem of racial profiling on the national agenda. What these journalists claimed was that driving, walking, or even flying while Black could be hazardous to one's health, or at the very least, to one's self-esteem.

In one story, reporters for an Atlanta television station followed up on a tip that suggested that Customs officials at the Atlanta airport had been systematically targeting African Americans for intrusive body searches for drugs (Russell and Larcom 2000). Initially, the reporters came to doubt the accuracy of the initial claim. When they examined the official records of the Customs office, they found that actually, more Whites than African Americans were being searched. When they reexamined the data with regard to the ways in which the decision to search had actually been made, a more striking disparity emerged. It seems that when drug sniffing dogs indicated a target, they tended to point to Whites; and the dogs were almost never wrong.

However, when the invasive searches were initiated in response to a human agent's call, two out of every three passengers tapped for a search were African Americans. Yet, 99 percent of those searches failed to produce any contraband. When the most invasive searches were requested (a search requiring a trip to the hospital), 90 percent of the people searched were African American. And despite the inconvenience, embarrassment, and actual risk involved in conducting these searches, only 20 percent of the people examined were found to be concealing drugs.

Investigative reporters are motivated by a desire to do good by exposing evil. They do so often with the hope of shaping the form and force of law (Gandy 1982). Indirectly, they also influence the flow of information to other journalists and policy entrepreneurs. One investigative series, "The Color of Money" not only won its author William Dedman the Pulitzer Prize in 1989, but it generated a host of follow-on stories by newspapers in other cities. This increased attention to lending practices eventually led to important changes in the reporting requirements of lenders. The passage of the Home Mortgage Disclosure Act meant that journalists, as well as academic researchers, would be able to investigate differences in lending rates by race, gender, and income, as well as by other factors that might reflect differences in the nature of the real estate markets in different communities (Leven and Sykuta 1994).

Media critics have charged the news media with failing to pay sufficient attention to the nature of racial inequality in the criminal justice system (Westfeldt and Wicker 1998). There have been some important exceptions. It seems likely that widespread media attention that was drawn to the problem of racial profiling has brought about important policy changes. Media coverage has led to demands by citizens at local, state, and federal levels for the government to collect data about the racial and ethnic identity of individuals stopped by police as they pursued the "war on drugs" (Allen-Bell 1997; Jenkins 1999). Indeed, growth in the number and variety of these data-gathering efforts led the Department of Justice (DOJ) to publish a "resource guide" in an effort to ensure the quality of the data being compiled (Ramirez, McDevitt, and Farrell 2000).

Among the concerns expressed in the DOJ report was an apparent need to guard against threats to the integrity of these data. DOJ consultants suggested that the same police officers who would be responsible for collecting the data were also likely to be the targets of criticism regarding racial profiling. Investigative reporters and others recognize that when statistical data have the possibility of reflecting poorly upon an administrative agency, there will be powerful incentives for data gatherers to engage in "flexible accounting." The police are no exception (Ericson and Haggerty 1997). The police officers who were accused of shooting four young African American men during a traffic stop along the New Jersey Turnpike were eventually charged with falsifying the racial identification of other persons they had stopped in the past (Davis 1999).

Crime statistics also reflect the influence of political opportunism. The nature of that influence is rarely reflected in journalistic interpretation of crime statistics. The cyclical phenomenon we recognize as "crime waves" can best be understood as reflecting the efforts of politicians to generate support for their reelection. As a result of the pressure that mayors and other elected officials impose on police administrations, the rise and fall in the number of arrests of persons charged with "quality-of-life" crimes is often highly correlated with turning points in municipal electoral campaigns.

On occasion, the flow of public attention actually moves toward focusing on the police as the source of crime. In something of a classic example of publishing the right story at the right time, an investigative report about police brutality in Chicago helped mayoral candidate Harold Washington to mobilize an angry electorate in support of his reform-oriented campaign (Protess et al. 1991). The mobilization of police activity following the assaults on the World Trade Towers and the Pentagon in September 2001 is also likely to transform the character and substance of crime-related statistics.

PUBLIC INTELLECTUALS

Although journalists are the means through which the general public comes to be informed about racial disparity and its causes, it is public intellectuals who bear much of the responsibility for interpreting the data, and for assessing the meaning of the more "objective" analyses that journalists tend to produce. It is the liberal public intellectual who is supposed to remind us that racial profiling actually *inflates* the statistics that are likely to be used by conservatives as validation of their claims regarding the distribution of criminal tendencies among African Americans. It is the same public intellectual who is most likely to help us understand the nature of the vicious circles that help to generate the crime statistics that are then used to justify racial profiling and increased attention to the activities of African American males. Randall Kennedy's commentaries on racial profiling stand as a prime example.

Kennedy noted that for some police officers "racial profiling is a sensible, statistically based tool that enables them to focus their energies efficiently for the purpose of providing protection against crime to law-abiding folk" (Kennedy 1999, 30). Kennedy then cited some of the crime statistics that are often used by police and their supporters as a justification for using race as an index of criminality.

Arguments in support of racial profiling that are based on crime statistics often point to the "fact" that "blacks, who are only about 13 percent of the population, make up '35 percent of all drug arrests and 55 percent of all drug convictions,'" implying that African Americans are responsible for a "disproportionate share of the crime" (Muharrar 1999, 8).

It then falls to public intellectuals like Kennedy to remind us that not only is the implication that one is likely to draw from these statistics dangerously incorrect, in that arrest and conviction rates bear no necessary relationship to the commission of drug-related crimes, but that the social cost of using race to activate police surveillance exceeds the short-term benefits that the supporters of profiling might reasonably expect.

Kennedy (1999) suggests that each encounter that an "innocent" or nonoffending African American has with the police increases their sense of alienation, resentment, and disregard for the police and for the criminal justice system. Public opinion data support this claim, in that African Americans are more likely than Whites to hold unfavorable opinions of the police, with young Black men most likely to hold unfavorable opinions of their local police (Gallup 1999). This alienation feeds back into the system and weakens it, inviting high-level concern about the nature and extent of "jury nullification" and the reluctance among African Americans to participate in the imprisonment of still more young men (Cole 1999).

Most of what we have read about racial profiling has been framed in terms of the importance of the war against drugs (Allen-Bell 1997). The police and much of the general public have come to believe incorrectly that African Americans are far more likely to be users of illegal drugs than Whites. For many, the numbers of African Americans in prison for drug offenses supplies all the proof that anybody might need. But those "facts" deserve greater scrutiny.

If the truth is that African Americans are no more likely than Whites to be carrying drugs as they drive the New Jersey Turnpike (ACLU 1996), yet they are far more likely to be stopped and searched by the police, then the end result will be that more African Americans will be charged and convicted of drug-related charges (Cole 1999).

Public intellectuals are also likely to provide the "commonsense" understandings that ordinary citizens adopt as their own. The statistical claims made by these policy elites are more likely to move into the mainstream from the pages of periodicals and newspaper editorial pages, rather than from the lead paragraphs of investigative reports in the nation's leading newspapers (Michael 2000). Often, the circumstances that propel some of the less visible commentators into the mainstream debate is the broadly felt need to respond to some of the more highly visible, and thereby more dangerous interpretations of racial statistics by those who oppose traditional liberal responses to inequality.

The publication of *The Bell Curve* by Richard Herrnstein and Charles Murray (1994) generated an outpouring of barely civil critique, and much of it was focused on the flaws, distortions, and misrepresentations of the data that were at the core of the authors' analysis (Jacoby and Glauberman 1995). Equally flawed analyses have been allowed to pass on into history because they failed to achieve some requisite level of visibility.

EXPERT WITNESSES

It is often the expert witness, or consultant, who gathers or directs the collection of the statistical data that are used in the formulation of claims of discrimination or disparate impact when criminal or civil cases are brought before the nation's courts. The expert witness is often called upon to produce an analysis that describes a causal chain, and ultimately identifies a responsible party or agent who may be sued, or otherwise brought to justice.

There are great many ways in which suitable statistical evidence may be gathered in support of such a claim. Methods run from the randomized control group experiment through the variety of data-intensive epidemiological studies conducted in support of toxic tort claims. Each relies, to some degree, upon assumptions about the degree of certainty that can be derived from samples and compared against theoretical distributions (Zeisel and Kaye 1997). Indeed, ongoing debates about the appropriate models for assessing the probability of a match between samples of DNA represent another in a stream of troubling challenges to the ability of judges and juries to evaluate the counsel of experts (Faigman 1999).

The nature of the evidence and, most importantly, the nature of the procedures that are used to bring the data into being are especially troublesome when the evidence of disparate impact, and discriminatory intent has to meet a burden that is not well defined (Baldus and Cole 1980; DeGroot, Fienberg, and Kadane 1994). In some cases, bureaucratic agencies have established guidelines that are supposed to facilitate making a distinction between statistical and legal significance.

In the area of employment discrimination, for example, experts have argued in support of an "80% rule," whereby "the hire rate for the group allegedly discriminated against must be less than 80% of the rate for the most favored group" (Meier, Sacks, and Zabell 1994, 2). The use of such a rule of thumb is justified in part on recognition of the extent to which statistical significance can be affected by the size of the sample available for analysis. Large disparities observed in small samples can easily fail to achieve significance.

More problematic for determining which rules should govern the interpretation of statistical evidence is the lack of comparability in the circumstances under which choices and decisions are made. As we noted with regard to charges of discrimination in the mortgage markets, as more and more information about applicants, homes, and housing markets are introduced into multivariate models, the importance of racial classification tends to shrink toward nonsignificance. In the case of employment discrimination claims, comparable data about the selection process are rarely captured in the records available to the courts. They are even less likely to be available to petitioners who seek to convince the courts that some administration agency was motivated by racial animus when it approved the citing of hazardous waste facilities in one community rather than in another (Roberts 1998).

As Faigman (1999) reminds us, however, we have little basis for assuming that either judges or jurors are likely to appreciate the arguments made in support of toxic torts colored by racialized marketing schemes. Recently, the United States Court of Appeals (3rd Ct.) concluded that representatives of the class of African Americans who claimed that R. J. Reynolds, Inc. had unlawfully targeted them in order to promote the consumption of a dangerous product (mentholated cigarettes) were not supported by the statistical evidence and arguments presented on their behalf (*Brown v. Philip Morris* 2001).

In his impassioned dissent, district judge Milton Shadur argued that his colleagues didn't understand, and thereby failed to reject what he described as the "hypocritical" and "deceptive" use of statistics by the defense. By emphasizing the fact that 69 percent of menthol cigarettes are consumed by non-Blacks, the defendants sought, in his opinion, to distract the court's attention from the more compelling fact that African Americans, who represented somewhat more than 10 percent of the population, nevertheless consumed 31 percent of the defendants' dangerous product.

Judge Shadur made reference to another so-called rule of thumb that was supposed to be used in establishing "proof" of discrimination in the case of large samples—a difference between the observed and expected statistic that is "more than 2 or 3 standard deviations." Judge Shadur estimated that the difference between 10 percent and 31 percent in this particular case was some 7 standard deviations, an outcome marked by a likelihood of chance occurrence "so small to beggar the imagination: 1.28 in a trillion." (*Brown v. Philip Morris* 2001, 50). Unfortunately, not all courts have been as willing, as Judge Shadur implied, to accept guidelines based on standard deviations, standard errors, or P-values (Baldus and Cole 1980; DeGroot, Fienberg, and Kadane 1994; Zeisel and Kaye 1997, 79–98).

Somewhat greater success has been observed with regard to racial profiling. John Lamberth, a psychology professor from Temple University, provided the data and analysis that the ACLU used in arguing that only the use of racial profiles could explain the remarkable disparity between the treatment of White and Black drivers along Interstate 95. Central to Lamberth's task was (1) the need to establish the prevalence of African Americans among all drivers, and (2) the extent to which African Americans were behaving in ways that made them more or less likely to be stopped and then searched.

Lamberth developed a number of creative techniques for gathering evidence in the field. Observational data from static and moving vehicles were used to establish the extent to which African American, Latino, and other drivers were exceeding the speed limit. Lamberth used state police records of traffic stops and searches for evidence of risk and the efficiency and fairness of their strategies. As the expert witness for the ACLU, Lamberth had to demonstrate that disparities in the relative risk of being stopped by the highway patrol, which was higher for African Americans, could not be explained by chance variations in selectivity.

Lamberth argued that the difference between the number of Black drivers eligible to be stopped on the basis of their behavior and those actually stopped and searched exceeded thirty-four standard deviations! This was a difference that he claimed should not have occurred by chance more than once in one quintillion samples (ACLU 1996). Lamberth's analysis of stop-and-search records from the Maryland State Police found virtually indistinguishable success rates when White and Black motorists' vehicles were searched. African Americans were "holding" 28.4 percent of the time, and Whites were in possession of contraband 28.8 percent of the time.

Here, of course, it would be up to the journalists, and the public intellectuals to use these data to point out how stopping and searching more

African Americans would necessarily produce more arrest, conviction, and time behind bars for young Black men.

ENGAGING THE REASONABLE RACIST

Unfortunately, it is not by data alone that the expert witness shapes the sense of injustice that African Americans derive from their knowledge of the workings of the criminal justice system. Expert witnesses have helped to establish the standards of "reasonableness" with which defendants might justify their discriminatory treatment of African Americans. Armour (1997) examines the concept of reasonableness primarily with regard to claims of self-defense, but he does so in terms that can readily be applied to many of the routine encounters that define "everyday racism" (Essed 1991). In Armour's view, these standards of reasonableness are likely to be based on flawed reasoning and inappropriate statistical comparisons.

Armour notes that legal scholars and jurists these days seem to be broadly committed to introducing Bayesian statistical reasoning into the courtroom (Gigerenzer et al. 1989, 263–69). Armour identifies the so-called Intelligent Bayesian as one the three types of "reasonable racists" who are likely to justify visiting violence upon, or avoiding contact with African Americans because they are believed to represent an unacceptably high risk.

Whereas racial stereotypes may no longer be used as an explicit justification for discriminatory acts, the Bayesian makes use of statistics (of the sort likely to be cited by public intellectuals, and quoted by journalists) to support his actions as being reasonable, rather than racist. Unfortunately, Bayesian estimates of probability are subjective, rather than based on experiments, or samples. More problematic still is the likelihood that Bayesian jurors will rely upon wildly varying sources of base rates in the "calculation" of their "posterior probabilities" of risk.

As noted earlier, journalists may inadvertently distract their readers from the base-rate information that they provide in their stories by using a purposively chosen, but unrepresentative exemplar as a lead for their story. When journalists are motivated by a policy goal, or when they have been influenced by issue activists, they tend to "err on the side of exaggeration" in presenting relevant facts (Best 2001, 34). They may do this by choosing a "representative" of the problem, even if the chosen representative is, in fact, unrepresentative of the facts that matter most. In an analysis of stories in news magazines, Zillman and Brosius (2000, 21) found that 25 percent of the stories included exemplars that were inconsistent with the focus of the story. Rather than providing precise quantities or statistical measures, 56 percent of the stories in television news magazines made "comparatively vague assertions, such as that the incidence 'is skyrocketing,' . . . or 'is increasing at an alarming rate'" (25).

Imprecision and exaggeration are likely to influence the probability estimates of Bayesian jurors, especially if these impressions happen to interact with and reinforce existing stereotypes of African Americans. Gilens (1996) observed the misuse of exemplars in the press in ways that might lead jurors to make at least two sorts of biased estimates of the prevalence of African Americans among the poor. Gilens found that the photographs used in stories about poverty in weekly news magazines overrepresented African Americans among the poor. In addition, the images that were used tended to underrepresent African Americans among the so-called deserving or sympathetic poor, such as the elderly and the physically handicapped. The African Americans used to illustrate stories about poverty seemed to be able-bodied, and such representations are likely to invite victim-blaming attributions of individual responsibility.

CONCLUSION

While Armour (1997) holds out the hope that "rationality-enhancing group references" might come to replace the distortions that "intelligent Bayesians" and statistical illiterates may introduce into the courts and the legislative process, other signs invite greater caution about the future of the law and social policy (Habermas 1998).

On the one hand, we have observed that the evidentiary requirements that must be met by those who would pursue a charge of discrimination have been raised by a series of court decisions that have concluded that a disparate impact is not enough (Cole 1999). At the same time we have observed an increase in the rhetoric of markets and the efficient pursuit of wealth, which suggests that racial discrimination may be rational, and thereby justified in a broad range of contexts (Kuttner 1999).

While communication scholars appeal for us to pay greater attention to the ways in which journalists and editors present statistics and interpret their social meaning (Best 2001; Zillman and Brosius 2000), there are others who suggest that the nature of competition and an increased concern with the bottom line in the media industry does not bode well for the pursuit of traditional journalistic standards (Sparks and Tulloch 2000). Indeed, the emergence of the Internet as an alternative source of ideological critique, and a medium with even less of a tradition of fairness and balance, is seen by some observers as leading to even greater polarization and less opportunity for direct comparison of the facts and figures that support competing views (Sunstein 2001).

As Gerd Gigerenzer and his colleagues (1989) have argued, probability and statistics have come to rule the world. The application of statistical reasoning to the concerns of the public sphere has helped to produce an uncertain, and on occasion troubling state of affairs. As a product of "La technique" (Ellul 1964) racial statistics have taken on a life of their own. They enable discrimination at the same time that they provide evidence of its existence, and estimates of its social cost.

It seems unlikely that statistical literacy will keep pace with the opportunities for its strategic misuse. The most we can hope for is the occasional reminder that the resolution of uncertainty about what is just is a goal that cannot really be achieved (Hochschild 1981).

19

Crime Statistics, Disparate Impact Analysis, and the Economic Disenfranchisement of Minority Ex-Offenders

Regina Austin

In the conclusion of his chapter, "Deracializing Social Statistics: Problems in the Quantification of Race," sociologist Tukufu Zuberi writes: "[T]he racialization of data is an artifact of both the struggles to preserve and to destroy racial stratification. Before the data can be deracialized, we must deracialize the social circumstances that created race. Statistical research can go beyond racial reasoning if we dare to apply the methods to the data appropriately" (Zuberi 2000, 183). Unfortunately, "[r]ace-based beliefs about human behavior continue to linger in the public mind and seek legitimacy through so-called value-free scientific inquiry" (Spigner 1998, 360). As a result, when racial statistics are interpreted or discussed, race is very often treated as if it were *a cause of*, rather than merely *a factor associated with*, social phenomena (Spigner 1998). In most instances, though, race-specific data should be "unpacked" and viewed in conjunction with causal social variables such as poverty, unemployment, and discrimination (Spigner 1998). The data should prompt further inquiry into the relationship between race and the likely causes of negative social phenomena, not less.

I wish that I could say that the law always uses racialized data in the appropriate way, but I cannot. I hope to illustrate this by examining the use of race-based crime statistics in connection with a concrete legal problem, the economic disenfranchisement of ex-offenders. As used in this chapter, the term "economic disenfranchisement" refers to the effect of laws, regulations, and unregulated private practices that negatively impact the ability of ex-offenders to function as economic actors. Included in this category are barriers that impede ex-offenders' access to employment and occupational pursuits, credit, housing, education, and social welfare benefits.[1]

ECONOMIC DISENFRANCHISEMENT OF MINORITY EX-OFFENDERS

One of the most significant disabilities burdening the economic advancement of blacks and Latinos today is the tendency to link their race and/or ethnicity with crime and violence, a linkage that statistics seemingly confirm. For example, although Blacks represent roughly 12.8 percent of the population, they constitute 28.6 percent of persons arrested, 27.7 percent of persons convicted in federal courts, 44 percent of those convicted of felonies in state courts, 37.8 percent of those incarcerated by federal authorities, and 46.5 percent of those incarcerated by state authorities.[2] Similarly, Latinos, who represent roughly 11.9 percent of the population and may be of any race, are 27.3 percent of federal inmates and 17 percent of state inmates (Bureau of Justice Statistics 2000; U.S. Census Bureau 2000).[3]

All manner of social and economic consequences follow from the mistaken significance attached to such racialized criminal justice data. Because minorities are disproportionately represented among those arrested, convicted, and incarcerated, it is assumed that any individual minority person is more likely to engage in criminal behavior than any individual White person. It is accordingly thought to be rational for actors or decision makers in political, economic, or even social settings to avoid contact or interaction with minority persons who might use the encounter as an opportunity to commit a crime. There are many problems with this approach. For one thing, it is an erroneous interpretation of the gross criminal justice statistics. Even if the data are taken at face value, the percentage of the minority population engaged in criminal behavior is still quite small and so are the chances that any random minority individual poses a threat of criminal behavior (Armour 1997, 38–39, 165 n.10).[4] More importantly, action predicated on misinterpretations of racialized crime data produces grave social, political, and economic consequences that contravene norms of fairness and equality. The burdens imposed on Blacks and Latinos because of the inappropriate interpretation of crime data extend beyond racial profiling by law enforcement officers, a practice nearly universally condemned.[5] For example, statistical discrimination and the exaggerated fear of minority criminality have impaired the ability of law-abiding minority citizens to engage in such mundane activities as shopping in a retail establishment without being closely watched, having a pizza delivered to their door (because deliverymen fear being mugged), or paying for a purchase by check (because merchants fear that the checks will bounce) (Austin 2000; Linstedt 2000).[6]

As difficult as the suspicion of criminal activity may make economic life for the law-abiding, however, those who have actually run afoul of the law have it much worse. Both formal legal prohibitions and informal practices prevent minority ex-offenders from achieving full participation in the economy after they have paid whatever price the criminal justice system has directly imposed on them as punishment. Thus, by law, a person with a criminal record, especially one involving drug offenses, may be denied the right to get or keep a job, obtain public assistance and food stamps, or receive a student loan (U.S. Congress 1998; Allard 2002; Golden 2001; Mukamal 2000; Rudenstine 1979; Schemo 2001).[7] Informal discrimination by private employers, landlords, and lenders against ex-offenders is even more ubiquitous than that produced by state-imposed prohibitions, but it may be effectively beyond the reach of antibias measures. Various justifications have been offered in support of these collateral, extrajudicial civil penalties, among them retribution, stigmatization, and notions of moral desert (Demleitner 1999). (These will be discussed more fully below.) A more frequently invoked explanation, though, is the suspicion or fear of future lawbreaking by, and the recidivist proclivities of, ex-offenders (Demleitner 1999).[8] Civil penalties or disabilities theoretically bar ex-offenders from gaining access to economic rights or entitlements that might become launching pads for further criminal behavior. Recidivism statistics would appear to support the proposition that minority ex-offenders pose a substantial threat of future lawbreaking.[9] Taken all together, the collateral penalties and related private practices pose a significant obstacle to the reintegration of minority ex-offenders into the formal economy and prevent many of them from gaining access to the resources they need in order to become economically contributing members of their communities.

The gross criminal justice statistics cited above, however, suggest that the adverse burden of conditioning economic entitlements or opportunities on an applicant's or a recipient's having a clean criminal record will fall disproportionately on Blacks and Latinos.[10] If the law is sensitive to the disparate impact of private practices burdening minorities, then the crime statistics that promote stereotypes about the criminal proclivities of minorities in general should trigger individualized inquiries that should ameliorate some of the discrimination and economic hardship experienced by those with criminal records. An economic decision maker or actor who chooses to rely on arrest and conviction records would have to explain the necessity for doing so in the particular instance and would not be able to rely on gross racialized criminal data as an excuse. The decision maker or actor would have to go beyond the numbers to focus on the personal characteristics and social circumstances of the specific minority ex-offender that make her or him likely to perpetrate crime in the future. The crime data would, in essence, be used affirmatively to initiate an inquiry that should lead to its own critical deconstruction. Moreover, if employment plays a significant role in desistance from crime, as is widely suggested, then case-by-case assessments of employability and the resulting reduction in employment discrimination against minority ex-offenders should alter the very socioeconomic conditions that are the source of the crime statistics.

But the negative power of the highly misunderstood association between race/ethnicity and crime should not be underestimated. Racialized crime data is routinely misinterpreted and its import highly exaggerated. As a result, enforcement of antibias measures favoring ex-offenders appears to require that economic decision makers (prospective employers, lenders, or landlords) choose between seemingly amorphous discrimination against the ex-offender on the one hand and seemingly palpable danger to itself, its customers, and the population in general on the other. For many people, the choice is easy: it is better to avert the danger than to avoid the discrimination. There is, of course, a strong counterargument that the danger posed by ex-offenders is overblown and that the consequences of bias are quite severe and widespread in that they impact not only the ex-offender, but her or his family and community too. At this point in time, however, the society is not favorably disposed toward the protection of the interests of ex-offenders.

There should be little wonder, then, that minority ex-offenders find it difficult to prove that they have been the victims of racial/ethnic discrimination because they have been denied a job or a loan on account of their criminal records. Courts may reject the relevance of generalized crime data as proof that reliance on criminal histories disproportionately affects minorities and demand that an ex-offender claimant come up with more specific statistical evidence of a disparate impact on a smaller subset of the minority population of which she or he is a member. Furthermore, even if a disparate impact is established, a court may refuse to go beyond the statistics to consider factors that produce the correlation between race/ethnicity and crime, such as individual agency, social milieu, and structural factors like poverty, unemployment, and discrimination. Thus, the courts do not always use race statistics appropriately and disparate impact analysis under the antidiscrimination laws applicable to employment and lending, for example, does not always provide a basis for challenging decisions that effectively disenfranchise minority ex-offenders from full participation in the economy.

THE FUTILITY OF DISPARATE IMPACT ANALYSIS

A.B. and S. Auto Service, Inc. v. South Shore Bank of Chicago illustrates this point nicely. The plaintiff in the case, a Black man, owned an auto repair shop. He applied for a loan of $230,000 from the defendant bank, which had a loan production office in his neighborhood, after he had been turned down by another financial institution. In connection with his application, the plaintiff was required to complete a Small Business Administration form that asked him to disclose his record of arrests and convictions. Roughly ten years before applying, he had been arrested for domestic violence and for possession of a controlled substance. During the same period, he was convicted of aggravated battery for a stabbing that occurred when he defended himself and his wife from an attack by a number of assailants. Roughly five years before seeking the loan, he had been arrested once for disorderly conduct and for possession of a controlled substance. Four or five months prior to seeking the loan, he had been charged with possession of a stolen car. In all then, the plaintiff had a record of five arrests and one conviction (*A.B. and S. Auto v. S. Shore* 1997, 1057–58).

The opinion leaves out some information that is important to understanding this case from the plaintiff's perspective. According to the plaintiff's lawyer, the plaintiff ran a fairly large, successful operation.[11] He had been in business for ten years, employed roughly ten to fifteen workers, and had sufficient collateral to back the loan and a clear credit record. He wanted the loan so that he could buy equipment that would enable him to do auto insurance work. Though he might have had a defense to the aggravated assault charge, his attorney at the time told him to plead guilty and accept probation. Finally, the stolen vehicle charge, which was dropped, stemmed from the plaintiff's use of the automobile of a customer who failed to pay for its repair.

An African American vice president of the defendant bank recommended that the plaintiff's loan request be approved. The loan committee, however, decided to reject it on the ground that the plaintiff's criminal record "reflect[ed] poorly on [his] judgment and character" (*A.B. and S. Auto v. S. Shore* 1997, 1058). The bank did not as a matter of policy reject persons with criminal records; rather it considered "an applicant's criminal history and the surrounding facts on a case-by-case basis . . . in evaluating the applicant's character and judgment which, in turn, [was] used in assessing the ability and willingness of the applicant to repay the loan" (*A.B. and S. Auto v. S. Shore* 1997, 1058). The bank had made loans to three borrowers with criminal records, one of whom was an African American. Of course, the bank did not maintain data on the loan applicants it rejected because of their criminal records.

In advancing a claim under the Equal Credit Opportunity Act (ECOA), the plaintiff had to present evidence of a disparate impact on black loan applicants arising from the bank's reliance on arrest records, before the bank would be required to justify its practice (Equal Credit Opportunity Act 2000).[12] The plaintiff offered expert testimony to the effect that any decision based on arrest records would adversely and disparately impact or affect blacks because of their disproportionately higher arrest rates (*A.B. and S. Auto v. S. Shore* 1997, 1058–59). The plaintiff's theory was that the percentage of loan applicants who would be disqualified by the reliance on criminal histories correlated with the percentage of Blacks who have arrest records. The plaintiff's expert argued that higher arrest rates did not necessarily indicate that Blacks commit a higher percentage of crime than others. He further asserted that his research also revealed that many qualified Blacks were rejected for loans for reasons other than not being creditworthy, including consideration of arrest records. The expert, however, could not cite any study that showed that consideration of arrest records adversely impacted Black applicants for credit of any kind, including business loans (*A.B. and S. Auto v. S. Shore* 1997, 1062).

There were essentially two ways in which the plaintiff could have proven disparate impact. First, the plaintiff could have relied on general arrest statistics, provided that he could show that the applicant pool for small business loans had roughly the same characteristics as the general population with regard to law breaking. Alternatively, he could have satisfied the threshold requirement by proving that reliance on criminal records would have had a disparate impact on the pool of actual or potential loan applicants who would have otherwise been considered qualified for a loan. The plaintiff was in essence required to establish either of two propositions that run counter to normal class expectations: (1) that the class of entrepreneurial Blacks seeking small business loans breaks the law as much as the general population, or (2) that there exists a class of entrepreneurial Blacks who break the law yet are, but for their criminal records, qualified for loans. The plaintiff proved neither.

The court ruled that general population statistics were insufficient to establish disparate impact under the ECOA without proof that the pool of qualified loan applicants possessed characteristics roughly equivalent to those of the general population (*A.B. and S. Auto v. S. Shore* 1997, 1063). Plaintiff's attorney and his expert were not totally unreasonable in thinking that general criminal data would be sufficient to show that the bank's reliance on an applicant's record of arrests and convictions would disproportionately disadvantage potential Black small business borrowers. They were assuming the homogeneity of Blacks across classes and occupational groupings, at least with regard to their vulnerability to being ensnared by the machinations of a criminal justice system that seems permeated by racism. Younger, poorer urban males may be more vulnerable than others, but the arbitrary nature of the administration of justice puts nearly everyone at risk. Pervasive racism, if not race, seemingly trumps whatever might otherwise divide Black offenders; this is especially true where drug law enforcement is concerned.

It is broadly taken for granted, at least by minorities, that crime statistics reflect the impact of racial discrimination both as to the causes of criminal behavior and its severity, as well as to the ways in which Blacks are dealt with throughout the criminal justice system. If minorities are more likely to commit crime, it is because of factors such as social strain and social disorganization that disproportionately affect the victims of White supremacy and ethnocentricity (Walker, Spohn, and DeLone 2000). The greater presence of criminals and the higher incidence of crime in minority communities also feed on themselves to increase the rates of criminal behavior among minorities. In regard to the criminal justice system itself, arrest rates reflect not only the incidence of crime perpetrated by Blacks and Latinos, but also the priority given to the policing of minority communities by the authorities and the degree of discretion that individual police officers have regarding whom they arrest.[13] As with any self-fulfilling prophecy, the police particularly find more drug-related crime where they look for it. The disparate arrest rates experienced by Blacks and Latinos contribute in turn to disparate rates of conviction and incarceration. Moreover, success at each stage of the process keeps the cycle of disparate arrests, convictions, and incarcerations going. In addition, discrimination in the criminal justice system is not limited to the activity of the police. Racial discrimination would appear to be implicated in the nature and the quality of legal representation minority defendants can afford and/or obtain gratis from the state, in their ability to make bail and participate in the preparation of their defenses or to avoid being sentenced to time served, in the stringency of the charges filed against them or the generosity of the plea bargains offered them by prosecutors, in young defendants' assignment to adult court as opposed to juvenile court, in the juries' assessments of the defendants' guilt, and in sentencing judges' assessments of the defendants' culpability and responsibility, especially where the victim is White.[14]

Statistical studies might be helpful in unraveling the extent to which discriminatory practices at various levels (structural, contextual, and individual) of the criminal justice process is producing racial and ethnic disparities in the rates of arrest, conviction, and incarceration, but the data is inconclusive.[15] At the very least, though, it appears that at numerous points in the criminal justice process minorities are disparately and adversely impacted by state action. To rely on criminal records in deciding to make a small business loan, then, adds another layer to an already tall stack of disparate impacts befalling Blacks who run afoul of the law. Just as it is impossible to unpack the cumulative disparate impacts that produce the gross arrest and conviction data, there is little point to trying to separate out a discrete segment of the Black offending population (i.e., entrepreneurial Blacks) from the whole in an attempt to show that it is better off, worse off, or about the same as the rest.

Given that the plaintiff was unable to rely on general arrest data, the court said that he was required to establish "(1) how many African-Americans with convictions or arrests [were] otherwise qualified for the loan; and (2) how many African-Americans [were] deterred from applying because of the bank's practices" (*A.B. and S. Auto v. S. Shore* 1997). The court acknowledged that, since creditors are prohibited by the ECOA from inquiring about an applicant's race, the plaintiff was in the near impossible position of "trying to prove disproportionate impact without any access to [the] creditor's statistical lending profile" (*A.B. and S. Auto v. S. Shore* 1997). Finally, the court indicated that the plaintiff's ability to establish a link between the allegedly discriminatory criterion (reliance on criminal records) and loan denials would be hampered by the absence of a blanket disqualification by the defendant bank of all applicants with criminal records (*A.B. and S. Auto v. S. Shore* 1997).

Basically, the plaintiff had to prove disparate impact by satisfying criteria similar to those applicable in Title VII actions. Under such an approach, the claimant must first demonstrate that the lender's policy or practice has a substantial adverse impact on the class of *financially qualified* loan applicants protected by the law. This class may consist of either those qualified persons who actually applied for a loan from the defendant institution (the applicant flow approach) or all of those qualified persons in the market for loans, including those who were deterred from applying because of the use of the contested policy or practice (the virtual or proxy market approach).[16] The claimant must establish that this class bore the unfavorable consequences of the disputed lender practice disproportionately as compared with the class of nonprotected applicants who are similarly situated.

Thus, where a disappointed Black borrower challenges a lender's reliance on her or his arrest and conviction information, the borrower must have data establishing the dimensions of the protected class of Black, otherwise qualified actual or potential loan applicants, the impact that the contested policy had or would have on their loan approval rate based on data on the incidence of arrests and convictions experienced by this class, and finally the extent of the disparity between the policy's impact on such a protected class and its impact on the class of similarly situated Whites (*A.B. and S. Auto v. S. Shore* 1997, 1063). Unfortunately, the plaintiff in *A.B. and S. Auto Service* offered no such statistical support for his claim.

Consider the predicament confronting the plaintiff in constructing the class of qualified borrowers. The plaintiff, who was himself otherwise fully qualified for a loan, had to prove that there was some actual or virtual group of Black loan applicants as to whom he was the rule, rather than the exception, a task not so easily performed in light of the hardships borne by Black small business entrepreneurs, regardless of their criminal histories, in establishing their entitlement to credit. Creditworthiness is fairly subjective and may be affected by racial inequality beyond that evidenced by the lender practice in dispute. Consider the number of Black businesses that were never established because of the use of questionable loan criteria other than criminal records, or the number that resorted to informal or illegal credit markets because the formal market seemed foreclosed to them, or the number that started with inadequate capital and failed as a result. Some of these concerns might have been creditworthy and theoretically should be included in the class of protected applicants whose criminal histories would have been considered.

Because of discrimination, there are any number of characteristics ostensibly related to creditworthiness that are disproportionately lacked by Blacks and other minorities in general, let alone by ex-offenders in particular. The phenomenon of compound disparate impacts applies here too. But the plaintiff seems to have been foreclosed from pursuing that line of inquiry. The way I read the opinion, the court is saying that before the plaintiff can rely on disparate impact analysis with regard to *one factor* she or he has to either accept the assumption that there are no disparate impacts operating with regard to *any other factor* relevant to creditworthiness or prove that disparate impact analysis applies to *each and every such factor*. If a claimant lives by disparate impact analysis, so to speak, she or he also dies by disparate impact analysis. The court's reliance on an "all other things being equal" standard makes resort to disparate impact analysis a totally unwinnable strategy. Success for the claimant is dependent on the collection of ever more specific race-based data. It is unclear whether there will ever be enough data to override the assumption that "neutral" forces like the market or individual irresponsibility explain the disparities in economic and social well-being minorities suffer on a gross basis.

The defendant bank did not collect data regarding applicants with a record of arrests and convictions or the dispositions of their loan requests. Arrest rates for Blacks in general can be found in publicly maintained sources, but the plaintiff needed data on the arrest rate for the subset of qualified entrepreneurial Blacks who would apply for a small business loan, and that data is no doubt very hard, if not impossible, to come by.[17] Moreover, he would have had to compile much the same data for Whites because it is possible that White business owners are more likely to have criminal records than the White population in general. If so, the increase in their involvement in criminal behavior might offset the disparity that exists between the arrest rates of Blacks and Whites in the general population and thereby undermine a plaintiff's ECOA claim.

For all of these reasons, then, the plaintiff's attempt to prove discrimination via the disparate impact of the lender's reliance on loan applicants' criminal records based on race statistics was futile. Given the standards employed by the court, it could not have been otherwise.

MAKING SENSE OF CRIMINAL RECORDS

To assure itself of the correctness of the defendant bank's judgment call, the court went on to consider whether the bank's decision bore a manifest relationship to the plaintiff's creditworthiness. The court was not required to make this inquiry since the plaintiff could not establish that use of an applicant's criminal history had a disparate impact on Blacks, but it chose to do so anyway (*A.B. and S. Auto v. S. Shore* 1997). Generally, if the claimant establishes a disparate adverse impact, the defendant may prove that the practice in question serves a legitimate business purpose. If the defendant succeeds in making this showing, the claimant may nonetheless prevail by demonstrating that an alternative practice would be equally as effective in achieving the defendant's business purpose as the challenged practice, but would have a less disproportionate effect.

The court in *A.B. and S. Auto Repair* first noted that the Small Business Administration required the bank to inquire into an applicant's criminal record as part of an assessment of her or his character, reputation, and credit history.[18] Consideration of an applicant's background was therefore a legitimate factor related to creditworthiness. Moreover, the plaintiff admitted that "the charges for possession of a controlled substance, domestic abuse, and disorderly conduct . . . involved an exercise of bad judgment and reflected negatively on his character" (*A.B. and S. Auto v. S. Shore* 1997, 1058 n. 2). The court concluded that the bank had accordingly "demonstrated that its practice has a manifest relationship to the extension of credit" (*A.B. and S. Auto v. S. Shore* 1997, 1064).

Plaintiff's admission notwithstanding, almost any criminal behavior, particularly where the criminal is so inept as to get caught, reflects on a person's judgment and character. But in this case, some of that bad judgment occurred long before plaintiff applied for a loan. There is no indication of what his life circumstances were at the time of his arrests or what changes he had made in his ways since then. It is not clear how the bad judgment he displayed as a lawbreaker who was arrested but not convicted related to his ability to run a legitimate auto repair business or his capacity to repay a loan on time. The stolen vehicle possession charge might be worrisome were there no explanation for it, but the other acts of which the plaintiff was accused do not bespeak dishonesty or theft.

An argument can be made that if criminal records, particularly arrest records, are relevant at all in a case such as *A.B. and S. Auto*, then, the decision maker's discretion should be constrained and the inquiry should be broadened to require consideration of not only the nature of the offenses and their seriousness (with more weight being given to convictions, felonies, crimes involving moral turpitude, and offenses punishable by incarceration), but also the applicant's age at the time of their commission, the circumstances surrounding their commission, the amount of time that has elapsed since their commission, the efforts the applicant has made toward rehabilitation (including educational attainment, changes in marital or family status, prior employment, treatment for substance abuse or psychological counseling, membership in social organizations or participation in community activities, or receipt of a state-issued certificate of rehabilitation), and any other factors that are relevant to determining whether the offenses bear a substantial relationship to her or his creditworthiness or are otherwise legitimately related to the extension of credit (Mukamal 2001; Rudenstine 1979). The last factor is a broad one. It would justify consideration of whether the applicant is likely to engage in further crime and jeopardize the interests of the lender or persons with whom the applicant will come into contact if a favorable decision is granted.[19] Also, the actor (whether it be an employer or lender) should specifically inquire as to whether a favorable decision will provide an opportunity for the recurrence of criminal behavior. That may depend on whether the circumstances that resulted in the prior criminal behavior are still present or whether the applicant has maintained connections or ties with prior victims or accomplices.

The SBA form on which plaintiff revealed his criminal past stated, "'The fact that you have an arrest or conviction record will not necessarily disqualify you'" (*A.B. and S. Auto v. S. Shore* 1997, 1057). The only way to insure the truth of this statement is to constrain the decision maker's discretion by opening up the inquiry it must make. Of course, were a claimant to make such a proposal in an ECOA case, she or he might have to establish with statistics that constrained discretion is more effective at identifying bad loan candidates and has a less discriminatory effect than the open-ended consideration of an applicant's prior criminal history without more.

The real danger associated with requiring or allowing unfettered consideration of an applicant's record of arrests and convictions in cases such as this is that it invites an assessment of her or his social or moral entitlement to a loan. The additional scrutiny might ostensibly be justified on a number of grounds. Loans are a scarce or precious social resource that must be rationed. Receiving a loan is, after all, a privilege, not a matter of right. Loans are rewards for good behavior, while denials are the just deserts of someone who has erred in a way that warrants social ostracism and economic marginalization in addition to time served. As a result, the lender gets the opportunity to make an independent assessment of the applicant's crime based on factors that bear no relationship to the applicant's capabilities as a legitimate business owner who can pay her or his debts.

Aside from the failure of such an approach to leave room for the possibility of rehabilitation, it begs the ultimate question of the extent to which society can hold an individual's mistakes against him or her while at the same time admitting to the existence of systemic wrongs that impact the opportunity structure of the minority group of which that person is a member. Parceling out blame between individual agency or responsibility, on the one hand, and structural determinism, on the other, is a political, not a scientific, matter. Not every crime committed by a minority person is an act of submission to political, economic, or social forces beyond her or his control, but some crimes are. Not every failure to award a loan to a minority applicant reflects a pattern of economic discrimination, but some refusals do. Surely, a compromise between holding the system totally accountable and subjecting a former lawbreaker to perpetual social and economic estrangement is plausible. It must be acknowledged that the incentives for compromise are not substantial at this point. The society is less willing to accept responsibility for discrimination than it once was and even less willing to admit the role that structural factors play in minorities' criminal behavior. This seems true despite the fact that it is becoming more and more apparent that the criminal justice system is creating a caste of black and brown inmates whose bodies are the fodder fueling the growth of the so-called "prison industrial complex" (Donzinger 1996; Schlosser 1998). A new form of bondage is creating economic wealth for prison construction firms, private prison operators, investment companies that sell the bonds used to finance prison construction, security firms that arm and equip the prisons and the guards, commissary suppliers who provide the prisoners with everything from Twinkies to pornographic magazines, users of prison labor, prison guards who are organized in powerful unions, and economically depressed rural, White working-class enclaves that look upon a non-polluting prison as a godsend. The prison-industrial complex is supported by a highly effective social denigration regime that extends to justifying stripping otherwise unconditionally released ex-offenders of important social and economic entitlements and opportunities, which increases their chances of recidivism. Race is an essential component of the stigmatization. Writes law professor David Cole:

> There is a mutually reinforcing relationship between criminal stigmatization of blacks and racial subordination: the criminal stigmatization of blacks perpetuates and justifies their subordination as a group and the status of blacks as a segregated, subordinated group makes it easier to insist on ever-more-stringent stigmatizing measures in criminal law. Cast as criminals, blacks deserve prison, not redress. (Cole 1999, 177)

Employers and lenders are not immune from the effects of this stigmatization and indeed participate in the labeling process when they summarily reject job and loan applicants based on the mere fact that the latter have criminal records (Bushway 2000).

The cycle of stigmatization and subordination through criminalization must be broken. Recognition of the many ways in which the supposedly neutral operation of the criminal justice system disparately impacts minorities would interrupt the process. Challenging the stigmatization that taints economic decisions that interfere with the ability of ex-offenders to assume productive roles as wage earners and entrepreneurs in their communities is a good place to begin.

It might be claimed, however, that liberal use of disparate impact analysis, with its reliance on racialized crime data, will only confirm the stereotyping and stigmatization that many law-abiding minorities have worked so hard to counter. The interests of the noncriminal majority might be better served by a political stance whereby it distances itself from ex-offenders rather than identifies with them (Austin 1992).

Consider the court's analysis in *EEOC v. Carolina Freight Carriers Corp* (1989). The case involved Francisco Rios, a Hispanic-American who, after working for the defendant as a casual or part-time driver for more than four years, was not hired for a full-time position because he had previously been convicted of receiving stolen property and of larceny, the latter conviction having resulted in eighteen months of incarceration (1989, 741).[20] Not only did the EEOC fail to establish disparate impact, but the defendant trucking company was also able to prove that it had a legitimate nondiscriminatory justification for its policy of not hiring individuals with a record of "felony, theft or larceny convictions within the applicant's lifetime which resulted in an active prison or jail sentence" (738).[21] The court accepted the defendant's assertion that its policy was intended to reduce the incidence of losses due to employee theft (752–54). The court concluded that "[i]t is exceedingly reasonable for an employer to rely upon an applicant's past criminal history in predicting trustworthiness" (753). The employer's policy would certainly have a disparate impact on thieves; it was immaterial that some of those thieves were Hispanic. "If Hispanics do not wish to be discriminated against because they have been convicted of theft then, [*sic*] they should stop stealing." An employer may "refuse to hire persons convicted of a felony even though it has a disparate impact on minority members." Concluded the court, "To hold otherwise is to stigmatize minorities by saying, in effect, your group is not as honest as other groups." The solution "is not to lower the employer's standards, but to raise the qualifications of Hispanics applying for jobs" (754).

Hispanics are already stigmatized by the data the plaintiff presented in support of his disparate impact claim. Stereotyping already exaggerates its significance. The court's approach does little to counter the misconceptions; it is not a corrective. Going beyond the data to investigate the relationship between the claimant's record and the requirements of the job would have done more to deconstruct the tie between race and ethnicity, on the one side, and crime, on the other, than the court's wholesale dismissal of the plaintiff's disparate impact challenge. The fact that the claimant had done the job for four years without incident suggests that the employer may not have had a sufficient justification for a lifetime ban on employment. The worker was apparently better qualified than his criminal record suggested. Stigma is not a substitute for legitimate standards. The seeming neutrality of the employer's reliance on a hiree's record of convictions belies the reality of the criminal justice system. Race or ethnicity may not cause criminal behavior, but racial and ethnic discrimination certainly have some bearing on whether a person is arrested and incarcerated. The court might have done more to ensure that the employee was disqualified from the job on account of who he was and what he might do in the future rather than on what group he belonged to and what he had done in the past. Where employment decisions are an issue, courts should acknowledge that discrimination plays an indeterminate role in the criminal justice system and seek to achieve substantive equality as a goal.

An employer or lender does not have only its own interests to consider, of course. Liability for negligent hiring or lending is a matter of concern.[22] Negligent hiring, for example, exists when a reasonably prudent employer, who knows or should know of an applicant's criminal record, would not have hired the person because she or he was unfit for the job or would have taken appropriate measures to eliminate or minimize the unreasonable risk of harm she or he posed to others (Restatement [Second] of Torts Sec. 307 1965). Nonetheless, the cause of action for negligent hiring should not undermine the effort to eliminate discrimination against minority ex-offenders. It should not be assumed that the law is working at cross-purposes. An employer can reduce the risk of liability by pursuing a reasonably diligent hiring process (including background or criminal records checks where the job involves special access to the persons and real or personal property of others); employing a referral agency that screens and works with the ex-offenders to support and facilitate their desistance from crime; and procuring fidelity bonds to cover losses arising from employer misconduct (Miller and Fenton 1991; Mukamal 2001).

Mistakes will be made. Some minority ex-offenders who receive the benefit of the doubt produced by rejection of statistical discrimination will commit crimes, but so will some minorities who have no history of prior offenses and so will some nonminorities possessing the same or similar characteristics. As Professor Jody Armour argues in his book *Negrophobia and Reasonable Racism* (1997):

> We simply do not live in a risk-free society, nor are we willing to sacrifice the values and conveniences that a dramatically less risky society would cost. Viewing our risk-laden social existence from this broader perspective, incremental

race-based risks are not meaningfully different from thousands of other incremental risks we assume every day in return for a comfortable, convenient, decent, and democratic way of life. Accordingly, we must accept incremental race-based risks as the price of living in a just, humane, democratic society, as just, humane, democratic citizens. (56–57)

CONCLUSION

Racialized crime statistics have the ability either to reinforce or to challenge racial and ethnic stratification and subordination. To the extent that the law takes disparate impacts into account, it seems to be saying that racial effects statistically revealed are vulnerable to further analysis and amelioration. Yet, when evidence of such effects is produced the courts sometimes reject the criminal statistics' potency and demand more and more data that claimants (as opposed to their opponents) should not really be expected to gather. In other instances, the courts prove themselves to be little better able than the defendants appearing before them to get beyond the stereotypes produced by the gross association between minorities and crime. They refuse to explore thoroughly the relationship between an ex-offender's criminal record and her or his ability to participate fully in economic life by holding a job or obtaining a loan. The law ceases to be an instrument for correcting the inequality produced by the misuse of racialized crime statistics when it adopts the very same cursory approach as its own and forgoes the chance to deconstruct the statistics by focusing on what are assumed to be the causes of crime and desistance: individual agency, social milieu, and the structural context.[23]

All racialized crime statistics should be published, read, or interpreted with the following explicit or implicit disclaimer:

> Racial and ethnic data must be treated with caution because of the varying circumstances under which such information is recorded or reported. . . . Race and ethnicity may be recorded from observation or from self-identification. The use of racial or ethnic descriptions may reflect social custom rather than genetic or hereditary origins. Moreover, existing research on crime has generally shown that racial and ethnic identity is not predictive of crime behavior within data which has been controlled for social and economic factors such as education levels, family status, income, housing density, and residential mobility. (Minnesota Department of Public Safety 2000)

Stated more succinctly, descriptive racialized crime statistics that are not controlled for social and economic factors are "not sufficient for causal analysis and should not be used as an indicator of the role of race and criminality in economic decision making" (Walker, Spohn, and DeLone 2000).

NOTES

1. See note 7 and accompanying text. The term "disenfranchisement" does not pertain exclusively to the loss of the right to vote. "To disenfranchise" or to "disfranchise" is "to deprive one of a right, privilege, immunity, or pleasure" (Gove et al. 1993, 649). The benefit of which a person may be disenfranchised is generally one granted by the state, either by statute or constitution, but it need not be. Moreover, the benefit may be economic or social, rather than strictly political. In addition to the loss of the right to vote, conviction of a crime, particularly a felony, may carry with it such political disabilities as the loss of the right to hold political office, to serve on a jury, to possess a firearm, or to join the armed services, and such civil or social disabilities as the loss of the right to custody of one's children, to preserve one's marriage, or to drive an automobile. See generally David Rudenstine (1979); offering an overview of civil disabilities imposed on ex-offenders; Office of the Pardon Attorney (1996); cataloging the impact of a federal conviction on the civil and political rights of an individual under the laws of the fifty states and the federal government (hereinafter *Civil Disabilities of Convicted Felons*); and Olivares, Burton, and Cullen (1999, 10). Requirements that ex-offenders register with their local police have also become more prevalent, especially for those convicted of sex crimes (Olivares, Burton, and Cullen 1999, 15). Activists and academic commentators have devoted much more attention to the denial of the vote to ex-offenders and its disproportionate impact on the Black electorate than to the other forms of disenfranchisement. See, for example, Sentencing Project and Human Rights Watch (1998); Allard and Mauer (2000); Flecther (1999); and Harvey (1994).

2. See Bureau of Justice Statistics (2000) table 4.10, "Arrests: By Offense, Charged, Age Group, and Race, United States 1999" (366); table 5.17, "Federal Defendants Convicted in U.S. District Courts"(427); table 5.41, "Felony Offenders Convicted in State courts" (457); and table 6.38, "Characteristics of Prisoners in State and Federal Correctional Institutions" (519).

3. "Population estimates by race and Hispanic origin are published each year for the U.S. Race categories changed beginning with Census 2000. . . . There are two Hispanic origin categories—Hispanic or Latino and Not Hispanic or Latino. Race and Hispanic origin are considered two separate concepts and therefore Hispanics may be of any race or races" (U.S. Census Bureau 2000). See also Bureau of Justice Statistics (2000, 519) table 6.38.

Arrest data for persons of Hispanic ethnicities are not kept for all offenses. However, Hispanics represent 38.1 percent of those arrested by the Drug Enforcement Administration. See also table 4.42, "Characteristics of Persons Arrested by the Drug Enforcement Administration," in Bureau of Justice Statistics (2000, 403).

4. Armour challenges the rationality of discrimination based on racialized crime statistics with estimates that less than 1 percent of the Black population and less than 1.86 percent of the Black male population was arrested for violent crime in 1994).

5. See Harris (2002). Racial profiling exists when race is one of the personal or behavioral characteristics law enforcement officers rely on in attempting to predict criminal behavior (11). The term is most commonly associated with pretextual traf-

fic stops of minority drivers that become the excuse for initiating consensual searches of their vehicles for drugs and other contraband. This practice is sometimes referred to as "Driving while Black/Brown" or "DWB" (11). Racial profiling is thought to be efficacious because of the gross statistical assumption that minorities are disproportionately involved in crime (11). There is little support, however, for the proposition that profiling actually leads to higher apprehension rates (78–84). Blacks, of course, are not the only group victimized by racial/ethnic profiling. Latinos, who are stereotyped as undocumented immigrants, Asian Americans, who are stereotyped as gang members, and Arab or Muslim-Americans, who are stereotyped as terrorists, are also targeted (130–35, 135–39, 139–44).

6. See generally Austin (1994), analyzing the ways in which Black consumption is treated like deviance; Main (2000), reviewing cases involving retail discrimination and the efficacy of the various theories plaintiffs have invoked in response. See also Austin (2000), citing instances of discrimination, law suits, and a Justice Department agreement stemming from the refusal of some pizza delivery franchise outlets to deliver in minority communities, and, for example, Linstedt (2000, A7), announcing a settlement ending a retailer's practice of rejecting checks at stores in communities with large minority populations; Schalch (2000), reporting on an action challenging a retailer's discriminatory check acceptance policy, which the company attributed to its actual negative experience with bad checks, not demographics.

7. The employment opportunities of ex-offenders are subject to a panoply of state laws that erect barriers of various degrees of strictness. See generally Rudenstine (1979, 71–103) (describing employment restrictions imposed on ex-offenders, as well as laws protecting their right to employment); Office of the Pardon Attorney (1996), outlining, state-by-state, laws relating to the impact of a federal conviction on an ex-offender's employment opportunities; and Mukamal (2000), outlining the legal framework applicable to ex-offender employment. Ex-offenders may be absolutely barred from holding certain positions or from obtaining the necessary license to pursue certain vocations or professions. Alternatively, ex-offenders may be conditionally barred from certain jobs or licensed activities. The bar may depend on whether the ex-offender committed a crime of moral turpitude or one that is contrary to justice and good morals. The bar may also depend on whether the ex-offender committed a crime that is directly or substantially related to the job for which he/she is applying or being considered. Conversely, the ex-offender may be protected by an antidiscrimination provision, which is conditional. The conditions may pertain to the nature of the job, the prior offenses' relationship to the employment under consideration, or the ex-offender's trustworthiness or bondability. Title VII of the Civil Rights Act of 1964 (1994), prohibits absolute bars on the hiring of minority ex-offenders, but permits rejection where the applicant actually engaged in the conduct for which he was arrested, it is job related, and it was relatively recent (see EEOC 1990). These provisions are problematic for ex-offenders in that some of them impose absolute bars that are broader than is justified or warranted given the nature of the employment involved, while others impose conditional bars that are not well defined or are too broadly construed. See, for example, *Nixon v. Comm.*, A.2d, 2000 WL 33656044 (Pa. Cmwlth. Ct. 2001) (sustaining a challenge under the state constitution of a provision of the Older Adults Protective Services Act, which

absolutely barred for life certain ex-offenders from employment in health care facilities and agencies, on the ground that the provision was a deprivation of the right to engage in employment that was not reasonably related to the state's interest in protecting senior citizens from abuse; named claimants had been barred from employment by convictions that were nearly thirty years old). Moreover, many employers reject ex-offenders for positions solely on account of their criminal records despite antidiscrimination measures that prohibit such a response.

Whatever the legislative scheme, ex-offenders have a hard time finding employment in a tight labor market. See generally Kilborn (2001), describing the difficulties ex-offenders recently released from prison encounter in the job market. See also, Personal Responsibility and Work Opportunity Reconciliation Act of 1996 (2000), granting the states the option of imposing a ban on the receipt of food stamps and TANF (Temporary Assistance for Needy Families) benefits by persons with drug-related felony convictions. See also *Turner v. Glickman* (2000), rejecting a constitutional challenge of the denial of benefits to persons convicted of drug offenses where Congress acted for the purpose of deterring drug use and reducing the incidence of fraud. Available evidence suggests that the ban disproportionately affects poor Black and Latino ex-drug felons who are mothers. See Allard (2002), detailing the expected adverse consequences of the ban on female ex-offenders in light of the fact that only eight states have opted not to enforce the measure in full or in part. In a related area, public housing authorities are also entitled to deny rental units to persons convicted of drug-related offenses (Housing Opportunity Program Extension Act of 1996 [1994 ed., Supp. V 2000]. Moreover, entire families can be dispossessed for the drug-related activities of one member of the household, whether the leaseholder knows of or can control such behavior, under lease terms required by § 6(*l*)(6) of the U.S. Housing Act of 1937 (1994 ed., Supp. V 2000). See *HUD v. Ruker* (2002), upholding no-fault "one-strike" evictions as mandated by Congress and written into public housing leases.

8. See generally von Hirsch and Wasik (1997), mounting a normative argument in favor of imposing employment-related civil disqualifications only on a narrow deterrence basis.

9. Data on recidivism and desistance from crime would appear to be more relevant with regard to the likelihood that an ex-offender will commit further crimes on the job than general crime statistics. The data, however, is more equivocal than ordinary citizens might suspect. For example, a recent study indicates that only about 16 percent of those released from federal prison return within three years, though Blacks return at a higher rate (24.4 percent) than do Whites (13.4 percent) and Hispanics (17 percent) (Bureau of Justice Statistics 2000, 540, table 6.67). Most of the returnees (60 percent) have committed technical violations of their release terms (Sabol et al. 2000). Offenders convicted of violent offenses (as opposed to drug offenses, property crimes, or immigration violations) and offenders who had served five or more years prior to release returned at higher rates than did others (Sabol et al. 2000, 3, 5). See also Gonnerman (2002), describing the debate in the corrections community over the futility of a parole system that involves little supervision and sends many parolees back to prison for technical violations. Data regarding ex-offenders released from state prisons is more pessimistic. A study of recidivism that tracked more than 250,000 state prisoners released in 1994 indicated that, within

three years, 67.5 percent had been arrested, 46.9 percent had been convicted, and 25.4 percent had been sentenced to prison for new crimes (Langan and Levin 2002, 3). More than one-half of the former inmates were back in prison on account of either new offenses or technical violations of the terms of their release (2002,7). Blacks were more likely than Whites to be arrested (72.9 percent to 62.7 percent), convicted (51.1 percent to 43.3 percent), and reincarcerated (28.5 percent to 22.6 percent) for new crimes (2002). Offenders who had committed property crimes like burglary and auto theft had higher recidivism rates (73.8 percent) than those released after committing violent (61.7 percent), drug (66.7 percent), or public-order offenses (62.2 percent) (2002, 8).

10. The EEOC has so held. See EEOC (1990, 1–2).

11. Telephone conversation with Armand L. Andry, attorney for A.B. and S. Auto Service, Inc., December 1998.

12. The ECOA provides, in relevant part, that "it shall be unlawful for any creditor to discriminate against an applicant, with respect to any aspect of a credit transaction . . . on the basis of race, color, religion, national origin, sex or marital status, or age (provided the applicant has the capacity to contract)." (Equal Credit Opportunity Act 2000).

13. See Walker, Spohn, and DeLone (2000, 73, 83), describing various theories explaining the impact of inequality on crime and concluding that most predict higher rates of criminal behavior among the poor and among racial and ethnic minorities. For example, the so-called War on Drugs prompted many police departments to focus on low-income minority communities as sites of heightened, visible drug enforcement activity. Unlike suburbanites who can sell and procure their drugs in locations hidden from police view, people in poor urban minority neighborhoods conduct their business in the streets. Open-air markets and drug houses prompted neighbors to complain and ask for police intervention. Police departments, once criticized for failing to respond to crime in poor minority communities, stepped up their drug enforcement there. See Mauer (1999, 148). Though the incidence of drug crimes may be greater in White communities, it will not be reflected in arrest rates because the policing is focused elsewhere.

14. For a general description of the way in which the seemingly neutral criminal justice process produces substantive racial inequality, see Cole (1999).

15. See generally Walker, Spohn, and DeLone (2000, 37), providing a detailed survey of statistical studies assessing the impact of race discrimination at various stages of the criminal justice process. Data suggests that arrest rates reflect differential offending and greater disrespect of the police, though there is some evidence of discrimination. (Walker, Spohn, and DeLone 2000, 102).

16. Cf. Baker (2000).

17. Black small business ownership may be such that Black business people often run afoul of the law. For example, they too may be the targets of racial profiling by tax authorities or business regulators, in addition to the police. This an area in which there is little or no data, either qualitative or quantitative. It should also be noted that auto repair may be a business that is especially subject to crime in the form of insurance fraud. This was nowhere mentioned in the opinion, however.

18. The court cited in support of its conclusion 13 C.F.R. § 120.150 and SBA form 912 Statement of Personal History which inquires whether an applicant has "ever

been charged with or arrested or convicted for any crime other than a motor vehicle violation. . . ." (*EEOC v. Carolina Freight Carriers Corporation* 1989, 1057, 1064).

19. See generally Josephine R. Pututo (1980), discussing the guidelines for application of the "direct relationship test" set forth in the Model Sentencing and Corrections Act.

20. The employee did not disclose his record on his application, but he did disclose it in a polygraph examination (*EEOC v Carolina Freight Carriers Corp* 1989, 741). It apparently escaped notice before he was hired. It resurfaced when the employee was considered for a permanent position (737, 739, 741).

21. The court accepted the EEOC's contention that a lifetime employment ban based on conviction and incarceration for theft would disproportionately impact Hispanics because Hispanics have higher rates of conviction than non-Hispanic Whites. It nonetheless concluded that the EEOC had not proven the existence of the pool of qualified Hispanic drivers whom defendant might have hired and the percentage of those drivers who would have been disqualified by the conviction bar (*EEOC v Carolina Freight Carriers Corp* 1989, 751–52).

The prohibition against the hiring of persons with convictions was a term of a consent decree the defendant entered into with the United States Department of Justice (*EEOC v Carolina* 1989, 737-38). The decree did not bar Rios's action because the decree contained a provision preserving the rights of individuals asserting discrimination claims. (*EEOC v Carolina* 1989, 748).

22. See generally Miller and Fenton (1991).

23. See generally Laub and Sampson (2001).

VII

CONCLUSION

20

Telling the Real Tale of the Hunt

Toward a Race Conscious Sociology of Racial Stratification

Tukufu Zuberi and Eduardo Bonilla-Silva

> Until lions tell the tale, the story of the hunt will always glorify the hunter.
>
> —African Proverb

> To the real question, how does it feel to be a problem? I answer seldom a word.
>
> —W. E. B. Du Bois, *The Souls of Black Folk* (1903, 44)

Sociological hunters still parade the game they collect (data and arguments about people of color) with their objective rifles (White methods) and it is very likely they will continue doing so in the near future. However, in this volume the prey had a chance to tell the tale of the hunt. And the "prey" ("prey" from the perspective of the hunters) showed the weaknesses of the hunters as well as the many calibration problems of their rifles.[1] In this conclusion we attempt to bring it all together and we proceed as follows. First, we outline the contours of an alternative epistemology to the White logic. Second, we suggest the need to deracialize the analysis of race matters by conducting research not on the infamous "race effect," but on how racial stratification produces disparate outcomes among racialized groups. Our specific intent in this chapter is to spark new thinking on methods so as to turn the sociological tables on the sociology that made us, people of color, into a problem. Lastly, we speculate aloud on the kind of politics[2] we believe will be necessary for the epistemology and methodologies we advocate to become dominant in the wild (social scientific) kingdom.

TOWARD AN EPISTEMOLOGY OF RACIAL EMANCIPATION

> *Lo otro no existe*: tal es la fe racional, la incurable creencia de la razón humana. Identidad = realidad, como si, a fin de cuentas, todo hubiera de ser, absolutamente *uno y lo mismo*. Pero lo *otro* no se deja eliminar; subsiste, persiste; es el hueso duro de roer en que la razón se deja los dientes.
>
> (*The other does not exist*: such is rational faith, the incurable belief of human reason. Identity = reality; as if, all in all, everything had been absolutely *one and the same*. But the *other* does not allow itself to be eliminated; it subsists, persists; it is the hard bone in which reason loses its teeth.)
>
> —Antonio Machado, *Juan de Mairena* (1963)

The authors in this volume, along with a number of other scholars (see, for example, the excellent collections by Stanfield and Dennis 1993; and Stanfield 1993, Twine and Warren 2000, and Bulmer and Solomos 2004; see also the many books by critical race theory scholars in the field of education on epistemology and methodology) are engaging in discussions that help us understand that race need not determine the structures that organize the distribution of life chances and well-being. This important line of scholarship in the social sciences demands we change our view of race and how we use it in our research. This new view embraces diversity, multiplicity, and heterogeneity (Zuberi 2001a; Collins 2007).

Unfortunately (or, maybe, predictably), because the social sciences were part of what Foucault (1973) labeled "the sciences of Man," the knowledge they produced was implicated in the "matrix of domination" (the race, class, gender, and sexual order of things) (Collins 2007), and fundamentally geared toward "social control" (Ross 1990).[3] Hence, from the beginning, sociology—as all the social sciences—produced knowledge about "Others" (workers, people of color, gays and lesbians, etc.) as "deviants" from the "norm" (defined as White, heterosexual, bourgeois, and male). Furthermore, social statistics were created as researchers sought to formally define these "deviant" others of color (Zuberi 2001a). Difference was not regarded in the social sciences as a salutary sign of human heterogeneity, but as clear proof of the inferiority of the "deviants" from the natural "order of things" (Foucault 1973; Zuberi 2001a, 2006). From a statistical point of view this meant that normalcy could be defined by the use of a so-called bell curve (Zuberi 2001a).

Based on this "(White) gaze" (Foucault 1979), sociology explained racial inequality mostly as the outcome of the "deficiencies" of people of color whether they be construed as natural (i.e., biological) or cultural. In fact, African Americans and other people of color have been historically central to disciplines such as sociology for this reason exclusively: they have served, alongside women and workers, as the "abnormal," "deviants," and "problem people" (Du Bois 1934; Zuberi 2006); they have served as the "object of study" as well as subjects for practicing social engineering and "reforms" of all sorts (Bhabha 1994). Whereas anthropology found most of its "savages" abroad (Said 1979; but see Baker 1998), sociology "found" them within (Zuberi 2006). Indeed, "The Art of Savage Discovery" has a long history in the social sciences (Ryan 1972).

But sociology and the social sciences have always had their discontents.[4] Women such as Ida B. Wells and Jane Addams, men of color such as W. E. B. Du Bois, and a few White men such as W. I. Thomas (see Bonilla-Silva, Baiocchi, and Horton forthcoming), challenged White supremacist standards early on and offered more nuanced interpretations of inequality (racial and otherwise) in society (Zuberi 2006). And almost all the sociological dissidents of yesteryears as well as those of today (Essed and Goldberg 2002) have been connected to larger causes and movements.[5] Their specific confrontations in sociology derived from the intellectual foundations of the social movements they were part of, such as the antilynching campaigns (Ida B. Wells), the suffragist and feminist movement (Ida B. Wells and Jane Addams), Pan-Africanism (Du Bois), and many other movements in the early part of the twentieth century.[6]

The critique of what has been known as "the sociology of race relations" has thus been intrinsically connected to the politics of resistance and decolonization projects. Whereas mainstream sociology has advocated, since the work of Robert Park, "assimilation" as the solution to America's (and the world's) racial "problems,"[7] critical minority sociologists have insisted on fundamental changes to the social order as the only way to eliminate "the color line" (Du Bois 1903; Crenshaw 1988); whereas sociology and the social sciences have offered at best a slow, piecemeal, evolutionary process of racial change, analysts of color have insisted on the need for radical or revolutionary change.[8] African and African Diaspora scholars such as W. E. B. Du Bois (1934) and Oliver Cox (1948), for instance, long held that only by understanding decolonization and deracialization could one understand the development of capitalism and modern society. Rather than "civilization" (the language of sociology in the early years), "modernity" (the language of sociology from the 1940s to the 1960s), or "development" (the language of sociology since the 1960s), people of color enduring colonial, neocolonial, or internal colonial domination have historically demanded freedom, equality, and respect as the way out of the bubbling racial cauldron.

Therefore, we position our efforts as part of the long (and still woefully incomplete) march for racial redemption and propose that what is needed to uproot the White logic that has organized the sociology of race relations is an *epistemology of liberation* (Moya 1997; Feagin and Vera 2001; De Sousa Santos 2006). We advocate for a new epistemology expressive of the movement to abolish White supremacy and liberate us all—White and non-White—from the racial prison we have inhabited for 500 years. Such epistemology is a corrective to the Tarzanic logic[9] that has inspired (sometimes vocally, but most often, silently) sociological inquiry into racial matters that made Whites into heroes and Blacks into primitives, villains, and criminals (Young 1990). Below we provide the outline of such an epistemology fully aware that the precise content of any epistemology of social change will ultimately be shaped by the politics, values, and emotions of the movement it embodies—in this case, the movement to end White supremacy once and for all and, hopefully, achieve in the process "social emancipation."[10]

In the introductory chapter to this volume we defined "White logic" as "the epistemological arm of White supremacy." Rather than leading to a science of objectivity, White logic has fostered an ethnocentric orientation. Most researchers have embraced the assumptions of White supremacy. In fact, many researchers of color (Dinesh D'Souza and John McWhorter come to mind) are in agreement with White supremacy at the epistemic level; however, scholars of color are potentially much closer to being objective or unbiased in research on racial stratification. This point has been well argued by Iris M. Young, Paula Moya, and more recently, by Charles W. Mills. According to Mills, expressing a view to which we subscribe wholeheartedly, "hegemonic groups characteristically have experiences that foster illusory perceptions about society's functioning, whereas subordinate groups characteristically have experiences that (at least potentially) give rise to more adequate conceptualizations" (1998, 28). Therefore, our claim for the need of an epistemology of racial liberation is not just a claim for just another "perspective." We are not arguing that there is an "ontological symmetry between whiteness and blackness" (Headley 2004, 87). Instead, we contend that viewing racial stratification from the position of people of color (Bonilla-Silva 2001) is a privileged perspective.

At the same time, we reject the ontological and fixed existence of racial identity. Racial identity embodies the basis and nature of modern racism and White supremacy. Sociology from this point of view sees the persons of color when they are in conflict with the existence of the racism that sustains White supremacy (see Zuberi 2006; and several of the chapters in this volume on this point). While we see the confrontation with White supremacy as important, we do not see it as a totalizing experience. Overcoming White supremacy is possible for all people within its realms of domination; however, it would be foolish to act as if we did not live in a society in which the implications of race are all too real.

Second, although modernity constructed the notion of *the* subject as "a self-present origin outside of and opposed to objects of knowledge—

autonomous, neutral, abstract, and purified of particularity . . . an abstract idea of formal reason, disembodied and transcendent" (Young 1990, 125), we argue that all subjects are part of the social process and, therefore, denote epistemologically their place in the power structure—some express domination, while others express resistance to domination. In this light, as postmodern, feminist, and critical commentators have argued, the modern Cartesian subject is not truly universal, but an idealized White, bourgeois, male, atomistic, heterosexual construct.[11] Hence, an epistemology of racial emancipation makes explicit its foundational nexus to people of color, that is, it is both *race conscious* and *race-affirming*.

And to anticipate two easy criticisms, first, being "race conscious" does not mean we essentialize race.[12] To be race conscious is to be aware of the system of racial stratification, and to recognize the acts of survival and creativity of those marginalized by the racial hierarchy. Like other scholars of color (Ladson-Billings 2000), we recognize that racial "Others" are internally fractured along class, gender, and sexual-orientation lines as well as by the multiplicity of histories that comprise the people we call "Latinos," "Asian Americans," "American Indians," and even "Blacks." For us, having a race-conscious standpoint means that we openly acknowledge the positionality of our episteme; we do not hide the fact that the epistemology we advocate reflects the "racialized identity" and the common history of oppression shared by people of color (Ladson-Billings 2000; Collins 1998). We knowingly take the risk of using race as a category because we know that "'race' in a racist society bears profound consequences for daily life, identity, and social movements" (Fine et al. 2003, 176). Furthermore, because of its emancipationist goal, this epistemic alternative *must* be race conscious so as to validate the standing, views, and even aesthetic of people of color in the "ecology of knowledges" (De Sousa Santos 2006).[13] Second, to those who will accuse us of advocating divisive "identity politics" we respond with: We reject the view of those who wish to erase difference without first erasing the structure that produces differences in life chances (i.e., inequality and exclusion) and in identities. We advocate a move from race as soon as the conditions of racial stratification no longer exist.

Instead of the so-called universal programs and universal politics (by which authors often mean using class as the category around which to build a coalition) advocated by liberals and many progressives alike (Greenberg and Skocpol 1999), we believe it is imperative for this episteme to be openly race conscious. Such a standpoint is better suited for producing realistic knowledge about racial matters, for ultimately helping to develop *real* communication across racial boundaries, and for producing the knowledge and practices that will ultimate help abolish race as a category of exclusion (Gooding-Williams 2001).[14] In this we stand strong, like Frantz Fanon,

Sojourner Truth, W. E. B. Du Bois, Ida B. Wells, and so many others; we stand strong and proud of who we are and tell sociologists and other social scientists exactly what Fanon said in his *Black Skin, White Masks*:

> I am not a potentiality of something. I am wholly what I am. I do not have to look for the universal. No probability has any place in me. My Negro consciousness does not hold itself out as a lack. It *is*. It is its own follower. (1967, 135)

Third, the epistemology of racial liberation is unabashedly "political" in the sense that it is deeply reflective of and rooted in the liberation movements of the past, present, and future. "Knowledge," as Scraton has argued, "including the formalized 'domain assumptions' and boundaries of academic disciplines is neither value-free nor neutral . . . but is derived and reproduced in, historically and contemporaneously, in the structural relations of inequality and oppression that characterize established social orders" (Scraton 2004, 179). Hence the challenge for a critical epistemology like the one we are endorsing here "is to provide knowledge which engages the prevailing social structures . . . oppressive structures [such as] those based on class, gender, and race" (Harvey 1990, 2). Accordingly, the epistemology of racial emancipation is fundamentally geared toward the production of knowledge that is socially and politically relevant (Essed and Nimako 2006) and, hence, derides the current state of affairs in sociology and the social sciences where too many scholars do "small-scale research backed by large-scale grants" (Duberman 1999, 193).

Once again, to avoid easy criticisms, by "political" we do not mean doing politicized, one-sided, sloppy research. We mean that, like feminist and Marxist scholarship, research based on the epistemology of racial emancipation examines the practices of White supremacy and their effects and, more significantly, works toward the elimination of both.

Lastly, the epistemology of racial emancipation is global, multicultural, and in conversation and solidarity with all social movements of emancipation. It is *global* because the world system has been racialized for at least 500 years (Winant 2001; Balibar and Wallerstein 1988) and, therefore, the house race built must be demolished everywhere. It is *multicultural* because it aspires to learn from, understand, and validate the knowledge produced by the experiences of the many racialized groups in the world system suffering from the various incarnations of White supremacy. And it is in *solidarity* with the aspirations for social justice of oppressed people everywhere.

Although rooted on the racial problematic, the epistemology of racial liberation is not blind to other forms of oppression and works *with* and *for* the liberation of all oppressed people in the world. It works toward racial justice but is mindful that "racial justice is only a part of justice; one could have a society that is racially just, but unjust in other ways" (Mills 2003, 196).

People doing research in this tradition work with others in the struggle for human emancipation; they work to demolish the monstrous and complex prison built by systems of racial and class domination, by patriarchy, by heterosexism, and by other forms of domination; and, finally, they hope to learn from—as well as to teach to—other subordinated groups and peoples in struggle. But the epistemology of racial emancipation does not empty itself a priori into universal projects based on human rights, world citizenship, or class, because such projects, and the categories upon which they are based, are still partial and have historically worked to subsume projects of racial liberation (e.g., the case of Cuba [Sawyer 2006] and South Africa [Schutte 1995]). The strategy we favor for coalition building is based on the notion of *radical democratic pluralism*, a stand that acknowledges and affirms group differences "as a means of ensuring the participation and inclusion of *everyone* in social and political institutions" (Young 1990, 168. See also Laclau and Mouffe 1985. Our emphasis).

TOWARD A METHODOLOGY FOR ACHIEVING RACIAL JUSTICE

The epistemology of racial emancipation has as its goal the elevation of the human by the elimination of White supremacy. As part of that process, we have urged in this volume for a relentless critique of the traditional methods, quantitative and qualitative alike, used to produce racial knowledge. We have urged analysts to search for alternative methodologies to comprehend how racial stratification produces racial inequality, and, more significantly, we have called for *deracializing* the analysis of racial stratification. Since this last point seems to contradict our call for a race conscious sociology of racial stratification, we will explain here what we mean by a deracialized analysis of race matters.

A deracialized perspective has great potential for helping us to understand society (also see Zuberi 2001a; 2006). If race is not biological, then it is not a good proxy for understanding biological processes (Marks 2002). If race is, as has been argued by the authors in this volume, a signifier for the impact of racial stratification, then we may well learn much by developing better measures of social and economic processes. Cultural differences among different populations do exist; however, race is not a satisfactory measure of these differences (Marks 1995, 2002).

We, the authors of this volume included, have argued that race is a social construct. Within this construct, the person of color does not exist outside of his or her otherness. Here we are not simply being critical in our view of racial research; we are also creatively suggesting a way forward (Zuberi 2006). Race is constructed for the purpose of maintaining a racial hierarchy.

Race does not exist as a neutral attribute of each individual. Race exists as a signifier of group and individual social status. Race is real in its social consequences. If race existed only on its condition of being believed, its life would have ceased long ago. Our desire is not to diminish the social significance of race, but to bring into view the reality of racial stratification, the reality of the experience of race, and the rationality of those who study racial dynamics and processes. We are not advancing the idea that race is the most important form of oppression. We agree with Stuart Hall who suggests a "non-reductive approach to questions concerning the interrelationship between class and race" (Hall 1986). By not reducing the problem to a single determining articulation of oppression—class or race—we avoid making circular and dogmatic arguments. To view the problem purely from a class perspective limits our ability to understand the dynamics of race. Likewise, by viewing the problem from a perspective that privileges race over class we enter into the pitfalls of racial reasoning. The solution to the problem of oversimplification may reside in a perspective that considers "intersectionality within the matrix of domination" (Collins 2000,18, 274–76). This perspective suggests that examining how racism, sexism, classism, and other forms of domination are organized within the matrix of oppressive circumstances.

It is in the collective belief that humans are divided into races, built into the experience of everyday life, that the idea of race to which we are subordinate gains its place in the "real world." Creative critical thinkers have long been aware of the limits of racial reasoning (see Fanon 1963, 1967; Césaire 1972). In order to elevate our understanding of racial stratification we must reject the ontological and fixed existence of racial identity. From this perspective both whiteness and blackness are social problems produced by the European partitioning of humanity into races. In order to understand and to evaluate whom humans are—and specifically, for our purposes—we must look beyond our own personal or historical experience. And in order to change the place of race in the world, we must change not merely our own thinking but also the social conditions of everyday life that facilitate beliefs in race.

This volume has focused more sharply on the concepts of research methods by directing our attention onto the actions of researchers, and the power of the researcher, in conducting research. Deracialization of our research methods sets out to change the social world. Deracializing our methods will require that we disarrange the current social order. The social and economic realities of race must be changed by our actions. Deracializing our research methods is a process by which two forces—by definition opposed to each other—culminate in the rearticulation of what it means to be human. The first aspect of this process concerns how and why people are raced at, and between, birth and death. Secondly, mutual understanding or developing friendships across racial groupings cannot change racial realities; the erasure of humanity that race has brought to bear cannot be clearly understood except in the exact measure that we engage in social research to transform its social basis.

We propose an idea to produce in us a new state of consciousness in which we describe in detail the basic concepts we use in our research of racial stratification. Empirically (from ethnography to statistical analysis of census data) oriented persons have no reason to reject such reflections, for that would imply that their empiricism is, in reality, an apriorism with its sign reversed. And to commit this mistake is to violate the very foundation of the logic of scientific analysis. There is no reason for rejecting reflection.

Most research on race lacks a critical evaluation of racist structures that encourage pathological interpretations (Zuberi 2001a). These pathological interpretations have had a profound impact on our theories and methods. Our theories of society, not our empirical evidence, guide how we interpret racial stratification. Fancy methods come and go. We need a better understanding of how our methods relate to society. We are not suggesting that we discredit research findings because they lead to unwanted political conclusions. We are suggesting that we have a better understanding of the political and theoretical ideas that motivate different interpretations of social science results.

The Civil Rights, Black Power, and National Liberation movements are all forms of deracialization. Like the philosopher Charles W. Mills's (1998) idea of the "racial contract," our idea of deracialization is a critique of the nature of the "White logic" that has given rise to the misconception that we have labeled "White methods." In the tradition represented by literary critic Henry Louis Gates Jr.'s (1988) concept of signifying, deracialzation marks the sense of difference from the sociology as practiced under White logic and applied in the form of White methods.

Unlike Fanon, whose classic analysis in *The Wretched of the Earth* focused on the moment or "onset" of decolonization, our new methods must allow us to focus on the process of the rise of these new social relations, the social, demographic, and political trends that follow the end of White supremacy (or the anticipation of its end), and the possibilities that are implied. Deracializing our research methods is fundamentally important if we are to turn back the tide and bring the human back into the picture.

Deracialization of our research methods is a social act, and it requires that the researcher participate in the modification of social reality. It privileges the human over the racialized individual. These new methods will need to be created by a new self-conscious action, and they will introduce a new language as part of a new social reality. The racialized and the racializer will both be humanized by the process.

Accordingly, the challenge we pose to the sociology of race relations is preeminently a political one. We preach to newcomers (and old-timers who can still listen) in sociology to refuse normativity in race research and urge them to rely on alternative paradigms and methodologies. As does Headley (2004), we advocate for the "teleological suspension" of whiteness and White logic. Although we must continue exposing the multiple problems of research done from the White logic perspective and critiquing the racial knowledge produced through White methods, the new generation of analysts must prioritize their efforts and develop new projects, orientations, approaches, practices, and knowledge about racial stratification. To do this effectively we must all work hard to decolonize our own sociological imagination (Oliver 2004); to unlearn received truths about race, "race relations," and race research; to unlearn received truths even about ourselves and our own potential. The new generation of race scholars must do their work without much concern for *"el que dirán"* (what others will say). We must do a "For-Us" social science (Mendoza 2006) on racial affairs and let the representatives of whiteness continue finding, again and again, that race "is declining in significance." The race rebellions of the future will awaken them from their dream as the race rebellions of the sixties forced many of them to admit they actually knew very little about racial matters in America.[15]

We are extremely aware that in this age where social science data on race has become crucial (maybe even more important than data from the biological sciences) for the reproduction of racialization and racism (Dumm 1993), critical social scientists[16] must do whatever they can to be active in the various social movements against White supremacy. Even if our engagement with these movements is only as supporters (but we plead to social scientists so that they become scholar activists in these movements), we should not evade our historic responsibility;[17] we cannot continue business as usual and act as mere reporters of racial matters. Our ethical and political neutrality on these matters, given the *herrevolk* moral terrain of America and the world (Mills 1998), leaves our folks trapped in *"el laberinto de la soledad"* (the labyrinth of solitude).

Critical social scientists on race matters can provide data, arguments, counternarratives, and all sorts of intellectual ammunition against dominant representations about racial groups and racial inequality. And to provide better ammunition for the movements against White supremacy, the sociological and social scientific efforts in this field must be race conscious and engaged in a systematic analysis of racial stratification and its effects. A neutral, or even liberal, sociology will not do the trick, as neutrality on race matters usually means "support of the racial status quo" and liberal sociology fosters at best charitable views about people of color and reformist policies on behalf of the "problem people" (Du Bois 1903). If the social sciences are going to assist in the emancipation of people of color, their efforts, therefore, must be clearly on the side of the racially oppressed for "[i]f there is a hell for social scientists, it is precisely that they only manage to be objective if they are directly involved in a struggle, and that they have no way of escaping, even through wishful thinking (Casanova 1981, 3). Our committed practice *for* people of color and *for* the elimination of White supremacy in the social sciences (the need for outing the institutionally dominant White, male, heterosexual *homus academicus* is still desperately urgent)[18] and elsewhere will help lift the veil that has prevented Whites (and some people of color) from truly seeing and understanding how racial stratification affects the life chances of people of color. Only then will the tale of the hunt reflect what truly happened in the hunt.

NOTES

1. Our metaphoric choice here (the notion of "the hunt") is neither casual nor poetic. As the authors of a recent book state in their introduction, "The visceral, embodied experiences of domination and control—the immediate manifestation of colonial corporeality—were an integral part of governmental practices of codifying, categorizing, and racializing difference" (Rao and Pierce 2006, 5). Hence, we believe that racial others have been "hunted" for years in the social sciences and that this is a space for "the prey" to fight back.

2. Most social scientists deride anyone who claims politics are part of the scientific process. We contend that politics, with a small *p*, are part and parcel of all social action, scientific or otherwise. In the case of sociology, this social fact can be corroborated by even the most cursory reading of texts on the history of the discipline, such as Bernard and Bernard's *Origins of American Sociology* (1943) or Craig Calhoun's (ed.) recent *Sociology in America: A History* (2007).

3. A word of caution must be inserted here. We are not suggesting that all sociology, or any other disciplinary-based knowledge for that matter, is useless ideology. We believe, following some of Latour's ideas on science studies (1999), that all discovery is arrived at in a way that *potentially* combines ideology and science. The alternatives to this view are the *externalist* view, which holds that science is all ideology/politics (a position that cannot explain scientific advances) or the *internalist* view, which holds that science and scientists are somehow above the social process (a position that cannot explain how humans can work in a nonhuman or nonsocial way). Hence, sociologists may discover "social facts," but analysts must examine to what extent these "social facts" have the imprint of the social world and what components of that world they reflect.

4. Sociology, like all disciplines, has a center, a mainstream, or a normative component. But this also means that it has margins or a periphery. Thus, domination within the field of sociology (or, better, *hegemony*) has never been complete or total. This is why alternative views and analyses of racial matters have always existed in sociology and in the various disciplines.

5. Yet far too many members of subaltern communities have assimilated to the norms of sociology, as the alternative—imperiling their careers or working in "secondary" institutions—is unsavory. In yesteryears, for example, Black scholars in the social sciences before the birth of the African American Studies movement of the 1960s and 1970s (Aldridge and Young 2000) found "success" only by capitulating

"often uncritically, to the prevailing paradigms and research programs of the White bourgeois academy" (West 1993, 72). And although the confrontations derived from the intellectual foundations of the social movements for decolonization and deracialization, such as Pan-Africanism, Negritude, Civil Rights, Black Power, and the National Liberation movements of the 1940s to the 1960s had a tremendous impact on the study of the African Diaspora (Zuberi 2006), the (White-led) academy produced serious counterattacks on the credibility, validity, and usefulness of this (Allen 1974) and other related disciplines such as Women Studies, Chicano Studies, and Ethnic Studies programs. As we finish this book, those attacks remain potent and many of those programs and the faculty that labor in them feel under siege. For example, the dismissal of Professor Ward Churchill, a professor of Ethnic Studies at the University of Colorado, in the summer of 2007 for supposed violations to "academic standards" (but see Mayer 2007), has had a chilling effect on all those who labor in similar programs and departments.

6. For later generations, the Negritude, Civil Rights, Black Power, and National Liberation movements in Africa served as the intellectual foundation for developing new sociological thinking, theory, methods, and politics (Zuberi 2006; Collins 2007).

7. The dominance of the assimilationist perspective has prevented sociologists from anticipating the possibility of the National Liberation and Civil Rights movements (McKee 1993). Likewise, the assimilationist perspective has precluded any consideration of the social effects of the Black Power movement within the United States, the Caribbean, and Latin America or the anticolonial movement in Africa (for a recent example, see Bourdieu's and Wacquant's (1999) critique of Hanchard's work).

8. Even "moderate" civil rights leaders, such as Martin Luther King, advocated for fast, profound, and deliberate change in the social order. See, for instance, his views on this matter in his "Letter from Birmingham Jail" in *Why We Can't Wait* (2000).

9. Much like in the adventures of "Tarzan of the Apes," White sociologists "discovered" the natives in America and worked hard at their civilizing mission. For a recent critical view of the creator of Tarzan, see Talisferro (2002).

10. In his *The Rise of the Global Left: The World Social Forum and Beyond* (2006), Boaventura De Sousa Santos articulates the need for a conception of social power that goes beyond the narrow confines of class analysis. Hence, rather than advocating for socialism as the cure of all ills in the world, De Sousa Santos proposes an agenda of "social emancipation as the aspiration to a society in which the different power relations are replaced by relations of shared authority" (De Sousa Santos 2006, 114). This view, which forces social analysts to have an intersectional approach to power and politics, is gaining momentum. It is forcing those of us who still do race-, or gender-, or class-based analysis to realize that given the complexities of the matrix of domination typical of all modern societies, our old "one-cause" approach to social change may be necessary, but it is definitely not sufficient.

11. Ladson-Billings (2000) makes this point beautifully by counterposing at the outset of her piece on epistemology the bourgeois White notion of Decartes ("I think, therefore I am") versus an African proverb (*Unbuntu*, which means, "I am because we are").

12. Again, the work of Iris M. Young is instructive on this point (but see also Moya 1997). As she argues, recognizing "group differences" does not necessarily mean one ends essentializing those differences. Differences are indeed "ambiguous,

relational, shifting without clear borders" and do not exclude the reality of overlapping experiences (1990, 171). Difference ought to be viewed as meaning "not otherness, exclusive opposition, but specificity, variation, heterogeneity" (1990, 171). Difference signifies the relations between groups, their differential patterns of interaction, and their positions within institutions.

13. Scholars of color and feminists are likely to understand this point because women and people of color (particularly women of color) are rarely cited, rarely appreciated, rarely recognized as sources of authority even in the fields they presumably ought to master. On this, see Charles V. Willie, "Dominant and Subdominant People of Power: A New Way of Conceptualizing Minority and Majority Populations" (2002).

14. In recent years, scholars such as Walter Benn Michaels (2006), Todd Gitlin (1995), and authors associated with the "new ethnicity paradigm school" such as Roger Waldinger, Loïc Wacquant, and Rogers Bruebaker and Frederick Cooper (2000), among many others, have discredited politics and analyses centered on what they label as "identities" by which they mean, race, gender, and sexual orientation, all categories they believe are of lesser or secondary importance as compared to class, nation, or citizenship. This stand has made many of these authors celebrities in the academy (Michaels and Gitlin in particular), but celebrity and popularity do not equal correctness. History, we believe, will not be kind to the liberal academic productions of these scholars.

15. One of the few sociologists who openly acknowledged the limitations of how social analysts saw race matters in the 1960s was Everett C. Hughes. His insights and commentary, many of which we believe are still valid, can be read in his 1963 presidential address to the American Sociological Association titled "Race Relations and the Sociological Imagination."

16. The critical tradition has been deeply connected to the work of Frankfurt School scholars such as Theodore Adorno, Herbert Marcuse, and Max Horkheimer among others. But that "tradition" has been safely expanded and revised to include the work and ideas of many in the Black Radical Tradition. For efforts in expanding the former, see Joe Kincheloe and Peter Mclaren (2000), "Rethinking Critical Theory and Qualitative Research." For a magisterial work on the latter, see Cedric J. Robinson (2000), *Black Marxism: The making of the Black Radical Tradition*.

17. This point reminds us of discussions with fellow minority graduate students and with junior colleagues when we were junior professors who insisted they would not do "politics" until they were "safe." We told them such approach was a betrayal of those who struggled for our right to be where we were and led to accommodation and, ultimately, cooptation by the system that had excluded us for so long. Now twenty years or so later, these colleagues have become part of mainstream sociology and have still not done anything "political" (that is, they have not raised concerns about racism in academia).

18. This point was well made referring to queer studies by Joshua Gamson (2003).

References

A.B. and S. Auto Service, Inc. v. South Shore Bank of Chicago. 1997. 962 F. Supp. 1056 N.D. Ill.

Abbott, Andrew. 1999. *Department and discipline: Chicago sociology at one hundred.* Chicago: University of Chicago Press.

Abrahams, Roger D. 1964. *Deep down in the jungle.* Chicago: Aldine Publishing Company.

ACLU. (American Civil Liberties Union) 1996. (Memorandum in support of plaintiffs' motion for enforcement of settlement agreement and for further relief. Civ. A No.l CCB-93-468 1996. Available from wwww.aclu.org/court/mpset.html.

Adorno, Theodore W. 1950. *The authoritarian personality*. New York: Harper and Row.

Agger, Ben. 2002. *Postponing the postmodern: Sociological practices, selves, and theories.* Lanham, MD: Rowman and Littlefield.

Aguirre, Adalberto, Jr. 2000. *Women and minority faculty in the academic workplace: Recruitment, retention, and academic culture*. New York: Jossey-Bass.

Alba, Richard, John Logan, and Brian Stults. 2000a. How segregated are middle-class African Americans? *Social Problems* 47:543–58.

——. 2000b. The changing neighborhood contexts of immigrant metropolis. *Social Forces* 79:587–21.

Alba, Richard, and Victor Nee. 2003. *Remaking the American mainstream: Assimilation and contemporary immigration*. Cambridge: Harvard University Press.

Alba, Richard, Ruben Rumbaut, and Karen Marotz. 2005. A distorted nation: Perceptions of racial/ethnic group sizes and attitudes toward immigrants and other minorities. *Social Forces* 84 (2): 873–900.

Aldridge, Delores P., and Carlene Young, eds. 2000. *Out of the revolution: The development of Africana Studies*. Lanham, MD: Lexington Books.

Alexander, J. C. 1988. *Action and its environments: Toward a new synthesis*. New York: Columbia University Press.

Alexander, M. Jacqui, and Chandra Tapade Mohanty. 1997. Introduction: Genealogies, legacies, movements. In *Feminist genealogies, colonial legacies, and democratic futures*, ed. M. Jacqui Alexander and Chandra Tapade Mohanty, xiii–xlii. New York: Routledge.

Allard, Patricia. 2002. *Life sentences: Denying welfare benefits to women convicted of drug offenses*. Washington, DC: The Sentencing Project.

Allard, Patricia, and Marc Mauer. 2000. *Regaining the vote: An assessment of activity relating to felon disenfranchisement laws*. Washington, DC: The Sentencing Project.

Allen, Richard L. 1974. Politics of the attack on African-American studies. *Black Scholar* 6.

Allen, Walter, and Angie Y. Chung. 2000. Your blues ain't my blues: Race, ethnicity, and social inequality in America. *Contemporary Sociology* 29 (6): 796–805.

Allen, Walter R., Marguerite Bonous-Hammarth, and Robert Teranishi. 2002. *Stony the road we trod: The black struggle for higher education in California*. Research Report. Los Angeles: CHOICES: Access, Equity and Diversity in Higher Education, University of California–Los Angeles.

Allen-Bell, Angela. 1997. The birth of the crime: Driving while black (DWB). *Southern University Law Review* 25:195–225.

Allport, Gordon W. 1954. *The nature of prejudice*. New York: Beacon Press.

American Sociological Association. 2002. Statement of the American Sociological Association on the importance of collecting data and doing social scientific research on race. August 9.

Andersen, Margaret. 2003. Whitewashing race: A critical perspective on whiteness. In *White out: The continuing significance of race*. ed. Ashley W. Doane and Eduardo Bonilla-Silva, 21–35. New York: Routledge.

Anderson, Barbara, Brian Silver, and Paul Abramson. 1988. The effects of the race of the interviewer on race-related attitudes of Black respondents in SRC/CPS national election studies. *Public Opinion Quarterly* 52 (Autumn), 3:289–324.

Anderson, Elijah. 1989. Sex codes and family life among poor inner-city youth. *Annals of the Academy of Political and Social Science* 501: 59–78.

——. 1990. *Streetwise: Race, class, and change in an urban community*. Chicago: University of Chicago Press.

——. 1999. *Code of the street: Decency, violence, and the moral life of the inner city*. New York: W.W. Norton & Company.

Anderson, Margo, and Stephen E. Fienberg. 1999. *Who counts? The politics of census taking in contemporary America*. New York: Russell Sage.

Anderton, Douglas L., Andy B. Anderson, John Michael Oakes, and Michael R. Fraser. 1994. Environmental equity: The demographics of dumping. *Demography* 31 (2): 229–48.

Annis, Robert, and B. Corenblum. 1986. Effect of test language and experimenter race on Canadian Indian children's racial and self-identity. *The Journal of Social Psychology* 126 (6): 761–73.

Antonio, Anthony Lising. 2002. Faculty of color reconsidered: Reassessing contributions to scholarship. *The Journal of Higher Education* 73 (5): 582–602.

Aponte, Robert. 1990. Definitions of the underclass: A critical analysis. In *Sociology in America*, ed. Herbert Gans. Newbury Park, CA: Sage Publications.

Armour, Jody David. 1997. *Negrophobia and reasonable racism: The hidden costs of being black in America*. New York: New York University Press.

Aronson, J., M. Lustina, C. Good, K. Keough, C. Steele, and J. Brown. 1999. When white men can't do math: Necessary and sufficient factors in stereotype threat. *Journal of Experimental Social Psychology* 35:29–46.

Auletta, Ken. 1982. *The underclass.* New York: Random House.

Austin, Regina. 1992. The Black community, its lawbreakers, and a politics of identification. *Southern California Law Review* 65:1769–1817.

——. 1994. A nation of thieves: Securing black people's right to shop and to sell in white America. *Utah Law Review* 1:147–77.

——. 2000. "Bad for business": Contextual analysis, race discrimination, and fast food. *John Marshall Law Review* 34:207–43.

Babbie, E. 1998. *The practice of social science research*. Belmont, CA: Wadsworth.

Baca Zinn, Maxine. 1979. Field research in minority communities: Ethical, methodological and political observations by an insider. *Social Problems* 27 (2).

Baca Zinn, Maxine, et al. 1986. The costs of exclusionary practices in women's studies. *Signs: Journal of Women and Culture in Society* 11 (2): 290–303.

Bache, Meade. 1895. Reaction time with reference to race. *Psychological Review* 2 (5): 475–86.

Badillo, Jalil Sued. 1978. *Los Caribes: Realidad o fábula*. Río Piedras, Puerto Rico: *Editorial Antillana*.

Bah, Sulaiman. 2002. Deaths in South Africa that are due to HIV/AIDS and related causes, 1993–2000. Unpublished document.

Baker, Houston. 1993. *Black studies, rap, and the academy*. Chicago: University of Chicago Press.

Baker, Lee D. 1998. *From savage to Negro: Anthropology and the construction of race, 1896-1954*. Berkeley: University of California Press.

Baker, Scott. 2000. Defining "otherwise qualified applicants": Applying an antitrust relevant market analysis to disparate impact cases. *University of Chicago Law Review* 67:725.

Baldus, David C., and James W. L. Cole. 1977. Quantitative proof of intentional discrimination. *Evaluation Quarterly* 1 (1): 53–86.

——. 1980. *Statistical proof of discrimination*. New York: McGraw-Hill.

Baldwin, James. 1955. *Notes of a native son*. Boston: Beacon Press.

Balibar, Etienne, and Immanuel Wallerstein. 1988. *Race, nation, and class: Ambiguous identities*. London: Verso.

Ballard, Allen B. 1973. *The education of black folk: The Afro-American struggle for knowledge in white America*. New York: Harper & Row.

Bamshad, M. 2005. Genetic influences on health: Does race matter? *Journal of the American Medical Association* 294 (8): 937–46.

Bansak, Cynthia, and Steven Raphael. 2001. Immigration reform and the earnings of Latino workers: Do employer sanctions cause discrimination? *Industrial and Labor Relations Review* 54 (2): 275–95.

Barringer, Herbert, Robert W. Gardner, and Michael J. Levin. 1993. *Asians and Pacific Islanders in the United States.* New York: Russell Sage Foundation.

Bar-Tal, Daniel. 1990. Causes and consequences of delegitimization: Models of conflict and ethnocentrism. *Journal of Social Issues* 46 (1): 65–81.

Barth, Fredrik. 1969. *Ethnic groups and boundaries: The social construction of organizational difference.* Boston: Little, Brown and Company.

Barthelow, Bruce, Cheryl Dickter, and Marc Sestir. 2006. Stereotype activation and control of race bias: Cognitive control of inhibition and its impairment by alcohol. *Journal of Personality and Social Psychology* 90 (2): 272–87.

Bashi V., and A. McDaniel. 1997. A theory of immigration and racial stratification. *Journal of Black Studies* 27:668–82.

Baumgartner, Frank, and Bryan Jones. 1993. *Agendas and instability in American politics.* Chicago: University of Chicago Press.

Becker, Gary S. 1957. *The economics of discrimination.* Chicago: University of Chicago Press.

Beggs, John J., Wayne J. Villemez, and Ruth Arnold. 1997. Black population concentration and black-white inequality: Expanding the consideration of place and space effects. *Social Forces* 76 (1): 65–91.

Bellamy Foster, John. 2003. Kipling, "the white man's burden," and U.S. imperialism. *Monthly Review*, November.

Bendick, Marc Jr., Lauren Brown, and Kennington Wall. 1999. No foot in the door: An experimental study of employment discrimination. *Journal of Aging and Social Policy* 10 (4): 5–23.

Bendick, Marc Jr., Charles W. Jackson, and Victor A. Reinoso. 1999. Measuring employment discrimination through controlled experiments. In *Race and ethnic conflict: Contending views on prejudice, discrimination, and ethnoviolence*, ed. Fred L. Pincus and Howard J. Ehrlich, 140–51. Boulder, CO: Westview Press.

Benson, Lee, Ira Harkavy, and John Puckett. 2007. *Dewey's dream: Universities and democracies in an age of education reform: Civil society, public schools, and democratic citizenship.* Philadelphia: Temple University Press.

Berger, Bennet M. 1960. *Working class suburb: A study of auto workers in suburbia.* Berkeley: University of California Press.

Berinsky, Adam. 1999. The two faces of public opinion. *American Journal of Political Science* 43 (4): 1209–30.

——. 2002. Political context and the survey response: The dynamics of racial policy opinion. *Journal of Politics* 64 (2): 567–84.

Bernard, L. L., and Jessie Bernard. 1943. *Origins of American sociology.* New York: Thomas Y. Crowell Company.

Besag, Frank. 1981. Social darwinism, race, and research. *Educational Evaluation and Policy Analysis* 3 (1): 57–69.

Best, Joel. 2001. *Damned lies and statistics.* Berkeley: University of California Press.

Bhabha, Homi K. 1994. *The location of culture.* London: Routledge.

Bickel, P. J., E. A. Hammel, and J. W. O'Connell. 1975. Sex bias in graduate admissions: Data from Berkeley. *Science* 187:398–404.

Biernat, Monica, and Diane Kobrynowicz. 1997. Gender- and race-based standards of competence: Lower minimum standards but higher ability standards for devalued groups. *Journal of Personality and Social Psychology* 72 (3): 544–77.

Billingsley, Andrew. 1968. *Black families in white America.* Englewood Cliffs, NJ: Prentice-Hall.

Billson, Janet Mancini. 1996. *Pathways to manhood: Young black males' struggle for identity.* New Brunswick, NJ: Transaction.

Blackwell, James E., and Morris Janowitz. 1974. *Black sociologists: Historical and contemporary perspectives*. Chicago: University of Chicago Press.

Blair, Irene. 2001. Implicit stereotypes and prejudice. In *Cognitive social psychology*, ed. Gordon Moskowitz, 359–74. Mahwah, NJ: Lawrence Erlbaum.

Blalock, H. M. Jr. 1962. Four variable causal models and partial correlations. *American Journal of Sociology* 68:182–94.

——. 1964. *Causal inferences in nonexperimental research*. Chapel Hill: University of North Carolina Press.

——. 1968. Theory building and causal inferences. In *Methodology in social research*, ed. H. M. Blalock Jr. and A. B. Blalock. New York: McGraw-Hill.

——. 1971. *Causal models in the social sciences*. Chicago: Aldine-Atherton.

——. 1979. *Black-white relations in the 1980s: Toward a long-term policy*. New York: Praeger.

Blalock, H. M. Jr., and A. B. Blalock. 1968. *Methodology in social research*. New York: McGraw-Hill.

Blau, Francine D., and Marianne A. Ferber. 1987. Discrimination: Empirical evidence from the United States. *The American Economic Review* 77 (2): 316–20.

Blau, Judith. 2003. *Race in the schools: Perpetuating white dominance?* Boulder, CO: Lynne Rienner Publishers.

Blau, Peter M., and Otis Dudley Duncan. 1967. *American occupational structure*. New York: Wiley.

Blauner, Robert. 1969. Internal colonialism and ghetto revolt. *Social Problems.* 16 (4): 393–408.

——. 1989. *Black lives, white lives: Three decades of race relations in America*. Berkeley: University of California Press.

Blee, Kathleen. 2001. *Inside organized racism: Women and men in the hate movement*. Berkeley: University of California Press.

Bluhm, Philip, and Wallace Kennedy. 1965. Discrimination reaction time as a function of incentive-related DRQ anxiety and task difficulty. *Perceptual Motor Skills* 20 (1): 131–34.

Blumenthal, Arthur. 1977. *The process of cognition*. Englewood Cliffs, NJ: Prentice-Hall.

Blumer, Herbert. 1958. Race prejudice as a sense of group position. *Pacific Sociological Review* 1:3–7.

——. 1969. *Symbolic interactionism: Perspective and method*. Berkeley: University of California Press.

Boardman, Jason D., Daniel A. Powers, Yolanda C. Padilla, and Robert A. Hummer. 2002. Low birth weight, social factors, and developmental outcomes among children in the United States. *Demography* 39 (2): 353–68.

Bobo, Lawrence. 1999. Prejudice as group position: Microfoundations of a sociological approach to racism and race relations. *Journal of Social Issues* 55:445–72.

Bobo, Lawrence, and Cybelle Fox. 2003. Race, racism, and discrimination: Bridging problems, methods, and theory in social psychological research. *Social Psychology Quarterly* 66 (4): 319–32.

Bobo, Lawrence, James Kluegel, and Ryan Smith. 1997. Laissez faire racism: The crystallization of a kinder, gentler, antiblack ideology. In *Racial attitudes in the 1990s: Continuity and change*, ed. Steven A. Tuch and Jack Martin, 15–42. Westport, CT: Praeger.

Bobo, Lawrence, and Ryan Smith. 1998. From Jim Crow racism to laisse-faire racism: The transformation of racial attitudes. In *Beyond pluralism: The conception of groups and group identities in America*, ed. Wendy Freedman, Ned C. Landsman, and Andrea Tyree. Urbana: University of Illinois Press.

Bobo, Lawrence D., and Mia Tuan. 2006. *Prejudice in politics: Group position, public opinion, and the Wisconsin treaty-rights dispute*. Cambridge, MA: Harvard University Press.

Bobo, Lawrence, and Camille Zubrinsky. 1996. Attitudes on residential integration: Perceived status differences, mere in-group preference or racial prejudice. *Social Forces* 74:883–909.

Bond, H. M. 1927. Some exceptional negro children. *The Crisis* 34:257–59.

Bonilla-Silva, Eduardo. 1997. Rethinking racism: Toward a structural interpretation. *American Sociological Review* 62 (3): 465–80.

———. 1999. The essential social fact of race: A reply to Loveman. *American Sociological Review* 64:899–906.

———. 2001. *White supremacy and racism in the post–civil rights era*. Boulder, CO: Lynne Rienner Publishers.

———. 2003. *Racism without racists: Color-blind racism and the persistence of racial inequality in the United States*. Lanham, MD: Rowman and Littlefield.

———. 2006. *Racism without racists: Color-blind racism and the persistence of racial inequality in the United States*. 2nd edition. Lanham, MD: Rowman and Littlefield.

Bonilla-Silva, Eduardo, and Gianpaolo Baiocchi. 2001. Anything but racism: How sociologists limit the significance of racism. *Race and Society* 4:117–31.

Bonilla-Silva, Eduardo, Gianpaolo Baiocchi, and Hayward D. Horton. Forthcoming. *Anything but racism: How social scientists minimize the impact of race*. London: Routledge Press.

Bonilla-Silva, Eduardo, and Tyrone Forman. (2000). I'm not a racist, but . . . : Mapping white college students' racial ideology in the USA. *Discourse & Society* 11 (1): 50–85.

Bonilla-Silva, Eduardo, Carla Goar, and David G. Embrick. 2006. When whites flock together: White habitus and the social psychology of whites' social and residential segregation from blacks. *Critical Sociology* 32 (2–3): 229–54.

Bonnett, Alastair. 1997. Constructions of whiteness in European and American antiracism. In *Debating cultural hybridity: Multi-cultural identities and the politics of anti-racism*, ed. Pnina Werbner and Tariq Modood. London: Zed Books.

Bordua, David J. 1961. Delinquent subcultures: Sociological interpretations of gang delinquency. *Annals of the American Academy of Political and Social Sciences* 228:120–36.

Bouchard T. J., D. T. Lykken, M. McGue, N. L. Segal, and A. Tellegen. 1990. Sources of human psychological differences: The Minnesota study of twins reared apart. *Science* 250:223–28.

Bourdieu, Pierre. 1990. *The logic of practice*. Cambridge: Cambridge University Press.

Bourdieu, Pierre, and Loic Wacquant. 1999. The cunning of imperialist reason. *Theory, Culture and Society* 16 (1): 41–58.

Bourgois, Philippe. 1995. In search of respect: Selling crack in el barrio. New York: Cambridge University Press.

Bradshaw, D., et al. 1998. New birth and death registration forms: A foundation for the future, a challenge for health workers? *South African Medical Journal* 88 (8): 971–74.

Bratter, J., and Tukufu Zuberi. 2001. As racial boundaries "fade": Racial Stratification and interracial marriage. *Race and Society* 4:133–48.

Braun, Gedahlia. 1993. Forgotten Black Voices. *American Renaissance* 4: 1.

Brezina, Timothy, and Kenisha Winder. 2003. Economic disadvantage, status generalization, and negative racial stereotyping by white Americans. *Social Psychology Quarterly* 66 (4): 402–18.

Brink, W., and L. Harris. 1963. *The Negro revolution in America*. New York: Simon and Schuster.

Brooks, Roy. 1990. *Rethinking the American race problem*. Los Angeles: University of California Press.

Brown, David D. 1994. *Critical theory and methodology*. Thousand Oaks, CA: Sage Publications.

Brown v. Philip Morris. 2001. No. 99-1931, 2001 U.S. App. LEXIS 9734.

Brown, Michael, Martin Carnoy, Elliot Currie, Troy Duster, David B. Oppenheimer, Marjorie Shultz, and David Wellman. 2003. *Whitewashing race: The myth of a colorblind society*. Los Angeles: University of California Press.

Brown, Tony N. 2001. Measuring self-perceived racial and ethnic discrimination in social surveys. *Sociological Spectrum* 21 (3): 377–92.

Brubaker, Rogers, and Frederick Cooper. 2000. Beyond "identity." *Theory and Society* 29: 1–47.

Bryk, Anthony S., Valerie E. Lee, and Peter B. Holland. 1993. *Catholic schools and the common good*. Cambridge, MA: Harvard University Press.

Bryk, Anthony S., Stephen Raudenbush. 1992. *Hierarchical linear models: Applications and data analysus methods*. Newbury Park, CA: Sage Publications.

Bullard, R. D. 1990. *Dumping in Dixie: Race, class, and environmental quality*. Boulder, CO: Westview Press.

Bulmer, Martin, and John Solomos. 2004. *Researching race and racism*. London: Routledge.

Burchard, E. G., E. Ziv, N. Coyle, S. L. Gomez, H. Tang, A. J. Karter, J. L. Mountain, E. J. Pérez-Stable, D. E. Sheppard, and N. Risch. 2003. The importance of race and ethnic background in biomedical research and clinical practice. *New England Journal of Medicine* 348 (12): 1170-75.

Bureau for Information (BI). 1991. Statistics on population groups essential. Press release by the News Service. Pretoria: CSS, February 6.

Bureau of Justice Statistics. 2000. Sourcebook of criminal justice statistics. U.S. Washington, DC: Department of Justice, 366, 427, 457, 519.

Bushway, Shawn D. 2000. The stigma of criminal history records in the labor market. In *Building violence: How America's rush to incarcerate creates more violence*, ed. John P. May. Thousand Oaks, CA: Sage Publications.

Caditz, Judith. 1976. *White liberals in transition: Current dilemmas of ethnic integration*. New York: Spectrum Publications.

Calhoun, Craig, ed. 2007. *Sociology in America: A history*. Chicago: University of Chicago Press.

California Department of Education (CDE). 2002. Department Data. http://dq.cde .ca.gov/dataquest/.

California Postsecondary Education Commission. 2002. Student Data. www.cpec.ca.gov/OnLineData/OnLineData.asp.

Camic, Charles, Franklin D. Wilson, Andrew Walder, Judith Howard, David Weakliem, Evelyn Glenn, Denise Bielby, and Charles Halaby. 2001. A dialogue about American Sociological Review: The Editorial Team Talks. *American Sociological Review* 66 (1): v–ix.

Campbell, Angus, and Howard Schuman. 1968. *Racial attitudes in fifteen American cities*. Ann Arbor, MI: Survey Research Center.

Campbell, Bruce. 1981. Race of the interviewer effects among Southern adolescents. *Public Opinion Quarterly* 45 (Summer), 2:231–44.

Campbell, Donald, and Julian Stanley. 1963. *Experimental and quasi-experimental designs for research*. Chicago: Rand McNally.

Canady, Horace. 1936. The effect of "rapport" on the I.Q.: A new approach to the problem of racial psychology. *Journal of Negro Education* 5:209–19.

Cancio, A. Silvia, T. David Evans, and David J. Maume, Jr. 1996. Reconsidering the declining significance of race: Racial differences in early career wages. *American Sociological Review* 61 (4): 541–56.

Carmines, Edward G., and Richard A. Zeller. 1979. *Reliability and validity assessment*. Beverly Hills, CA: Sage Publications.

Carter, Prudence L. 2005. *Keepin' it real: School success beyond black and white*. Oxford: Oxford University Press.

Carter, Stephen L. 1991. *Reflections of an affirmative action baby*. New York: Basic Books.

Casanova, Pablo. 1981. *The fallacy of social science research: A critical examination and new qualitative model*. New York: Pergamon Press.

Césaire, Aimé. 1972. *Discourse on colonialism*. New York: Monthly Review Press.

Cell, John W. 1982. *The highest stage of white supremacy: The origins of segregation in South Africa and the American South*. New York: Cambridge University Press.

Central Statistical Services (CSS). 1994. *Annual report 1994*. Pretoria: Central Statistical Services.

Charles Darwin Research Institute. 2000. Press release, July 11. www.charlesdarwin research.org.

Cheeseboro, Anthony Q. 1999. Conflict and continuity: E. Franklin Frazier, Oliver C. Cox and the Chicago school of sociology. *Journal of the Illinois State Historical Society*, Summer.

Cherry, Robert. 2001. *Who gets the good jobs? Combating race and gender disparities*. New Brunswick, NJ: Rutgers University Press.

Childs, Erica Chito. 2005. *Navigating interracial borders: Black-White couples and their social worlds*. New Brunswick, NJ: Rutgers University Press

Chin, Jeffrey C. 1986. Divergent trends in white racial attitudes toward blacks. *International Journal of Sociology and Social Policy* 6 (1): 25–38.

Christopher, A. J. 1983. Official land disposal policies and European settlement in southern Africa, 1860. 1960. *Journal of Historical Geography* 4 (4): 369–83.

———. 1992. Segregation levels in South Africa cities, 1911. 1985. *The International Journal of African Historical Studies* 25 (3): 561–82.

——. 1994. *The atlas of Apartheid.* London: Routledge.

Chronicle of Higher Education. 2000. January 14, A24.

Civil Rights Act of 1964. 1994. 42 U.S.C. Sec. 2000e-2.

Clack, B., J. A. Dixon, and C. Tredoux. 2005. Eating together apart: Patterns of segregation in a multiethnic cafeteria. *Journal of Community and Applied Social Psychology* 15:1–16.

Clark, W. A. V. 1992. Residential preferences and residential choices in a multiethnic context. *Demography* 29:451–66.

Clay, Kenneth Y. 1998. The impact of federal civil rights policy of black economic progress: Evidence from the Equal Employment Opportunity Act of 1972. *Industrial and Labor Relations Review* 51 (4): 608–32.

Clayton, J. E. 1964. Anti-rights bill lobby is best-financed ever. *Washington Post,* March 22, A9.

Clogg, C. C., and A. Haritou. 1997. The regression method for causal inference and a dilemma confronting this method. In *Causality in crisis? Statistical methods and the search for causal knowledge in the social sciences,* ed. S. P. Turner, 83–112. Notre Dame, IN: Notre Dame University Press.

Cloward, Richard A., and Lloyd E. Ohlin. 1960. *Delinquency and opportunity: A theory of delinquent gangs.* New York: Free Press.

Coate, Stephen, and Glenn C. Loury. 1993. Will affirmative-action policies eliminate negative stereotypes? *The American Economic Review* 83 (5): 1220–40.

Cohen, Albert K., and Harold M. Hodges. 1963. Characteristics of the lower bluecollars class. *Social Problems* 10 (4): 303–34.

Cohn, Victor. 1989. *News and numbers: A guide to reporting statistical claims and controversies in health and other fields.* Ames: Iowa State University Press.

Cole, David. 1999. *No equal justice: Race and class in the American criminal justice system.* New York: The New Press.

Coleman, J. S. 1966. *Equality of educational opportunity.* Washington, DC: U.S. Government Printing Office.

Collins, Chiquita A., and David R. Williams. 1999. Segregation and mortality: The deadly effects of racism? *Sociological Forum* 14 (3): 495–523.

Collins, Patricia Hill. 1998. Fighting words: Black women and the search for justice. Minneapolis: University of Minnesota Press.

——. 1999. Learning from the outsider within: The sociological significance of black feminist thought. In *Feminist approaches to theory and methodology: An interdisciplinary reader,* ed. Sharlese Hesse-Biebr, Christina Gilmartin, and Robin Lyndenberg, 155–78. New York: Oxford University Press.

——. 2000. *Black feminist thought.* New York: Routledge.

——. 2007. Pushing the boundaries or business as usual? Race, class, and gender studies and sociological inquiry. In *Sociology in America: A history,* ed. Craig Calhoun, 572–604. Chicago: University of Chicago Press.

Comeaux, Eddie, and Tara Watford. 2006. Admissions and omissions: How "the numbers" are used to exclude deserving students: 2005–2006 CAPAA findings. *Bunche Research Report,* 3 (June). Ralph J. Bunche Center for African American Studies, UCLA.

Conley, D. 1999. *Being black, living in the red: Race, wealth, and social policy in America.* Berkeley: University of California Press.

Cooley, Charles Horton. 1909. *Social organization: A study of the larger mind.* New York: C. Scribner's Sons.

Cortese, Charles F., R. Frank Falk, and Jack C. Cohen. 1976. Further considerations on the methodological analysis of segregation indices. *American Sociological Review* 41:630–37.

Cose, E. 1993. *The rage of a privileged class.* New York: HarperCollins.

Coser, Lewis. 1965. The sociology of poverty. *Social Problems* 13 (2): 140–48.

Cousins, C. W. 1923. Cited in *Census of the union of South Africa 1921*, Union Government, 15 (1): 11.

Covington, Jeannette. 2002. Racial classification in criminology. In *2001 Race odyssey: African Americans and sociology*, ed. Bruce Hare, 178–202. Syracuse, NY: Syracuse University Press.

Cox, David R. 1992. Causality: Some statistical aspects. *Journal of the Royal Statistical Society* 135 (2): 291–301.

Cox, Earnest S. 1923. *White America.* Richmond, VA: White America Society.

———. 1925. *Let my people go.* Richmond, VA: White America Society.

Cox, Oliver. 1948. *Caste, class, and race: A study in social dynamics.* New York: Doubleday and Company.

Crane, A. L. 1923. Racial differences in inhibition: A psychological study of the comparative characteristics of the Negro and the white man as measured by certain tests, with special reference to the problem of volition. *Archives of Psychology* 63:9–84.

Cready, C. M., and R. Saenz. 1997. The nonmetro/metro context of racial/ethnic outmarriage: Some differences between African Americans and Mexican Americans. *Rural Sociology* 62:335–62.

Crenshaw, Kimberly. 1988. Race, reform, and retrenchment: Transformation and legitimation in anti-discrimination law. *Harvard Law Review* 101:1331–87.

Cukor-Avila, Patricia, and Guy Bailey. 2001. The effects of the race and the interviewer on sociolinguistic fieldwork. *Journal of Sociolinguistics* 5 (1): 254–70.

Dalmage, Heather. 2000. *Tripping the color line: Black-white multiracial families in a racially divided world.* New Brunswick, NJ: Rutgers University Press.

Danso, Henry, and Victoria Esses. 2001. Black experimenters and the intellectual test performance of white participants: The tables are turned. *Journal of Experimental Social Psychology* 37:158–65.

Darity, William A. 1982. The human capital approach to black-white earnings inequality: Some unsettled questions. *The Journal of Human Resources* 17 (1): 72–93.

Darity, William Jr., and Samuel Myers. 1998. *Persistent disparity: Race and economic inequality in the United States since 1945.* Cheltenham, UK: Edward Elgar Publishing.

Davenport, Charles B. 1911. *Heredity in relation to eugenics.* New York: H. Holt and Company.

Davenport, T. R. H. 1991. *South Africa: A modern history.* 4th edition. London: Macmillan Press.

Davis, Allison. 1946. The motivation of the underprivileged worker. In *Industry and society*, ed. William F. Whyte. New York: McGraw-Hill.

Davis, Darren. 1997a. Nonrandom measurement error and race of interviewer effects among African-Americans. *Public Opinion Quarterly* 61 (1): 183–207.

———. 1997b. The direction of race-of-interviewer effects among African Americans: Donning the black mask. *American Journal of Political Science* 41 (1): 309–22.

Davis, Darren, and Brian Silver. 2003. Stereotype threat and race-of-interviewer effects in a survey on political knowledge. *American Journal of Political Science* 47 (1): 33–45.

Davis, F. James. 1991. *Who is black? One nation's definition*. University Park: The Pennsylvania State University Press.

Davis, J. A. 1966. The campus as frog pond: An application of the theory of relative deprivation to career decisions of college men. *American Journal of Sociology* 72:1–17.

Davis, Marcia. 1999. Traffic violation: Racial profiling is a reality for black drivers, but momentum is building to put on the brakes. *Emerge*, June, 42–48.

Daymont, Thomas N., and Robert L. Kaufman. 1979. Measuring industrial variation in racial discrimination using log-linear models. *Social Science Research* 8 (1): 41–62.

Degler, Carl. 1986. *Neither black nor white: Slavery and race relations in Brazil and the United States*. Madison: University of Wisconsin Press.

de Graft-Johnson, K. T. 1988. Demographic data collection in Africa. In *The state of African demography*, ed. Etienne van de Walle, Patrick O. Ohadike, and Mpembele D. Sala-Diakanda, 13–28. Liège: International Union for the Scientific Study of Population.

DeGroot, Morris, Stephen Fienberg, and Joseph Kadane, eds. 1994. *Statistics and the law*. New York: John Wiley & Sons.

Demleitner, Nora V. 1999. Preventing internal exile: The need for restrictions on collateral sentencing consequences. *Stanford Law and Policy Review* 11:153.

Demos, Vasilikie. 1990. Black family studies in the *Journal of Marriage and the Family* and the analysis issue of distortion: A trend analysis. *Journal of Marriage and Family*. 52:603–12.

DeSena, Judith. 1990. *Protecting one's turf: Social strategies for maintaining urban neighborhoods*. Lanham, MD: University Press of America.

——. 1994. Local gatekeeping practices and residential segregation. *Sociological Inquiry* 64: 307-21.

De Sousa Santos, Boaventura. 2006. *The rise of the global left: The world social forum and beyond*. London: Zed Books.

de Tocqueville, Alexis. 2004. *Democracy in America*. New York: Library of America.

DiTomaso, Nancy, Rochelle Parks-Yancy, and Corinne Post. 2003. White views of civil rights: Color blindness and equal opportunity. In *White out: The continuing significance of race*, ed. Ashley Doane and Eduardo Bonilla-Silva. New York: Routledge Press.

Doane, Ashley, and Eduardo Bonilla-Silva, eds. 2003. *White out: The continuing significance of race*. New York: Routledge.

Doane, Woody. 2003. Rethinking whiteness studies. In *White out: The continuing significance of race*. New York: Routledge.

Dodoo, F. Nii-Amoo. 1997. Assimilation differences among Africans in America. *Social Forces* 76 (2): 527–46.

Dollard, John. 1957 [1949]. *Caste and class in a southern town*. Garden City, NY: Doubleday.

Donzinger, Steven. 1996. The prison-industrial complex: What's really driving the rush to lock 'em up? *Washington Post*, March 17, C3.

Douglas, Mary. 2002. *Purity and danger: An analysis of the concept of pollution and taboo*. New York: Routledge.

Douglass, Frederick. 2003. *My bondage and my freedom*. New York: Penguin Books.

Dovidio, John, and Samuel Gaertner. 2000. Aversive racism and selection decisions: 1989 and 1999. *Psychological Science* 11 (4): 319–23.

Drake, St. Clair. 1987. *Black folk here and there: An essay in history and anthropology*. Vol. 1. Los Angeles: University of California Press.

Drake, St. Clair, and Horace Cayton. 1993 [1945]. *Black metropolis: A study of Negro life in a northern city*. Chicago: University of Chicago Press.

D'Souza, Dinesh. 1995a. *The end of racism: Principles for a multiracial society*. New York: The Free Press.

———. 1995b. Racism: It's a White (and Black) thing. *Washington Post*, September 24, C1-C2.

Du Bois, W. E. B. 1899 [1996]. *The Philadelphia Negro: A social study*. Philadelphia: University of Pennsylvania Press.

———. 1903. *The souls of black folk*. New York: Knopf.

———. 1934 [1995]. *Black reconstruction in America, 1860–1880: An essay toward a history of the part which black folk played in the attempt to reconstruct democracy in America*. New York: Atheneum.

———. 1939. *Black folks then and now: An essay in the history of sociology of the Negro race*. New York: H. Holt and Co.

———. 1940. *Dust of dawn*. New York: Schocken.

———. 1985. *Against racism: Unpublished essays, papers, addresses, 1887-1961*. Amherst: University of Massachussetts Press.

———. 2006. The souls of white folk. In *Darkwater: Voices from within the veil*, 55–77. New York: Humanity Books.

Duberman, Martin. 1999. *Left out: The politics of exclusion/essays/1964–1999*. New York: Basic Books.

Dubow, Saul. 1995. *Scientific racism in modern South Africa*. New York: Cambridge University Press.

Dumm, Thomas L. 1993. The new enclosures: Racism in the normalized community. In *Reading Rodney King, reading urban uprising*, 178–95. New York: Routledge.

Duncan, Otis Dudley. 1968. Inheritance of poverty or inheritance of race? In *On understanding poverty*, ed. Daniel Patrick Moynihan, 85–110. New York: Basic Books, Inc.

Duncan, Otis, and Beverly Duncan. 1955. A methodological analysis of segregation. *American Journal of Sociology* 96:1226–59.

Duneier, Mitchell. 1992. *Slims's table: Race, respectability, and masculinity*. Chicago: University of Chicago.

———. 1999. *Sidewalk*. New York: Farrar, Straus and Giroux.

———. 2002. What kind of combat sport is sociology? *American Journal of Sociology* 107 (6): 1551–76.

Dyer, James, Arnold Vedlitz, and Stephen Worchel. 1989. Social distance among racial and ethnic groups in Texas: Some demographic correlates. *Social Science Quarterly* 70 (3): 607–16.

Dyer, Richard. 1997. *White*. New York: Routledge.

Eckstein, Susan. 1977. *The poverty of revolution: The state and the urban poor in Mexico*. Princeton, NJ: Princeton University Press.

Edgeworth, Francis Ysidro. 1885. Methods of statistics. *Jubilee Volume of the Statistical Society*, 181–217.

Edmonston, B., Sharon M. Lee, and Jeffrey Passel. 2002. Recent trends in intermarriage and immigration and their effects on the future racial composition of the U.S. population. In *The New Race Question: How the Census counts multiracial individuals*, ed. Joel Perlmann and Mary Waters, 227–55. New York: Russell Sage Foundation.

Edwards, Jeffrey R. 1992. A cybernetic theory of stress, coping, and well-being in organizations. *The Academy of Management Review* 17:238–74.

EEOC v. Carolina Freight Carrier Corporation. 1989. 734 S.D. Fla.

EEOC. 1990. Notice No. N-915-061. Policy guidance on the consideration of arrest records in employment decisions under title VII of the Civil Rights Act of 1964, as amended, 42 U.S.C. Sec. 2000e et. seq. Sept. 7. (1982).

Eichler, Margarit. 1991. *Nonsexist research methods: A practical guide*. New York: Routledge.

Eliasoph, Nina. 1999. Everyday racism in a culture of political avoidance: Civil society, speech, and taboo. *Social Problems* 46:479–502.

Ellul, Jacques. 1964. *The technological society*. Trans. John Wilkinson. New York: Vintage Books.

Emerson, Michael, George Yancey, and Karen J. Chai. 2001. Does race matter in residential segregation? Exploring the preferences of white Americans. *American Sociological Review* 66:922–35.

Emirbayer, Mustafa. 1997. Manifesto for a relational sociology. *American Journal of Sociology* 103 (2): 281–317.

Epstein, Joshua M., and Robert Axtell. 1996. *Growing artificial societies: Social science from the bottom up*. Washington, DC: Brookings Institution Press.

Equal Credit Opportunity Act. 2000. 15 U.S.C. Sec. 1691 et seq.

Ericson, Richard V., and Kevin D. Haggerty. 1997. *Policing the risk society*. Toronto: University of Toronto Press.

Erikson, K. 1966. *Wayward Puritans*. New York: Wiley.

Espiritu, Yen Le. 1992. *Asian American panethnicity: Bridging institutions and identities*. Philadelphia: Temple University Press.

Essed, Philomena. 1991. *Understanding everyday racism*. Newbury Park, CA: Sage Publications.

Essed, Philomena, and David T. Goldberg. 2002. Introduction: From racial demarcations to multiple identfications. In *Race critical theories: Text and context*, ed. Philomena Essed and David T. Golberg, 1–11: Oxford: Blackwell.

Essed, Philomena, and Kwame Nimako. 2006. Designs and (co)incidents: Cultures of scholarship and public policy on immigrants/minorities in the Netherlands. *International Journal of Comparative Sociology* 47 (3–4): 282–312.

Estudios Avanzados. 2004. As pesquisas na Bahia sobre os afros-brasileiros: Entrevista de Waldemir Freitas Oliveira. *Estudios Avanzados* 18 (50): 127–34.

Evans, I. 1997. *Bureaucracy and race: Native administration in South Africa*. Berkeley: University of California Press.

Faigman, David. 1999. *Legal alchemy: The use and misuse of science in the law*. New York: W. H. Freeman.

Fanon, Frantz. 1965. *A dying colonialism*. New York: Grove Press.

——. 1967. *Black skin, white masks*. New York: Grove Press.

Farkas, George, and Keven Vicknair. 1996. Appropriate tests of racial wage discrimination require controls for cognitive skill: Comment on Cancio, Evans, and Maume. *American Sociological Review* 61 (4): 557–60.

Farley, Reynolds. 1977. Residential segregation in urbanized areas of the United States. *Demography* 14:497–518.

——. 1984. *Blacks and whites, narrowing the gap?* Cambridge, MA: Harvard University Press.

——. 1996. *The new American reality*. New York: Russell Sage Publishers.

Farley, Reynolds, and Walter R. Allen. 1987. *The color line and the quality of life in America*. New York: Russell Sage Publishers.

Farley, Reynolds, and W. Frey. 1994. Changes in the segregation of whites from blacks during the 1980s: Small steps towards a more integrated society. *American Sociological Review* 59:23–45.

Farley, R., C. Steeh, M. Krysan, and K. Reeves. 1994. Stereotypes and segregation: Neighborhoods in the Detroit area. *American Journal of Sociology* 100:750–80.

Fay, Brian. 1996. *Contemporary philosophy of science: A multicultural approach*. Oxford: Blackwell.

Feagin, Joe R. 1981. Documenting and measuring race and sex discrimination. *Civil Rights Research Review* 9 (1–2): 1–9.

——. 1994. A house is not a home: White racism and the U.S. housing practices. In *Residential apartheid: The American legacy*, ed. R. D. Bullard, J. E. Grigsby, and C. Lee, 17–48. Los Angeles: CAAS.

——. 2000. *Racist America: Roots, current realities, and future reparations*. New York: Routledge.

——. 2001. Social justice and sociology agendas for the twenty-first century. *American Sociological Review* 66:506–28.

——. 2006. *Systemic racism: A theory of oppression*. New York: Routledge.

Feagin, Joe R., and Hernán Vera. 2001. *Liberation sociology*. Boulder, CO: Westview Press.

Featherman, David L. 1971. A research note: A social structural model for the socioeconomic career. *American Journal of Sociology* 77: 293–304.

Featherman, David L., and Robert M. Hauser. 1976. Changes in the socioeconomic stratification of the races. *American Journal of Sociology* 82:621–51.

Ferguson, George O. 1916. *The psychology of the Negro: An experimental study*. Wesport, CT: Negro Universities Press.

Ferguson, Ronald F. 1998. Teacher's perception and expectations and the black-white test score gap. In *The black-white test score gap*, ed. C. Jencks and M. Phillips. Washington, DC: Brookings Institution Press.

Fields, Barbara. 1990. Slavery, race and ideology in the United States of America. *New Left Review* 181:95–118.

Fine, Michelle, and Lois Weis. 1998. *The unknown city: Lives of poor and working class young adults*. Boston: Beacon Press.

Fine, Michelle, Lois Weis, Susan Weseen, and Loonmun Wong. 2003. For whom? Qualitative research, representations, and social responsibilities. In *The Landscape of Qualitative Research*, ed. Norman K. Denzin and Yvonna S. Lincoln, 167–207. Thousand Oaks, CA: Sage Publications.

Finkel, Steven, Thomas Guterbock, and Marian Borg. 1991. Race of interviewer effects in a preelection poll: Virginia 1989. *Public Opinion Quarterly* 55 (Autumn), 3:313–30.
Firebaugh, Glenn. 1997. *Analyzing repeated surveys*. Sage University Paper Series on Quantitative Analysis, series no. 07-115. Beverly Hills, CA: Sage Publications.
Firebaugh, Glenn, and Kenneth E. Davis. 1988. Trends in antiblack prejudice, 1972–1984: Region and cohort effects. *American Sociological Review* 94:251–72.
Fischer, Claude S., Michael Hout, Martín Sánchez Jankowski, Samuel R. Lucas, Ann Swidler, and Kim Voss. 1996. *Inequality by design: Cracking the bell curve myth*. Princeton, NJ: Princeton University Press.
Fischer, Claude S., Gretchen Stockmayer, Jon Stiles, and Michael Hout. 2004. Distinguishing the geographic levels and social dimensions of U.S. metropolitan segregation, 1960–2000. *Demography* 41 (1): 37–59.
Fisher B. J., and D. J. Hartmann. 1995. The impact of race on the social experience of college students at a predominantly white university. *Journal of Black Studies* 26 (2): 117–33.
Fisher, Ronald A. 1925. *Statistical methods for research workers*. London: Oliver and Boyd.
——. 1935. *The design of experiments*. London: Oliver and Boyd.
Fitzhugh, George. 1854. *Sociology for the South or the failure of free society*. Richmond, VA: A. Morris, Publisher.
Flectcher, George P. 1999. Disenfranchisement punishment: Reflections on the racial uses of infamia. *UCLA Law Review* 46:1895.
Foner, Eric. 2002. Expert report for *Gratz et al. v. Bollinger, et al.*, 1–24:.2
Fordham, Signithia. 1996. *Blacked out: Dilemmas of race, identity, and success at Capital High*. Chicago: University of Chicago.
Fossett, Mark A., and Theodore Seibert. 1997. *Long time coming: Racial inequality in the nonmetropolitan South, 1940–1990*. Boulder, CO: Westview Press.
Foucault, Michael. 1972. *The archaeology of knowledge and the discourse or language*. New York: Pantheon Books.
——. 1973. *The order of things: An archeology of the human sciences*. New York: Vintage Books.
——. 1979. *Discipline and punish: The birth of the prison*. New York: Vintage Books.
——. 1980. *Power/Knowledge: Selected interviews and other writings, 1972–1977*. New York: Pantheon.
Francis, Samuel. 1995. Prospects for racial and cultural survival. *American Renaissance* 6:1-7.
——. 1999. Race and the American identity. *American Renaissance* 10 (2): 5–8.
Frankenberg, Ruth. 1993. *White women, race matters: The social construction of whiteness*. Minneapolis: University of Minnesota Press.
Frazier, Edward Franklin. 1927. The pathology of race prejudice. *Forum* 70: 856–62.
——. 1932. *The Negro family in Chicago*. Chicago: University of Chicago Press.
——. 1934. Traditions and patterns of Negro family life in the United States. In *Race and culture contacts*, ed. E. B. Reuter. New York: McGraw-Hill.
——. 1945. My most humiliating experience with Jim Crow. *Negro Digest* 4:81–82.
——. 1962. The failure of the Negro intellectual. *Negro Digest* (February).

——. 1968. *On race relations.* Chicago: University of Chicago Press.

Fredrickson, George M. 1971. *The black image in the white mind.* New York: Harper and Row.

——. 1981. *White supremacy: A comparative study in American and South African history.* New York: Oxford University Press.

Freedman, David A. 1987. As others see us: A case study in path analysis. *Journal of Education Statistics* 12 (2): 101–28.

Frey, William H., and Dowell Myers. 2005. *Racial segregation in U.S. metropolitan areas and cities, 1990–2000: Patterns, trends, and explanations.* Population Studies Center Research Report 05-573. Ann Arbor: University of Michigan.

Fryer, Roland G. Jr., and Paul Torelli. 2005. An empirical analysis of "acting white." Working Paper, Harvard University.

Fu, V. 2001. Interracial marriage pairings. *Demography* 38:147–59.

Gallagher, Charles A. 1997. Redefining Racial Privilege in the United States. *Transformations* 8 (1): 28–39.

——. 2003a. Miscounting race: Explaining whites' misperceptions of racial group size. *Sociological Perspectives* 46 (3): 381–96.

——. 2003b. Color-blind privilege: The social and political functions of erasing the color line in post race America. *Race, Class and Gender* 10 (4): 22–37.

——. 2006a. Color blindness: An obstacle to racial justice. In *Mixed messages: Multiracial identities in the "color-blind" era,* ed. David L. Brunsma. Boulder, CO: Lynne Reiner.

——. 2006b. The challenge to public sociology: Neo-liberalisms illusion of inclusion. In *Public Sociologies,* ed. Judith Blau and Keri Iyall Smith. Lanham, MD: Rowman and Littlefield.

Gallup. 2004. Civil rights and race relations. Poll sponsored by AARP. January 2004.

Galster, George. 1988. Residential segregation in American cities: A contrary review. *Population Research and Policy Review* 7:93–112.

Galton, Francis. 1892. *Hereditary genius: An inquiry into its laws and consequences.* Gloucester, MA: Peter Smith.

——. 1874. *English men of science: Their nature and nurture.* London: Macmillan.

——. 1875. Statistics by intercomparison, with remarks on the law of frequency of error. *Philosophical Magazine* 49:33–46.

——. 1889. *Natural Inheritance.* London: Macmillan.

Gamson, Joshua. 2003. Sexualities, queer theory, and quantitative research. In *The landscape of qualitative research,* eds. Norman K. Denzin and Yvonna S. Lincoln, 540–68. Thousand Oaks, CA: Sage Publications.

Gandy, Oscar H. 1982. *Beyond agenda setting: Information subsidies and public policy.* Norwood, NJ: Ablex.

——. 1996. If it weren't for bad luck: Framing stories of racially comparative risk. In *Mediated messages and African-American culture: Contemporary issues,* ed. Venise T. Berry and Carmen L. Manning-Miller, 55–75. Thousand Oaks, CA: Sage Publications.

Gandy, Oscar H., Katharina Kopp, Tanya Hands, Karen Frazer, and David Phillips. 1997. Race and risk: Factors affecting the framing of stories about inequality, discrimination, and just plain bad luck. *Public Opinion Quarterly* 6 (1): 158–82.

Gans, Herbert. 1962. *Urban villagers.* New York: Free Press.

——. 1969. Class in the study of poverty: An approach to anti-poverty research. In *On understanding poverty: Perspective from the social sciences*, ed. Daniel P. Moynihan. New York: Basic Books.

——. 1995. *The war against the poor: The underclass and anti-poverty policy*. New York: Basic Books.

——. 1999. The possibility of a new racial hierarchy in the twenty-first-century United States. In *The cultural territories of race: Black and white boundaries*, ed. Michael Lamont. Chicago: University of Chicago Press and Russel Sage Foundation.

Garrett, Henry E. 1961. The scientific racism of Juan Comas. *Mankind Quarterly* 2:106

——. 1962. Letter to the editor. *Science* 135:984.

——. 1966. Lesson in Bias. *Newsweek*, May 30, 63.

——. n.d. *Breeding down*. Richmond, VA: Patrick Henry Press.

——. n.d. *How classroom desegregation will work*. Richmond, VA: Patrick Henry Press.

Garrison, Bruce. 1998. *Computer-assisted reporting*. Mahwah, NJ: Lawrence Erlbaum.

Gates Jr., Henry Louis. 1988. *The signifying monkey: A theory of African-American literary criticism*. New York: Oxford University Press.

Geertz, Clifford. 1973. *The interpretation of cultures*. New York: Basic Books.

George, Douglass, and George Yancey. 2004. Taking stock of America's attitudes on cultural diversity: An analysis of public deliberation on multiculturalism, assimilation, and intermarriage. *Journal of Comparative Family Studies* 35:1–19.

George, Wesley Critz. 1955. *The race problem from the standpoint of one who is concerned about the evils of miscegenation*. Pamphlet distributed by the American States Rights Association, Birmingham, AL.

——. 1962. *The biology of the race problem*. New York: Putnam National Letters Committee.

Gerhart, Gail M. 1978. *Black power in South Africa: The evolution of an ideology*. Berkeley: University of California Press.

Gibson, Campbell, and Emily Lennon. 1999. *Historical census statistics on the foreign-born population of the United States 1850–1990*. Washington, DC: Population Division, U.S. Bureau of the Census. www.census.gov/population/www/documentation/twps0029/twps0029.html.

Giddens, Anthony. 1984. *The constitution of society: Outline of a theory of structuration*. Cambridge: Polity Press.

Gigerenzer, Gerd, Zeno Swijtink, Theodore Porter, Lorraine Daston, John Beatty, and Lorenz Kruger. 1989. *The empire of chance*. Cambridge: Cambridge University Press, 1989.

Gilbert, Dorie J. 1998. The prejudice perception assessment scale: Measuring stigma vulnerability among African American students at predominantly Euro-American universities. *Journal of Black Psychology* 24 (3): 305–21.

Gilens, Martin. 1996. Race and poverty in America: Public misperceptions and the American news media. *Public Opinion Quarterly* 60 (4): 515–41.

Giliomee, Hermann. 1995. The growth of Afrikaner identity. In *Segregation and apartheid in twentieth-century South Africa*, ed. William Beinart and Saul Dubow, 189–205. New York: Routledge.

Gilroy, Paul. 2000a. *Against race*. Cambridge, MA: Belknap Press of Harvard University Press.

——. 2000b. *Between camps: Race, identity and nationalism at the end of the colour line.* London: Allen Lane.

Giroux, Henry. 1998. *Channel surfing: Race talk and the destruction of today's youth.* New York: St. Martin's Press.

——. 2003. Spectacles of race and pedogogies of denial: Anti-black racist pedagogy under the reign of neoliberalism. *Communication Education* 52 (3–4): 191–211.

Gitlin, Todd. 1995. *The twilight of common dreams: Why America is wracked by culture wars.* New York: Henry Holt and Company.

Glenn, Evelyn Nakano. 2002. *Unequal freedom: How race and gender shaped American citizenship and labor.* Cambridge, MA: Harvard University Press.

Goar, Carla, and Jane Sell. 2005. Using task definition to modify racial inequality within task groups. *The Sociological Quarterly* 46 (3): 525–43.

Goldberg, David Theo. 1997. *Racial subjects: Writing on race in America.* New York: Routledge.

——. 2006. The global reach of raceless states. In *The globalization of racism,* ed. Donaldo Macedo and Panayota Gounari, 45–67. Boulder, CO: Paradigm Publishers.

Golden, Daniel. 2001. Up in smoke: Tougher Bush stance on obscure law hits students seeking aid. *Wall Street Journal.*

Gonnerman, Jennifer. 2002. Life without parole? *New York Times Magazine,* May 19, 40.

Gooding-Williams, Robert. 2001. Race, multiculturalism, and democracy. In *Race and racism,* ed. Bernard Boxill, 422–47. Oxford: Oxford University Press.

Gordon, Linda. 1999. *The great Arizona orphan abduction.* Cambridge, MA: Harvard University Press.

Gornick, M. E., Paul W. Eggers, Thomas W. Reilly, Renee M. Mentnech, Leslye K. Fitterman, Lawrence E. Kucken, and Bruce C. Vladeck. 1996. Effects of race and income on mortality and use of services among Medicare beneficiaries. *New England Journal of Medicine* 335 (11): 791–99.

Goshorn, Kent, and Oscar H. Gandy. 1995. Race, risk, and responsibility: Editorial constraint in the framing of inequality. *Journal of Communication* 45 (2): 133–51.

Gould, Mark. 1992. Law and sociology: Some consequences for the law of employment discrimination deriving from the sociological reconstruction of economic theory. *Cardozo Law Review* 13 (5): 1517–78.

——. 1999. Race and theory: Culture, poverty, and adaptation to discrimination in Wilson and Ogbu. *Sociological Theory* 17 (2): 171–200.

Gould, Stephen Jay. 1996. *The mismeasure of man.* New York: Norton.

Gouldner, Alvin. 1961. Ati-minotaur: The myth of a value-free sociology. *Social Problems* 9:199–213.

Gove, Phillip Babcock et al., eds. *Webster's Third New International Dictionary.* Springfield, MA: Merriam Webster, 649.

Graham, Stephen, and Simon Marvin. 2001. *Splintering urbanism.* London: Routledge.

Grannis, Rick. 1998. The importance of trivial streets: Residential streets and residential segregation. *American Journal of Sociology* 103 (6): 1530–64.

——. 2002. Discussion: Segregation indices and their functional inputs. *Sociological Methodology* 32:69–84.

Graves, Joseph L. Jr. 2001. *The emperors new clothes: Biological theories of race at the millennium.* New Brunswick, NJ: Rutgers University Press.

——. 2004. *The Race Myth: Why we pretend race exists in America*. New York: Penguin Books.

Greenberg, Stanley B., and Theda Skocpol. 1999. *The new majority*. New Haven, CT: Yale University Press.

Grier, William H. 1968. *Black rage*. New York: Basic Books.

Grimes, S. 1993. Residential segregation in Australian cities: A literature review. *International Migration Review* 27 (1): 103–20.

Grodsky, Eric, and Devah Pager. 2001. The structure of disadvantage: Individual and occupational determinants of the black-white wage gap. *American Sociological Review* 66 (4): 542–67.

Guinier, Lani. 1995. The representation of minority interests. In *Classifying by race*, ed. P. E. Peterson, 21–49. Princeton, NJ: Princeton University Press.

Guthrie, Robert. 1998. *Even the rat was white: A historical view of psychology*. Boston: Allyn and Bacon.

Habermas, Jürgen. 1998. *Between facts and norms: Contributions to a discourse theory of law and democracy*. Trans. William Rehg. Cambridge, MA: MIT Press.

Hacker, A. 1992. *Two nations: Black and white, separate, hostile, unequal*. New York: Scribner.

Hackett, R. K., P. W. Holland, M. Pearlman, and D. T. Thayer. 1987. *Test construction manipulating score differences between black and white examinees: Properties of the resulting tests*. RR-87-30. Princeton, NJ: Educational Testing Service.

Hall, Stuart. 1981. The whites of their eyes: Racist ideologies and the media. In *Silver linings: Some strategies for the eighties*, ed. G. Bridges and R. Brunt. London: Lawrence and Wishart Ltd.

——. 1986. Gramsci's relevance for the study of race and ethnicity. *Journal of Communication Inquiry* 10:5–27.

——. 1988. New ethnicities. In *Black film, British cinema*, ed. K. Mercer. New York: Scribner.

Halsell, Grace. 1999. *Soul sister*. Washington, DC: Crossroads International Publishing.

Hampton, Robert L., and Richard Gelles. 2000. Violence toward black women in a nationality-representative sample of black families. In *Structured inequality in the United States: Discussions on the continuing significance of race, ethnicity, and gender*, ed. Adalberto Aguirre and David Baker. Upper Saddle River, NJ: Prentice Hall.

Hanchard, Michael George. 1994. *Orpheus and power: The movimento negro of Rio de Janeiro and São Paulo, Brazil, 1945–1988*. Princeton, NJ: Princeton University Press.

Hannerz, Ulf. 1969. *Soulside*. New York: Columbia University Press.

——. 1972. What ghetto males are like: Another look. In *Black psyche*, ed. Stanley Guterman. Berkeley, CA: The Glendessay Press.

——. 1974. Research in the black ghetto: A review of the sixties. *Journal of Asian and African Studies* 9 (3–4): 139–59.

Harding, R. M., E. Healy, A. J. Ray, N. S. Ellis, N. Flanagan, C. Todd, C. Dixon, A. Sajantila, I. J. Jackson, M. A. Birch Machin, and J. L. Rees. 2000. Evidence for variable selective pressures at MC1R. *American Journal of Human Genetics* 66:1351–61.

Harding, Sandra. 1991. *Whose science? Whose knowledge?* Ithaca, NY: Cornell University Press.

——. 1993. *The racial economy of science: Toward a democratic future*. Bloomington: Indiana University Press.

——. 2006. *Science and social inequality: Feminist and postcolonial issues*. Urbana: University of Illinois Press.

Harlow, Roxanna. 2003. Race doesn't matter, but . . . : The effect of race on professor's experiences and emotion management on the undergraduate college classroom. *Social Psychology Quarterly* 66 (4): 348–63.

Harrington, Michael. 1962. *The other America: Poverty in the United States*. New York: Touchstone.

Harris, David A. 1999. Property values drop when blacks move in because . . . : Racial and socioeconomic determinants of neighborhood desirability. *American Sociological Review* 64:461–79.

——. 2001. Why are whites and blacks averse to black neighborhoods? *Social Science Research* 30:100–16.

——. 2002. *Profiles in injustice: Why racial profiling cannot work*. New York: New Press.

Harris, Melvin. 1964. *Patterns of race in the Americas*. New York: W.W. Norton.

Hartigan, John Jr. 1997. Locating white Detroit. In *Displacing whiteness: Essays in social and cultural criticism*, ed. Ruth Frankenberg, 204. Durham, NC: Duke University Press.

——. 2005. *Odd tribes: Toward a cultural analysis of white people*. Durham, NC: Duke University Press.

Harvey, Alice E. 1994. Comment, ex-felon disenfranchisement and its influence on the black vote: The need for a second look. *University of Pennsylvania Law Review* 142:1145.

Harvey, Lee. 1990. *Critical social research*. London: Sage Publications.

Hatchett, Shirley, and Howard Schuman. 1975. White respondents and race-of-interviewer effects. *Public Opinion Quarterly* 39 (Winter), 4:523–28.

Hawe, Penelope, and Alan Shiell. 2000. Social capital and health promotion: A review. *Social Science and Medicine* 51:871–85.

Hayes, James R. 1973. Sociology and racism: An analysis if the first era of American sociology. *Phylon* 34 (4): 330–41.

Hayward, Mark D., Eileen Crimmins, Toni P. Miles, and Yu Yang. 2000. The significance of socioeconomic status in explaining the racial gap in chronic health conditions. *American Sociological Review* 65:910–30.

Hayward, Mark D., and Melonie Heron. 1999. Racial inequality in active life among adult Americans. *Demography* 36 (1): 77–92.

Headley, Clevis. 2004. Delegitimating the normativity of "whiteness": A critical Africana philosophical study of the metaphoricity of "whiteness." In *What whiteness looks like: African-American philosophers on the whiteness question*, ed. George Yancy. New York: Routledge.

Heaton, T. B., and C. K. Jacobson. 2000. Intergroup marriage: An examination of opportunity structures. *Sociological Inquiry*, 70:30–41.

Heckman, James J., and Peter Siegelman. 1993. The Urban Institute audit studies: Their methods and findings. In *Clear and convincing evidence: Measurement of discrimination in America*, ed. S. Fix and R. Struyk, 187–258. Washington, DC: The Urban Institute Press.

Heise, D. R. 1969. Problems in path analysis and causal inference. In *Sociological Methodology 1969*, ed. E. F. Borgatta. San Francisco: Jossey-Bass.

Herrnstein, Richard J., and Charles Murray. 1994. *The bell curve: Intelligence and class structure in American life*. New York: The Free Press.

Higganbotham, A. Leon Jr. 1978. *In the matter of color: Race and the American legal process*. Oxford: Oxford University Press.

Higher Education Act of 1965. 1998. 20 U.S.C. 1091 (r) (199x).

Hill, A. B. 1965. The environment and disease: Association or causation? *Proceeding of the Royal Society of Medicine* 58:295–300.

Hill, Robert B. 1972. *The strengths of black families*. New York: National Urban League.

Hochschild, Jennifer L. 1981. *What's fair: American beliefs about distributive justice*. Cambridge, MA: Harvard University Press.

———. 1995. *Facing up to the American dream*. Princeton, NJ: Princeton University Press.

Hodgson, Godfrey. 1976. *America in our time*. Garden City, NY: Doubleday.

Holland, Paul W. 1986. Statistics and causal inference. *Journal of the American Statistical Association* 81 (396): 945–70.

———. 1988a. Causal inference, path analysis and recursive structural equations models. In *Sociological Methodology*, ed. Clifford C. Clogg, 449–84. Washington, DC: The American Sociological Association.

———. 1988b. Causal mechanism or causal effect: Which is best for statistical science? *Statistical Science* 3:149–95.

———. 2001. The causal interpretation of regression coefficients. In *Stochastic Causality*, ed. M. C. Galavotti, P. Suppes, and D. Costantini, 173–88. Stanford, CA: CSLI Publications.

Holland, P. W., and H. Wainer. 1993. *Differential item functioning*. Hillsdale, NJ: Earlbaum Associates.

hooks, bell. 1984. *Feminist theory: From margin to center*. Boston: South End Press.

———. 2001. *All about love: New Visions*. Boston: Harper Paperbacks.

Horton, Hayward Derrick. 1992. Race and wealth: A demographic analysis of black homeownership. *Sociological Inquiry* 62:480–89.

———. forthcoming. Toward a critical demography of race and ethnicity: Introduction of the "r" word. In *Critical demography: Critical demography and racism*, ed. Hayward Derrick Horton. Vol. 1. New York: Plenum Press.

Horton, Hayward Derrick, Beverlyn Lundy Allen, Cedric Herring, and Melvin E. Thomas. 2000. Lost in the storm: The sociology of the black working class, 1950 to 1990. *American Sociological Review*, Special millennial issue 65 (1): 128–37.

Horton, Hayward Derrick, and Melvin E. Thomas. 1998. Race, class and family structure: Differences in housing values for black and white homeowners. *Sociological Inquiry* 68:114–36.

Horvat, Erin McNamara, and Carla O'Connor, eds. 2006. *Beyond acting white: Reframing the debate on black student achievement*. Lanham, MD: Rowman and Littlefield.

Housing Opportunity Program Extension Act of 1996. Pub. L. No. 104-120. 42 U.S.C. Sec 13661 (Supp. V 2000).

Houston, Brant. 1999. *Computer-assisted reporting: A practical guide*. 2nd ed. Boston: Bedford/St. Martin's.

HUD v. Ruker. 2002. 122 S. Ct. 1230.

Hughes, Everett C. 1963. Race relations and the sociological imagination. *American Sociological Review* 28 (6): 879–90.

Hunt, Darnell M. 1997. *Screening the Los Angeles "riots": Race, seeing, and resistance.* Cambridge: Cambridge University Press.

———. 1999. *O. J. Simpson facts and fictions: New rituals in the construction of reality.* New York: Cambridge University Press.

Hunt, Matthew. 2000. Status, religion, and the belief in a just world: Comparisons of African-Americans, Latinos, and Whites. *Social Science Quarterly* 81:325.

Hunt, Matthew, Pamela Brown, Brian Powell, and Lala Steelman. 2000. Color-blind: The treatment of race and ethnicity in social psychology. *Social Psychology Quarterly* 63 (4): 352–64.

Hurtado, Sylvia, Jeffrey Milem, Alma Clayton-Pedersen, and Walter R. Allen. 1999. *Enacting diverse learning environments: Improving the climate for racial/ethnic diversity in higher education.* Washington, DC: ASHE-ERIC Higher Education Report.

Hwang, S. S., R. Saenz, and B. Aguirre. 1997. Structural and assimilationist explanations of Asian American intermarriage. *Journal of Marriage and the Family* 59:758–72.

Hyman, Herbert. 1954. *Interviewing in social research.* Chicago: University of Chicago Press.

Hyman, H. H., and P. B. Sheatsley. 1964. Attitudes toward desegregation. *Scientific American* 211:16–23.

Ignatiev, Noel. 1995. *How the Irish became "white."* New York: Routledge.

Ignatiev, Noel, and John Garvey. 1996. *Race traitor.* London: Routledge.

Jackman, Mary. 1994. *The velvet glove: Paternalism and conflict in gender, class, and race relations.* Berkeley: University of California Press.

Jackman, M. R., and M. Crane. 1986. Some of my best friends are black . . .: Interracial friendships and whites' racial attitudes. *Public Opinion Quarterly* 50:459–86.

Jackson, Fatimah L. C. 2000. Anthropological measurement: The mismeasure of African Americans. *The Annals of the American Academy of Political and Social Sciences* 568:154–71.

Jacobs, J. 1961. *The death and life of great American cities.* New York: Vintage Books.

Jacoby, Russell, and Naomi Glauberman. 1995. *The bell curve debate: History, documents, opinions.* New York: Times Books.

Jaggar, Alison. 1983. *Feminist politics and human nature.* Totowa, NJ: Rowman and Allanheld.

Jakubs, John F. 1979. A consistent conceptualization definition of the index of dissimilarity. *Geographical Analysis* 11:315–21.

James, David R., and Karl E. Taeuber. 1985. Measures of segregation. *Sociological Methodology* 15:1–32.

Jasso, Guillermina, and Nura Resh. 2002. Exploring the sense of justice about grades. *European Sociological Review* 18 (3): 333–51.

Jencks, Christopher. 1972. *Inequality: A reassessment of the effect of family and schooling in America.* New York: Basic Books.

Jencks, Christopher, and Meredith Phillips. 1998. *The black-white test score gap.* Washington, DC: Brookings Institution Press.

Jenkins, Alan. 1999. See no evil: Bans on racial data collection are thwarting antidiscrimination efforts. *Nation*, June, 15.

Jensen, Arthur R. 1981. *Straight talk about mental tests.* New York: Free Press.

Jensen, Robert. 2005. *The heart of whiteness: Confronting race, racism, and white privilege.* San Francisco: City Lights Books.

Johnson, Allan G. 1997. *The forest and the trees: Sociology as life, practice, and promise.* Philadelphia: Temple University Press.

———. 2001. *Power, privilege, and difference.* Mountain View, CA: Mayfield.

Johnson, Charles S. 1934a. Negro personality and changes in a southern community. In *Race and Contacts,* ed. E. B. Reuter. New York: McGraw-Hill.

———. 1934b. The cultural development of the negro. In *Race Relations,* ed. Willis D. Weatherford and Charles S. Johnson. Boston: D.C. Heath and Company.

———. 1934c. Can there be a separate Negro culture. In *Race relations,* ed. Willis D. Weatherford and Charles S. Johnson. Boston: D.C. Heath and Company.

———. 1934d. *Shadow of the plantation.* Chicago: University of Chicago Press.

———. 1941. *Growing up in the black belt: Negro youth in the rural south.* Washington, DC: American Council on Education.

———. 1993. Gender and formal authority. *Social Psychology Quarterly* 50:193–210.

———. 1994. Gender, legitimate authority, and leader-subordinate conversations. *American Sociological Review* 59:122–35.

Jones, F. L., and Jonathan Kelley. 1984. Decomposing differences between groups: A cautionary note on measuring discrimination. *Sociological Methods and Research* 12 (3): 323–43.

Jones, James. 1999. Cultural racism: The intersection of race and culture in intergroup conflict. In *Cultural divides: Understanding and overcoming group conflict,* ed. Deborah Prentice and Dale Miller, 465–90. New York: Russell Sage Foundation.

Jones, Lewis Wade. 1962. *Cold rebellion: The south's oligarchy in revolt.* London: MacGibbon & Kee.

Jones, Rhett S. 1972. Proving blacks inferior: The sociology of knowledge. In *The death of white sociology,* ed. Joyce Ladner, 114–35. New York: Random House.

Jordan, Winthrop D. 1968. *White over black: American attitudes toward the Negro, 1550-1812.* New York: Norton.

———. 1974. *The white man's burden: Historical origins of racism in the United States.* London: Oxford University Press.

Kalmijn, M. 1993. Trends in black/white intermarriage. *Social Forces* 72:119–46.

Karter, A. J. 2003. Race and ethnicity: Vital constructs for diabetes research. *Diabetes Care* 26 (7): 2189–93.

Katende, Charles. 1994. *Population dynamics in Africa.* Doctoral dissertation. University of Pennsylvania.

Kawakami, Kerry, and Kenneth L. Dion. 1992. The impact of salient self-identities on relative deprivation and action intentions. *European Journal of Social Psychology* 23:525–40.

Keil, Charles. 1966. *Urban Blues.* Chicago: University of Chicago Press.

Kelley, Robin G. 1996. *Race rebels: Culture, politics, and the black working class.* New York: Free Press.

———. 1997. *Yo' mama's disfunktional.* Boston: Beacon Press.

Kennedy, Bruce, Ichiro Kawachi, and Deborah Prothrow-Stith. 1998. Social capital, income inequality, and firearm violent crime. *Social Science and Medicine* 47:7–17.

Kennedy, Randall. 1999. Suspect policy. *New Republic,* September 13, 30–35.

———. 2003. *Interracial intimacies: Sex, marriage, identity, and adoption.* New York: Pantheon.

Kessler, Ronald C., Kristin D. Mickelson, and David R. Williams. 1999. The prevalence, distribution, and mental health correlates of perceived discrimination in the United States. *Journal of Health and Social Behavior* 40 (3): 208–30.

Kevles, Daniel J. 1985. *In the name of eugenics: Genetics and the uses of human heredity*. Berkeley: University of California Press.

Kilborn, Peter T. 2001. Ex-convicts seen straining U.S. labor force. *New York Times*, March 15, A16.

Killian, Lewis. (1990). Race relations and the nineties. *Social Forces* 69 (1): 1–13.

Kincheloe, Joe, and Peter Mclaren. 2000. Rethinking critical theory and qualitative research. In *The landscape of qualitative research*, ed. Norman K. Denzin and Yvonna S. Lincoln, 433–88. Thousand Oaks, CA: Sage Publications.

Kinder, Donald R., and Lynn M. Sanders. 1996. *Divided by color: Racial politics and democratic ideals*. Chicago: University of Chicago Press.

King, Martin Luther Jr. 1996. Letter from a Birmingham jail. In *African intellectual heritage*, ed. Molefi Asante and Abu Abarry, 740–50. Philadelphia: Temple University Press.

——. 2000. *Why we can't wait*. New York: Signet Classics.

Kivel, Paul. 2007. Social service or social change. In *The revolution will not be funded: Beyond the non-profit industrial complex*, ed. INCITE! Women of Color Against Violence, 129–50. Boston: South End Press.

Kleinpenning, Gerard, and Louk Hagendoorn. 1993. Forms of racism and the cumulative dimension of ethnic attitudes. *Social Psychology Quarterly* 56 (1): 21–36.

Klinenberg, E. 2002. *Heat wave: A social autopsy of disaster in Chicago*. Chicago: University of Chicago Press.

Kluegal, James, and Aliot Smith. 1982. White's beliefs about blacks' opportunity. *American Sociological Review* 47:518–32.

Kramer, Betty J. 1993. Expanding the conceptualization of caregiver coping: The importance of relationship-focused coping strategies. *Family Relations* 42:383–91.

Krivo, Lauren, and Ruth Peterson. 2000. The structural context of homicide: Accounting for race differences in process. *American Sociological Review* 64 (4): 547–59.

Kuhn, Peter. 1987. Sex discrimination in labor markets: The role of statistical evidence. *The American Economic Review* 77 (4): 567–83.

Kuttner, Robert. 1999. *Everything for sale: The virtues and limits of markets*. Chicago: University of Chicago Press.

Laclau, Ernesto, and Chantal Mouffe. 1985. *Hegemony and socialist strategy*. London: Verso.

Ladner, Joyce A. 1973. *The death of white sociology*. New York: Random House.

Ladson-Billings, G. 2000. Racialized discourses and ethnic epistemologies. In *Handbook of qualitative research* (2nd edition), ed. N. Denzin and Y. Lincoln. Thousand Oaks, CA: Sage Publications.

Laird, Bob. 2005. *The case for affirmative action in university admissions*. Berkeley, CA: Bay Tree Publishing.

Lamont, Michele, ed. 1999. *The cultural territories of race: Black and white boundaries*. Chicago: University of Chicago Press.

——. 2000. *The dignity of working men: Morality and the boundaries of race, class, and immigration*. New York: Russell Sage Foundation.

Lamont, M., and V. Molnar. 2002. The study of boundaries in the social sciences. *Annual Review of Sociology* 28:167–95.

Lane, Charles. 1995. Letter to the editor. *Commentary* 16.
Langan, Patrick A., and David J. Levin. 2002. *Recidivism of prisoners released in 1994.* Washington, DC: Bureau of Justice Statistics.
Latack, Janina C. 1986. Coping with job stress: Measures and future directions for scale development. *Journal of Applied Psychology* 71:377–85.
Latour, Bruno. 1999. *Pandora's hope: Essays on the reality if science studies.* Cambridge, MA: Harvard University Press.
Laub, John H., and Robert J. Sampson. 2001. Understanding desistance from crime. *Crime and Justice* 28:11.
Lazarus, Richard S., and Susan Folkman. 1984. *Stress, appraisal, and coping.* New York: Springer.
Lee, Jennifer, and Frank D. Bean. 2004. America's changing color lines: Immigration, race/ethnicity, and multiracial identification." *Annual Review of Sociology* 30.
Leven, C. L., and M. E. Sykuta. 1994. The importance of race in home mortgage loan approvals. *Urban Affairs Quarterly* 29 (3): 479–89.
Lewis, Amanda. 2001. There is no "race" in the schoolyard: Colorblind ideology in an (almost) all white school. *American Educational Research Journal* 38 (4): 781–812.
———. 2003. *Race in the schoolyard: Negotiating the color line in classrooms and communities.* New Brunswick, NJ: Rutgers University Press.
Lewis, D. K. 1973. *Counterfactuals.* Cambridge: Harvard University Press.
Lewis, David Levering. 1993. *W. E. B. Du Bois: Biography of a race.* New York: Henry Holt and Company.
Lewis, Oscar. 1959. *Five families: Mexican case studies in the culture of poverty.* New York: Basic Books.
———. 1961. *The children of Sanchez.* New York: Random House.
———. 1966. *La vida: A Puerto Rican family in the culture of poverty, San Juan and New York.* New York: Random House.
———. 1968. The culture of poverty. In *On Understanding Poverty,* ed. Daniel P. Moynihan, 187–200. New York: Basic Books.
Lieberson, Stanley. 1980. *A piece of the pie: Blacks and white immigrants since 1880.* Berkeley: University of California Press.
———. 1985. *Making it count: The improvement of social research and theory.* Berkeley: University of California Press.
Liebow, Elliot. 1967. *Tally's corner: A study of Negro streetcorner men.* Boston: Little, Brown.
Linder, F. 1981. Problems of improving vital registration systems in developing countries. *International Population Conference, Manila 1981.* Vol. 3. Liège, Belgium: IUSSP.
Lipset, Seymore Martin. 1996. *American exceptionalism: A double-edged sword.* New York and London: W.W. Norton.
Livesay, T., and C. Louttit. 1950. Reaction time experiments with certain racial groups. *Journal of Applied Psychology* 14 (6): 557–65.
Lofland, John, and Lyn H. Lofland. 1984. *A guide to qualitative observations and analysis.* Belmont, CA: Wadsworth Publishing Company.
Logan, John R., B. J. Stults, and Reynolds Farley. 2004. Segregation of minorities in the metropolis: Two decades of change. *Demography* 41 (1): 1–22.
López, Ian Haney. 1996. *White by Law: The legal construction of race.* Critical America Series. New York: New York University Press.

Loring, Marti, and Brian Powell. 1988. Gender, race, and DSM-III: A study of the objectivity of psychiatric diagnostic behavior. *Journal of Health and Social Behavior* 29 (1): 1–22.

Loury, Glenn C. 1995. *One by one from the inside out: Essays and reviews on race and responsibility in America.* New York: Free Press.

Lovell, Peggy. 1999. Development and the persistence of racial inequality in Brazil. *Journal of Developing Areas* 33:395–418.

Loveman, Mara. 1999. Is "race" essential? *American Sociological Review* 64 (6): 891–98.

Lowery, Brian, Miquel Unzueta, Eric Knowles, and Phillip Goff. 2006. Concern for the in-group and opposition to affirmative action. *Journal of Personality and Social Psychology* 90 (6): 961–74.

Lucas, Jeffrey. 2003. Theory-testing, generalization, and the problem of external validity. *Sociological Theory* 21 (3): 236–53.

Ludwig, Jack. 2004a. Acceptance of interracial marriage at a record high. The Gallup Organization, June 1, 106.

Lundberg, Shelly J. 1991. The enforcement of equal opportunity laws under imperfect information: Affirmative action and alternatives. *The Quartile Journal of Economics* 106 (1): 309–26.

Lyman, Stanford M. 1972. *The black American in sociological thought.* New York: Capricorn Books.

———. 1993. Race relations as social process: Sociological resistance to a civil rights orientation. In *Race in America: The struggle for equality*, ed. Herbert Hill and James E. Jones, 377. Madison: University of Wisconsin Press.

———. 1994. *Color, culture, civilization: Race and minority issues in American society.* Urbana: University of Illinois Press.

Machado, Antonio. 1963. *Juan de Mairena: Epigrams, maxims, memoranda, and memoirs of an apocryphal professor.* Berkeley: University of California Press.

Maddox, Keith B., and Stephanie A. Gray. 2002. Cognitive representations of black Americans: Reexploring the role of skin tone. *Personality and Social Psychology Bulletin* 28 (2): 250–59.

Magubane, Bernard Makhosezwe. 1979. *The political economy of race and class in South Africa.* New York: Monthly Review Press.

Main, Amanda G. 2000. Note, racial profiling in places of public accommodation: Theories of recovery and relief. *Brandeis Law Journal* 39:289.

Majors, Richard G., and Janet Billson. 1992. *Cool pose.* New York: Lexington Books.

Mamdani, M. 1996. *Citizen and subject: Contemporary Africa and the legacy of late colonialism.* Princeton, NJ: Princeton University Press.

Marable, Manning. 1983. *How capitalism underdeveloped black America: Problems in race, political economy, and society.* Boston: South End Press.

Marcuse, Herbert. 1964. *One-dimensional man: Studies in the ideology of advanced industrial society.* Boston: Beacon.

Mare, Robert. 1995. Changes in educational attainment and school enrollment. In *State of the union: America in the 1990s.* Volume 1: *Economic Trends*, ed. R. Farley. New York: Russell Sage Foundation.

Marini, M. M., and Singer, B. 1988. Causality in the social sciences. In *Sociological Methodology*, ed. Clifford C. Clogg, 347–410. Washington, DC: The American Sociological Association.

Mark, Melvin M., and Robert Folger. 1984. Response to relative deprivation: A conceptual framework. *Review of Personality and Social Psychology* 5:192–218.

Marks, Jonathan. 1994. Black, white, other: Racial categories are cultural constructs masquerading as biology. *Natural History*, December, 32–35.

Marks, Jonathan. 1995. *Human biodiversity: Genes, race, and history*. New York: Aldine De Gruyter.

——. 2002. *What it means to be 98% chimpanzee*. Berkeley: University of California Press.

Marley, Bob. 1979. Babylon system. In *Survival*. Island Records.

Marshall, Gloria. 1993. Racial classifications: Popular and scientific. In *The racial economy of science: Toward a democratic future*, ed. Sandra Harding. Bloomington: Indiana University Press.

Marx, Gary T. Undercover. 1988. *Police surveillance in America*. Berkeley: University of California Press.

Mason, Heather. 2003. Equal-opportunity education: Is it out there? The Gallup Organization, July 1, 79.

Massey, Douglas, and Mary Fischer. 1999. Does rising income bring integration? New results for blacks, Hispanics, and Asians. *Social Science Research* 28:316–26.

Massey, Douglas, and Nancy Denton. 1985. Spatial assimilation as socioeconomic outcome. *American Sociological Review* 50:94–106.

——. 1988. The dimensions of residential segregation. *Social Forces* 67 (2): 281–315.

——. 1993. *American apartheid: Segregation and the making of the underclass*. Cambridge, MA: Harvard University Press.

Mauer, Marc. 1999. *Race to incarcerate*. New York: New Press.

Mauro, John. 1992. *Statistical deception at work*. New York: Lawrence Erlbaum Associates.

Mayer, Tom. 2007. The plagiarism charges against Ward Churchill. Posted June 19, 2007, in Ward Churchill Solidarity Network www.wardchurchill.net/.

Mazzuca, Josephine. 2004. For most Americans, friendship is colorblind. The Gallup Organization, July 13, 99.

McAllister, P. H. 1993. Testing, DIF, and public policy. In *Differential item functioning*, ed. P. W. Holland and H. Wainer, 389–96. Hillsdale, NJ: Earlbaum Associates.

McCall, Leslie. 2001. Sources of racial wage inequality in metropolitan labor markets: Racial, ethnic, and gender differences. *American Sociological Review* 66 (4): 520–41.

McCann-Mortimer, P., Augoustinos, M., and LeCouteur, A. (2004) "Race" and the Human Genome Project: Constructions of scientific legitimacy. *Discourse Society* 15:409–32.

McConahay, John. 1986. Modern racism, ambivalence, and the modern racism scale. In *Prejudice, discrimination, and racism*, ed. John F. Dovidio and Samuel L. Gaertner, 91–125. Orlando, FL: Academic Press.

McCorkel, Jill, and Kristen Myers. 2003. What difference does difference make? *Qualitative Sociology* 26 (2): 199–231.

McCulloch, Richard. 1995. The preservationist imperative: Why separation is necessary for survival. *American Renaissance*, June 6.

McDaniel, Antonio. 1995a. Dynamic racial composition of the United States. *Daedalus* 124:179–98.

——. 1995b. *Swing low, sweet chariot: The mortality cost of colonizing Liberia in the nineteenth century*. Chicago: University of Chicago Press.

——. 1996. Fertility and racial stratification. *Population and Development Review* 22, Supplement: Fertility in the United States: New Patterns, New Theories: 134–50.

——. 1998. The "Philadelphia Negro" then and now: Implications for empirical research. In *W. E. B. Du Bois, race, and the city: "The Philadelphia Negro" and its legacy*, ed. M. B. Katz and T. J. Sugrue, 155–93. Philadelphia: University of Pennsylvania Press.

McGraw, M. 1931. A comparative study of a group of Southern white and Negro infants. *Genetic Psychology Monographs* 10:1–105.

McGregor, Alan. 1981. Group conflict: An evolutionary residual? *Mankind Quarterly* 22: 43–48

——. 1986. The evolutionary function of prejudice. *Mankind Quarterly* 26: 277–84.

——. 1993. The double nature of prejudice. *Mankind Quarterly* 33:423–32.

McKee, James B. 1993. *Sociology and the race problem: The failure of a perspective*. Urbana: University of Illinois Press.

McKim, Vaughn R., and Stephen P. Turner. 1997. Causality in crisis? Statistical methods and the search for causal knowledge in the social sciences. In *Studies in science and the humanities from the Reilly Center for Science, Technology, and Values*. Vol. 4. Notre Dame, IN: University of Notre Dame Press.

McWhorter, John. 2000. *Losing the race: Self-sabotage in black America*. New York: The Free Press.

McWhorter, Ladelle. 1995. Scientific discipline and the origins of race: A Foucaltian reading of the history of biology. In *Continental and postmodern perspectives in the philosophy of science*, ed. Babette E. Babich, Debra B. Bergoffen, and Simon V. Glynn, 173–88. Aldershot UK: Avebury.

Meier, Paul, Jerome Sacks, and Sandy Zabell. 1994. What happened in Hazelwood: Statistics, employment discrimination and the 80% rule. In *Statistics and the law*, ed. Morris DeGroot, Stephen Fienberg, and Joseph Kadane. New York: John Wiley.

Memmi, Albert. 2000. *Racism*. Minneapolis: University of Minnesota Press.

Menaghan, Elizabeth G., and Esther S. Merves. 1984. Coping with occupational problems: The limits of individual efforts. *Journal of Health and Social Behavior* 25:406–23.

Menchik, P. L. 1993. Economic status as a determinant of mortality among black and white older men: Does poverty kill? *Population Studies* 44 (3): 427–36.

Mendoza, S. Lily. 2006. New frameworks in Philippine postcolonial historiography: Decolonizing a discipline. In *Race and the foundations of knowledge: Cultural amnesia in the academy*, ed. Joseph Young and Jane Evans Braziel, 155–73. Urbana: University of Illinois Press.

Merton, Robert K. 1941. Intermarriage and social structure: Fact and theory. *Psychiatry* 4:361–74.

Meyer, Philip. 2001. *The new precision journalism*. Lanham, MD: Rowman and Littlefield.

Michael, John. 2000. *Anxious intellects: Academic professionals, public intellectuals, and Enlightenment values*. Durham, NC: Duke University Press.

Miller, Gary D., and James W. Fenton Jr. 1991. Negligent hiring and criminal record information: A muddled area of employment law. *Labor Law Journal* 42:186–92.

Miller, Walter B. 1958. Lower-class culture as a generating milieu of gang delinquency. *Journal of Social Issues* 14 (3): 5–19.

Mills, C. Wright. 1959. *The sociological imagination*. New York: Oxford University Press.

Mills, Charles. 1997. *The racial contract*. Ithaca, NY: Cornell University Press.

———. 1998. *Blackness visible: Essays on philosophy and race*. Ithaca, NY: Cornell University Press.

———. 2000. Race and the social contract tradition. *Social Identities* 6 (4): 441–62.

———. 2001. White supremacy as sociopolitical system: A philosophical perspective. In *Off-white: Readings on race, power, and society*, ed. Michelle Fine, Lois Weis, Linda Powell, and L. Mun Wong. New York: Routledge.

———. 2003. White supremacy as sociopolitical system: A philosophical perspective. In *White out: The continuing significance of racism*, ed. Woody Doane and Eduardo Bonilla-Silva, 35–48. New York: Routledge.

Mills, Kathryn, and Pamela Mills. 2000. *C. Wright Mills: Letters and autobiographical writings*. Berkeley: University of California Press.

Milner, David. 1975. *Children and race*. London: Penguin.

Minnesota Department of Public Safety. 2000. *General arrest information, offense and race of persons arrested for 2000*. St. Paul, MN: Bureau of Criminal Apprehension, Criminal Justice Information Systems.

Moffat, J. B. 1911. Letter to E. D. Durand, director of the Census Bureau, Department of Commerce and Labour, U.S.A., December 8. Pretoria: RSA State Archives, File No. A1/13 "Permanent Census Office: Views Regarding" in SES A1/5/2.

Montagu, Ashley. 1942. *Man's most dangerous myth: The fallacy of race*. New York: Columbia University Press.

Moody, JoAnn. 2004. *Faculty diversity: Problems and solutions*. New York: Routledge.

Morawski, Jill. 1997. White experimenters, white blood, and other white conditions: Locating the psychologist's race. In *Off white: Readings on race, power, and society*, ed. Michelle Fine, Lois Weis, Linda Powell, L. Mun Wong. New York: Routledge.

———. 2005. Reflexivity and the psychologist. *History of the Human Sciences* 18 (4): 77–105.

Moreland, R. L., and S. Beach. 1992. Exposure effects in the classroom: The development of affinity among students. *Journal of Experimental Social Psychology* 28: 255–76.

Morris, Aldon. 1993. Centuries of black protest: Its significance for America and the world. In *Race in America: The struggle for equality*, ed. Herbert Hill and James E. Jones, 19–69. Madison: University of Wisconsin Press.

———. 2002. The historical black freedom struggle. In *2001 race odyssey: African Americans and sociology*, ed. Bruce Hare, 295–315. Syracuse, NY: Syracuse University Press.

———. 2007. Sociology of race and W. E. B. Du Bois: The path not taken. In *Sociology in America: A history*, ed. Craig Calhoun, 503–34. Chicago: University of Chicago Press.

Mossakowski, Krisia. 2004. Coping with perceived discrimination: Does ethnic identity protect mental health? *Journal of Health and Social Behavior* 44 (3): 318–31.

Mouw, Ted. 2000. Job relocation and the racial gap in unemployment in Detroit and Chicago, 1980 to 1990. *American Sociological Review* 65 (5): 730–53.

Moya, Paula M. L. 1997. Postmodernism, "realism," and the politics of identity: Cherrie Moraga and Chicana feminism. In *Feminist genealogies, colonial legacies, and democratic futures*, ed. M. Jacqui Alexander and Chandra Tapade Mohanty, 125–50. New York: Routledge.

Moynihan, Daniel Patrick. 1965. *The Negro family: The case for national action*. Washington, DC: U.S. Government Printing Office.

Mueller, Charles, Munyae Mulinge, and Jennifer Glass. 2002. Interactional processes and gender workplace inequalities. *Social Psychology Quarterly* 65 (2): 163–85.

Muharrar, Mikhal. 1999. Taking sides: Differing media approaches to the problem of racial profiling. *Extra!* July/August, 7–8.

Mukamal, Debbie A. 2000. Confronting the employment barriers of criminal records: Effective legal and practical strategies. *Clearinghouse Review* 33:597.

——. 2001. *From hard time to full time: Strategies to help move ex-offenders from welfare to work*. Washington, DC: U.S. Department of Labor, 15–16.

Muntaner, Charles, John Lynch, and George Smith. 2000. Social capital and the third way in public health. *Critical Public Health* 10:107–24.

Murdock, Steve H., and David R. Ellis. 1991. *Applied demography: An introduction to basic concepts, methods, and data*. Boulder, CO: Westview Press.

Murray, Albert. 1973. White norms, Black deviation. In *The death of while sociology*, ed. Joyce Ladner, 96–114. New York: Random House.

Murray, Charles. 1984. *Losing ground: American social policy, 1950–1980*. New York: Basic Books.

——. 1999. *The underclass revisited*. Washington, DC: AEI Press.

Myers, Kristen. 1993 [2005]. *Racetalk: Racism hiding in plain sight*. Lanham, MD: Rowman and Littlefield.

Myers, Kristen, and, Passion Williamson. 2001. Race talk: The perpetuation of racism through private discourse. *Race & Society* 4 (1): 3–26.

Myrdal, Gunnar. 1944. *An American dilemma: The Negro problem and modern democracy*. New York: Harper and Brothers.

——. 1963. *Challenge to affluence*. New York: Pantheon Books.

Naples, Nancy. 2003. *Feminism and method: Ethnography, discourse, analysis, and activist research*. New York: Routledge.

Nascimento, Abdias do, and Elisa Larkin Nascimento. 2001. Dance of deception: A reading of race relations in Brazil. In *Beyond racism: Race and inequality in Brazil, South Africa, and the United States*, ed. Charles V. Hamilton, Lynn Huntley, Neville Alexander, Antonio Sérgio Alfredo Guimarães, and Wilmont James, 105–56. Boulder, CO: Lynne Rienner Publishers.

Neal, Derek A., and William R. Johnson. 1996. The role of premarket factors in black-white wage differences. *The Journal of Political Economy* 104 (5): 869–95.

Nelson, Debra, and Charlotte Sutton. 1990. Chronic work stress and coping: A longitudinal study and suggested new directions. *The Academy of Management Journal* 33:859–69.

Nelson, J. I. 1972. High school context and college plans: The impact of social structure on aspirations. *American Sociological Review* 37:143–48.

Newman, Katherine. 1999. *No shame in my game: The working poor in the inner city*. New York: Knopf and the Russell Sage Foundation.

——. 2002. No shame: The view from the left bank. *American Journal of Sociology* 107 (6): 1577–99.

Newport, Frank. 1999. Racial profiling is seen as widespread, particularly among young black men. Gallup News Service, December 9. Available from www.gallup .com/poll/reseases/pr991209.asp.

Nisbett, R., and T. Wilson. 1977. Telling more than we can know: Verbal reports on mental processes. *Psychological Review* 84:231–59.

Nixon v. Comm., ____*A.2d*____, 2000 WL 33656044. Pa. Cmwlth. Ct. 2001.

Nussbaum, Martha Craven. 1997. *Cultivating humanity: A classical defense of reform in liberal education*. Cambridge, MA: Harvard University Press.

O'Connor, Alice. 2001. *Poverty knowledge: Social science, social policy, and the poor in twentieth-century U.S. history*. Princeton, NJ: Princeton University Press.

Office of Census and Statistics (OCS). 1925a. The Union Census Office: Its organization and methods. Radio broadcast read on A.S. & T. Broadcasting Company Limited in April. Pretoria: Republic of South Africa State Archives, File No. A1/14.

———. 1925b. The Union Census Office: Its organization and methods (second talk). Radio broadcast read on A.S. & T. Broadcasting Company Limited in April. Pretoria: RSA State Archives, File No. A1/14 "Broadcasting" in SES A1/5/2. "Broadcasting" in SES A1/5/2.

Office of the Pardon Attorney. 1996. Civil disabilities of convicted felons: A state-by-state survey. Washington, DC: U.S. Department of Justice, October.

Ogbu, John U. 1974. *The next generation: An ethnography of education in an urban neighborhood*. New York: Academic Press.

———. 1978. *Minority education and caste*. New York: Academic Press.

———. 1983. Minority status and schooling in plural societies. *Comparative Education Review* 27 (2): 168–90.

———. 1987. Variability in minority school performance: A problem in search of an explanation. *Anthropology & Education Quarterly* 18 (4): 312–34.

———. 1990. Minority education in comparative perspective. *The Journal of Negro Education* 59 (1): 45–57.

———. 2003. *Black American students in an affluent suburb: A study of academic disengagement*. Mahwah, NJ: Lawrence Ehrbaum Associates.

Ogbu, John U., and Astrid Davis. 2003. *Black American students in an affluent suburb: A study of academic disengagement*. Mahwah, NJ: Lawrence Erlbaum Associates, Publishers.

Olivares, Kathleen M., Velmer S. Burton Jr., and Frances T. Cullen. 1999. The collateral consequences of a felony conviction: A national study of state legal codes 10 years later. *Federal Probation*, September, 10.

Oliver, Kelly. 2004. *The colonization of psychic space: A psychoanalytic theory of oppression*. Minneapolis: University of Minnesota Press.

Oliver, Melvin, and Thomas Shapiro. 1995. *Black wealth, white wealth: A new perspective on racial inequality*. New York: Routledge.

Omi, Michael, and Howard Winant. 1994. *Racial formation in the United States: From the 1960s to the 1990s*. New York: Routledge.

O'Neill, June. 1990. The role of human capital in earnings differences between black and white men. *The Journal of Economic Perspectives* 4 (4): 25–45.

Orfield, Gary, and Edward Miller, eds. 1998. *Chilling admissions: The affirmative action crisis and the search for alternatives*. Cambridge, MA: Civil Rights Project, Harvard University, Harvard Education Pub. Group.

Osofsky, Gilbert. 1964. Progressivism and the Negro: New York, 1900–1915. *American Quarterly* 16 (2)(1): 153–68.

Otis-Graham, L. 1995. *Member of the club*. New York: HarperCollins.

Pager, Devah. 2003. The mark of a criminal record. *American Journal of Sociology* 108 (5): 937–75.

Park, Robert Erza. 1926. The urban community as a spatial pattern and a moral order. In *Urban social segregation*, ed. C. Peach. London: Longman.

———. 1950. *Race and culture*. New York: The Free Press.

Patterson, Orlando. 1971. Rethinking black history. *Harvard Educational Review* 41 (3): 299–304.

———. 1998. *Rituals of blood: Consequences of slavery in two American centuries*. Washington, DC: Civitas/Counterpoint.

———. 1997. *The ordeal of integration: Progress and resentment in America's "racial" crisis*. Washington, DC: Civitas/Conterpoint.

Patterson, Sheila. 1975. Some speculations on the status and role of the free people of color in the western Cape. In *Studies in African social anthropology*, ed. Meyer Fortes and Sheila Patterson. New York: Academic Press.

Peach, Cetri. 1980. Ethnic segregation and intermarriage. *Annals of the Association of American Geographers* 70:371–81.

Pearl, J. 2000. *Causality: Models, reasoning and inference*. Cambridge: Cambridge University Press.

Pearlin, Leonard I., and Carmi Schooler. 1978. The structure of coping. *Journal of Health and Social Behavior* 19:2–21.

Pearson, Karl. 1948. *Karl Pearson's early statistical papers*. Cambridge: Cambridge University Press.

Pellow, D. 1996. *Setting boundaries: The anthropology of spatial and social organization*. Wesport, CT: Bergin & Garvey.

Persell, Caroline H. 1977. *Education and inequality: The roots and results of stratification in America's schools*. New York: The Free Press.

Personal Responsibility and Work Opportunity Reconciliation Act of 1996. Sec. 115, 21 U.S.C. Sec. 862a 2000.

Pettigrew, Thomas. 1980. Prejudice. In *Dimensions of ethnicity: Prejudice*, ed. Stephen Thernstrom, Ann Orlov, and Oscar Handlin, 1–29. Cambridge, MA: Harvard University Press.

———. 1985. New black-white patterns: How best to conceptualize them? *Annual Review of Sociology* 11:329–46.

———. 1997. The affective component of prejudice: Empirical support for the new view. In *Racial attitudes in the 1990s*, eds. Steven Tuch and Jack Martin, 76–90. Westport, CT: Praeger.

Phelps, Edmund S. 1972. The statistical theory of racism and sexism. *The American economic review* 62 (4): 659–61.

Philippot, Pierre, and Yanelia Yabar. 2005. Stereotyping and action tendencies attribution as a function of available emotional information. *European Journal of Social Psychology* 35 (4): 517–36.

Phillips, Meredith, James Crouse, and John Ralph. 1998. Does the black-white test score gap widen after children enter school? In *The black-white test score gap*, ed. Christopher Jencks and Meredith Phillips. Washington, DC: Brookings Institution Press.

Pierce, Jennifer. 2003. Racing for innocence: Whiteness, corporate culture, and the backlash against Affirmative Action. In *White out: The continuing significance of race*, ed. Ashley Doane and Eduardo Bonilla-Silva. New York: Routledge.

Pinkney, Alphonso. 1984. *The myth of black progress*. Cambridge: Cambridge University Press.

Pogrund, Benjamin. 1990. *How man can die better: Sobukwe and apartheid*. London: Peter Halban.

Portes, Alejandro. 1998. Social capital: A review. *Annual Review of Sociology* 24:1–24.

Poulantzas, Nicos. 1972. The problem of the capitalist state. In *Ideology and social science*, 238–64. New York: Pantheon Books.

Powell, Adam, Nyla Branscombe, and Michael Schmitt. 2005. Inequality as group privilege of outgroup disadvantage: The impact of group focus on collective guilt and interracial attitudes. *Personality and Social Psychology Bulletin* 31 (4): 508–21.

Powers D. A., and Ellison C. G. 1995. Interracial contact and black racial attitudes: The contact hypothesis and selectivity bias. *Social Forces* 74 (1): 205–26.

Proctor, Robert. 1991. *Value-free science? Purity and power in modern knowledge*. Cambridge, MA: Harvard University Press.

Protess, David L., Fay Lomax Cook, Jack C. Doppelt, James S. Ettema, Margaret T. Gordon, Donna R. Leff, and Peter Miller. 1991. *The journalism of outrage: Investigative reporting and agenda building in America*. New York: Guilford Press.

Putato, Josephine R. 1980. A model proposal to avoid ex-offender employment discrimination. *Ohio State Law Journal* 41 (77): 101–4.

Putnam, Robert. 2001. Civic disengagement in contemporary America. *Government and Opposition* 36:135–56.

Qian, Z. 1997. Breaking the racial barriers: Variations in interracial marriage between 1980 and 1990. *Demography* 72:263–76.

———. 1999. Who intermarries? Education, nativity, region, and interracial marriage, 1980 and 1990. *Journal of Comparative Family Studies* 34:263–76.

Quillian, Lincoln, and Mary E. Campbell. 2003. Beyond black and white: The present and future of multiracial friendship segregation. *American Sociological Review* 68:540–66.

Rainwater, Lee. 1970. *Behind ghetto walls: Black families in a federal slum*. Chicago: Aldine.

Rambo, Lewis. 1969. Effects of experimenter bias on attitudes toward controversial issues. *Journal of Negro Education* 38 (Autumn), 4:384–94.

Ramirez, Deborah, Jack McDevitt, and Amy Farrell. 2000. A resource guide on racial profiling data collection systems. Washington, DC: U.S. Department of Justice.

RAND Report. 1992. *Educational matchmaking: Academic and vocational tracking in comprehensive high schools*, ed. Jeannie Oakes, Molly Selvin, Lynn A. Karoly, Gretchen Guiton. Santa Monica, CA: RAND Corporation.

Rao, Anupama, and Steven Pierce. 2006. Discipline and the other body: Humanitarianism, violence, and the colonial exception. In *Discipline and the other body: Correction, corporeality, and colonialism*, ed. Steven Pierce and Anupama Rao, 1–35. Durham, NC: Duke University Press.

Raudenbush, Stephen, and Robert J. Sampson. 1999. "Ecometrics": Toward a science of assessing ecological settings, with application to the systematic social observation of neighborhoods. *Sociological Methodology* 29:1–41.

Reese, Stephen D., Oscar H. Gandy, and August E. Grant, eds. 2001. *Framing public life*. Mahwah, NJ: Lawrence Erlbaum.

Republic of Bophuthatswana (RB). 1991. *1991 Population census*: 1(2).

Republic of South Africa (RSA). 1961. *Population census 6th September, 1960: Geographical distribution of the population*. Vol. 1. Pretoria: The Government Printer.

———. 1968. *Urban and rural population of South Africa: 1904 to 1960*. Report No. 02-02-01. Pretoria: The Government Printer.

———. 1992a. *Population census 1991: Adjustment for undercount*. Report No. 03-01-26 (1991). Pretoria: Central Statistical Service.

———. 1992b. *Population census 1991: Age by development region, statistical region and district*. Report No. 03-01-03 (1991). Pretoria: Central Statistical Service.

———. 1997. *The people of South Africa: Population census 1996, calculating the undercount in census '96*. Report No. 03-01-18 (1996). Pretoria: Statistics South Africa.

Reskin, Barbara. 2003. 2002 Presidential Address: Including mechanisms in our models of ascriptive inequality. *American Sociological Review* 68 (1): 1-21.

Reuter, E. B. 1938. *The American race problem: A study of the Negro*. New York: Thomas Y. Crowell Company.

Riesman, David, with Nathan Glazer and Reuel Denney. 1950. *The lonely crowd: A study of the changing American character*. New Haven, CT: Yale University Press.

Riessman, Frank. 1962. *The culturally deprived child*. New York: Harper.

Roberts, R. Gregory. 1998. "Environmental justice and community empowerment: Learning from the civil rights movement." *American University Law Review* 48 (October): 229.

Roberts, R., and Cedric J. Robinson. 2000. *Black Marxism: The making of the black radical tradition*. Chapel Hill: University of North Carolina Press.

Robinson, Vaughan. 1981. Segregation and simulation: A reevaluation and case study. In *Social interaction and ethnic segregation*, ed. Peter Jackson and Susan J. Smith, 137-61. New York: Academic Press.

Rodman, Hyman. 1963. The lower-class value stretch. *Social Forces* 42:205-15.

Rodriguez, Clara E. 2000. *Changing race: Latinos, the census, and the history of ethnicity in the United States*. New York: New York University Press.

Rodriguez, Clara, and Hector Cordero-Guzman. 1992. Placing race in context. *Ethnic and Racial Studies* 15:523-42.

Roediger, David. 1993. *The wages of whiteness*. New York: Verso Press.

———. 1994. *Towards an abolition of whiteness: Essays on race, politics and the working class*. New York: Verso Press.

———. 2005. *Working toward whiteness: How America's immigrants became white: The strange journey from Ellis Island to the suburbs*. New York: Basic Books.

Rogers, Richard G. 1992. Living and dying in the U.S.A.: Sociodemographic determinants of death among blacks and whites. *Demography* 29 (2): 278-303.

Rose, Arnold M. 1951. *The roots of prejudice*. Paris: UNESCO.

Rosenbaum, Paul R. 1984. From association to causation in observational studies: The role of tests of strongly ignorable treatment assignment. *Journal of the American Statistical Association* 79 (38): 41-47.

Rosenfeld, M. J. 2001. The salience of pan-national Hispanic and Asian identities in the U.S. marriage markets. *Demography* 38:161-75.

Rosenthal, Robert, and Lenore Jacobson. 1968. *Pygmalion in the classroom*. New York: Holt, Reinhart and Winston, Inc.

Ross, C. E., and J. Mirowsky. 2001. Neighbourhood disadvantage, disorder, and health. *Journal of Health and Social Behaviour* 42 (3): 258–76.

Ross, Dorothy. 1990. *The origins of American social science*. Cambridge: Cambridge University Press.

Ross, Roberts. 1989. The cape of good hope and the world economy, 1652–1835. In *The shaping of South African society, 1652–1840*, ed. Richard Elphick and Hermann Giliomee, 243–80. Middletown, CT: Wesleyan University Press.

Rossiter, Margaret W. 1982. *Women scientists in America: Struggles and strategies to 1940*. Baltimore: John Hopkins University Press.

Royster, Deirdre A. 2003. *Race and the invisible hand: How white networks exclude black men from blue-collar jobs*. Berkeley: University of California Press.

Rucinski, Dianne. Personalized bias in news: The potency of the particular. *Communication Research* 19 (1): 91–108.

Rudenstine, David. 1979. *Rights of ex-offenders: An American civil liberties handbook*. New York: Avon Books.

Ruggles, Steven, Matthew Sobek, Trent Alexander, Catherine A. Fitch, Ronald Goeken, Patricia Kelly Hall, Miriam King, and Chad Ronnander. 2004. Integrated public use microdata series: version 3.0 [Machine-readable database]. Minneapolis: Minnesota Population Center. http://usa.ipums.org/usa/.

Rushton, J. Philippe. 1995. *Race, evolution and behavior*. New Brunswick, NJ: Transaction Press.

———. 1999. *Race, evolution, and behavior*, special abridged edition. New Brunswick, NJ: Transaction Press.

Russell, Dale, and Mindy Larcom. 2000. Airport harassment. *The IRE Journal*. 12–13.

Ryan, William. 1972. *Blaming the victim*. New York: Vintage Books.

Sabol, William J. et al. 2000. *Offenders returning to federal prison, 1986–97*. Washington, DC: Bureau of Justice Statistics & The Urban Institute, September, 4–5.

Sadie, J. L. 1949. The political arithmetic of the South Africans population. *Journal of Racial Affairs* 1: 3–8.

———. 1988. *A reconstruction and projection of demographic movements in the RSA and TBVC countries*. Pretoria: University of South Africa, Bureau of Market Research. Report No. 148.

Said, Edward. 1979. *Orientalism*. New York: Vintage.

Sampson, Robert J., and Steve Raudenbush. 1999. Systematic social observation of public spaces: A new look at disorder in urban neighborhoods. *American Journal of Sociology* 105:603–51.

Sanjek, Roger. 1994. Intermarriage and the future of races. In *Race*, ed. Steven Gregory and Roger Sanjek, 103–30. New Brunswick, NJ: Rutgers University Press.

Santiago-Valles, Kevin A. 1994. *Subject people and colonial discourses: Economic transformation and social disorder in Puerto Rico, 1898-1947*. Albany: State University of New York Press.

Sastry, Narayan, and Jon M. Hussey. 2003. An investigation of racial and ethnic disparities in birth weight in Chicago neighborhoods. *Demography* 40 (4): 701–25.

Sawyer, Mark Q. 2006. *Racial politics in post-revolutionary Cuba*. New York: Cambridge University Press.

Schalch, Kathleen. 2000. Class action lawsuit filed against KB Toys after stores in predominately black neighborhoods refused to take checks. National Public Radio, March 6. Available at www.npr.org/templates/story/story.php?storyId=1071227.

Schemo, Diana Jean. 2001. Students find drug law has big price: College aid. *New York Times*, May 3, 12.

Schermerhorn, Richard. 1970. *Comparative ethnic relations: A framework for theory and research*. New York: Random House.

Schiller, Mayer. 1995. Separation: Is there an alternative? *American Renaissance*, 6:1–5.

Schlosser, Eric. 1998. The prison-industrial complex. *Atlantic Monthly*, December, 51.

Schoen, R. 1988. *Modeling multigroup populations*. New York: Plenum Press.

Schulz, Amy, David Williams, Barbara Israel, Adam Becker, Edith Parker, Sherman A. James, and James Jackson. 2000. Unfair treatment, neighborhood effects, and mental health in the Detroit metropolitan area. *Journal of Health and Social Behavior* 41 (3): 314–32.

Schulz, David. 1969. *Coming up black: Patterns of ghetto socialization*. Englewood Cliffs, NJ: Prentice-Hall.

Schuman, Howard. 2000. The perils of correlation, the lure of labels, and the beauty of negative results. In *Racialized politics*, ed. David Sears, J. Sidanius, and L. Bobo, 302–22. Chicago: University of Chicago Press.

Schuman, Howard, and Jean Converse. 1971. The effects of Black and White interviewers on Black responses in 1968. *Public Opinion Quarterly* 35 (Spring), 1:44–68.

Schuman, Howard, Charlotte Steeh, Lawrence Bobo, and Maria Krysan. 1997. *Racial attitudes in America*. Cambridge, MA: Harvard University Press.

Schutte, Gerhard. 1995. *What racists believe: Race relations in South Africa and the United States*. London: Sage Publishers.

Schwalbe, Michael, Sandra Godwin, Daphne Holden, Douglas Schrock, Shealy Thompson, and Michele Wolkomir. 2000. Generic processes in the reproduction of inequality: An interactionist analysis. *Social Forces* 79 (2): 419–52.

Schwendinger, Herman. 1974. *The sociologists of the chair: A radical analysis of the formative years of North American sociology (1883–1922)*. New York: Basic Books.

Scott, Daryl Michael. 1997. *Contempt and pity: Social policy and the image of the damaged black psyche 1880–1996*. Durham: University of North Carolina Press.

Scott, Joan W. 1999. The evidence of experience. In *Feminist approaches to theory and methodology: An interdisciplinary reader*, ed. Sharlese Hesse-Biebr, Christina Gilmartin, and Robin Lyndenberg, 79–99. New York and Oxford: Oxford University Press.

Scraton, Phil. 2004. Speaking truth to power. In *Researchers and their subjects: Ethics, power, knowledge, and consent*, ed. Marie Smyth and Emma Williamson, 175–94. Bristol, UK: The Policy Press.

Sears, D. O. 1988. Symbolic racism. In *Eliminating racism*, ed. P. Katz and D. Taylor, 53–85. New York: Plenum Press.

Sears, David, and P. J. Henry. 2003. The origins of symbolic racism. *Journal of Personality and Social Psychology* 85 (2): 259–75.

———. 2005. Over thirty years later: A contemporary look at symbolic racism. *Advances in Experimental Social Psychology* 37:95–150.

Sears, David O., Jim Sidanius, and Lawrence Bobo. 2000. *Racialized politics: The debate about racism in America*. Chicago: University of Chicago Press.

Sen, Amartya. 1992. *Inequality reexamined*. Cambridge, MA: Harvard University Press.

Sengupta, Ni. 1944. Studies in race: Sensory traits and reaction times. *Indian Journal of Psychology* 19:50–53.

Sentencing Project and the Human Rights Watch. 1998. Losing the vote: The impact of felony disenfranchisement laws in the United States. www.hrw.org/reports98/vote/.

Sewell, William H., and J. Michael Armer. 1966. Neighborhood context and college plans. *American Sociological Review* 31 (2): 159–68.

Sewell, William H., Archibald O. Haller, and Alejandro Portes. 1969. The educational attainment and early occupational attainment process. *American Sociological Review* 34 (1): 82–92.

Sewell, William H., and Robert Hauser. 1972. Causes and consequences of higher education: Models of the status attainment process. *American Journal of Agricultural Economics* 54 (5): 851–61.

———. 1980. The Wisconsin longitudinal study of social and psychological factors in aspirations and achievement. *Research in Sociology of Education and Socialization* 1:59–99.

Shelton, J. Nicole. 2000. A reconceptualization of how we study issues of racial prejudice. *Personality and Social Psychology Review* 4 (4): 374–90.

Shermer, Michael. 1997. *Why people believe weird things: Pseudoscience, superstition, and other confusions*. New York: W.H. Freeman.

Shulman, Steven. 1989. A critique of the declining discrimination hypothesis. In *The question of discrimination: Racial inequality in the United States labor market*, ed. S. Shulman, and W. Darity Jr. Middletown, CT: Wesleyan University Press.

Sidanius, James. 1989. Racial discrimination and job evaluation: The case of university faculty. *National Journal of Sociology* 3 (2): 223–56.

———. 1999. *Social dominance: An intergroup theory of social hierarchy and oppression*. Cambridge: Cambridge University Press.

Sigelman, L., T. Bledsoe, S. Welch, and M. W. Combs. 1996. Making contact? Black-white social interaction in an urban setting. *American Journal of Sociology* 101 (5): 1306–32.

Simon, H. A. 1957. Spurious correlation: A causal interpretation. In *Models of Man*, ed. H. A. Simon. New York: Wiley.

Simpson, E. H. 1951. The interpretation of interaction in contingency tables. *Journal of the Royal Statistical Society* 13 (2): 238–41.

Skerry, Peter. 2000. *Counting on the census? Race, group identity, and the evasion of politics*. Washington, DC: Brookings Institutional Press.

Skinner, David. 2006. Racialized futures: Biologism and the changing politics of identity. *Social Studies of Science* 36 (3): 459–88.

Smith, Eliot. 1993. Social identity and social emotions: Toward new conceptualizations of prejudice. In *Affect, cognition, and stereotyping: Interactive processes in group perception*, ed. Diane Mackie and David Hamilton, 297–315. San Diego: Academic Press.

Smith, Heather J., and Daniel J. Ortiz. 2002. Is it just me? The different consequences of personal and group relative deprivation. In *Relative deprivation: Specification, development, and integration*, ed. I. Walker and H. J. Smith. Cambridge: Cambridge University Press.

Smith, Herbert L. 1990. Specification problems in experimental and non-experimental social research. *Sociological Methodology* 20:59–91.

Smith, Linda Tuhiwai. 1999. *Decolonizing methodologies: Research and indigenous peoples*. New York: Zed Books.

Smith, Sandra Susan. 1998. Mobilizing social resources: Race, ethnic, and gender differences in social capital and persisting wage inequalities. *Sociological Quarterly* 41:509–37.

Sniderman, Paul M., and Thomas Piazza. 1993. *The scar of race*. Cambridge, MA: Harvard University Press.

Sobel, Michael E. 1994. Causal inference in latent variable models. In *Latent variables analysis: Applications for developmental research*, ed. Alexander von Eye and Clifford C. Clogg, 3–35. Thousand Oaks, CA: Sage Publications.

——. 1995.Causal inference in the social and behavioral sciences. In *Handbook of statistical modeling for the social and behavioral sciences*, ed. Gerhard Arminger, Clifford C. Clogg, and Michael E. Sobel, 1–38. New York: Plenum Press.

South, S. J. 2001. Time-dependent effects of wives employment on marital dissolution. *American Sociological Review* 66:226–45.

Sowell, Thomas. 1978. Three black histories. In *Essays and data on American ethnic groups*, ed. Thomas Sowell, 7–64. Washington, DC: The Urban Institute.

——. 1983. *The Economics and politics of race*. New York: William Morrow and Company.

——. 1984. *Civil Rights: Rhetoric or reality?* New York: Quill.

——. 1998. *Race, culture, and equality*. Stanford, CA: Hoover Institution on War, Revolution and Peace.

Sparks, Colin, and John Tulloch, eds. 2000. *Tabloid tales: Global debates over media standards*. Lanham, MD: Rowman and Littlefield.

Spigner, Clarence. 1998. Race, class, and violence: Research and policy implications. *International Journal of Health Services* 28:349–60.

Stack, Carol. 1974. *All our kin: Strategies for survival in a black community*. New York: Harper and Row.

Stanfield, John H. II. 1982. The "Negro problem" within and outside the institutional nexus of pre–World War I sociology. *Phylon* 43:187–201.

——. 1985a. The ethnocentric basis of social science knowledge production. *Review of Research in Education* 12:387–415.

——. 1985b. *Philanthropy and Jim Crow in American social science*. New York: Greenwood Press.

——. 1987. *Charles S. Johnson, Bitter Canaan, an introductory essay*. Piscataway, NJ: Transaction Books.

——. 1988. Absurd assumptions and false optimism mark race relations social science. *Chronicle of Higher Education* 34:132.

——. 1993. *A history of race relations research: First generation recollections*. Thousand Oaks, CA: Sage Publications.

——. 1994a. The nebulous state of American race relations theories: Paradigmatic erosion and decline, research on race and ethnic studies. *JAI Press Annual*.

——. 1994b. Ethnic modeling in qualitative research. In *Handbook of qualitative research*, ed. Norman Denzin and Yvonna Lincoln. Thousand Oaks, CA: Sage Publications.

——. 1997. Black radical sociological thinking. In *Research and Ethnic Relations* 10:13–34.

——. 1999. Slipping through the front door: Social science evaluation research in the people of color century. *American Journal of Evaluation* 20 (3): 415–31.

——. 2006a. The restorative justice functions of qualitative research methods. *The International Journal of Qualitative Studies in Education* 40.

——. 2006b. Ethnicity and race as resource mobilization in American civic life and participation: Traditional and emerging concerns. In *Handbook on community movements and local organizations*, ed. Ram A. Cnaan amd Carl Milofsky. New York: Springer Publishers.

——. 2006c. Contrasting experiencing race in larger society to the academic disappearance of race in academic sociological paradigms: An African American public sociologist visiting South Africa in 2006 (unpublished paper submitted for publication).

Stanfield, John H. II, and Rutledge M. Dennis. 1993. Race and ethnicity in research methods: Methodological Reflections. In *Epistemological Considerations*, 3–15. Thousand Oaks, CA: Sage Publications.

——. 1995a. Not all that bright. *Journal of Negro Education* 64:214–17.

——. 1995b. The myth of race and the human sciences. *Journal of Negro Education* 64:218–31.

Stanley, Christine A. 2006. *Faculty of color: Teaching in predominantly white colleges and universities*. Bolton, UK: Anker.

Stanton-Salazar, Ricardo D. 2001. *Manufacturing hope and despair: The school and kin support networks of U.S.-Mexican youth*. New York: Teacher's College, Columbia University.

Stanton-Salazar, Ricardo, and Sanford M. Dornbusch. 1995. Social capital and the reproduction of inequality: Information networks among Mexican-origin high school students. *Sociology of Education* 68:116–35.

Statistical Council (SC). 1921. Minutes of a meeting of the Statistical Council held at Pretoria on Monday the 14th November. State Archives, Transvaal Depot. Ref #: SES, 5/10/5.

Statistics South Africa. 2002. *Causes of death in South Africa, 1997–2001*. Pretoria: Statistics South Africa. Publication No. P0309.2: 33–34.

Steele, Claude. 2003. Stereotype threat and African-American student achievement. In *Young, gifted and black: Promoting high achievement among African-American students*, ed. T. Perry, C. Steele, and A. Hilliard III, 109–30. Boston: Beacon Press.

Steele, Claude, and J. Aronson. 1995. Stereotype threat and the intellectual test performance of African-Americans. *Journal of Personality and Social Psychology* 69:797–811.

Steele, Shelby. 1990. *The content of our character: A new vision of race in America*. New York: St. Martin's Press.

Stepan, Nancy Leys. 1982. *The idea of race in science: Great Britain, 1800–1860*. London: McMillan.

Stephan, Walter. 1999. *Reducing prejudice and stereotyping in schools*. New York: Teachers College Press.

Stewart, Quincy Thomas. 2006. Reinvigorating relative deprivation: A new measure for a classic concept. *Social Science Research* 35 (3): 779–802.

Stigler, Stephen M. 1986. *The history of statistics: The measurement of uncertainty before 1900*. Cambridge, MA: Belknap Press of Harvard University.

Sugrue, Thomas. 1996. *The origins of the urban crisis*. Princeton, NJ: Princeton University Press.

Sullivan, M. L. 1989. *Getting paid: Youth crime and work in the inner city*. Ithaca, NY: Cornell University Press.

Sunstein, Cass. 2001. *Republic.com*. Princeton, NJ: Princeton University Press.

Suttles, G. D. 1968. *The social order of the slum: Ethnicity and territory in the inner city*. Chicago: Chicago University Press.

Swain, Carol M. 1996. *Race versus class: The new affirmative action debate*. Lanham, MD: University Press of America.

———. 2002. *The new white nationalism in America: Its challenge to integration*. Cambridge: Cambridge University Press.

———. 2003. *Contemporary voices of white nationalism in America*. Cambridge: Cambridge University Press.

Swidler, Ann, and Jorge Arditi. 1994. The new sociology of knowledge. *Annual Review of Sociology*, August 20: 305–29.

Taeuber, K. E., and A. F. Taeuber. 1965. *Negroes in cities: Residential segregation and neighborhood change*. Chicago: Aldine Publishing Company.

Talisferro, John. 2002. *Tarzan forever: The life of Edgar Rice Burroughs, creator of Tarzan*. New York: Scribner Books Company.

Tarski, Alfred. 1941 [1995]. *Introduction to logic: And to the methodology of deductive sciences*. New York: Dover.

Taylor, Howard F. 1973. Playing the dozens with path analysis: Methodological pitfalls in Jencks et al. *Inequality Sociology of Education* 46: 433–50.

———. 1980. *The IQ game: A methodological inquiry into the heredity-environment controversy*. New Brunswick, NJ: Rutgers University Press.

Telles, Edward E. 1992. Residential segregation by skin color in Brazil. *American Sociological Review* 57:186–97.

———. 1995. Race, class, and space in Brazilian cities. *International Journal of Urban and Regional Research* 19:395–406.

Thernstrom, Stephan, and Abigail Thernstrom. 1997. *America in black and white*. New York: Simon and Schuster.

Thoits, Peggy A. 1995. Stress, coping, and social support processes: Where are we? What next? *Journal of Health and Social Behavior*, Extra Issue: 53–79.

Thomas, William Isaac. 1904. The psychology of race-prejudice. *American Journal of Sociology* 9:593–611.

Thompson, Leonard. 1995. *A history of South Africa*. Revised edition. New Haven, CT: Yale University Press.

Thorndike, Edward. 1912. The measurement of educational products. *School Review* 20:289–99.

———. 1922. Intelligence tests and their use. *21st Yearbook of the National Society for the Study of Education, Parts I and II*. Chicago: National Society for the Study of Education.

Tilly, Charles. 1998. *Durable inequality*. Berkeley: University of California Press.

———. 2004. Social boundary mechanisms. *Philosophy of the Social Sciences* 34 (2): 211–36.

Timberlake, J. 2000. Still in black and white: Effects of racial and class attitudes on prospects for residential integration in Atlanta. *Sociological Inquiry* 70:420–45.

Tinsley, H. E. A., and D. J. Weiss. 2000. Interrater reliability and agreement. In *Handbook of applied multivariate statistics and mathematical modeling,* ed. H. E. A. Tinsley and S. D. Brown, 95–124. San Diego, CA: Academic Press.

Tobias, Phillip V. 1953. The problem of race determination: Limiting factors in the identification of the South African races. *Journal of Forensic Medicine* 1 (2): 113–23.

———. 1970. Brain-size, grey matter and race—fact or fiction? *American Journal of Physical Anthropology* 32:3.

———. 1985. History of physical anthropology in southern Africa. *Yearbook of Physical Anthropology* 28:1–52.

Tougas, Francine, and Ann M. Beaton. 2002. Personal and group relative deprivation: Connecting the "I" to the "we." In *Relative deprivation: Specification, development, and integration,* ed. I. Walker and H. J. Smith. Cambridge: Cambridge University Press.

Tucker, William H. 1994. *The science and politics of racial research.* Chicago: University of Illinois Press.

———. 2002. *The funding of scientific racism: Wickliffe Draper and the Pioneer Fund.* Urbana: University of Illinois Press.

Ture K., and C. Hamilton. 1967 [1992]. *Black power.* New York: Vintage Books.

Turner v. Glickman. 2000. 207 F.3d 419. 7th Cir.

Twine, France Winddance, and Jonathan W. Warren. 2000. *Racing research, researching race: Methodological dilemmas in critical race studies.* New York: New York University Press.

Udjo, Eric O. 2005. Fertility levels, differentials, and trends. In *The demography of South Africa,* eds. Tukufu Zuberi, Amson Sibanda, and Eric Udjo, 40–65. Armonk, NY: M.E. Sharpe.

Union of South Africa (USA). 1911. *Statutes of the Union of South Africa, 1910–1911.* Pretoria: The Government Printers.

———. 1950a. *Statutes of the Union of South Africa, 1950.* Pretoria: Parow.

———. 1950b. Act No. 30 of 1950—Population Registration Act. *Statutes of the Union of South Africa, 1950.* Pretoria: Parow, 275–99.

U.S. Census Bureau. 2000. *National population estimates, annual population estimates by sex, race, and hispanic origin.* Washington, DC: U.S. Census Bureau.

U.S. Housing Act of 1937. 2000. Sec. 6(l)(6) as amended, 42 U.S.C. Sec. 1437d(l)(6) (1994 ed., Supp. V 2000).

University of California. 2004. *Final report to the president.* University of California, April 2004.

Valentine, Charles. 1968. *Culture and poverty: Critique and counter-proposals.* Chicago: University of Chicago Press.

Valenzuela, A., and S. M. Dornbusch. 1994. Familism and social capital in the academic achievement of Mexican origin and Anglo adolescents. *Social Science Quarterly* 75:18–36.

van den Oord, E. J. C. G., and D. C. Rowe. 2000. Racial differences in birth health risk: A quantitative genetic approach. *Demography* 37 (3): 285–98.

van Wyk, D. H. 1984. Race. In *The law of South Africa,* ed. W. A. Joubert and T. J. Scott, 21:385–421. Durban and Pretoria: Butterworth Publishers.

van Zyl, Johan. 1994. *History, scope and methodology of fertility and family planning surveys in South Africa*. Paper presented at the Population Association of America annual meeting in Miami, Florida, May 5–7.

Vanman, Eric, and Norman Miller. 1993. Applications of emotion theory and research to stereotyping and intergroup relations. In *Affect, cognition, and stereotyping: Interactive processes in group perception*, ed. Diane Mackie and David Hamilton, 213–38. San Diego, CA: Academic Press.

Vanneman, Reeve D., and Thomas F. Pettigrew. 1972. Race and relative deprivation in the urban United States. *Race* 13:461–86.

Vinson, Ben III, and Bobby Vaughn. 2004. *Afroméxico: El pulso de la problación negra en México: Una historia recordada, olvidada y vuelta a recordar*. México, D.F.: Centro de Investigación y Docencia Económicas, Fondo de Cultura Económica.

von Hirsch, Andrew, and Martin Wasik. 1997. Civil disqualification attending conviction: A suggested conceptual framework. *Cambridge Law Journal* 56:599.

Wacquant. Loïc. 2002. Scrutinizing the street: Poverty, morality, and the pitfalls of urban ethnography. *American Journal of Sociology* 107 (6): 1468–1532.

——. 2004. *Body and soul: Notebooks of an apprentice boxer*. New York: Oxford University Press.

——. 2005a. Shadowboxing with ethnographic ghosts: A rejoinder. *Symbolic Interaction* 28 (3): 441–47.

——. 2005b. Carnal connections: On embodiment, apprenticeship, and membership. *Qualitative Sociology* 28 (4): 445–74.

Wade, Peter. 1993. *Blackness and race mixture: The dynamics of race identity in Colombia*. Baltimore: John Hopkins University Press.

——. 1997. The meaning of race and ethnicity. In *Race and ethnicity in Latin America*, ed. Peter Wade, 5–24. London: Pluto Press.

Waldinger, Roger. 1995. The "other side" of embeddedness: A case-study of the interplay of economy and ethnicity. *Ethnic and Racial Studies* 18:555–80.

——. 1996. *Still the promised city? African-Americans and new immigrants in postindustrial New York*. Cambridge, MA: Harvard University Press.

Walker, Iain, and Leon Mann. 1987. Unemployment, relative deprivation and social protest. *Personality and Social Psychology Bulletin* 13:275–83.

Walker, Samuel, Cassia Spohn, and Miriam DeLone, eds. 2000. *The color of justice: Race, ethnicity, and crime in America*. Belmont, CA: Wadsworth Publishing.

Waters, Mary C. 1990. *Ethnic options: Choosing identities in America*. Berkeley: University of California Press.

——. 1999. *Black identities: West Indian immigrant dreams and American realities*. New York: Russell Sage Foundation.

Waters, Ronald. 1973. Black sociology: Toward a definition of theory. In *The death of white sociology*, ed. Joyce Ladner. New York: Random House.

Watson, Graham. 1970. *Passing for white: A study of racial assimilation in a South African school*. London: Tavistock Publications.

Weber, Max. 1949. *The methodology of the social sciences*. New York: The Free Press.

Webster, M., and J. Driskell. 1978. Status generalization: A review and some new data. *American Sociological Review* 43:220–36.

Weis, Lois, and Michelle Fine. 2004. *Working method: Research and social justice*. New York: Routledge.

West, Candace, and Sarah Fenstermaker. 1995. Doing difference. *Gender and Society* 9 (1): 8–37.

West, Cornel. 1993. The new cultural politics of difference. In *The cultural studies reader*, ed. Simon During, 212. New York: Routledge.

——. 1994. *Keeping faith: Philosophy and race in America*. New York: Routledge.

Westfeldt, Walter, and Tom Wicker. 1998. *Indictment: The news media and the criminal justice system*. Nashville, TN: First Amendment Center.

Wetherell, M., and J. Potter. 1992. *Mapping the language of racism: Discourse and the legitimation of exploitation*. London: Harvester/Weatsheaf.

Weyher, Harry F. 1998. Contributions to the history of psychology: CXII. Intelligence, behavior genetics, and the Pioneer Fund. *Psychological Reports* 82:1347–74.

——. 1999a. The Pioneer Fund, the behavioral sciences, and the media's false stories. *Intelligence* 26:319–36.

——. 1999b. Reply to Tucker: Defending early IQ researchers. *Psychological Reports* 84:487.

Wheeler, S., W. Jarvis, and R. Petty. 2001. Think unto others: The self-destructive impact of negative racial stereotypes. *Journal of Experimental Social Psychology* 37:173–80.

Whyte, William Foote. 1943. *Street corner society: The social structure of an Italian slum*. Chicago: University of Chicago Press.

Willer, Judith. 1971. *The social determination of knowledge*. Englewood Cliffs, NJ: Prentice-Hall.

Williams, David. 1999. Race, socioeconomic status, and health: The added effects of racism and discrimination. *Annals of the New York Academy of Sciences* 896: 173–88.

Williams, David R., and M. Harris-Reid. 1999. Race and mental health: Emerging patterns and promising approaches. In: *A Handbook for the Study of Mental Health*, ed. A. Horwitz, and T. L. Scheid, 295–314. New York: Cambridge University Press.

Williams, David R., Yan Yu, James S. Jackson, and Norman B. Anderson. 1997. Racial differences in physical and mental health: Socio-economic status, stress and discrimination. *Journal of Health Psychology* 2 (3): 335–51.

Williams, Eric. 1944. *Capitalism and slavery*. Chapel Hill: The University of North Carolina Press.

Williams, Robin. 1988. Racial attitudes and behavior. In *Surveying social life: Papers in honor of Herbert H. Hyman*, ed. Hubert O'Gorman, 331–52. Middletown, CT: Wesleyan University Press.

Williamson, Joel. 1984. *New people: Miscegenation and mulattoes in the United States*. New York: New York University Press.

Willie, Charles V. 2002. Dominant and subdominant people of power: A new way of conceptualizing minority and majority populations. In *2001 Race Odyssey*, ed. Bruce R. Hare, 277–94. Syracuse, NY: Syracuse University Press.

Wilson, Edward O. 1998. *Consilience: The unity of knowledge*. New York: Alfred A. Knopf.

Wilson, William J. 1978. *The declining significance of race: Blacks and changing American institutions*. Chicago: University of Chicago Press.

——. 1987. *The truly disadvantaged: The inner-city, the underclass, and public policy*. Chicago: University of Chicago Press.

——. 1991. Studying inner-city dislocations: The challenges of public agenda research. *American Sociological Review* 56:1–14.

——. 1992. The plight of the inner-city black male. *Proceedings of the American Philosophical Society* 136 (3): 320–25.

——. 1993. *The ghetto underclass*. Newbury Park, CA: Sage Publications.

——. 1996. *When work disappears*. New York: Alfred Knopf.

Winant, Howard. 2000. Race and race theory. *Annual Review of Sociology* 26:169–85.

——. 2001. The world is a ghetto: Race and democracy since World War II. New York: Basic Books.

——. 2007. The dark side of the force: One hundred years of the sociology race. In *Sociology in America: A history*, ed. Craig Calhoun, 535–71. Chicago: University of Chicago Press.

Winfrey, L. 1964. Anti-rights fight costs $120,000. *Memphis Commercial Appeal*, January 30.

——. 2003. Introduction. In *Critical race feminism: A reader*. 2nd ed., ed. Adrien Katherine Wing, 1–22. New York: New York University Press.

Winston, Andrew S. 1998. Science in the service of the far right: Henry E. Garrett, the IAAEE, and the Liberty Lobby. *Journal of Social Issues* 54:182.

Wood, K., and Jewkes, R. 1998. Opportunities and threats in proposed changes to birth and death registration. *South African Medical Journal* 88 (1): 28–29.

Wood, Wendy, and Stephen Karten. 1986. Sex differences in interaction style as a product of perceived sex differences in competence. *Journal of Personality and Social Psychology* 50:341–47.

Woodson, Carter Godwin. 1933. *The mis-education of the Negro*. Washington, DC: Associated Publishers AMS Press.

Wray, Matt, and Annalee Newitz. 1997. *White trash: Race and class in America*. New York: Routledge.

Wright, Erik O. 1985. *Classes*. London: Verso.

——. 1997. *Class counts: Comparative studies in class analysis*. Cambridge: Cambridge University Press.

Wuthnow, Robert. 1987. *Meaning and moral order: Explorations in cultural analysis*. Berkeley: University of California Press.

Wuthnow, Robert, and Marsha Witten. 1988. New directions in the study of culture. *Annual Reviews of Sociology* 14:49–67.

Yerushalmy, J., and C. E. Palmer. 1959. On the methodology of investigations of etiologic factors in chronic diseases. *Journal of Chronic Diseases* 10:27–40.

Yinger, John. 1993. Access denied, access constrained: Results and implications of the 1989 housing discrimination study. In *Clear and Convincing Evidence: Measurement of Discrimination in America*, ed. S. Fix and R. Struyk, 69–112. Washington, DC: The Urban Institute Press.

Young, Alford A. Jr. 1999. "The (non) accumulation of capital: Explicating the relationship of structure and agency in the lives of poor black men. *Sociological Theory* 17 (2): 201–27.

——. 2000. On the outside looking in: Low-income black men's conception of work opportunity and the "good job." In *Coping with poverty: The social contexts of neighborhood, work, and family in the African American community*, ed. Sheldon Danziger and Ann Chin Lin, 141–71. Ann Arbor: University of Michigan Press.

——. 2004. *The minds of marginalized black men: Making sense of mobility, opportunity, and future life chances*. Princeton, NJ: Princeton University Press.

——. 2006. Low-income black men on work opportunity, work resources, and job training programs. In *Black males left behind,* ed. Ronald Mincy, 147–84. Washington, DC: Urban Institute Press.

Young, Iris M. 1990. *Justice and the politics of difference.* Princeton, NJ: Princeton University Press.

Yule, George Udny. 1897. On the theory of correlation. *Journal of the Royal Statistical Society* 60:812–54.

——. 1899. An investigation into the causes of changes in pauperism in England, chiefly during the last two intercensal decades. *Journal of the Royal Statistical Society* 62:249–95.

Zeisel, Hans, and David Kaye. 1997. *Prove it with figures. Empirical methods in law and litigation.* New York: Springer-Verlag.

Zerubavel, Eviatar. 1997. *Social mindscapes: An invitation to cognitive sociology.* Cambridge, MA: Harvard University Press.

Zillmann, Dolf, and Hans-Bernd Brosius. 2000. *Exemplification in communication: The influence of case reports on the perception of issues.* Mahwah, NJ: Lawrence Erlbaum Associates.

Zorbaugh, H. W. 1929. *The gold coast and the slum: A sociological study of Chicago's north side.* Chicago: University of Chicago Press.

Zuberi, Tukufu. 2000. Deracializing social statistics. *The Annals of the American Academy of Political and Social Science* 568:172–85.

——. 2001a. *Thicker than blood: How racial statistics lie.* Minneapolis: University of Minnesota Press.

——. 2001b. The population dynamics of the changing color line. In *Problem of the century: Racial stratification in the United States,* ed. Elijah Anderson and Douglas S. Massey, 145–67. New York: Russell Sage Foundation.

——. 2001c. One step back in understanding racial differences in birthweight. *Demography* 38 (4): 569–71.

——. 2003. Racial statistics and public policy. Special issue, *Race and Society* (mistakenly listed as 2001 on volume cover) 4(2).

——. 2004. W. E. B. Du Bois: "The Philadelphia Negro" and social science. *The Annals of the American Academy of Political and Social Science* 595:146–56.

——. 2006. Sociology and the African diaspora experience. In *A Companion to African American Studies,* ed. Lewis Gordon and J. Gordon, 246–64. New York: Blackwell Publishers.

Zuberi, Tukufu, and Akil K. Khalfani. 1999. *Racial classification and colonial population enumerations in South Africa.* African Census Analysis Project Working Paper Series #6. Philadelphia: University of Pennsylvania.

Zuberi, Tukufu, Amson Sibanda, and Eric Udjo, eds. 2005. *The demography of South Africa.* Volume 1 of the General Demography of Africa series. New York: M.E. Sharpe.

Index

About the Editors and Contributors

Walter R. Allen is the Allan Murray Cartter Professor in the Graduate School of Education and Information Studies at UCLA. His research specialties and interests include comparative race, ethnicity and inequality, diversity in higher education, and family studies.

Regina Austin is the William A. Schnader Professor at the University of Pennsylvania Law School. Her scholarship focuses on civil injustices based on race, class, and gender discrimination. She is currently completing a book of essays on documentaries and the law.

Sulaiman Bah was trained in Sierra Leone, Ghana, and Canada. In Sierra Leone he obtained his bachelor of science in mathematics and physics in 1983. He changed his career path and obtained his MA and MPhil degrees from the University of Ghana. His MPhil thesis was on the influence of cause-of-death structure on age patterns of mortality in Mauritius for the period 1969–1986. Subsequent to his MPhil research, the analysis of data on causes of death became one of Professor Bah's major research preoccupations. In furthering this research interest, he took graduate courses in epidemiology, biostatistics, survival models, mathematical demography, and social demography at the University of Western Ontario (Canada) and graduated with a PhD in 1993. Professor Bah has lectured at the University of Zimbabwe, the University of Swaziland, and the University of Pretoria. He worked at Statistics South Africa from 1997 to 2003 in the section dealing with the compilation, analysis, and publication of births and causes of death statistics. He joined the Department of Epidemiology at the University of Limpopo, Medunsa Campus, in April 2003. He was head of the Department of Epidemiology from April 2005 to January 2007, after which he moved to King Faisal University in Saudi Arabia, where he became head of the Research Support Unit at the College of Applied Medical Sciences. Professor Bah has written many papers on different aspects of mortality and causes of death. His current area of research is on multiple causes of death. Professor Bah is married and lives with his family in Al-Khobar, Saudi Arabia.

Gianpaolo Baiocchi is associate professor of sociology and international studies at Brown University. He writes on politics, culture, race, and cities, with a focus on Brazil and Latin America. He is currently engaged in a project on race and human rights violations in Salvador, Brazil, in addition to research on the diffusion of participatory ideas. His last book was *Militants and Citizens* (2005).

Brent Berry is an assistant professor of sociology at the University of Toronto in Ontario, Canada. He specializes in the sociological study of health inequalities, race and ethnic relations, and urban issues. He has also published work on residential segregation, social theory, and family intergenerational support. A general intellectual problem that motivates much of his work is how complex causal processes operate over time to shape stratification and inequality. He is also interested in using innovative methods to provide a fresh perspective on social problems.

Eduardo Bonilla-Silva is a professor of sociology at Duke University. He is the 2007 recipient of the Lewis A. Coser Award for Theoretical Agenda-Setting in sociology. His books include *White Supremacy and Racism in the Post-Civil Rights Era* (2001), *Racism without Racists: Color-Blind Racism and the Persistence of Racial Inequality in the USA* (2003, 2006), and *White Out: The Continuing Significance of Racism* (with Woddy Doane, 2003). His 1996 article in the *American Sociological Review*, "Rethinking Racism: Towards A Structural Interpretation," has become a classic in sociology. Professor Bonilla-Silva is currently working on a methodology book and on a project examining the future of racial stratification in the United States.

Jenifer L. Bratter is an assistant professor of sociology at Rice University. Dr. Bratter's research explores the dynamics of interracial family formation and multiracial identity. She has recently published work on the events that facilitate the formation of an interracial marriage (in *The Sociological Quarterly*) and the mental health of interracial married couples (in *Social Science Research*), and is currently investigating the rates of disruption of interracial couples compared to mono-racial couples. Additionally, her work explores how self-identified multiracial adults navigate the "color line" when racially classifying their children (forthcoming in *Social Forces*). She is currently investigating how multiracial adults select spouses/partners and the relationships between parent-child interactions and racial identity in mixed-race households.

Charles A. Gallagher is an associate professor in the Department of Sociology and the race and urban studies concentration director at Georgia State University. He has published articles on the sociological functions of color-blind political narratives, how racial categories expand and contract within the context of interracial marriages, race theory, racial innumeracy, and how one's ethnic history shapes perceptions of privilege. He is currently examining how white communities mobilize to protect their material and symbolic interests and the various strategies they employ to maintain the color line through seemingly color-blind discourse.

Oscar H. Gandy Jr. is professor emeritus at the Annenberg School for Communication at the University of Pennsylvania. He is author of *The Panoptic Sort* and *Beyond Agenda Setting,* two books that explore issues of information and public policy. A recent book, *Communication and Race,* explores the structure of media and society, as well as the cognitive structures that reflect and are reproduced through media use. A coedited volume, *Framing Public Life,* examines the role of media in shaping public understanding. A book in progress, *If It Weren't for Bad Luck,* will examine the ways in which probability and its representation affect the lives of different groups in society.

Carla Goar is an associate professor of sociology at Northern Illinois University. Her research has focused on the ways that racial inequality is negotiated, challenged, or perpetuated in small groups. Her recent work examines ways that structural modifications might decrease such inequality.

Gloria González is a professor of sociology at Pomona College. She completed her PhD in sociology from the University of California–Los Angeles in 2007. Her research includes race, ethnicity, gender, and education. Gloria González's current work examines body image and adolescent girls, focusing on Mexican-origin girls. This research examines body satisfaction and perceptions of weight, body shape and size, and skin color.

Paul W. Holland holds the Frederic M. Lord Chair in Measurement and Statistics (retired) in the Research and Development Division at the Educational Testing Service in Princeton, New Jersey. His educational background includes an MA and a PhD in statistics from Stanford University, 1966, and a

BA in mathematics from the University of Michigan, 1962. His association with ETS began in 1975. In 1979 he became the director of the Research Statistics Group. In 1986 Holland was appointed ETS's first distinguished research scientist. He left ETS in 1993 to join the faculty at the University of California–Berkeley as a professor in the Graduate School of Education and the Department of Statistics, but returned in 2000 to his current position at ETS. He has made significant contributions to the following applications of statistics to social science research: categorical data analysis, social networks, test equating, differential item functioning, test security issues, causal inference in nonexperimental research, and the foundations of item-response theory. His current research interests include kernel equating methods, population invariance of test linking, software for item-response theory, and causal inference in program evaluation and policy research.

Hayward Derrick Horton is the associate dean of graduate studies and a professor in the Department of Sociology and the School of Public Health at SUNY–Albany. He also is the director of the Critical Demography Project, and director of the Capitalize on Community Project.

Angela James is an assistant dean in the Graduate Division at UCLA. Her research centers on demographic understandings of family change, race, and education. She has just finished an article, cowritten with Holly Furdnya and M. Belinda Tucker, that examines relationship satisfaction among dual-earner marriages. She is currently working on several projects that assess the efficacy of doctoral education.

Akil Kokayi Khalfani is the director of the Africana Institute and of the Urban Issues Institute, as well as an associate professor of sociology at Essex County College. He is president and founder of ATIRA Corp, a think tank that develops solutions for the problems that people of African descent face globally. He is the vice chair for the Solutions Organizational Network, a New Jersey–based grassroots umbrella organization.

Pali J. Lehohla is the first statistician-general for the Republic of South Africa. He is the head of Statistics South Africa and a vice president of the International Association for Official Statistics (IAOS).

Carole Marks is a professor of sociology at the University of Delaware. Her books include *Farewell, We're Good and Gone* (1989), *A History of Blacks in Delaware and the Eastern Shore of Maryland* (1997), *The Power of Pride: Style Makers and Rule-Breakers of the Harlem Renaissance* (1999), and *Moses and the Monster and Miss Anne: Three Dangerous Women of the Eastern Shore* (forthcoming). Her 2003 article on the "Great Migration" and a reprint of *Farewell*

We're Good and Gone appear in the award-winning Schomburg digitized collection, *In Motion: The African American Migration Experience*. Professor Marks is currently working on *Subversive Representations*, a book on African American art from a sociology-of-art perspective.

John H. Stanfield II is professor of African American and African Diaspora studies with senior faculty status in American studies, philanthropic studies, and sociology at Indiana University–Bloomington, with affiliated faculty status with the University of Cape Town in South Africa. He is president of Stanfield Consultants International, LLC and the founding director of the African Diaspora Seminar. As an alumnus of the Salzburg Seminar, and other august international scholarly activities, he is also the 2007–2008 Distinguished Fulbright Chair in American Studies–Brazil. Professor Stanfield has researched extensively American and cross-national epistemological and intellectual histories of academic racism in the social sciences and is presently involved in cross-national race and restorative-justice scholar-practitioner projects.

Quincy Thomas Stewart is a Robert Wood Johnson Scholar in Health Policy Research at the University of Michigan and an assistant professor of sociology at Indiana University–Bloomington. His research interests pertain to demography, social inequality, and methodology. Specifically, he is interested in the social processes that create inequalities in socioeconomic status, health, and mortality, and the methods that social scientists use to examine inequality, mortality, and other aspects of social life.

Susan A. Suh is a doctoral candidate of sociology at UCLA. She has collaborated with Walter Allen, Lawrence Bobo, and others on various articles and reports regarding higher-education experiences and racial attitudes. Her research interests include race/ethnicity theory, higher education, workplace experiences, and race/class/gender perspectives. Her MA thesis, "Impacts of Gender, Racial Group, and Class in Perceptions of Workplace Discrimination," may be found in *Prismatic Metropolis: Inequality in Los Angeles* (Melvin Oliver and Lawrence Bobo, editors, 2002). Ms. Suh is completing her dissertation work on the significance of race in the workplace experiences of Asian American academics. Prior to her interests in academia, she worked as an engineer after receiving a BS from Columbia University. She is the proud mother of Mina and Malcolm.

Lori Latrice Sykes received her PhD in sociology from State University of New York–Albany. Her areas of specialization are demography, race and ethnicity, race and wealth, and community development.

William H. Tucker is a professor of psychology at Rutgers University–Camden, whose research focuses on the misuse of science to support oppressive social policies. His 1994 book, *The Science and Politics of Racial Research,* received the Anisfield-Wolf Award given by the Cleveland Foundation for books that have made important contributions to our understanding of racism and the Ralph J. Bunche Award given by the American Political Science Association for a scholarly work that explores the phenomenon of ethnic pluralism. His 2002 book, *The Funding of Scientific Racism,* received Honorable Mention in the History of Science category from the Association of American Publishers. His current project is a book on the controversial psychologist, Raymond Cattell.

Joshua Yang is a member of the faculty at University of California–San Francisco.

Alford A. Young Jr. is Arthur F. Thurnau Professor and associate professor of sociology in the Center for Afro-American and African Studies at the University of Michigan. His books include *The Minds of Marginalized Black Men: Making Sense of Mobility, Opportunity, and Future Life Chances* (2004) and a coauthored work entitled *The Souls of W. E. B. Du Bois* (Paradigm Publishers, 2006). He has published articles in *Sociological Theory, The Annual Review of Sociology, Symbolic Interaction, Ethnic and Racial Studies,* and other journals. Professor Young is completing a book entitled *From the Edge of the Ghetto: African Americans and the World of Work.*

Tukufu Zuberi is Lasry Family Professor of Race Relations and the director of the African Census Analysis Project (ACAP) at the University of Pennsylvania. His recent books include *Thicker Than Blood: How Racial Statistics Lie* (2001) and *Swing Low, Sweet Chariot: The Mortality Cost of Colonizing Liberia in the 19th Century* (1995). He has published numerous articles in peer-reviewed journals and as book chapters. Professor Zuberi is currently working on a book and documentary film on African development, and he is the series editor of *A General Demography of Africa.*